Mass Media Writing

COMMUNICATION
TEXTBOOK SERIES
Jennings Bryant — Editor

Journalism
Maxwell McCombs — Advisor

BERNER • Writing Literary Features

FENSCH • The Sports Writing Handbook

TITCHENER • Reviewing the Arts

FENSCH • Writing Solutions:
Beginnings, Middles,
and Endings

SHOEMAKER • Communication
Campaigns About Drugs:
Government, Media,
and the Public

STEPP • Editing for Today's
Newsroom

BOGART • Press and Public: Who
Reads What, When, Where,
and Why in American
Newspapers, Second Edition

FENSCH • Associated Press Coverage
of a Major Disaster: The
Crash of Delta Flight 1141

GARRISON • Professional
Feature Writing

FENSCH • Best Magazine Articles: 1988

DAVIDSON • A Guide
for Newspaper Stringers

GARRISON • Professional
News Writing

SLOAN • Makers of the
Media Mind: Journalism Educators
and Their Ideas

FENSCH • Nonfiction for the 1990s

LESTER • Photojournalism: An
Ethical Approach

PROTESS/McCOMBS • Agenda Setting:
Readings on Media,
Public Opinion, and Policymaking

McCOMBS/EINSIEDEL/WEAVER • Contemporary
Public Opinion: Issues
and the News

PARSIGIAN • Mass Media Writing

Mass Media Writing

Elise K. Parsigian
University of Michigan—Dearborn

LEA   LAWRENCE ERLBAUM ASSOCIATES, PUBLISHERS
1992   Hillsdale, New Jersey   Hove and London

Lawrence Erlbaum Associates, Inc., Publishers
365 Broadway
Hillsdale, New Jersey 07642

Cover design by Rosalind Orland

Library of Congress Cataloging-in-Publication Data

Parsigian, Elise K.
    Mass media writing / by Elise K. Parsigian.
       p. cm. — (Communication textbook series. Journalism)
    Includes bibliographical references (p.   ) and index.
    ISBN 0-8058-1130-3 (cloth). — ISBN 0-8058-1131-1 (paper)
    1. Mass media—Authorship.   I. Title.   II. Series.
P96.A86P37   1992
808'.06607—dc20   91-35265
                                               CIP

Printed in the United States of America
10 9 8 7 6 5 4 3 2 1

In memory of my parents
Levon and Zabel Keoleian
and for
Linda, Ellen, and David

Preface

Professional writers are disciplined thinkers. They win copy approvals because they are mentally organized performers. Whether they write for print, broadcast, public relations, or advertising organizations, media writers employ a common strategy and critical method. Their strategy and critical thinking habits constitute the focus of this book. Because that strategy and method of thinking represent on-the-job refinements of the professional approach, the purpose of this book is to provide inexperienced writers with this knowledge before entering the work world, whether they enter it as an intern, a new hire, or a free-lancer.

After producing copy for all types of mass media organizations for more than two decades, I am convinced of a number of things. One of them is that the work habits of professional writers are not as disorderly as they seem. The best news journalists in both print and broadcast work and writers in public relations and advertising are highly disciplined performers whose work procedures are remarkably more similar than they are different. Even though news, magazine, public relations, and advertising writers serve different purposes, and print and broadcast writers communicate through different channels, all follow a common method.

Having taught news journalism and mass media writing, I am also convinced that students can write with confidence in a variety of media situations once they learn the specific strategy and skills professional writers have learned through trial and error on the job. With practice, novices develop an ability to manage information systematically, to reach into personal reservoirs of creativity, and to evaluate their own writing critically.

Another one of my convictions is that in these uncertain times it is unrealistic for students to expect on-the-job training. More directly, it is downright foolhardy. At one time, editors and senior writers were the best teachers outside the classroom. Today, organizations cannot afford to assign their experienced writers to train novices. Competition is too keen, money is too tight, and time is very limited. Even when a staff member is assigned to a trainee, that staffer usually has a demanding project to complete and little time or energy to devote to a beginner. These days, the media writer in demand is the one who enters the work world capable of demonstrating independence, critical ability, and versatile performance.

The teaching of a systematic and critical approach to mass media writing has received little attention in the past. However, more than ever before, that approach has become an absolute necessity. Today's issues and events are extremely complex and command more than casual attention to the numerous forces surrounding them. Novices need a guide to direct their way through thorny writing problems and these seem to multiply daily as we approach the 21st century.

This book was written, not only to meet that need, but for other reasons as well. I was alarmed by the increasing numbers of undergraduate students who came into my classes unable to think systematically and logically. Students had difficulty determining what to write about, what information required investigation, what to do with information collected, which factors needed consideration. They chose sources indiscriminately and relied too heavily on interviews for "evidence." Instead of being active evaluators of received information, they were passive absorbers of the written and spoken word. I was also concerned about student inability to organize and synthesize a body of verified information down to its common denominator and to write to the point of a matter in an engaging way for a particular audience.

Writing, first and foremost, is critical thinking. If the information is flawed and the writer duplicates those flaws in the copy, the reader is quick to detect the weakness. Editors have too much on their minds to catch writers' errors. The bottom line is that the writer is responsible.

Still another reason for this book was my failure to find a suitable classroom text. I wanted a book that lent itself to the disciplined process I wanted to teach, one that explicitly outlined the core strategy and cognitive thinking skills that applied to diverse areas of mass media work. Although many texts were available, none met that requirement. This book fills the void.

Unlike other media writing texts, this one suggests that in the seemingly chaotic world of media, where systematic performance is supposed to be nonexistent, professional writers are as methodical as those who practice the disciplines of science. That does not mean media writers are scientists, or vice versa. It just means professional writers work as systematically as those who are specifically trained to proceed in a methodical way (see Fig. 1).

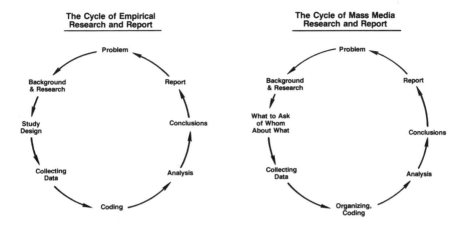

FIG. 1.   Two patterns of inquiry compared.

The similarity was demonstrated recently in an exploratory study of nearly 100 media professionals who had volunteered to take part in the survey and who represented all areas of mass media. Results showed that, at least among these media professionals, a significant number of them practiced a common strategy resembling the methodical work patterns of scientists in the social, behavioral, and communication sciences, and that they repeated the pattern in varying degrees of breadth and depth across all types of mass media assignments. Yet few could say how they had learned the strategy and believed it must have been an unconscious effort after many trial-and-error experiences on the job.[1]

A host of scientists, journalists, and educators have long recommended adoption of scientific methods for mass media work. Some have noted the similarities of systematic procedure that professional media writers share with scientists and that other practitioners might adopt (Bogart, 1968; Levine, 1980; Tankard, 1976; Webb & Salancik, 1966). Several observers have translated some key procedures of science and suggested ways they could apply them to mass media work (Grey, 1972; Meyer, 1979; Palmer, 1982; Rivers, 1975; Tankard, 1976; Williams, 1978).

The movement is headed in the right direction, but thus far the available literature for media writers has focused on procedural patterns far afield

---

[1]An exploratory survey of 48 news journalists at six of the nation's largest metropolitan newspapers in the midwest (conducted between December 1985 and January 1986) revealed that a majority number within this group practiced a pattern of work behavior and recursive activity across all types of news stories that paralleled the standards of examination and report accepted and practiced by scientists in the social, behavioral, and communication sciences (Parsigian, 1987). The same survey, conducted in 1988–1989, revealed similar results with an equal number of other writers at midwest newspapers, television stations, public relations and advertising companies.

from the codified methods of science, or they cover only parts of media work procedure. The fact is, the work strategy professional media writers share with disciplined minds is an already established model, well documented in the literature of the social, behavioral, and communication sciences and needs little alteration here for our purposes.[2] Yet, adaptation of that model to the needs of media students and practitioners seems to have escaped full development as a practical guide for writers.

For those interested in developing a professional approach to their work, the suggestions made in this book should serve them well. The advantage to the novice is knowing what to do with an assignment before entering the offices of a mass media organization, not after the fact.

This book is not meant to replace texts detailing the unique characteristics that separate print news, broadcast, public relations, and advertising work from one another. It is, instead, a handbook about the dynamics of mass media writing. It details the strategy and critical thinking habits all professional writers rely on to write a mass media piece, whether it is for a news, magazine, broadcast, public relations, or advertising company. Media students will discover that the medium alone does not determine the message. The message is also the sum total of what the writer has put into it: sources used, how the collected information was evaluated, organized for analysis, and composed. All these shape the message for any medium. The way the message is delivered to media consumers is another factor, but it all begins with the writer.

The notion of similarity across all mediums is more easily appreciated if one looks on each mass media product as a narrative communication. The news story is a narrative of an incident, event, issue, thing, or person(s). A magazine piece is an expanded news story. A news broadcast is a compressed one. A public relations release is a narrative of a specific company's pronouncement about an incident, event, issue, group, or person associated with that company. A print or TV ad is a miniature narrative that aims to persuade the consumer to buy a product, or to evoke public support for a particular cause or person. Purpose, presentation, depth, and breadth differ, but the strategy for getting the job done remains the same (e.g., see McAdams & Sweeney, 1985).

Each chapter in this book represents a sequential step in the common strategy, includes an integrated series of critical questions to raise, and provides the means to answer them. Wherever necessary, examples, feedback, and models are provided to direct attention to specific factors

---

[2]The model is outlined in different ways in several texts devoted to the methods of conducting systematic social, behavioral, and communication research stuides. For example, see Kaplan (1964); Platt (1962); Runkel and McGrath (1972); Selltiz, Jahoda, Deutsch, and Cook (1959); Selltiz, Wrightsman, and Cook (1976); and Wimmer and Dominick (1983).

discussed in the chapter. At the end of chapters 2, 3, 4, 7, 11, and 12 you will also find excerpts from interviews held with print and broadcast news, public relations, and advertising writers. The work habits of these professionals illustrate the importance of systematic and critical thinking procedures outlined in this book. Additional interviews held with writers in video and film production may be found in Appendices B and C.

The movement is from steps, questions, and clues to rational decisions at each point of the strategy. The novice begins to appreciate how these functions play a significant role in developing systematic habits and the cognitive process of critical thinking and writing.

Although this book is designed for use by students in print and broadcast news, magazine, public relations, and advertising courses, it can be used by students in other courses where writing is a requisite. The nature of writing for mass media encompasses so many different types of writing (observational, explanatory, expository, exploratory, investigative, argumentive, persuasive, creative) that this book would be useful in a variety of subject areas as well as mass media courses: English, business, political science, history, philosophy, education, psychology, sociology, anthropology, and the like.

Teachers of tomorrow's teachers will find the text especially useful because it manifests the methodical work and critical thinking habits future teachers aim to instill in their students. The text can also be used as the focus of courses in study–work development skills, or in courses designed specifically to teach critical thinking and writing.

This book is the result of a need in the media classroom, but it is written to guide anyone in the disciplined habits of professional writers. The techniques this text seeks to develop are those that any interested person will want to acquire if the intent is to improve one's writing or to produce a piece of either minor or major length worthy of publication.

ACKNOWLEDGMENTS

My first thanks must go to the people I studied—media professionals in print and broadcast news, public relations, and advertising. They are too numerous to list here, but they know who they are. Without their help, this book could not have been written. They generously gave up time in the midst of their busy lives to participate in two surveys, laboring at times to answer my probing questions. Some talked beyond the survey hour, others for less, all gave me invaluable assistance. A few of the many who were interviewed are presented in this book.

I owe special thanks to Charles F. Cannell, professor of communication emeritus and research scientist emeritus of the Institute for Social Research,

University of Michigan. When I discussed this project with him some years ago, he recognized its merit and advised me to build on my ideas. Since then he has generously counseled and provided suggestions I could not have done without. I am indebted, as well, to Robert H. Giles, editor and publisher of *The Detroit News,* who reviewed my first chapters and whose insightful comments helped me redirect my course away from a doubtful start.

I was able to complete this manuscript because many good people willingly shared their expertise to help clarify its content. Some gave their time and knowledge or provided useful reference materials; some patiently sat through lengthy interviews; others read portions of the manuscript and made important suggestions that refined the writing and strengthened the material. Each made a contribution for which I am grateful: David R. Brimm in the Department of Management, College of Business at Eastern Michigan University; Karl Leif Bates, staff reporter at the *Ann Arbor News*; Karen D. Bartscht, MD, MPH, formerly in the Division of Gynecology, University of Michigan Medical Center, and now in private practice; Reynolds Donovan, executive producer, and Lisa L. Whiting, producer, Michigan Public Broadcasting; John E. Gannon, PhD, section chief of Habitat and Contaminant Assessment for the U.S. Fish and Wildlife Service; Peter F. Landrum, PhD, research chemist for the Great Lakes Environmental Research Laboratory, National Oceanic and Atmospheric Administration at the U.S. Department of Commerce; Donald G. Langsley, MD, executive vice-president with the American Board of Medical Specialities; David J. Smith, Jr., MD, associate professor of Surgery and section head of Plastic and Reconstructive Surgery, University of Michigan Medical Center; Frederick Steeper, principal at Market Strategies, Inc.; Judith Tomer, RD, dietician with the Nutrition Counseling Center, Department of Dietetics, University of Michigan Medical Center; and Michael W. Traugott, program director of the Center for Political Studies, Institute for Social Research, University of Michigan.

And to my husband and our children, Linda, Ellen, and David, I owe equal thanks for the encouragement and supportive environment they provided.

Writing this book was an exciting and enriching experience because all those named here helped make it so.

Elise K. Parsigian

1 On Being a Mass Media Writer[1]

Without any idea of what sort of process is at work, how is one to comprehend why certain conditions enhance understanding whereas others hamper it? And how is one to discover the best methods of training the mind for its profession?

—Rudolph Arnheim (1969)

Media writers are critically tuned conduits of information. Information is their stock in trade, but it is information of a verifiable kind, not hearsay, not fiction. Unlike fiction writers, who are free to write from the depths of their imagination, journalists are expected to write from a bank of information checked and re-checked through a series of valid sources in the real world. Without substantiated information, they have nothing to communicate.

To build that bank of information, professional media writers read all types of print materials. They are practiced at absorbing information with a discriminating mind. They observe people, events, and situations. They listen to speeches, comments, and testimonies. They read fine literature as well as general materials. The latter may include books, newspapers,

---

[1]The term *journalist* frequently includes all mass media writers, that is, those who write print news and magazine articles, broadcast news and special features, print or broadcast public relations and advertising copy. However, *journalist* in this sense is not yet a term in general use. *Media writer*, therefore, is our more frequent reference in this text, but when the terms *journalist*, *journalism*, or *journalistic* are used, they are meant to include the various classes of media named in this footnote. For a discussion concerning the expanded definition of journalism to other areas of mass media, see Weaver and Wilhoit (1986, pp. 44-45).

magazines, press releases, newsletters, manuals, government documents, business reports, professional journals, and the like. All these are composed by people who want the reader to accept what they have written.

Because media writers bring so much of their background reading to their writing, they first take account of their own biases before determining whether the information they hear or see is accurate, a sham, biased, or controversial. These writers are, therefore, astute judges of information. Applying certain critical skills, they have learned how to separate the counterfeit from the genuine. For example, one conservationist claims uncontrolled forest fires minimize new growth. Another claims some fires allowed to run their natural course maximize new and diverse growth. Two witnesses give conflicting accounts of the same event. Checks on statements made by sources or witnesses fail to square with the record. Information in different records concerning the same matter proves contradictory.

In the last analysis, it is the writer who must decide what information is valid and how to write about it. That holds true for all areas of the media, whether the written work is produced for a 12-inch news article, a full-length magazine piece, a 20-second radio or TV spot, a 60-minute video, a press release, or a full-page advertisement. The accuracy and merit of information communicated is the professional writer's greatest concern.

Of course, a writer may choose to accept received information without question. But then that is the writer who is a passive thinker and an unwitting participant in surface appearances and the claims of others. In addition, the produced copy is more than likely to prove meaningless, inaccurate, incomplete, perhaps even libelous.

There is an alternative choice. The writer can adopt the professional practice of methodical and critical behavior. To act methodically, experienced media writers rely on a systematic strategy. To think critically, they raise relevant questions to evaluate what they observe and what others write or say. They have learned controlled methods of getting answers and thinking critically to produce reliable copy that is creatively written for a mass audience. The professional media writer is, therefore, an active thinker and a critical conduit of information received and communicated. After studying and practicing the principles outlined in this book, the novice will be able to:

- determine the requirements of a writing assignment,
- develop an internal gauge of judgment about received information,
- organize time and the writing task to meet deadlines and reduce stress,
- discover insights that contribute substance to copy,
- write accurate, relevant, creative copy that speaks to an audience, and
- win an editor's confidence.

When confronted with information requiring a decision, the intellectual independence and self-confidence that accrues from practicing disciplined thinking is rewarding, particularly when that thinking manifests itself in writing. Because critical discipline fosters intellectual freedom, many writers discover that controlled thinking stimulates ideas for creative treatment of what is essentially objective data. Today's sophisticated public expects objective information not fiction from media writers, but they also expect media writers to engage their interest. Your aim is to produce creative copy that is grounded in objective data. However, one's imagination need not recede into cold storage. Imagination has a role in mass media writing, but that role comes into play only after a great deal of objective data has been accumulated, evaluated, and digested.

ON THE ISSUE OF OBJECTIVITY

The aim of media professionals is to be objective. That is, they aim to present the facts without bias. Print and broadcast writers are obliged to de-bias themselves and to present accurate information or face litigation. These days public relations and advertising writers must do as much or face angry consumers and clients.

Because media writers deal with complex social matters and people with varying viewpoints, they avoid making snap decisions. They know employers, clients, media consumers, and writers tend to gravitate toward causes and explanations consistent with personal views, and that individual preferences and decisions often reflect tenaciously held values and motives. The forces on human perception and behavior are so complex, scholars of mass media communication are unable to agree on definitions for *objectivity*, *fact*, *truth*. And an approved standard against which media writers can measure objective evidence is still awaiting discovery.

In the physical sciences, researchers answer questions about the world with greater confidence. They measure things: the speed of light, the depth of ocean waters, the age of an unearthed relic. Human behavior is less dependable. Media writers know objectivity is often beyond their grasp, but they also try to get as close to it as possible.

For this reason, professional writers try to be cognizant of motives and values and critically weigh the evidence received. They start with their own biases. They acknowledge them, recognize there is more than one side to any issue, realize even reasonable people will disagree on any matter, and try to determine why they disagree. The ability to recognize one's own biases, raise relevant questions, identify and organize the most substantial evidence from various sides, and still present objective copy creatively requires skill and practice. It is a methodical and critical skill professionals struggle to perfect because mass media audiences demand it.

THE IMPORTANCE OF AUDIENCE

Before writers undertake any media project, they ask: *Who cares or is interested in this?* The answer identifies the audience and indicates whether the subject matter will serve the interests and needs of that audience.

Once the audience is known, the writer tries to anticipate the questions the audience will want answered because what the writer needs to know about the subject of a media project is usually what the audience needs to know as well. To identify your audience and its needs, ask these basic questions:

- *Who cares or is interested in this problem* (issue or question)*?*
- *Why do they need or want to know about it?*
- *What does my audience need or want to know about this problem?*
- *What do I need or want to know about it?*

Other self-inquiries throughout this book will help you write for an audience instead of writing writing, which means writing to satisfy your ego instead of fulfilling the expectations of media consumers.

MEDIA VOICES AND VARIATIONS

Audiences expect media writers to speak in a voice appropriate to the purpose of the message and the medium. For example, the purpose of the news and magazine writer is to inform without fabrication, error, or bias because their audiences expect accurate, complete, and relevant information.

Public relations (PR) audiences, however, know the purpose of PR is to promote the image of a company, its personnel, its product. Like news readers, PR audiences expect accurate information, but they also know that the PR writer discloses only what the company chooses to disclose. Because the purpose of PR work is to persuade, emphasis is placed on information that portrays the company in a favorable light. Unfavorable information is usually put on hold. However, in recent years, the trend in PR is to tell it like it is when a crisis strikes and to explain what the company is doing, or at least planning to do, to correct a bad situation.

The purpose of advertising, like PR, is to persuade. Here, too, the consumer audience expects accurate information about an advertised product, but like PR audiences, they do not expect an impartial appeal. Consumers realize ads are designed to play on buyers' emotions. They will accept varieties of and varying degrees of honest hyperbole, comedy, and fantasy depending on personal preference or tolerance.

Professional media writers understand these differences in voice, but still rely on verified data to write in whatever creative scope their medium allows. In short, all writers in media have patrons — current, temporary, or prospective — whose attention they must capture, inform, and in some cases convince. However, PR and advertising writers are usually far more selective about information relayed than news and magazine writers. Still, all must be very sure about the information they do relay, or at least indicate its tentative or questionable nature.

PRACTICE IS IMPORTANT

Systematic and critical thinking habits do not happen over night. You learn the skills of professional writers by practicing them, not by being told what to do. It is much like learning how to get a tennis ball over the net or how to play the piano. It takes practice. Acquiring the skills of experienced writers is not easy, but the reward of insight into management of a media assignment is the gratifying outcome.

Refer frequently to the examples and models in this book. They illustrate how the strategy and critical self-inquiries work as a unit to produce a media product worthy of publication. Apply the strategy and self-inquiries next time you undertake a writing assignment.

CONCERNING VOCABULARY AND SENTENCE STRUCTURE

One way to build your vocabulary and become familiar with good sentence structure is to read the work of good writers. Professional media writers have large vocabularies because they *read*. They are competent writers because they experience good literature. When they are not reading materials related to their writing assignments, they read nonfiction as well as fiction, the classics, stage plays and, yes, even poetry. Reading good literature, more than listening, develops vocabulary and sensitivity to readable copy because seeing the copy imprints images of easily read and clearly understood sentences on the mind.

Try the readings suggested in Appendix A. This is where you will also find some "do's" about sentence structure and criteria for evaluating your written work. In addition, keep some reliable references on grammar, punctuation, and sentence structure within reach. Suggestions for these are also listed in Appendix A.

English is a fluid language and exceptions to its rules are numerous and confusing. It is best to refer to more than one reference because not every reference answers all problems, nor do these references always agree. The ultimate test is whether the choices you have made promote understanding of the message.

This book is designed principally to make you more aware of your methodical and critical thinking abilities and to help you cultivate them. The habit of systematic procedure and critical thinking helps you recognize weaknesses in the written and spoken word and draws your attention to flaws in your own copy. Because good writing is essentially good thinking, you will find the means to work systematically and to think critically throughout this book, also how to use those means to become a more competent and creative writer.

THE DYNAMICS OF MASS MEDIA WRITING

The strategy of professional media writers is outlined at the end of the next section. A figure illustrating the process appeared in the Preface and you probably noticed that it was recursive (a continuous line to indicate a process that permits repetition) rather than linear (a horizontal line that has an end point). In both recursive and linear strategies each step is completed before movement to the next step can occur. In both strategies frequent returns to one or more completed steps are possible to accommodate modifications as new information is obtained. However, a recursive strategy, rather than a linear one, applies more directly to mass media writing, because a recursive model indicates not only accruing data and turning back in the opposite direction, it also suggests continuation. That is, the media assignment rarely ends with one story, one press release, one ad. There is always another angle, another focus, another episode to write about on the same problem or issue.

ABOUT THE TIME CRUNCH

A frustrating factor in mass media work is time allowed for completion of an assignment. Although no step in the strategy should be circumvented, deadlines and assignment complexity determine the depth of attention given to any one step.

Short deadlines necessarily limit the time spent at certain stages of the strategy and the whole process is, therefore, greatly compressed. Stages in the strategy meld together as one function as they are performed mentally and on the run. But the details in this book are expressly called out to expand that compressed accordion of functions so the novice can see all key segments of the media strategy.

The functions become more obvious to the eye on long deadline assignments because extended deadlines permit depth attention to the parts and often permit elaborately drawn plans and data organizations instead of mental or simplified ones. The whole process is, in comparison, expanded.

Compressed or expanded, on the run or at the office, each of the functions and mental processes follow a natural sequence. By the time you complete the chapters in this book you will be able to adapt the strategy to any media assignment, any deadline.

The *right strategy, right questions* outlined here represent an overview of the dynamics of mass media writing and illustrate the critical thinking steps necessary before other steps can take place. It all adds up to scientific reporting and writing, but in plain English it is fundamentally a detailed breakdown of good work habits, a methodical response to writing assignments, which is the common practice of professional writers in any medium of communication. With practice and experience, you will discover that the strategy and its questions have become an unconscious reflex action, a second nature. You will not think twice about the strokes it takes.

By itself, and as it appears here, the strategy is no more than a map showing a starting point and spot locations to a destination. You are the one who directs the action. This means you must know what self-inquiries to raise at each reference point on the map in order to propel your activity forward to the next point. The questions you raise to generate that action are presented here. The means to answer them are provided in the chapters that follow.

OVERVIEW: RIGHT STRATEGY, RIGHT QUESTIONS

I. Stating the Problem.
   Critical Self-Inquiry 1: *What is the problem, issue, or question?* (chapter 2).

II. Backgrounding and Researching the Problem.
   Critical Self-Inquiry 2: *What information has been and/or is currently documented and known by whom?* (chapter 3).
   Critical Self-Inquiry 3: *What is the working statement?* (chapter 4).
   Critical Self-Inquiry 4: *What information fails to stand up to question?* (Part I: chapter 5; Part II: chapter 6).

III. Designing the Interview Plan.
   Critical Self-Inquiry 5: *What do I need to ask who about what and how shall I ask it?* (Part I: chapter 7; Part II: chapter 8).

IV. Conducting the Interview.
   Critical Self-Inquiry 6: *What data,[2] prepared questions, and*

---

[2]The terms *data* and *information* are used interchangeably in this text. Both words define

interview techniques must I review in order to identify inadequate and/or inaccurate responses, and to raise impromptu questions? (chapter 9).

V. Organizing and Coding the Data.
   Critical Self-Inquiry 7: *What are the units of information in the collected data?* (chapter 10).

VI. Analyzing the Data.
   Critical Self-Inquiry 8: *Where are the similarities, differences, anomalies, gaps and unknowns; where are the agreements, disagreements or conflicts; where are the links indicating relationships, correlations, patterns, or trends; where does the weight and importance of evidence fall and why?* (chapter 11).

VII. Drawing a Conclusion(s).[3]
   Critical Self-Inquiry 9: *What is the statement inherent in and manifested by the body of verified and evaluated data?* (chapter 11).

VIII. Presenting and Writing the Copy.
   Critical Self-Inquiry 10: *What appropriate and effective presentation ideas are manifest in the synthesis statement?* (chapter 12).
   Critical Self-Inquiry 11: *What organization of the copy will render a clear and balanced elaboration of the synthesis statement and its presentation?* (chapter 12).
   Critical Self-Inquiry 12: *What information for elaboration is relevant, informative, interesting, provides a thorough and balanced account, and stands up to question?* (chapter 12).

Also in this book, you will meet eight media professionals whose work procedures and critical thinking habits reflect the pattern of activity outlined here. Those procedures and habits make up the dynamic that mass media writing demands. The professionals interviewed include two each from print news, broadcast news, public relations, and advertising.

Excerpts from interviews held with these professionals appear at the end of chapters detailing specific stages of the strategy: chapters 2, 3, 4, 7, 11 and 12. Chapter 2 introduces you to the first two media writers, then in chapter 3 two more add to the first pair, and so on, until all eight appear in

---

"evidence," which includes information from such materials as records, research reports, documents, minutes, books, references, manuals, journals, and statements from informed individuals.

[3]In this text, *conclusion(s)* refers to the *outcome* suggested by the available and current evidence. The outcome is a product of the strategy and critical process described throughout this text. It is not meant to denote a final judgment. The plural in *conclusion* denotes that the reasoning process may reveal more than one outcome.

chapter 7 and at the end of chapters 11 and 12 (chapter 10 is a companion unit of chapter 11).

Chapter 5 describes the means for evaluating general reading materials and chapter 6 does the same with research studies. Chapters 8 and 9 elaborate on interviewing techniques and introduce a few of the scientifically tested reasons for their use.

In Appendix A, you will find some ways to correct frequently made writing errors, a list of references on English usage, criteria for evaluating your own copy, and a suggested reading list. For two additional interviews with experienced video and film writers, see Appendices B and C. For backgrounds on all 10 professionals, see Appendix D.

2 Stating the Problem, Issue, or Question

Identifying and articulating a statement of the problem is probably the most critical part of the whole writing task.[1] If you are unable to identify and state the problem in specific terms, you will find yourself running in place. To identify the problem, you should be able to place it in some subject category and call out the specific topic within that subject category that you need or wish to write about. In some cases, the problem itself identifies the subject and topic to be explored. In other cases, the subject category may be obvious enough, but its topics so many in number or its issues so complex that a narrowing process must take place before a workable topic statement is found.

To get started, ask yourself the following question, even when the problem subject and topic appear obvious to you. Voicing the question somehow gets the mental wheels moving a little faster. Ask Critical Self-Inquiry 1: *What is the problem, issue, or question?*

Aside from bringing the media assignment into better focus, asking the question out loud is still another means of thinking about and identifying your audience, a crucial factor, as you will see, in the ultimate outcome of your work. In the examples listed here, note how stating the problem at the

---

[1]In this book, *problem* refers to a need or situation requiring consideration or answers, but it is also meant to include report of incidents and events of a general nature and incidents and events that may involve a complex problem and/or persons(s). *Issue* refers to a point or matter under dispute. *Question* is closely related to the terms *problem* and *issue*. It is included here to allow for occasions when posing a direct question is useful. Here also, we consider *problem*, and its related terms, to represent the broad area of a general *subject* and *topic* as a specific subset of that subject wherein many other specific topics may be found.

10

same time identifies its audience. No secrets here. All the clues are in the problem.

News

- *Assignment — Problem.* There's a fire at No. 2 Zed Street. Cover it. *Audience:* general news readers.
- *Observation — Problem:* Why were public telephone booths removed from Main Street? *Audience:* general news readers, especially patrons of public phones.
- *Tip — Problem:* The city treasurer is allegedly spending public funds to build a home swimming pool. Is he? Look into it. *Audience:* city taxpayers.
- *Journal — Problem:* Increasing amounts of toxics are being discharged into state waters, according to *Water Conservation Journal.* Check it out for a feature. *Audience:* ecologists, tourists, fishing industry, outdoor enthusiasts, seafood lovers, environmental violators.

Public Relations

- *Assignment — Problem:* Harley Jones was named vice-president of quality control. Send out a press release. *Audience:* business community via area newspapers, newsletters, trade journals, and the like, and employees via house magazine or newspaper.
- *Observation — Problem:* Bill Samson won the employee award for best cost control idea. Good story for the company. *Audience:* same as above.
- *Tip — Problem:* State distributor reports product tampering. Look into it. *Audience:* company officials and employees via internal communication systems, product consumers via local and national news media.

Advertising

- *Assignment — Problem:* The client wants a jazzier approach in the next Sudsy Soap campaign, but asks us to retain emphasis on its chemical-free feature. See what you can come up with. *Audience:* women, teen-agers, mothers of newborn babies, men and women with sensitive skin.
- *TV Commercial — Problem:* Competitor ABC claims its deodorant lasts longer than ours. Does it? Check it out. *Audience:* men, women, teen-agers.

- *Survey—Problem:* According to XYZ Polls, the teenage buying market has increased by 38%. Find out what's going on. If true, we need a wider magazine coverage for Lovely Lotion. Show me some sample ads. *Audience:* teen-agers.

Value of Problem Definition

These are fairly straightforward writing tasks in which the stated problem and audience are well defined. The boundaries of *preliminary* research are also fairly clear. For example, research for the first case should concern all circumstances and people connected with the fire on Zed Street. For the PR tip, research should cover the distribution area, its personnel, product packaging control, and other people and factors relevant to the problem. Research for the Lovely Lotion assignment should include study of the survey, other related surveys, review of the client's past and current advertising regarding skin care where product content was ignored or included, a look at what other advertisers are doing to attract the teen-age market and, if available, survey results from a *focus* group of teen-agers to find out what they expect from your product (advertisers rely on *focus* groups to test consumer needs or to test a new product or a new campaign approach).

In short, having articulated the problem, you now know what the subject area is, who you are writing for, and the initial information you need to get started. This is preliminary backgrounding and research. To obtain this initial information, you raise questions relevant to the problem subject because having stated the problem you noticed information that required research in order to write about the subject. It is from that backgrounding and research that you will find the topic focus that grabs your attention and requires *primary* backgrounding and research.

The Elusive Problem

If you are assuming all writing assignments originate with an editor, you are only partially right. Sometimes you are the source. That is, you could and should generate your own writing projects, something that engages your attention and moves you with a deep curiosity or unrest about it. All you need do to generate ideas is to notice the events, objects, and people around you. Or, let your curiosity work for you when you read or hear something that captures your interest. Be an enterprising writer. Do some preliminary research and present the findings to your editor in the form of a proposal, either verbally or, preferably, in writing. Editors may not always give you a go ahead, but they do expect enterprise and remember writers who demonstrate initiative.

However, with enterprise projects, and often with complex assignments, the problem is not as well defined as those in the examples listed previously. Consequently, the problem is not so easily articulated. When this happens, do exactly what you would do for an assignment where the problem is less elusive: Do a preliminary study of the subject.

Review past and current information on record concerning the subject. Conduct preliminary interviews with people who have had and currently have experience with it. Preliminary research is important because it primes you with basic information concerning the problem subject and tells you whether you have a project worthy of audience attention. It also provides a context of knowledge that can trigger an idea on which to focus and often leads to a fresh view concerning the problem.[2]

For example, a popular subject in mass media is the problem of water pollution. In your preliminary research you might discover that a subset problem of that subject is chemical waste discharged into state waters by industries. You may learn that this topic, too, has its subset problem: the effect of chemical waste on water wildlife. Additional preliminary research may uncover a subset of this topic, as well: the effect on a particular species of fish that is a favorite of seafood lovers and an important national industry. It is the process of narrowing a broad or complex subject area down to a workable topic area. You could use any of these subsets if one of them inspired a *working statement* you could articulate.[3]

The point here is, if you want to write a narrative about either a simple or complex problem, you should narrow your focus to accommodate the parameters of related research. Otherwise, your problem topic will be ill defined and you will be researching everything and nothing.

Problem subjects in PR and advertising are different than those in newswriting, but the process of narrowing down to a topic focus to inform, convince, or persuade remains the same. For example, a PR release on the subject of a smooth ride in a passenger car may focus on the topic of a new tooling setup that improves the vehicle's suspension system to provide a smoother ride. An advertisement promoting a cereal product may focus on

---

[2]In this book, *focus* is synonomous with *problem* focus, *subject* focus, *topic* focus, *theme*, *concept*, or the *main idea*.

[3]Many new terms are creeping into the vocabulary of mass media writers, particularly *working statement*, sometimes called the *problem* or *tentative statement*, *hypothesis*, *principal* or *main question*, or *main idea*. During the author's interviews with them, newswriters repeatedly used these terms, as well as *preliminary/primary background and/or research*, *preliminary/primary interviews*. For example, see an interview with *Washington Post* reporter, Lou Cannon, in which he referred to his hypothesis as a "working statement" (in Biagi, 1987, p. 48). In some instances, PR writers substituted the terms *problem*, *issue*, *need*, *situation*, or *question* for *working statement*, and advertising writers used some of these along with *campaign theme*, *idea* or *concept*.

a special process that maintains Nature's vitamins in cereal grain and eliminates the need to add synthetic vitamins.

Once the problem, audience, boundaries of preliminary research, and topic focus are identified, the writer can formalize the problem into a working statement, which is best written out so elements requiring primary research may be seen. As suggested earlier, on short deadline or less complex assignments, the stated problem indicates the audience, areas of research, and very often the working statement. More complex assignments usually require a great deal of research before a working statement can be formulated.

But take note, that statement is *not* a hypothesis the writer sets out to confirm or disconfirm. It is *not* the conclusion. The working statement is merely a means to get started on the topic and to stimulate first questions and likely sources. It is a first guide to data collection on the topic, and because it is a starting point, the working statement may be modified, even negated and replaced, as new information demands at any point along the way. But before taking on any assignment, you need to organize your time, a crucial factor in meeting deadlines.

SCHEDULING AN ASSIGNMENT TO MEET
THE DEADLINE

When writing for the media, a cardinal rule is: Meet the deadline, but get it right. Editors, often clients, usually set the deadline and they expect the writer to conduct and complete the work before the deadline expires. In news work the spot news (or breaking) story is usually completed within hours. The depth story may have a deadline of anywhere from 2 days to 2 weeks to several months. Deadlines in public relations and advertising vary just as much.

Knowing the due date, professional writers orchestrate their time from the moment they receive an assignment. One common practice on assignments with extended deadlines is to list all the tasks that are necessary and then to work backward from the deadline date to the date the assignment was received, allotting time needed for each task through each day or week within that calendar period.

The model presented here is meant to demonstrate the principle of dividing time among all tasks required on any specific assignment. It is not meant to stand as a hard and fast standard. If the model helps you break up tasks into time slots for your particular assignment, use it. If you have another way of doing the same thing, nothing should stop you from following it.

The important thing is to realize that you have only a certain amount of time and that the time should be distributed wisely among all tasks required of you. Furthermore, depending on the medium, the nature of time efficiency plans will vary from one assignment to another and within a single medium, and so will the type of required tasks. For example, on a video assignment, besides attending conferences, researching, writing, revising, obtaining approvals and editing, you also may be asked to identify suitable locations, schedule production and shooting periods, make casting decisions, and perform other functions related to production. Time necessary to get any task completed for any assignment in any medium must be taken into account. Just as an example of how you could set up an assignment schedule, here is a suggestion on what you might do for a print news feature story.

Sample Assignment Schedule

Let's suppose you are on the staff of a metropolitan newspaper and your editor assigns you to do a story on pollution in the largest inland body of fresh water in the world, the Great Lakes. Your deadline is 3 weeks away. You know nothing about the Great Lakes or things that pollute the waterways. Your editor gives you an article from a journal regarding toxic waste discharges in the Great Lakes. There are a few clues here, but not enough to help you out. Your work schedule might look like the following plan. Just remember no plan ever works out just the way you want it to go. You will probably work overtime, maybe weekends, and make more than one schedule adjustment. But knowing what needs to be done, how far along you are and what is left to be done reduces much of the chaos and anxiety of setbacks, interruptions, and frustrations.

May

3, W: Call IJC, get their water quality report [noted in journal article].
        Send messenger to pick up report.
        Read library newsclips, check other house references.
        Make a note of relevant articles in news indexes, environmental journal data base, *Reader's Guide.*
        Note relevant publications in *Books in Print.*
        Set up questions for preliminary research.
        Read about Great Lakes, toxic pollutants in encylopedias.
        See data about GL in almanacs.
        Pull noted references from public/university library.
        Begin readings.

4, Th: Call DNR, find out who to contact about GL water quality, effects.
        Call EPA, State Dept. of Health re same, check interviewees' backgrounds.
        Continue readings.

process of critical/creative thinking. These professionals, all star performers in their particular medium, were unaware of their systematic approach. It was not until they were interviewed and compelled to reach back into personal experience for the sources of their creativity that they later realized craftsmanship originated in scientific methods and disciplined thinking.

As in surveys conducted with other professionals, these respondents chose the media assignments they wanted to discuss and were asked the same questions: What was their story about? How did they come to work on it? What did they do to get started? What did they do next? What did they do after that?, and so on. In the process of answering these questions, the respondents explained what they were trying to learn or explain, how they conducted their research, whether their working statement remained stable or was modified and, if it was modified, at what point and why. They also explained how they prepared for and conducted their interviews and how they organized, analyzed, and decided to present their data in written form.

Few respondents required probing questions, including those represented here. Most were able to describe their activities, tools, sources, and habits. Not surprisingly, after the interview was over and they were asked to name or categorize the functions they had just described, few could do so. Yet, when their activities were identified and repeated to them in the same progression they had described, including verifications and retraced steps, each confirmed the interviewer's feedback. Many of the media-related terms used in this text came out of the vocabulary used by the professionals interviewed.

If the responses you read here sound choppy and groping, remember speakers are trying to pierce through the surface of their minds to explain activities they have only now begun to think about consciously. So do not expect classic prose, just ordinary speech. Although most professionals provided detailed answers, only portions from their lengthy interviews are provided here due to limited space. Nevertheless, those portions illustrate the function involved, whereas the whole of all interviews together crystallize to reflect the outline model of the strategy. The critical self-inquiries listed with the model were formulated to help you get started on the particular function concerned and to help you generate the kind of critical questioning professionals demonstrated during the interviews.

Other guidelines in this book represent a consolidation of the techniques I learned on the job as a media writer and with which student writers seemed to require the most assistance. The unity of strategy, critical questions, and techniques is presented with one purpose in mind — to reduce the hardship of discovering a procedure and mode of thought the author and other professionals learned through painful trial and error.

These excerpts come from interviews held with two print journalists and concern subject matter in this chapter. Their responses relating to the next stage of the strategy carry through in the following chapter where two broadcast journalists are introduced along with their comments concerning the discussion in chapter 3 and the previous chapter. Responses from all four professionals continue into chapter 4 where two public relations writers are introduced. Their comments manifest use of techniques discussed in previous chapters and all six illustrate use of the technique discussed in chapter 4.

Chapters 5 and 6 deal with evaluating reference materials and enlarge on the functions of backgrounding and research discussed in chapters 3 and 4. Comments from the last two media writers, those in advertising, are included at the end of chapter 7 along with their accounts of subject matter described in chapters 2-4 and 7. Comments from the other six concerning the topic in chapter 7 are also included. The last phases of media work are discussed in chapters 10-11 and the writers' comments related to this discussion appear at the end of chapter 11. Then at the end of chapter 12, which details how to put data together for a story, the writers describe how they finally used their data to write their assignments.

Gradual introduction of the writers and excerpts from interviews with them allow an orientation to the type and background of each assignment they describe and avoids burdening the reader with all eight orientations at once.

*   *   *

HOW THE PROFESSIONALS DO IT

Stating the Problem

Print News: The Navy Story

David L. Ashenfelter

The following concerns a series of stories written by a two-person team of news journalists, David L. Ashenfelter and Sidney P. Freedberg, for which they were awarded the 1982 Pulitzer Prize for Meritorious Public Service. Mr. Ashenfelter is now an investigative news reporter at the *Detroit Free Press*, and Ms. Freedberg is currently a news reporter at the *Miami Herald*. They had worked on the series while both were still on the staff at *The Detroit News*.

The subject of the series concerned the deaths of six Navy seamen who had died while on peacetime duty aboard their assigned vessels. The topic of the series focused on the problems their families encountered when they asked the Navy to tell them how their sons died. Preceded by nearly 5 months of research and analytic work, publication of the stories began on September 27, 1981, and continued in seven additional installments through October, November, December, and January of the following year.

The story broke in April 1981 when a Michigan sailor, Paul Trerice, died in the Philippines of a heart attack brought on by heatstroke while performing punishment exercises aboard the aircraft carrier USS Ranger. The Navy initially described the incident as an unfortunate accident during routine punishment. However, the sailor's father, suspecting that he was getting the runaround, complained to his congressman and Michigan news reporters that his son died at the hands of brutal jailers aboard the carrier. Shortly after the April exposure, the two newswriters began investigation and publication of the mental and physical battering Trerice had endured hours before his death and the rampant abuse of other wayward sailors confined to the ship's two correctional facilities. These stories and those written by other Michigan reporters prompted the Navy to launch an investigation of Trerice's death.

Ms. Freedberg and Mr. Ashenfelter began to suspect that other families were encountering similiar evasiveness when parents pressed the Navy for details about their sons' deaths. While the Navy completed its investigation of the Trerice case and prepared for court martials and other disciplinary proceedings against Ranger officers and crewmen, the two newswriters investigated the deaths of six other sailors whose families were having difficulty obtaining straight answers from the Navy.

Written in a collaborative effort by *The Detroit News* team and entitled "Peacetime Deaths at Sea: The Navy's Unfinished Business," the series revealed a Navy policy of keeping parents and the public uninformed or misinformed about active duty deaths. It is from this Pulitzer Prize series that Mr. Ashenfelter drew one story to describe the team's activities on this news project.

As a result of the Ashenfelter-Freedberg stories, the Navy relieved the U. S. Marine Corps of guard duty in Navy brigs, a tradition dating back to 1775. The Navy also filed misconduct charges against more than 24 Ranger officers and enlisted men and issued a new policy manual setting standards for Navy correction units. The new manual stresses prisoner rehabilitation rather than punishment, forbids prisoner mistreatment and requires correctional units to be run by trained supervisors, consultants, and staff members. Finally, the Navy pledged improvement in its reporting methods to families about peacetime deaths.

In this case, outrage triggered the curiosity and dedication of these two writers. The manner in which Navy officials treated the deaths of peacetime servicemen disturbed Ms. Freedberg and Mr. Ashenfelter. The families were not getting straight answers from Navy officials; the writers felt that was the least the Navy could do; the team set out to find out why families were not getting the truth.

Throughout the investigation, the newswriters encountered many obstacles, but critical thinking, resourcefulness, and persistence brought them results. Those features characterize this team's effort. They raised questions constantly, noticed points of misinformation, contradictions, holes, confirmations, and worked around obstacles to their progress. They kept their superiors informed at crucial points in the investigation and brought facts to the table so editors could contribute solutions to research problems.

As new information developed, they returned to research sources, repeated verification functions, pre-interviewed and interviewed sources, and adjusted their problem statement several times before focus for the series was found. Such disruption in the sequence and the ensuing chaos always accompanies a complex media story that is elusive, but not impossible to get. Moreover, those returns and repetitions were necessary before a substantial data bank could be accumulated, before interviews with the opposition and others could take place, before reliable analysis could begin, before conclusions could be drawn, and before a creative piece of work worthy of a Pulitzer could be written.

Mr. Ashenfelter began by explaining how he became involved with this story:

Ashenfelter: The [*Detroit*] *Free Press,* think it was late April or early May of 1981, they carried a story. Basically, the story was about the father [Mr. Trerice] raising questions about his son's mysterious death. Sydney Freedberg started asking questions of our [*The Detroit News*] state desk: *What are we doing on this story? It's a good story.*

What ultimately happened was that the kid's body was returned home without any organs which immediately sent shock waves through the journalism community. Our initial instinct as reporters was that something's going on here that deserves some close attention.

My involvement on the story started a week after the initial reporting and Sydney did not have an editor that day. I was curious about the story, so I volunteered to be her editor.

That's when she told me about a phone call she'd gotten from this guy in Illinois telling her that when he was on the ship [Ranger] in 1976 three prisoners were either murdered or died in the brig. One was apparently marched off the end of the flight deck by Marines. Orner [the witness] could not tell us who the kid was, but he gave us a few names. Two were Detroit area kids. In the meanwhile, Sydney had tracked down two sailors through Mr. Trerice. The sailors had called expressing condolences. Both said they had witnessed beatings while they were in the brig, and one said he was beaten himself in the brig by a Marine guard. They gave us names of other guys. One said while he was down there [in the brig] a Marine guard had slapped him up on the ear and ruptured his ear drum. So what we suspected immediately as reporters was widespread prisoner abuse aboard the ship [Ranger].

An enterprise project developed for this pair because Ms. Freedberg noticed a story in a competing newspaper. She reacted to her own paper's indifference to the incident, first because it involved local servicemen and promised audience interest, and then because the circumstances surrounding the death of Mr. Trerice's son remained a mystery.

No less sensitive to the report, Mr. Ashenfelter reacted to the same elements in this tragic event and stepped up to the responsibility of editorship. Ms. Freedberg had already done some preliminary checking to see if the telephone tip she had received held any merit. But mystery surrounded the issue and prevented clear definition of the problem which, at this point, could only be stated as: *Serviceman in peacetime service is sent home in a coffin with all his organs missing. What's going on?*

Stimulated first by curiosity, then by outrage, the reporters knew there was a story here, but moved cautiously. They had some first suspicions, but realized the story needed more backgrounding and research beyond the preliminary sources Ms. Freedberg had contacted (see chapter 3).

Print News: The Ford Plant Fire

All news projects are not as complex as the Ashenfelter-Freedberg project. Some are just routine assignments that even experienced newswriters must often cover. They can be just as difficult and anxiety driven as the complex story, perhaps even more so, because of the short deadline, usually less than a 24-hour period. Still, the same tasks are performed just as they are in a complex story with a long deadline. The difference, of course, is that the breaking or spot news story is compressed into a narrower time frame that obscures the delineating lines between tasks because the strategy becomes more fluid. The following interview illustrates the compressed and fluid nature of the short deadline assignment.

Beyond following the strategy, the features that characterize this reporter's work is how he keeps up with the momentum of the emergency by raising a steady stream of self-inquiries, adjusts his research effort and questions to a constantly changing event, and how he covers details before going on to the next step in the process, yet returns quickly to a previous stage to fill in a missing detail or when the situation warrants a return. Initiative and self-reliance mark the nature of his news coverage on this assignment, and it is all done in the midst of a chaotic on-scene situation and within the squeeze of a few hours.

Stating the problem is less complicated in this instance than it was in the first case. The problem subject is clear: A five-alarm fire, obvious to anyone who noticed the smoked-filled sky over an industrial area between Ann Arbor, Michigan, and the nearby city of Saline. The problem is easily articulated once the source of the fire is learned, a Ford Motor Company plastics plant just outside of Saline.

Stephen Cain

Stephen Cain is a seasoned general assignment and investigative reporter for *The Ann Arbor News.* He quickly recognized the potential for this story, volunteered to cover the story and was one of two reporters assigned to it. Meanwhile, other staff members are assigned to do some preliminary backgrounding and research from the newsroom. Separated from his teammate by traffic at the very outset, Mr. Cain's coverage of the story is necessarily carried out independently.

Because he has had previous experience covering similar fires, Mr. Cain knew the possible consequences of such a fire. While driving the 12-mile distance between Ann Arbor and Saline, he automatically framed a statement of the problem in his mind: *A five-alarm fire at the Ford Motor plastics plant near Saline threatens wholesale loss of life and property.* At the same time, he planned his preliminary research questions.

Cain: It was in the middle of the afternoon. There was a very large black cloud that was visible from the office. They first directed Bill Treml to go out and cover. It was clear that this was a very large scale event, so I asked to go along, and they said, "Yes, you and Bill work together."

Because this was a chemical plant, I knew this before arriving and became much more aware of that later, explosions could tear the plant apart and wholesale loss of life and property was a possibility.

I was aware, as was Bill, that any story about this event would require quite a few things: *How and where did it start? How much damage was there? How much danger was there of the fire spreading and doing even greater damage? How well did these fire officials respond to contain the threat?* [In a fire like this] there is always the risk of having toxic poisons in the smoke, so other questions would be: *Who gets evacuated? How is that decision made? How great or not great was the risk?* These are the things you just know you're going to have to find out.

Answers to these questions had to wait until Mr. Cain arrived on the scene to conduct preliminary backgrounding and research by first observing and then making initial inquiries. But his subject matter is clear—a five-alarm fire at a major manufacturing auto plant filled with toxic materials. However, the topic focus awaits further observation and research (see chapter 3).

3 Backgrounding and Researching the Problem

Many writers regard backgrounding as research. Others prefer to differentiate the two. In a sense, both viewpoints are accurate because the two functions are unique, yet dependent on one another and are closely related. For those who like to see a differentiation, it can be said that backgrounding provides a context, or backdrop, for additional research, some of which may be more in-depth and complex. Whether you choose one viewpoint or the other, backgrounding and research on the subject must precede *primary* backgrounding and research on the topic. But do not be surprised if you have to return to subject research to understand something more about the topic. That is always a possibility. Still, both stages serve the same end. They lead to facts in the case and are necessary for focused writing. Moreover, topic focus is what editors expect to see in any copy work, accomplished only after you accrue some acquaintance with the general picture.

SIMILARITIES AND DIFFERENCES

Professional writers conduct preliminary research because they need to:

- Learn basic facts and terms related to the problem subject in order to assure accuracy and complete coverage when writing.
- Determine whether enough evidence is available to assure productive development of an assignment or enterprise project.

- Determine if the problem, event, issue, or question is worthy of the time and effort necessary for continued investigation.
- Locate answers to questions carried by the writer to preliminary research sources.
- Identify questions left unanswered by preliminary sources.
- Identify possible sources for preliminary and primary interviews.
- Identify a topic focus when one is needed.
- Accumulate baseline data for a report to the editor about the potential of the writing assignment or enterprise project.

The reasons for primary research are not much different, except that they concern a topic subset of the subject. Both preliminary and primary research involve a search through past and current records and references. Both involve questioning informed sources who have had experience with and/or are currently knowledgeable about your area of investigation.

It makes sense to conduct preliminary research on the subject before undertaking definitive investigation of the topic. Sometimes the information available is substantial. Sometimes it is much less, but more is gained than lost. In the process of absorbing information about a subject problem, you accrue the vocabulary and knowledge to warrant responsibility for writing about the topic. In fact, you need basic facts about both subject problem and topic problem in order to validate and verify initial information and before you can convince your editor, supervisor, or account executive that the project is worthy of development for print space or air time.

Whether preliminary or primary, backgrounding and research generate questions and sources related to the topic, particularly if you are able to formulate a working statement of the topic problem. For example, if you were assigned to do a feature story on the impact of pollution in the Great Lakes, for background your first subject categories in references would be "pollution," "consequences of," "Great Lakes." Examples of some first sources might be the:

- *World Almanac and Book of Facts.*
- *American Encyclopedia, World Book Encyclopedia, Water Encyclopedia.*
- *Books in Print, Book Review Digest, Reader's Guide.*
- Government reports on Great Lakes pollution.
- Databases that list journal articles concerning Great Lakes pollution.
- *The Washington Post, The New York Times, Los Angeles Times*, and Detroit and Chicago newspaper indexes.

If you are lucky enough to be in an organization with a research library, you will find most of these references in the house library. If not, you will find these and other references in the public library. If a specific government document is needed, the office where the document was produced is obliged to provide it under the Freedom of Information Act (FOIA).

Selection of references and informed sources for either preliminary or primary research will vary from assignment to assignment whether it is a news, PR, or advertising project. Morever, selection is largely dependent on the nature of the assignment and the problem in question. In some instances, the materials and persons used in the preliminary stage of research are also useful in the primary stage. In other instances, the references utilized in the primary stage may be of an entirely different nature than those used in preliminary research.

PR and advertising writers have some advantage over newswriters. Their companies may initiate a research study that often serves as a base from which the writer can identify a topic idea. These studies are conducted by research specialists, within or outside the PR or ad agency. The studies are mainly designed to test the market, product, or ad, and research results are made available to PR and ad writers.

Despite possible variances, many types of sources remain faithful standbys for all media writers. The ones listed here number among them. Whatever the assignment or medium, the professional writer asks Critical Self-Inquiry 2: *What information has been and/or is currently documented and known by whom?*

IMPORTANCE OF SEQUENCE

Keep in mind that preliminary research precedes primary research because it is an exploration and a test of the media assignment on short or long deadline. If preliminary research indicates additional work is unwarranted, do not junk the data collected. Just put the project on hold for further developments. You will be that much ahead when something does break to prove you were right about the project's promise. And then you can play off the original work to continue with primary research. In fact, that is precisely the value of a sequential strategy. Everything that follows plays off of preliminary work. No single step in the strategy can be accomplished efficiently unless the one preceding it has taken place. Furthermore, the presence of defined steps in a sequential, yet flexible, order allows the writer to recognize which step to return to in order to make the necessary adjustments. The process is orderly, but recursive and fluid.

HANDLING THE RESEARCH TASK

Neither the preliminary or primary research task is easy. However, the guidelines for systematic approach in this book should eliminate any sense of anxiety or confusion. Keep in mind that the working statement is often a given on short deadline assignments and that the self-inquiries concerning them are predetermined. This expedites research. On more complex assignments, the depth of research is determined by the complexity of the assignment, print space or broadcast time allowed, and the deadline given for completion. Research is bound to be more extensive when the working statement is at first elusive or contains uncertainties. Remember, too, that everything that follows plays off the research. Without it you have nothing, as one professional points out in an interview at the end of this chapter. Research is a learning experience and, if nothing else, should be enjoyed for the exposures it affords.

What to Look For

For background information begin by carrying the basic questions, introduced in chapter 1, to preliminary reference sources:

- *Who cares or is interested in this problem* (issue or question)*?*
- *Why do they need or want to know about it?*
- *What does my audience need or want to know about this problem?*
- *What do I need or want to know about it?*

List those questions on paper and carry them with you to the research sources. Look for answers to these questions as you read, notice, and absorb the information. At this point, your aim is to understand what the general subject is all about, to get background on the facts and issues involved. As you research you will notice names of persons who may be able to provide additional information and still other source names. Make a note of them. Anything you read in preliminary research, anyone with whom you check preliminary information can trigger a main idea for a working statement or material for interview questions.

For primary research, continue in the same manner, but look for answers to questions that are *relevant* to the working statement. This means noticing both supporting *and* opposing views on the subject and/or the topic focus. Use the following as a checklist for preliminary and primary research:

- Names of those identified as authorities and from whom you can obtain clarifications or confirmations (or disconfirmations) of what is in the record, and who may act as your primary interviewees, as well.
- Names of prospective interviewees other than those with whom you have already checked preliminary information.

- Specific facts and items that may be useful during interviews or in final writing (names, dates, places, events, historical data, laws, regulations, policy, etc.).
- Unfamiliar terms that need defining so you can use them correctly in your copy.
- Notice what information is confirmed, ambiguous, biased, or contradicts other received information.
- Notice what questions are left unanswered in the data you are reviewing.

Any or all of these will provide the details you will need in your data bank.

Researching the Interview Prospect

After noting down the names of informed persons for interviews, try to find out something about them. You need to know if they are qualified sources. And if you intend to interview them, it is to your advantage to know who is answering your questions. Look them up in biographical directories. Libraries have such references on persons in almost every area of major human endeavor. For not-so-famous people, talk to friends, relatives, neighbors, employers, co-workers.

Knowing something about your interviewees before you interview them may mean the difference between a successful or dismal interview. Find out about their work, education, associations, family, and friends, even their interests, values, prejudices, and preferences.

James Dean, the late movie star who won public acclaim for his performances in *East of Eden* and *Rebel Without a Cause,* understood this. Before each interview he researched the background of the interviewer! Equipped with information, Dean proceeded to charm the interviewer by transforming himself into whatever the actor thought would appeal to that person. The journalists loved Dean and he rarely drew a bad review.

TV broadcaster Barbara Walters, who has interviewed many of the world's most prominent personalities, never goes to an interview without first learning everything she can about her interviewee. She uses the information to establish rapport and has found that when the respondent is at ease answers flow more freely (Walters, 1970). Information about the respondent facilitates the interview process. It also helps the interviewer formulate questions the interviewee will be able to answer, a matter discussed in more detail in chapters 7-9.

If your research does not yield source names, look up your subject in an encyclopedia and note the names of the authors at the end of the article. If you look up these names in a biographical directory, you may be able to locate them for contact. Or, look in the phone directory for a government agency related to your subject. Find out who heads that agency and ask that person for source names. Or, call the local university and ask for the person knowledgeable about your subject and ask that person to either act as a source and/or to recommend the names of other persons. And on not-so-famous respondents, use the city directory to get a bead on where they live and take it from there.

Research on a media project or an interviewee is not a one time effort. It does not end with either preliminary or primary work. New questions always enter the picture at any time before writing, even during writing, and each question will lead you back to a former research source or interviewee or, perhaps, a new source or respondent.

Where the First Sources Are

Media writers customarily start with in-house sources before going out of one's own media organization for information. For in-house records, news and magazine writers rely on news and magazine clips filed in the house library. PR writers refer to various types of company manuals and product data records located in the company library or stored in departmental or client files. Advertising writers have access to similar data files.

These sources are studied first to learn what others inside and outside the organization have written about the problem in the past and company personnel have found worthy enough to keep on hand. Whatever questions are left unanswered in these materials are then carried to outside sources.

Where and in what the exploration continues is determined by the problem itself. For example, if a PR writer, employed by an environmental group, had to write a piece on pollution in the Great Lakes, the first source would be that office's files. A trip to the public library would follow with a search through general references concerning the problem, similar to the ones mentioned earlier.

Preliminary research need not be limited to references in public libraries. For all writers on any problem, research also involves observation, phone calls, or trips to association or government offices, to university and private libraries, or to PR offices of corporations, institutions, private organizations, and the like.

Evidence Defined

Collecting information is one thing, but obtaining solid information is another. Media writers look for *evidence*. Evidence is an object in reality, a physical presence that offers some probability, but no guarantee, the given information is true. That physical presence may be a government document, a police record, a receipt, a driver's license, minutes of a meeting, record of a court testimony, a research or focus group report, a mechanic's manual, the annual report of a corporation, and the like.

Documentation is no assurance that the information is authentic, complete, or even accurate. However, physical presence does permit comparison of related documents in order to test the merit of the evidence in any one document. Comparisons bring the writer closer to the truth.

If information demonstrates consensus in more than one document, it provides the researcher with fairly reliable data. If comparison demonstrates a contradiction of "fact," an error, or a controversy, the mismatch is cause for further exploration and could develop into an enterprise project. For example, *Detroit Free Press* investigative reporter, David L. Ashenfelter, reviewed computerized sentencing records of the Michigan Department of Corrections and after checking them against files at Corrections headquarters in Lansing, he found 2,573 wrong numbers. That turned out to be nearly 45% of the computerized sentencing records on 5,762 inmates paroled in 1983. Some 1,759 records had inaccurate sentencing dates, the wrong amount of credit for time served in jail before sentencing, or the wrong date that the sentence legally began. A total of 392 records, in which sentence calculation formulas were provided by the Department of Corrections, yielded a different date than was shown on the computer tapes, and 422 records showed a combination of the two former factors.

Some of the errors were traced back to clerical errors due to flaws in the computer program. Because of these errors many inmates with long prison sentences for committing heinous crimes were released earlier than they should have been. In one instance, Ashenfelter discovered that a prisoner sentenced to 40-60 years for armed robbery was released after 40 months because a clerk had typed the word "months" into the state computer instead of "years." This error, and a great deal more information, was described in a week-long series of stories published during September 1985, by the *Detroit Free Press* concerning the early release of hardened criminals and the problem of Michigan's overcrowded prisons (D. L. Ashenfelter, personal communication, May 1987).

Quotes set off the word "fact" in the third paragraph of this section because, as you already know, uncertainty and tentativeness always surround objective data. The controversy about genetic versus environmental influence on intellectual ability is still a matter of debate. So is the abortion issue. In August 1989, a Canadian woman defied a lower court injunction filed by her lover in an attempt to prevent her from aborting their child. While the Canadian Supreme Court deliberated on the legality of the injunction, the woman underwent an abortion. The higher court finally overturned the lower court's injunction after the fact and the woman was absolved of any violation of the injunction (presently there is no law in Canada restricting abortion).

Even judicial orders are not written in stone. Nevertheless, professional writers search out evidence because it is an existing proof by which comparisons are made and human decisions are possible, until those decisions are overturned by better information.

Reliance on documented information does not mean opinion, statement, anecdote, personal experience, and the like, should be ignored. They may have some basis in fact when tested against the agreement or disagreement of a number of named persons and, when used along with documented information, they take on additional credibility. But used alone or without named sources, they are simply not as legitimate because such information is not as convincing as recorded proof that can provide two of the standards of evidence—documentation and consensus.

In the last months of 1989, conjecture and rumor surrounded Detroit Police Chief William L. Hart for alleged diversion of Detroit Police Dept. funds to dummy corporations set up by former police deputy, Kenneth Weiner. Hart denied any wrong doing and Weiner ran. Weiner was eventually found and arrested for alleged criminal conduct.

Weiner's business associates reported having been allegedly bilked of $17 million in phony investment deals promoted by Weiner between 1983 and 1986. Evidence indicated those reports might be true and other evidence showed that Weiner had used money from his dummy corporate network to pay rent on a luxurious home in California for Hart's daughter and son-in-law. The Internal Revenue Service also wanted Weiner for tax evasion. Mayor Coleman Young declared his confidence in Police Chief Hart and refused to take either the rumors or the mounting evidence seriously until the evidence was judged in court.

In May 1991, Weiner was sentenced to 10 years in prison on 40 fraud counts in the case involving his business associates. Three months previous to this, both Weiner and Hart had been charged with conspiracy to embezzle $1.3 million from the secret police fund used to make drug purchases and pay informants. In September 1991, under a plea deal, Weiner pleaded guilty to this charge. At this writing, Hart is awaiting trial on the same charge against him.

Rumors and opinions sometimes turn out to have some basis in fact, but without supportive and evaluated evidence, they carry little weight. Because solid data take precedence over opinions, media writers look for relevant evidence. As suggested earlier, relevant evidence may be good or bad, supportive or in opposition, similar or in contrast to other known facts. Relevant evidence is also verified data, that is, a valid ID, a documented historic or recent event, or a record or document that has been doctored, is incomplete, errroneous, or even fraudulent. In short, relevant evidence is connected in one way or another to the subject problem or topic problem.

Recording Research Notes

Evidence is of little value, however, unless you note it down accurately. That is why professional writers are systematic note takers. Good management of notes is as much a protective measure as it is a means of providing you with good records. Editors, company officials, and clients frequently want to know who said what to whom, when, where, and sometimes even why and how it was communicated, that is, the tone of delivery and given under what conditions. Morever, if members of the audience choose to challenge the writer, and they often do, they will want the same information.

Another reason to note information efficiently and carefully is time. The need to return to a source will always occur. A good record of the details concerning the original search expedites re-access and eliminates another time-consuming process. Be systematic. Use these suggestions when noting from references, records, documents, and the like:

- Record the date, time, and place of your source.
- Note the reference title, author(s), publisher, place and year of publication, page numbers used from the source document (even the call number if it is a library reference and where you found it in the library). These notations are important because you may need to cite whatever information you take down. It saves a lot of grief and time if you have all these details on hand in the event you have to return for a check on something.
- List unfamiliar terms. Look them up now, not when you are about to write, and make a note of the definition (meanings of new terms have a way of slipping out of memory unless they are written down).
- Check your notations, including spelling, to make sure you have made an accurate record of source names, titles, affiliations, addresses, phone numbers, any detail that identifies the source of information.
- When quoting, take down the words exactly as the source presents them, use quotation marks and note in what source and context you found it. You may want to use the quote.[1]

---

[1]Editors prefer source names when an attribution of information is made. Use of "an informed source says," or "officials say," is usually unacceptable. For a reliable guide on what editors expect of newswriters, see Giles (1987).

"Survey Data," "Interviews/Jones," "Interviews/Smith," "Editor/ Client Meetings," "Budget," "Travel/Other Expenses," and so on. All these folders should be filed under the tabbed name of the project.

- Keep note sheets in three-ring binders titled under the project name and specific data under tabbed categories of information, source names, and tasks.
- Keep notes on 5x7 index cards filed under tabbed categories of information, source names, and tasks.
- Try a logical mix of the above. Or, if you have access to a VDT and a software program designed for organizing notes you enter into it, use that approach, or organize from a printout.

The important thing is to be methodical because, as mentioned earlier, you will probably have more than one project going at one time. Each project should have its own title and its own units of information, sources or tasks. With so much going on and other projects to deal with, memory can play tricks on the mind. Systematic method is more reliable than spontaneous recall.

Validating and Verifying Data

Whether your sources of information are in-house or out, validate and verify. That is, give your audience a reason to believe your information comes from a reliable and authentic source.

News, magazine, PR, and advertising writers are careful to assemble validated and verified data. Their professional reputations rest on how dependable they are as accurate writers. For *validity* they seek a body of *appropriate* and *reliable* information. For *verified* data, they seek *consensus*, which means the evidence is confirmed or denied in more than one document, by more than one authority. And, remember, agreement or denial does not necessarily guarantee truth. Remember, as well, that the verifying process can prove data once confirmed (or denied) are now found to be quite the opposite, or that an error has been made.

Choosing valid sources begins with a little common sense. For example, a text on ornithology is an appropriate reference for information about the Szechuan pheasant. A book on the history of China is not. An auto mechanic's manual or certified mechanic are appropriate sources for information on how parts of a passenger car engine operate. A manual on trailer trucks is not. The division of vital records, state department of health, is the appropriate source to look for a birth record. A recorder's court record is not. If your assignment concerns solid waste pollution, an expert on solid waste pollution is more appropriate than an expert on air pollution.

A polling organization known for its consistently trustworthy performance is a more reliable source than one that delivers satisfactory performance sporadically. A publication recognized by its readers as being accurate more often than others in the same media arena is predictably a reliable source. Certification by a board of one's peers, or association with a prestigious institution, is a fair measure of reliability. When an authority is held in high esteem by colleagues, that person is predictably a reliable source in that area of expertise. All very obvious, you say? You would be surprised how assignment anxiety can misdirect an otherwise rational mind.

Earlier we suggested you could verify information in researched materials and the IDs of individuals by comparing several documents from different sources. If you do this, you gain an accumulation, a *range of evidence*. You are then able to weigh one set of facts and figures against another to reach a decision about the reliability of the data. Ultimately, you look for *consensus* in the evidence before accepting it. If the source is validated and the evidence checks out, you can be fairly confident the data is reliable, meaning the information is accurate to date until something else develops to change the picture.

However, when consensus is absent and contradictions appear, it is a warning that the information is either untrustworthy or controversial. In the case of unreliable information, ask why. You may choose to discard it or set it aside until better information becomes available. If it is controversial, take the conflict into account and raise questions to find out why the controversy exists. An enterprise story may develop from such research.

The Matter of Authenticity

Too often novice writers assume an "official" document is an automatic guarantee of the document's authenticity as a reliable record. Clerks are human and make mistakes like the rest of us, but sometimes records are deliberately altered and documents are forged. Comparing similar documents often reveals such anomalies. In any case, review documents with a sharp eye and then record what you see. Here are a few anomalies to look for:

- Cross outs.
- Misplaced entries.
- Changes in handwriting or formating.
- Contradictions between entries in categories.
- Missing entries or information that obscures understanding of the data.

- Signatures initialed by someone other than the authorized signee.
- A single digit entry when all others are entered as double or triple digits.
- An entry under a category that does not seem to match with other entries in the same category, or with the same category in a similar document.

Very often authenticity concerns experts in a particular field. Although writers seek out informed statements and opinions from qualified people, the credentials these people hold are often a matter of controversy. Any single factor such as education, certification, position, contribution to society, professionalism, and the like, may raise doubt or challenge.

Currently, controversy surrounds the credentials of some surgeons who practice plastic and reconstructive surgery. In order to know who might serve as an authoritative voice on a matter concerning plastic and reconstructive surgery, it is necessary to learn about the complexities of accreditation involved.

This type of surgery is a medical specialty and authority for certification for all medical specialties is issued by the American Board of Medical Specialties (ABMS). ABMS has conferred exclusive rights on the American Board of Plastic Surgery (ABPS) to certify surgeons in plastic and reconstructive surgery. ABPS is the only ABMS approved certifying board that has the words "plastic surgery" in its name.

In addition, ABPS follows training standards set by the Residency Review Committee in Plastic Surgery. This committee is recognized by the Accreditation Council of Graduate Medical Education (ACGME) as the agency that accredits residency training programs for graduate medical training in plastic and reconstructive surgery. ACGME is composed of five national medical associations concerned with medical education. The residency review committees determine whether medical training programs meet the general and specific requirements of the essentials for accredited medical residencies.

Graduate surgeons certified by ABPS are qualified for plastic and reconstructive surgery on both head and body areas and many do both or specialize on certain parts, for example, face or breast reconstruction.

Nevertheless, surgeons in other disciplines who are certified by their particular specialties also practice plastic surgery techniques related to their specialty and learned during training in that specialty. But they are not certified in the broad scope of plastic surgery. Those specialties might include otolaryngology, dermatology, obstetrics-gynecology, and others. Still other surgeons certified by boards with the words "cosmetic" or "plastic" in them may also use plastic and reconstructive techniques. However, none of these boards are ABMS approved to certify in "plastic surgery."

The question of qualification came to a head recently before a Senate hearing committee after women reported disfigurement or damage to their health. In some cases, death was reported as a result of liposuction surgery (a type of plastic and reconstructive surgery that literally vacuums fat from the body). Some of these doctors were certified by boards, but not by ABPS (ABMS approved to certify for plastic surgery).

To remove some of the confusion surrounding this issue of certification, several states have passed laws and several others are considering laws or regulations that would require the individual claiming board certification to identify the board designation and to signify whether that board is ABMS approved to certify for plastic surgery.

In tests of source reliability and authenticity and when dealing with copy concerning complex issues such as plastic and reconstructive certification, a writer must take into account the distinctions made between the several groups and the differences in certification.

To defend against poor sources, use the following guidelines. Depending on the project you may be working on, raise any one, some, or all of the following questions when seeking validity, verification, or authenticity:

- *How reliable is the historical reference, record or document?*
- *How reliable is the publication/publisher?* (book, magazine, news-paper, or journal).
- *How reliable is the research group?*
- *How current is the record, document, or publication?*
- *What makes the record or document "official?"*
- *What are the anomalies in this particular record, document, or publication?*
- *What agreement and/or disagreement exists concerning entries, statements, etc., made in related documents, records, references composed by others?*
- *What information is missing?*
- *What are the authority's credentials?*
- *Are any credentials controversial? Why?*
- *What experts in the same field disagree with this authority's statements or evidence? Why?*

Every one of these questions may not apply in every instance. Use only those that apply to your specific problem of validation and verification. If the question you need is not listed, those given should give you a lead on how to frame the one you do need.

Asking Librarians for Help

Whether you carry your research problem to an in-house librarian or a librarian elsewhere, know precisely what you want and state your request specifically. For example, suppose you were given the assignment on chemical waste discharges into the Great Lakes. You discover you have only a vague idea of what constitutes mercury. Your first questions would be: *What do I need or want to know about mercury? What does my audience need or want to know about it?* Your next questions might then be: *What is mercury? How does its composition change once it has been processed, reduced to waste material and discharged into the Great Lakes? What is its effect on fish and wildlife? How dangerous is it to humans who eat the fish, other water wildlife?*

First tell the librarian what it is you are working on and set the context for your inquiry. Then ask a specific question: *I'm working on a problem concerning mercury-based discharges into the Great Lakes. I need to find out what mercury is and how dangerous it is to humans and wildlife in and around the Great Lakes. Where can I find this information?* Precise requests help the librarian direct you to the correct sources of information.

Asking Sources Other Than Librarians for Help

Suppose you were given the advertising assignment about attracting a teen-age audience for Lovely Lotion, and suppose one of your self-inquiries was: *What pop recording is a teen-age favorite?* There is probably a periodic publication of leading favorites in more than one magazine, or even in a database, but for our purposes, let's say you choose to call a disc jockey in your city.

If you did not know who that was, you could call one of the major radio stations in your city and ask the switchboard operator for the name of that station's leading disc jockey. Once you make contact, address the person by name, introduce yourself, explain what you are working on, why you want it, and indicate your specific need:

Hello, Mr. Johnson, my name is Alison Bond. I'm an advertising copywriter at the XYZ Agency and I'm working on a project that may include pop music favorites in the next video project for one of our products. I'm looking for the titles of a few recordings that teen-agers request most often. Could you please provide me with that information?

He gives you some titles and ratings and says the station publishes a list of these favorites in their newsletter and would you like a copy. You say: *Yes, thank you very much. I'd appreciate receiving it. Please address it to Alison Bond, XYZ Agency, 1170 Circle Plaza, zip 12345. And thanks again for your help.*

No matter who it is, librarian, authority, or general information source, use good manners. Use "please" and "thank you" generously. Speak in a pleasant rather than a demanding tone of voice. Courtesy wins cooperation and a precise request spoken politely makes it easier for the source to cooperate.

And if any source does not happen to have the information you seek, by all means ask: *Who can tell me about this?* Or, *Where can I find information on this?* Even if that source provides the information, ask: *Who else would you suggest I speak to about this?* Or, *What other references* (records, documents, etc.) *should I look at?* This is no time to be shy about picking the minds of your sources because at this point you need answers to Critical Self-Inquiry 2: *What information has been and/or is currently documented and known by whom?*

SUGGESTED RESEARCH AND SOURCE REFERENCES

Beaubien, A. K., Hogan, S. A., & George, M. W. (1982). *Learning the Library*. New York: R. R. Bowker.
Horowitz, L. (1984). *Knowing Where to Look*. Cincinnati, OH: Writer's Digest Books.
Ullmann, J., & Colbert, J. (Eds.). (1991). *The Reporter's Handbook: An Investigator's Guide to Documents and Techniques* (2nd ed.). New York: St. Martin's Press.

* * *

Like print newswriters, broadcast writers may have weeks to research and report a story, or just a few hours. Still, no part of the strategy is overlooked, even within the narrowest time frame.

For this reason broadcast writers, like print newswriters, keep a daily watch on what is going on in the world. They read books, newspapers, journals, magazines, newsletters, reports, and press releases. They listen to the radio, the competition's and their own network broadcasts. They take notes, save newsclips, keep articles in ready files on topics of public concern.

That sort of readiness avoids desperate efforts at the last minute and is one of the characteristics that comes through in the following interviews with two television newswriters. Another thing to note is their effort to produce a program that stands up to question, but is also geared to fulfill the needs of a local audience on an incident of international import in the first instance and on an incident of national concern in the second instance.

*   *   *

HOW THE PROFESSIONALS DO IT

Backgrounding and Research

Broadcast News: The TWA Hijack

Mort Meisner

This interview was held with Mort Meisner, news director at WJBK-TV2, Detroit (CBS). The story Mr. Meisner described was produced while he was with the NBC affiliate, KSDK-TV at St. Louis, and is about the hijacking of a TWA jet by Muslim terrorists on June 14, 1985. As assistant news director, Mr. Meisner had to know how events happening in other parts of the state, the nation, and the world related to residents of St. Louis. He explained that he reads more than half a dozen newspapers daily, as well as other publications, keeps tabs on the national and cable networks, and watches what TV stations elsewhere are doing. He was fully aware, for example, of past Arab terrorist activities that had occurred abroad. He also knew where Arab communities were located in this country. He had a ready file of background information, including the wire reports from the Middle East on the most recent incident he discussed here. Mr. Meisner was ready and ahead of the game on this one.

The TWA flight 847 was hijacked enroute from Cairo to Rome. Two Lebanese Shiite Muslim gunmen had escaped security detection and boarded the plane during a stop-over in Athens. In midair they took charge of the flight and held 153 passengers and crew, including 104 Americans, hostage. Over the next 17 days, the TWA pilots were forced to shuttle the Boeing 727 back and forth between Beirut and Algiers where they landed to obtain fuel and supplies. Several passengers were beaten and terrorized. A few were released from time to time and permitted to take passage home, including a pregnant St. Louis woman. One American, U.S. Navy diver Robert Dean Stethem, 23, of Waldorf, Maryland, was forced from the plane, beaten and fatally shot in the shadow of the plane's wing on the Beirut runway.

Other passengers were released in groups during ensuing touchdowns for fuel and supplies at the Beirut and Algiers airports. Most of the passengers, including American women, children, and the elderly were permitted to return home, but 79 male passengers were forced from the plane and taken to unknown Shiite strongholds in Beirut. A group of them were released on June 21, but 37 passengers, American men, and 3 crewmen were held until June 30. The hijackers' key demand was for the release of 766 prisoners, mostly Shiite, held by Israel in exchange for the freedom of the U.S. captives.

The hijacking was reported to have been carried out by a Shiite extremist group. Lebanon's more mainstream Shiite Amal militia leader, Nabih Berri, intervened and conducted some of the negotiations from Beirut. Israel said the government would free the Shiite detainees if President Reagan requested it, but the United States held to its policy of no concessions to terrorists. The day after the remaining hostages were released and flown to Frankfurt, Germany, for treatment at a hospital there, Israel released 300 Shiite prisoners. The hijackers claimed a victory. Israel later claimed the detainees were going to be released anyway.

During the period the hostages were held, Mr. Meisner and his staff generated nearly 30 stories for the 6 p.m. news hour. Final events were taped and aired on the same news hour and then an hour-long documentary was produced and broadcast on prime time the same night from the 6 p.m. news tapes. Mr. Meisner began his story by explaining what prompted him to work on this multiproject story. In this case, the event again identifies the problem: *Americans held hostage by Muslim terrorists in hijacking of TWA flight 847 enroute from Cairo to Rome.*

Preliminary research on reported information began immediately, mainly trying to find out if any local residents were passengers on the beseiged plane. Mr. Meisner first explained how he learned about the incident. Notice how he tested the problem subject for local use, the questions he raised in his initial research effort, and his persistence in verifying both the situation and its connection to St. Louis residents.

> **Meisner:** We became aware of this story through a TV network cut-in [an interruption for a special announcement during a regularly scheduled program]. That was about 4:30 in the afternoon, and we learned some of the hostages being held were from St. Louis. So here was a big story, an international and national story that had a local tie-in.
>
> We first had to confirm whether St. Louis people were really on that plane. So at that point we began making calls. Made a lot of phone calls, first of all, trying to determine if, indeed, there were St. Louis people on the plane, getting an airlines source to check names and numbers of passengers that were on the plane: *How many passengers? Who was on the plane? Where were they from? What's the status?* [of the hostage situation]. We talked to a source at the airlines to check names and numbers of passengers that were on the plane

We talked with the U.S. State Dept., types who were very unhelpful. All you can do on a story . . . and it's good that we're talking about this story because it's a classic example where it's very difficult with a government official who is stonewalling, that won't give you the information that you need. I circumvented them. Any time you have a plane crash, any time you have a hostage situation, they give very little information to the families or to the media under the guise of they don't want false information to get out. I did have a source in the government who was very helpful. But you circumvent the stonewallers.

As it turned out, passengers from St. Louis were among those on the hijacked TWA and that preliminary check along with other research sources who did cooperate with Mr. Meisner identified his particular news problem: *St. Louis residents are among hostages held in an international incident.* With a grasp on the problem, a focus for it and some basic background information concerning it, he moved on (see chapter 4).

Broadcast News: Illegal Use of Public Land

Robbie Timmons

The speaker in this interview is Robbie Timmons, anchorwoman and reporter at WXYZ-TV7, Detroit (ABC). She anchors the 5 p.m. newscast with Bill Bonds and researches, writes, and edits news stories daily. In this interview, Ms. Timmons described her work on another localized story that is related, not to terrorism in the sky or a distant land, but to an equally serious circumstance of our time—illegal use of U. S. recreational land by marijuana growers.

Her news documentary is a follow-up on a story that came out of California concerning campers and hikers on public land being shot at by people who were growing marijuana illegally on government property. Ms. Timmons wanted to know if there was a similar problem in Michigan.

She explained that she spent nearly 2 weeks researching, interviewing, validating, and verifying her data for the Michigan story. She spent another week pulling it all together and getting clearances before her serialized news documentary, "Terror in the Woods," was aired in March 1989 over three 2-minute newscasts during the 11 p.m. news hour. But that series might never have come about if Ms. Timmons had not been alert to the fact that anything concerning one area of the country very often has its parallel in your own area and is always a good source for an enterprise story.

In this case, Ms. Timmons had the advantage of ready material that affiliated ABC broadcasters in California shared with the Michigan station, a common practice. Still, her research for the localized story was thorough and her strategy thoughtfully carried out despite the limited time frame for completion.

> **Timmons:** We received information from a reporter in California that several incidents were taking place on public land where campers and hikers were being threatened by people wielding guns, and that some campers and hikers were being shot at [the California reporter had aired a TV news report regarding these incidents]. Some of these people in California turned out to be survivalists, others turned out to be drug farmers protecting their crops, or they happened to be squatters who felt the public land was theirs and they did not want any trespassers.

Again, the event establishes the problem statement: *Misuse of government land threatens safety of recreationers*. However, it is one thing to recognize a good story, it is another to track down a possible relationship to your local area. Ms. Timmons had to research some preliminary questions before she could move on.

Notice how carefully she researched the possible local links to the California incident. Nothing is left to chance. Assertions, as well as possibilities, are verified, not with just one source, but with many. Like Mr. Ashenfelter in the interview that follows, she created a range of sources in order to compare and weigh the various pieces of information. And whenever she hit a dead end, she asked that important question: *Who can tell me about this?* Or, *Where can I find this information?* The result? She finally connected with the appropriate information source. It was that source who supplied the necessary documents and provided the most informed answers to both preliminary and primary questions.

> **Timmons:** At this point, the question was: *Is this* [misuse of government land and recreationers at risk] *going on in Michigan? Do we have a story?* I really talked to a lot of people all over the country trying to get several different sources to either negate or affirm, that is, saying: *No, there wasn't, or yes, there was a problem in Michigan.* And I was trying to find the right person in Michigan to give me the definitive answer and who would be the best person to interview. It was very frustrating trying to find the right person. I only had a week to prepare before three days of airing.
>
> I probably spent days going from the Federal government on to the regional people to the different state people. All of them had information, but not specific enough to the problem here. I talked to people from the Treasury Dept., people from the Agriculture Dept., the U.S. Fish and Wildlife people, the Dept. of Natural Resources, the Michigan State Police, and then I finally

got down to the one person [a Michigan State Police lieutenant] who was in charge of the marijuana problem.

In Michigan the operation is called "Operation Hemp." He [the Michigan State Police lieutenant] was in charge of it and also the person who was aware of people being attacked on public land and was in charge of the law enforcement officers dealing with marijuana growers. This person was recommended to me and was known by people in the Federal government and different state agencies. So I got his name from several different sources as being the person who was the expert in this field. He showed me some records and I went through these for specific data on the problem in Michigan.

Preliminary research established there was a Michigan story and provided Ms. Timmons with both focus and sources on whom she could rely for additional backgrounding. She then moved on to the next phase of research (see chapter 4).

Print News: The Navy Story

The Ashenfelter-Freedberg team wanted to look behind the mystery of the seamen's deaths and began by raising preliminary questions. Notice Mr. Ashenfelter's reference to substantiated evidence when he indicated his personal suppositions about the Collum case were later set aside by the mounting data proving otherwise.

Ashenfelter: In the Trerice case, we suspected there was a lot more than the Navy was telling. You just don't send the body home without organs unless there was something going on. We suspected there may be negligence on the part of the Navy. We figured he [Trerice] may have been abused. In Trerice's case it was pretty much: *How did Paul Trerice die?* And our whole game plan was to answer that question. In the Terry Collum case it was: *Was Terry Collum murdered?* In the other five deaths, the bottom line on that initially was: *How did these kids die and could their deaths have been prevented?* In the Collum case and the other five cases, we were trying to find out: *How did they die and was the Navy negligent?* We started out with this basic hypothesis and tried to either prove it or disprove it.

In the Terry Collum case: *Was Terry Collum murdered?* . . . that turned out not to be true. After a lot of digging, what did turn out to be true was that the family did not get the truth about how he died.

On Orner's lead, the team made hundreds of phone calls all over the country and found more than a dozen former Ranger sailors who said a shipmate did go over the side. One in Florida was able to give them a name. They got the name of Collum's hometown from the Navy and under the Freedom of Information Act (FOIA) got hold of the Navy's Investigative

Service (NIS) report and tracked down 3 of 5 names that appeared in the report. The three informed the writers that Collum had been a prisoner with them in the Ranger brig. These sailors, themselves mistreated and abused, told how Collum had been beaten, forcibly exercised for hours in 100-degree heat and routinely denied food and drinking water.

None of this was in the Navy report and all this information was accumulated before Mr. Ashenfelter spoke to Collum's father. Mr. Collum could not verify Orner's allegation that Marine guards had marched his son off the end of the flight deck.

In this next comment, notice how the team located Seaman Collum's family and how data was compared, one set of information against another. Contradictions show up fairly quickly. In this case, it was apparent that the Navy's report to the family regarding Seaman Collum's death failed to match the evidence in other government records.

Mr. Ashenfelter then explained how they found another key to this mystery — Navy cruise books. These, along with other obtained government documents, turn out to be essential to more than one phase of the research effort.

Ashenfelter: We had called the Navy and asked them to tell us how these two kids [Trerice and Collum] had died. One was lost overboard and we figured that was our guy. The Navy gave us his [Collum's] parents' hometown. They weren't listed in the phone book. So we asked the local newspaper out there if they had an obituary on him [Seaman Collum] and they listed the father as a retired school teacher. So we got hold of the father through school district records.

We figured the same thing that happened to him [Collum] happened to Trerice. He [Collum] suffered a heatstroke and he just simply jumped in the water.

Roy [Collum's father] told us that the Navy had told him that his son was blown overboard by jet exhaust during flight operations on ship. He said that his son was one of the guys who worked on the flight deck.

Well, that completely contradicted what we understood to be true. Even if he [Collum] wasn't murdered, we knew that the next best story was one that the Navy had lied to the family, and that fit completely with what Trerice [the father] was going through because Trerice was claiming that the Navy was lying to him.

[Re the Collum case] . . . this guy in Florida, he didn't know the name of the kid who went overboard, but he said, "I think I can find out. I have a cruise book," which is like a yearbook from the cruise. And he said, "I'll look in the back of it because they've got a memoriam page." And it turned out there were two deaths.

Documents and sources are always available for research and verification. The point is to get to the right ones and if denied access to them, you outmaneuver the blockades. In this respect, the team demonstrated admirable ingenuity, particularly in their effort to gain access to certain records vital to research and verification needed concerning what they were beginning to discover about the Collum death. Interestingly, that effort led to still another revealing document, plus key sources necessary for the next phase of research.

Ashenfelter: There was no way I could look at any reports about his son's death, that is, uncensored ones, without his [Mr. Collum] authorization. Mr. Collum, he didn't know me, so he didn't believe me [that his son was in the brig and probably died because of Marine guard abuse]. We wanted to let him think it over. We sent Mr. Collum all our clips on Trerice. A couple involved stories that Sydney [Ms. Freedberg] had done about a couple of CCU [Correctional Custody Unit] prisoners that apparently went through so much punishment that rather than stay on ship they jumped over the side while the ship was under way in the middle of the ocean.

Six weeks later I went down there and incredibly he said, "I've been waiting for you." So we basically made a deal. I had made arrangements to go to a Navy records center in St. Louis. I couldn't look at those records without his authorization, so he gave me authorization and said if I could show from looking at those records that his son was a brig prisoner, he would give me full authorization to completely investigate the case.

It was a medical and personnel report that they showed me, and on one of the pages in one paragraph there was a notation that he [Collum] died after escaping from the brig and had jumped overboard. It also acknowledged the existence of a full-fledged investigation by the Navy of his death and that document was at the Pentagon.

[After Mr. Collum gave his permission] I proceeded to make arrangements [filed a FOIA request] to get the JAG [Judge Advocate General] investigation report and I went to the Pentagon and picked it up. It was a 266-page investigation report that the family had never seen. They didn't even know it existed. That's where I found the names of the guys who had spent time in the brig with Collum [Rogers, Off, and Augustyn]. There were telltale signs in the Collum report that he was on the verge of breaking, that he might be considering something desperate, that Collum had told the legal officer that the Marines hadn't been giving him any drinking water, that he didn't think he could go on. This was the night before he went over the side.

This backgrounding and research not only cleared the way to the next research effort, it also produced key witnesses to what was beginning to lift a corner on the shroud of mystery (see chapter 4).

Print News: The Ford Plant Fire

Mr. Cain began his research by observing what was going on and noting who was in charge to verify his observations. Meanwhile, other staff reporters in the newsroom were researching other factors related to this and other fires like it in order to provide an evidentiary database for Mr. Cain and Mr. Treml. But research by other staffers did not preclude additional research by Mr. Cain when he returned to the office. As in the previous cases, the characteristic series of self-inquiries is a recurring exercise in this instance as well.

> **Cain:** My first task was to get there as quickly as possible, to observe it with my own eyes, not rely on second-hand accounts about what happened. I cut through some back roads that took me directly behind the plant. I knew there would be a pileup on the roads, gawkers and what not, barricades to the entrance of the plant. Bill [Treml] never got through the plant gates, incidentally.
>
> Another reporter back at the office did other work. He talked to several professors at the university [University of Michigan] about the potential of the chemicals: *How toxic were they?* He talked to the environmental people, had access to our files on similar events and put together a sidebar dealing directly with all that. I instructed another reporter, who had been out in the community of Saline, to pin down the parameters of the evacuation. He did another sidebar dealing with the evacuation.
>
> When I got back, I pulled the file that we had on the Ford plant, *when it was built, how big it was, how many people were employed*, etc. There was some background on some other industrial fires [in-house news files] and I looked at that, too.

Once on the scene, Mr. Cain discovered his first fears about heavy losses in life and property at the Ford plant were unwarranted, and he quickly adjusted his original view of the problem as he observed the changing scene before him.

> **Cain:** It was clear, after I had been on the scene only a few minutes, that we weren't talking about plastics exploding the plant apart. They managed to get chemical cannisters out of the way. It [the fire] was much smaller than I had originally thought. That's something I checked on right away with people on the scene whose adrenalin was going through the roof.

Observation of the current situation led to verification of it and this permitted Mr. Cain to turn his attention to researching what was a revised problem focus (see chapter 4).

4 The Working Statement

Once you have identified the problem and the focus, give expression to it by formulating a *working statement*. Doing so reveals relevant questions and where you might find answers. The trick is to put the working statement together precisely and clearly so that it does all that for you. But make no mistake, it does not stay that way. The working statement is a preliminary, a tentative, and not a final statement you set out to prove, a base from which to begin specific work. In short, it is a means, not an end.

Following identification of the problem and completing some preliminary research concerning it, your next step is to ask Critical Self-Inquiry 3: *What is the working statement?*

FORMULATING THE WORKING STATEMENT

Although the media problem frequently suggests the working statement, there are as many occasions when the writer must formulate it. Ready-made statements develop spontaneously from short deadline assignments where focus is predetermined. For example, suppose a news editor assigns you to cover a story concerning a mother who allegedly battered her 2-year-old daughter. The editor has stated the problem and, at the same time, has defined the problem subject, *child abuse,* the problem focus and, in this case, the working statement: *Mother abuses child.* However, preliminary research at the scene reveals that the child was beaten by the boyfriend of a neighbor in whose care the mother had left the child. Same problem, same subject, modified focus and a new working statement: *Babysitter's boy-friend batters neighbor's 2-year-old daughter.*

Very often the problem is a question and substitutes as the working statement: *Why were telephone booths removed from Main Avenue?* After some preliminary research and a call to a phone company official, the reporter develops a new working statement: *Ace Telephone Group says repeated coin box thefts led to removal of pay phones on Main Street.*

As indicated in the previous chapter, when the problem fails to provide or suggest a focus, preliminary research will. For example, the advertising copy assignment—*produce a jazzy campaign approach for Sudsy Soap without sacrificing previous emphasis on its chemical-free feature*—that is the problem, but the editor expects you to find a topic focus and develop a working statement.

You begin with preliminary research through the agency's files. It contains samples of ads produced in the past by competitors and by your agency. The files also contain facts about Sudsy Soap's chemical-free properties. You learn Sudsy Soap has a natural fragrance ingredient. Something in your research triggers an idea on how to exploit that feature. You decide on a working statement with sensual appeal: *The spring-fresh fragrance of Sudsy Soap attracts handsome men to women of all ages who use this chemical-free soap.*

Test of a Productive Working Statement

Do not make the mistake of thinking that the working statement is the news lead, PR concept, advertising theme, or conclusion. It is not. It is simply a directional guide to specific first points of fact that ultimately lead to other areas of research, observation, and interview. What emerges from the sum total of all this effort is the beginning of an idea that develops into a catchy news lead, PR premise, advertising slogan, or the opening lines of a magazine piece.

If verified facts bear out the original working statement, then the statement stands on its merits. If the facts do not bear out the working statement, it is modified, sometimes even negated and reconstructed, and the direction of primary research is adjusted.

The working statement can be articulated, but it works best when it is written out. Writing it out allows you to look at the words and see if the statement will lead to a productive outcome. A working statement is productive when it is:

- *Feasible*: Documented information exists concerning the matter at hand and a representative sample of sources and interviewees are available and qualified to answer your questions.

- *Objective*: Exhibits freedom from value judgment.
- *Worthy*: Shows promise of making a contribution to general knowledge or to the well-being of its audience.
- *Declarative*: Contains nouns, a subject(s), verb(s), and object(s), is framed in the present tense, is expressed precisely, clearly, completely, and concisely.

Although the working statement can be a question, a declarative sentence is more efficient because it yields many more noun, subject, verb, and object names. It is from these names that research categories emerge and clues to relevant questions and information sources become apparent.

Types of Working Statements to Avoid

Try to avoid the "If . . . then" proposition because this type is usually too general, raises too many questions, and can be the source of faulty reasoning. For example: *If there are more cancer detection centers today than 10 years ago, then the incidence of cancer cases must have decreased.* What type of cancer? What areas of the country? What was the incidence of that type in those areas 10 years ago? What other reasons account for the decrease (or increase) in reported cancer cases? Although these questions lead to areas of research, too often there is a tendency to assume the statement stands on its merits and the questions that need answers are left unanswered.

Another type to avoid is the correlational working statement. It infers where inferences are not intended. For example, the following statement infers that increased sales of certain ice-cream bars are due to high temperatures: *When temperatures soar, sales of Frosty Bars increase.* A sales promotion held during the same temperature period may have contributed to increased sale of Frosty Bars. The statement leaves too much room for the competition to jump all over the faulty reasoning and they will do it to their advantage. Meanwhile, the writer has lost precious time with a questionable working statement.

Still another type to avoid is the comparative working statement: *Fifty-year-old men can run longer distances than 60-year-old men.* The statement is a value judgment about age: The younger you are the farther you "ought to" be able to run. There will always be a 70-year-old who will write or call in and say that he or she beat a 50-year-old runner-up in the last marathon and that anyone with any sense knows senior citizens in top form can be as vital as any person 20 years their junior.

Declarative statements not only provide more subject-verb-object categories to explore, they also avoid these blind alleys of faulty reasoning.

HOW WORKING STATEMENTS PRODUCE
FIRST DIRECTIONS

Let's use your assignment on pollution in the Great Lakes as an example. On the editor's direction, you read the article in *Water Conservation Journal* and set out to verify its claims. After some preliminary research, you learn that pollution in the Great Lakes is, indeed, threatening the purity of the Lakes. You wonder about the current impact on fish and other wildlife. There are some answers in preliminary research, but you also observed that several markets in your area no longer stock Great Lakes whitefish. You learn that store managers say whitefish is in short supply. Others claim it is contaminated. This arouses your curiosity.

So moving from subject problem to topic problem, you develop a working statement: *Discharges of chemical waste into the Great Lakes threaten food supply of Great Lakes whitefish.*[1] You have a workable statement that yields plenty of categories to get you started on primary research. It is stated precisely, clearly, completely, yet concisely. And it is a new approach to an exploited problem previously overlooked. That is, your preliminary research revealed discussions about the impact of toxic waste on trout, walleye, salmon, and other wildlife species, but nothing about whitefish.

Use the underlined words and phrases as categories under which to organize your researched information. Rely on the underlined words and phrases to generate primary research questions. The questions, in turn, will suggest likely sources. To generate those questions, do what media professionals do—*anticipate* questions the reader or listener might raise. Start with these:

- *What do I need or want to know about it?*
- *What does my audience need or want to know about it?*
- *What library, organization, institute, or government agency would have records that could supply answers?*
- *What authoritative persons could supply information?*

The following chart models one way you could organize categories for the working statement just given. Use the model if it works for you. Or, you may find that another organizational approach suits you better. Whatever the approach, ask the questions just listed.

If logical sources of information do not come to mind, the best mental stimulator is the telephone directory. Look under city, state, and U. S.

---

[1]This is a hypothetical statement and should not be regarded as representing any facts in reality.

government listings. Then refer to the index of listings in the yellow pages of the telephone directory and do not overlook your local Chamber of Commerce as an information source. For references, almanacs, indexes, and directories, contact public, university, or private libraries. If you hit blind alleys with your first calls, the persons contacted are still useful because they may be able to provide the best association, company, agency, reference, or person if you ask: *Who can give me information on this?* Or, *Where can I find information on this?* No matter how many blind alleys you hit (even those suggested by knowledgeable people) keep on asking that question. You will eventually find the correct information source. Also, refer to the suggested texts on reference sources listed in chapter 3.

Set up questions and sources in whatever manner is best for you to work with. If you are not quite sure what that set up might be, the sample model given here will help you get started until you find a device that suits you better. You may discover that some sources answer questions you have listed for others. Ask for their perspective anyway. Whatever device you employ, the questions you list should represent those left unanswered by preliminary research. The sample questions listed here are necessarily abbreviated to conserve space.

Sample Question and Source Plan

Project: Great Lakes Pollution

First Questions	First Sources
Toxic waste discharge:	
What types of toxic chemicals in GL?	Information Services,
Which types most damaging?	International Joint Commission
Rate of toxic loads per year?	(IJC), IJC *Report on GL Water*
Periods of highest discharge?	*Quality*; representative,
Places of highest discharge?	National Research Council.
By whom? What chemicals?	
What EPA controls on discharges?	Director, Environmental
When instituted? By whom?	Protection Agency (EPA), their
Who's been fined? Amount?	records.
Paid up? Why not?	
If not fined, why not?	Director, Dept. of Natural
What EPA criminal sanctions?	Resources (DNR), their records.
Any applied? Against whom?	
Outcome?	Director, Great Lakes Environ-
Any opposition to litigation?	mental Research Lab, U.S. Dept.
By whom? Why?	of Commerce, their records.

What correctives on pollution?
What problems other than toxic
   chemical waste?

Professor, School of Natural
Resources and Environmental
Sociology.

Great Lakes: ·
Size? Depth? Flow?
Turnover rate?

American, World Book and
Water Encyclopedias; *World
Almanac & Book of Facts.*

Threat to fish/whitefish population:
What fish species threatened?
What other wildlife threatened?
How discovered?
Where's most contamination found?
What's principal cause?
What's being done? Progress?
GL only source of whitefish?
What's catch now compared to 10,
   20, 30 years ago?
Why short supplies of whitefish?

IJC Report, EPA, DNR;
Director, U.S. Fish and Wildlife
Service (FWS), their records.

Director, National Wildlife
Federation, GL Natural Resource
Center (NWF), their records.

Threat to fish consumers:
What's effect on contaminated fish?
Any reports of human illness, death?
Any warnings issued against
   fishing, eating fish, swimming?
How many areas? Where?
Since when?
What are consumption limits?
Prognosis for banned recreational
   areas?

"Public Health Fish
Consumption Advisory,"
Michigan Fishing Guide; DNR,
EPA, Mich. Dept. of Health.

Professor of toxicology, Dept. of
Environmental and Industrial
Health.

Environmental epidemiologist,
Council for Environmental
Quality, Health Dept.

Note that questions for possible violaters are not listed. For all media writers, newswriters particularly, it is essential to obtain information from the opposition. However, at this point the writer is interested in getting background and some solid facts before facing the opposition. In the process, factors representing the opposition will emerge and stimulate questions relevant to their position in the overall picture.

As you accumulate information, you will find new data call for new questions and new sources, or returns to former ones. The point is, research is a continuing process and may occur more than once at any point in the strategy. And because this is the reality, the operation of validation and verification follows as a companion feature. Furthermore, you can expect checks on your work by either an editor or supervisor and readiness with substantiated evidence is your best safeguard against challenge.

It may appear as if the media writer collects more information from more sources than is necessary—not really. The whole is necessary in order to determine what portions of the accumulated body of data are relevant and of importance to the audience.

The working statement given earlier is useful whether a writer has to produce a two-column news feature, a 3,500-word magazine article, or a TV documentary. It would serve a PR or advertising writer as well. For example, the PR director of a lobbying group for the fishing industry might ask a staff writer to prepare an in-depth press release concerning the impact of toxic waste on the state's fish population.

The same organization may also be the client of an advertising agency. The lobbying group might ask the ad agency to develop a print and broadcast campaign to bring public attention to chemical pollution and its impact on the state's fishing industry. In either instance, the procedure for research and shaping the topic statement are the same. It is all solid homework for interviews and writing.

THE COMPLEX AND NOT-SO-COMPLEX ASSIGNMENT

The working statement regarding pollution is representative of an assignment at mid-range complexity. Questions and sources differ for such assignments because questions for these assignments cannot be predetermined. That is one of the major differences between the complex and not-so-complex assignment.

Some of the not-so-complex types of news events that occur repeatedly include fires, accidents, disasters, crimes, meetings, speeches, and press conferences. Questions for these types of events are predetermined because those questions are the ones most frequently raised in such instances. That does not mean they are the only questions. It does mean they have become standard fare through frequent use and are usually raised when covering these types of news events.

News and PR writers get a mix of the complex and not-so-complex. This is not always the case for magazine or advertising writers. Their assignments usually call for questions and sources that remain unknown until the problem is stated and the working statement is formulated.

To illustrate the questions usually raised for the not-so-complex assignment, frequently occurring news and PR events are presented here with a representative series of basic questions and information sources needed for copy content. The questions do not represent all the information it is possible to get. Some may not apply in every instance and the list of events is by no means a complete one. Nevertheless, apply the list for the events that are given and use it as a stimulant for other questions and sources on these types of assignments.

How much information is used by the writer, whether it is for a news, magazine, broadcast, PR, or advertising project, depends on what information is relevant to the problem and how much can be included within the given limits of space or air time. The point is, the writer works from an abundance of collected information in order to have a substantial sample from that body of information and still get the message across within the prescribed limitations.

First Questions and Sources for Short Deadline Assignments

News

Fire:

- Address and location of?
- When did the fire break out?
- How many, who were injured and/or died in the fire? (IDs).
- What was extent of injuries? Where hospitalized?
- What was extent of damage? In dollars? What valuables lost or saved?
- What was cause of fire? Where did it originate?
- Who owns building? (ID).
- Adequate fire safety measures? Why not?
- What weather or other conditions were contributing factors?
- How many engines, firefighters called to the scene?
- How long have firefighters been battling the blaze?
- When was fire reported?
- When did firefighters get there?

Sources.   On-the-scene fire department officials, firefighters, witnesses, relatives and their IDs (without interfering with the work of officials and firefighters and after introducing yourself and revealing whom you represent and getting permission to be there from the person in charge. Do the same for anyone else you talk to). Make a note of all observations. Double check your IDs. They are important for attribution purposes in any story, also for information that may be available soon.

Accident:

- What type of accident (auto, truck, train, plane, bus, boat, etc.)?

- When did accident occur? Where?
- How many, who were injured and/or died in the accident? (IDs).
- What injuries were incurred? Where hospitalized?
- How many vehicles involved? What was extent of damage?
- How did accident occur? What negligence involved? By whom? (IDs).
- Any arrests? What charges? Previous record?
- What corrections will be made by those responsible?
- What weather or other conditions were contributing factors?

Sources. On-the-scene police department officials, victims, witnesses and their IDs (same precautions as previously given). Note your observations.

Disaster:

- What type disaster (flood, tornado, ice storm, drought, earthquake, etc.)?
- When did tragedy occur? Where?
- How many, who were injured and/or died? (IDs).
- What injuries were incurred? Where hospitalized?
- What was damage or dollar loss (to public transport, to private or public property, utilities)?
- Who owns the property damaged or lost? (ID).
- Who was in charge? (ID).
- What weather or other conditions were contributing factors?

Sources. On-the-scene officials, rescuers, victims, witnesses and their IDs (again, same precautions here as previously given and in the following cases). Note your observations.

Crime:

- Who made the arrest (ID)?
- Who is involved (victim(s), perpetrator(s))? (IDs).
- If perpetrator(s) is unknown, any suspect(s)? Who (IDs)?
- What was crime (murder, shooting, theft, vandalism, rape, drug sales, etc.)?
- Where did it occur? When?
- How did it happen? Why?
- What weapons involved? Drug related? What kind?
- What injuries? How serious? Where hospitalized?
- What property losses, if any? What dollar value?

- What social situation, relationships, or other conditions were contributing factors?
- What charges will be brought against the perpetrator(s), suspect(s)?
- Any previous offenses? What?

Sources.   On-the-scene police officials or the arresting officer, and/or officer's filed report, also victims, suspects (if permitted), witnesses, neighbors, friends, relatives, and their IDs.

Meeting:

- Where, when was meeting held?
- What was said, questioned, or decided that is of importance to community?
- What was initiated, overruled, accomplished, or decided by whom? (IDs). How? Why? (ID of person(s)).
- Who attended? Who else worthy of note?
- Who was expected and did not appear? (IDs).
- Who voiced opposition and why? (ID).
- Who led the discussion? (ID).
- What were some memorable quotes?
- What interferences occurred to diminish or cancel meeting's purpose? To agenda items?
- What decisions were made to whose advantage/disadvantage? (ID of group or individuals concerned).
- What evidence presented at meeting confirms, misrepresents, or contradicts existing data?

Sources.   In this instance, preliminary research helps before going to the meeting. Contact the sponsoring group. They have information on who will attend, where, and when the meeting is to be held, purpose of meeting, specific items on the agenda. Other preliminary research will provide background on the issues, the sponsoring group and their vested interests, the opposition, past and current controversies. At the meeting, observe those present, listen, and take notes concerning the above. If given adequate time, interview supporters and opposers who did or did not attend the meeting to get individual reactions to the meeting's outcome. Relevant references or members of the sponsoring group or those attending can provide leads on who and where these sources may be found.

Speech:

- What is name, full ID of speaker?
- Where was speech delivered? When?

- Who sponsored event? For what reason?
- What was the most important point made by the speaker?
- What evidence did speaker present to support this major point?
- What were some of the minor points and the supporting evidence for these?
- What evidence given by speaker confirms, misrepresents, or contradicts existing data?
- What were some memorable quotes?
- What was the reaction of the audience?
- How many present?
- Who else was on the podium? (IDs). Who introduced the speaker? (ID). How?
- Who was expected and did not attend? Who appeared and was not expected? (IDs).

Sources. For this story, it helps to have some background on the speaker to understand his or her motivations and biases and to establish the speaker's authority on the subject at hand. Preliminary research along with a contact source for the sponsoring group will provide background on the topic, including clip files of the speaker's former appearances, for whom, where, and when. Make a note of the speaker's full name (how it is spelled), title, education, experience, honors, achievements, family background, purpose of appearance, background on the sponsoring group and their particular interests. Then at the event observe the speaker, others present, listen carefully and take notes concerning the above. Here again, when given adequate time, interview the supporters and opposers who did or did not attend for their reactions to the speaker's thesis.

Press conference:

- Where was conference held? When? Why? By whom? Who made the announcement? (ID).
- What announcement did the speaker make?
- Who else spoke? (ID). Why? What did the speaker(s) say?
- Was announcement(s) a surprise? Why? Why not?
- What mistaken expectations did the announcement correct?
- How were the corrections supported?
- What information given fails to square with existing data?
- What questions were raised? What answers were given? How? Not given? Why not? How avoided?

Sources. Again, preliminary research is a must. Find out about the subject matter and speaker(s) beforehand. Learn about other views on the matter. Prepare some questions in advance. Have a number of these in case another journalist asks a question on your list. Be prepared because in this case, unlike the speech or meeting assignment, you are a participant during the question-and-answer period. Get to the conference early enough to gain a visible position so you will be called on. Sometimes the purpose of the press conference is unknown. The press conference is called to reveal its purpose or to correct mistaken expectations or rumors. In such cases, homework on the issues and those involved will prepare you to raise relevant questions at the conference. Here, too, if deadline time permits, the writer will get supporter/opposer viewpoints on the announcement(s) made. Listen carefully, observe and note the speaker's manner of delivery during the announcement and question-and-answer session.

Public Relations

Announcement of promotion (press release):

- What is the person's full name, prior and present title, department, and responsibility?
- What is person's education, previous promotions, experience, achievements, honors?
- What is family background?
- Who will person report to now?
- Who is person being replaced? (ID). For what reason?
- What are promoted person's plans for new programs, other changes?

Sources.   Personnel records (with knowledge and permission of those concerned or in authority), interviews with superiors and person(s) involved.

Announcement of product recall (for press release or at press conference):

- What is specific purpose of press conference?
- Where will it take place? When? Who will make announcement? (ID).
- What is product?
- What are advantages to consumer of new product over former one?
- Why was improvement or change necessary?
- What changes in manufacturing process are planned?
- Who will be in charge of new product production?
- Who was responsible in the planning phase of new product?

- How many employees involved? What outside persons/groups?
- Who specifically was involved? (ID).
- What was the time, cost involved to develop the new product?
- What are its cost savings to the consumer?

Sources.   Company records, files, videotapes, interviews with company officials. Keep a record of IDs in case attribution is necessary.

Announcement of consumer complaint (for press release or conference):

- What is purpose of press conference?
- Where will it take place? When? Who will make announcement? (ID).
- What is product?
- What is the problem specifically?
- What are the allegations/charges brought against the company?
- How was the consumer threatened? If not, why the allegations/ charges?
- How did it happen? Why? Who was responsible? (ID).
- Who is in charge of correcting it? (ID).
- What is being done to correct it?
- What is planned to avoid future mishaps?
- When can the consumer expect use of product again?
- What is expected cost to company for correction? To consumer?

Sources.   Company records, newspaper files, videotapes of incident (if any), interviews with company officials. Keep a record of IDs in case attribution is necessary.

Advertising

Advertising assignments are so varied in nature that no one type of assignment has its particular set of questions and sources. Still, any ad assignment whether it is on short or long deadline will fall within the same self-inquiry principle illustrated earlier. As in news and PR work, the important thing in advertising is to keep your audience in mind, to raise the questions you would ask if you were the consumer, and to do so within the boundaries of relevancy to the assignment problem.

THINKING CRITICALLY UNDER PRESSURE

The media strategy applies to both short and long deadline assignments. But for short deadline assignments, although none of the procedures are omitted, the activities involved are highly concentrated. In any of the mediums, news, magazine, public relations or advertising, the time crunch may allow only a:

- Rapid search through company files and other reference sources.
- Quick calls to available authorities.
- Fast arrangement of data collected.
- Speedy review to absorb its essence.
- Phone interviews as you plan the writing.
- Checkbacks as you pull information together.
- Callbacks and double checks on prevailing questions at the very moment of final composition.

Time pressures create anxiety in any type of work. However, knowing the routine, knowing what you need to do first, next, and so on, helps reduce the stress. The process becomes much easier and goes much faster after you have gone through the strategy in its full-blown form several times. After a while, the deliberate and sequential steps in the strategy become one reflexive operation for both long and short deadline assignments.

Working competently under pressure is merely a matter of critical thinking as you carry out the routine. You are probably beginning to realize that even though thinking critically is a complex cognitive process, it is basically the habit of working methodically and adopting a questioning attitude. The trick is knowing what questions to ask of yourself, and to realize that you are the one who must find the answers. With practice, the *right strategy* and the *right questions* you are learning here for media work will increase your critical abilities in other situations. In time, you will be able to adapt the strategy to any writing assignment and to cope with the unexpected.

Keep in mind that all questions in this book are starter questions. The questions listed earlier for short deadline assignments are first questions to raise. Each incident, event, or subject will have its own unique characteristics requiring specific information related to them. For example, in the instance of the meeting assignment, you might find protesters on the street present a sharp contrast to the quiet order inside. In the instance of an ongoing drug story, the bail posted for a pusher may be the most recent occurrence and the current focus for this story. And in the incident regarding product defect, the consumer's withdrawal of the original complaint may require a press release with a whole new set of information.

All these call for such new questions as: *Who were the protesters? What are they protesting? Why were they barred from the meeting? Who posted bail for the arrested drug pusher? How much? What is that person's connection to the alleged pusher? Who was the buyer? Age? Occupation?*

What were instances of other consumer complaints against this manufacturer? What happened in those instances? Why was this complaint withdrawn? Will the company take any action against the complainant? What action?

Special circumstances command special questions and these cannot always be predetermined. The questions you learn to raise here and the questions you will be able to raise thereafter in unexpected situations represent more than just internal dialogue or brainstorming with someone else. They are self-inquiries about a subject/topic you have studied, observed, thought about a lot, perhaps even mulled over as you tried to sleep.

Once you articulate the questions, that ingested store of knowledge becomes the source for answers to some of them, the lead on where to get answers for the rest, and the inspiration for new questions. With practice, thinking critically about your assignments becomes part of your reactive response system whether the assignment is on long or short deadline. But, a word of caution. Tread carefully. As the process of refining your thinking skills bolsters your self-confidence, you will need to stand ready against personal biases that can easily creep in to weaken the power of your work.

HOW TO AVOID SELECTION AND CONFIRMATION BIAS

The traps of bias are many and always just a footfall away. Included among them are biases of *selection* and *confirmation*, terms created by cognitive psychologists to indicate perceptual errors and quirks of human cognitive processing. Psychologists have found that we can attend to only a relatively small amount of information at any one time, five to eight pieces at the most. Given this limitation, the mind makes use of certain personal preferences to guide selections. For example, we prefer to attend to and select information that is *consistent* with what we believe or what strikes a familiar chord. We take in information that is *salient*, meaning we attend to that which is novel, noticeable, recent, or foremost in our minds. Furthermore, we prefer to attend to and select information that *confirms* our own viewpoint or knowledge.

Such cognitive handicaps are a source of much error, conflict, and subjectivity in communication. Knowing this, professional media writers take precautions against cognitive blinders, their own and those of others. They are, above all, aware of personal biases and work at keeping those subjective tendencies at a safe distance from their work. They anticipate opposing positions and notice exceptions and the not so obvious. They seek out information from many sources in order to learn about more than one side of the problem. And they know how to differentiate substance from sham.

The internal eye and ear of the novice, however, is not so practiced. One way to avoid selection and confirmation bias is to set up an *alternative* to the working statement. Those trained in scientific methods do it as part of their formal procedure. Professional writers do it unconsciously. They might say: *It looks like _____ is the case. On the other hand, it may also be that _____ is true.* Or, the writer may have good reason to believe that something is actually the case, but in order to stay this side of bias, will say: *It looks like _____ is not the case.* In science research, the latter type of statement is known as the *null hypothesis*.

The alternative, or null, statement helps create a sensibility to opposing points of view and deters exclusive notice of information consistent with personal beliefs or the working statement. And whether written out or kept in mind, having an alternative or null statement[2] directs the mind to be receptive to exceptions or differences and, consequently, necessary modifications in the working statement.

Articulating the Alternative Statement

The alternative statement takes possibilities into account other than the one expressed in the working statement, or it denies the working statement. For example, concerning the working statement just described—*Discharges of chemical waste into the Great Lakes threaten food supply of Great Lakes whitefish*—the alternative might suggest an opposite: *Discharges of chemical waste into the Great Lakes do not threaten food supply of Great Lakes whitefish.*

In short, you have a working statement of the problem as current belief seems to suggest, along with an alternative (or alternatives) that could modify or contradict that belief. As with the working statement, preliminary research crystallizes what the alternative statement might be.

Note that elements in the alternative statement generate questions and information sources just as they do in the working statement. You will find alternatives are easier to think of when the working statement is written out in full view. Possibilities for other sides of the issue are then more easily seen.

Fighting Cognitive Bias

If you hold to a personal point of view, a working statement may not always stimulate an alternative. Without a guard against personal biases, the

---

[2]From hereon references to the alternative statement include the meaning of the null form as well.

research collected will serve your biases and not the problem at hand. In such a case, alternatives creep into the mind well after considerable investments of work and time. And if the evidence proves your original belief was way off, all that effort will have been wasted. Do not fall into that trap. Confront your biases and set them aside. Think of alternatives before and not after the fact. Because if you don't, your editors, managers, clients, or competitors will, and they will expect you to have some ready answers.

Alternatives may also escape the writer's consideration if articulating them means risking cancellation of the desired project, or having to write a less sensational piece. Media writers are under pressure to produce and the temptation to ignore alternatives is always present. The best defense is to anticipate challenges to your position. Anticipation helps equip you for challenging questions, but it also contributes to your being flexible to negation, contradiction, or exception to your biases.

Anticipation is a frame of mind expected of all mass media writers. If the news or magazine writer locks into one side of an issue, anyone could bring charges of bias against that writer. If the public relations officer fixes on rhetoric alone and fails to anticipate challenge from the opposition, members of the press will be quick to point it out. If the advertising writer insists on exaggeration to a point where certain restraints are ignored, the client or consumer will be among the first to object. It is a human tendency to blindly try to prove one's point. Vigilance against this weakness through anticipation is objective self-management and is one way you build a reputation for being a professional performer. Begin by asking Critical Self-Inquiry 3: *What is the working statement?* . . . and always with the realization that an alternative statement is also possible. Now see how professionals keep their perspectives in line.

*   *   *

On occasion even seasoned media writers write out working and alternative statements and plan their questions and sources. However, most of the time they are practiced enough to do all this in their heads. Experience has taught them to work from what some call a "main question" and to recognize the necessary areas of preliminary and primary research. Their aim is to guard against letting first suspicions or predictions rule their direction, to remain open to new and opposing issues, and to pursue objective, bias-free data.

Not until as much preliminary research as they have time to complete is finished do they begin formulating a tentative working statement. Some find it necessary to modify that statement even when they are in the last phases of their research, occasionally after interviews have been completed, sometimes after final review of the data and before writing begins. The key to sustaining that bias-free attitude, as you will see throughout the following interviews, is critical self-inquiry.

The novice writer needs a little help. A question or an informal working statement may fail to stimulate the kinds of questions and source persons or places to contact for answers. Nor would anything less than a formal working statement trigger an alternative statement to avoid confirmation bias. The professional has learned to respond automatically, even to statements that lack categories a novice needs to see on paper.

The first interviews shown here were held with media personnel in public relations departments, although few organizations call their public relations departments by that name any more. Some do, but more often you will find these departments under such names as the office of public information, community relations, public affairs, and other variations of the same. One reason for the variety of labels is that the scope of PR has widened to include many different activities beyond the customary production of press releases and newsletters. The advent of television and its impact on organizations serving the public has created new problems and placed new demands on PR departments. As organizations grew and distribution of their products widened, so did product problems and the need for more sophisticated PR.

Press releases are still written, of course, but added to these are video releases, employee and consumer magazines and newspapers, in-house product updates, reports of sales agent meetings, employee education and training programs, and the like. You might also be asked to organize exhibitions, participate in TV and radio interviews, manage a crises, make public speaking appearances, arrange community activities such as sports events, charity campaigns, public education programs, or write guidelines on how executives should conduct interviews under the gun of either a press conference or TV camera.

In large organizations, the PR department usually includes separate divisions where personnel handle a particular set of related functions, those mentioned here as well as others. But whether you find yourself in a small or large organization, be prepared to adapt your media skills on demand to meet some unexpected PR need. Such versatility and adaptability call for the solid thinking and systematic procedure described in this text.

The interviews that follow reflect two of the various activities PR writers perform today. The speakers are managers in the vast PR network of one of the world's largest automakers, the Ford Motor Company, whose world headquarters are located in Dearborn, Michigan. In the first case, the need was to respond quickly to an emergency situation. In the second case, the need was to reactivate Ford's long-time commitment to motorsports events.

* * *

HOW THE PROFESSIONALS DO IT

The Working Statement

Public Relations: The Converted Ambulance Crisis

Charles L. Snearly

This interview was held with Charles L. Snearly, manager of Public Affairs in the Lincoln-Mercury Division at the Ford Motor Company, Dearborn, Michigan. The interview took place in 1989 when he was still manager of Public Affairs, Ford Parts and Service Division, Dearborn, and just before he was promoted to his current position.

Mr. Snearly's role as manager of the Ford Parts and Service Division included coordinating public announcements concerning recalls and responding to public inquiries about recalls. Although most inquiries come from the media, questions also come from consumers, dealers, parts manufacturers, government agencies, and attorneys.

Here he discusses a problem Ford never anticipated. Ford vans, bought and converted into ambulances by conversion companies and then sold by them to ambulance companies, were somehow bursting into flames while on route during emergency calls. However, the media suggested the Ford Motor Company was solely responsible. As a consequence, Ford Motor bore the brunt of public hostility and attorney reaction.

The first incident occurred in the spring of 1986 and dozens more occurred in 1987. Throughout that period and into 1988 and 1989, the Ford Parts and Service Division and Mr. Snearly's PR staff worked together to correct the problem. Their stated problem was essentially: *The conversions are the source of the problem, but Ford Motor is catching it and has to do something about it.* The PR program launched in 1988 is the one Mr. Snearly described here.

> **Snearly:** We had a recall problem, and frankly, it's an ongoing one we've had with ambulances built on what we call our Econoline E-350, which is a van that we supply. We do not manufacture ambulances. What we do is sell the

vans [the vans go to dealers or directly to van conversion manufacturers], and a third party buys them and puts a lot of different electronic and medical equipment into them and then sells them to local medical emergency service people. Many of them [the third party companies that convert the Ford chassis into emergency ambulances] didn't follow our published guidelines for conversion. They were literally rebuilding them.

Preliminary research with engineers and government officials provided an initial data file that came in handy when both the management and the media began firing questions. Notice in Mr. Snearly's next comment, protection of the company image figures large in his tentative working statement, just as it does in the problem statement: *These aren't our vans, but they've got the Ford oval on them so we need to know: Why are these vans catching fire?*

At the same time, the working statement sets up other research questions, primary questions that Mr. Snearly knows from experience the media will ask and the management will surely raise. He suggests that it is all a matter of anticipating the opposition and raising critical self-inquiries before the opposition does so. In the meanwhile, that mode of thinking serves the PR purpose (sustaining the corporate image) and simultaneously fulfills the needs of his audience — the media and other critics.

Snearly: When we first got the reports of these fires, we immediately sent engineers out and began reviewing the situation and collecting some initial data. We lined up questions for the engineers, service mechanics, management, and the main question was: *These aren't our vans, but they've got the Ford oval on them, so we need to know: Why are they catching on fire?*

We talked to our Automotive Safety Office, got their statistics, and those from NHSTA [National Highway Safety Traffic Administration]. I keep a going file of information including what I call my Q&A [questions and answers] file. This has a list of questions I had been asked, questions I had asked of the engineers, our Safety Office, and NHTSA, questions I knew I would be asked by the media, anybody [including management]. Basically, you sit down and say: *Okay, what are the toughest questions we can think of? What was embarrassing? What would I want to know?*

As in news writing, little is left to guesswork, including what Mr. Snearly called *my assumptions*. Data is checked for accuracy and cleared by management at several levels before any public announcements are made. Aside from directing the research, Mr. Snearly also took on the task of briefing staff members in the event they were questioned by the media. And, as indicated earlier, he pre-coded incoming data in his Q&A file throughout the process in order to answer challenging questions from any quarter.

> **Snearly:** Data was cleared through an elaborate system of verification to get consistency in agreement for technical accuracy and my assumptions about policy and legal matters. Everything's checked with the engineers, my management in Public Affairs, our legal counsel, any Ford executive in the chain who might be involved. If I'm speaking on behalf of the Ford Motor Company, I want to make sure I'm saying the right thing. My management said to push hard for the data, and I did. That is, I was persistent.

The primary research work soon led to interviews with primary sources from whom it was necessary to obtain additional data and some hard figures (see chapter 7).

Public Relations: The Motorsports Promotion

Paul M. Preuss

Paul M. Preuss is manager of Public Affairs, Product and Technology Dept. at the Ford Motor Company, Engineering Complex, Dearborn. Since 1985, Mr. Preuss has supervised the product publicity launch for all Ford cars sold in North America. He is responsible, as well, for a related product project, Ford's motorsports publicity.

In this interview, Mr. Preuss described PR management of a motorsports event that the Ford Motor Company has sponsored since its founder, Henry Ford, initiated it in the 1900s. Today the Ford Motor Company enters its competition cars in a number of motorsports events at various tracks including those at Daytona, Florida; Brooklyn, Michigan; Talledega, Alabama; Watkins Glen, New York; also the streets of Detroit and Phoenix. Some of the company's entries include such racecar types as the open cockpit, stock, and Formula One, highly sophisticated racecars that compete around the world for the most prestigious championships in motorsports.

In the early 1900s, the first Henry Ford decided that a good way to promote his new product was to set speed records with it. He ran his Model-T car on the frozen waters of Lake St. Clair, set a speed record, and later hired the legendary race driver, Barney Oldfield, to drive Ford cars in competitions. The company's participation in motorsports here and abroad continued until 1970 when legislated standards for fuel economy, emissions, and safety were established and engineers turned their attention to perfecting Ford emission systems.

Mr. Preuss had joined the motorsports program in the 1960s, acting as a one-man PR bureau for the program, putting out news releases, filing photos, and handling media requests. When the company replaced sports events with other concerns in the 1970s, Mr. Preuss was given other PR assignments. But in 1981, when the program was reinstated, Mr. Preuss was again assigned to the motorsports program. The Mustang GT was in production then and the sports car look was beginning to take hold. Here, Mr. Preuss described how he developed the new PR program that was launched in 1982 and that laid the groundwork for PR activities conducted to this day.

There are a number of differences between this and the PR case described earlier. This one was not a reaction type PR response; it was not a new or unique situation; Ford's advertising group had already established an overall concept, *Win*, and this overall presentation idea was consolidated into a slogan for the motorsports event, *Racing Into the Future*. Mr. Preuss took all this into account. Furthermore, the project was not totally an in-house PR effort. An outside PR firm was engaged and directed by Mr. Preuss to assist him and his staff while they handled other PR projects for the motorsports event.

Times and consumer needs had changed since the 1970s when the motorsports event was put on hold. Demands on the motorsports program were now much greater. Mr. Preuss and his newly enlarged staff had to produce something different than what he had done in the past and what everybody else was doing currently in motorsports promotion.

Preuss: I knew from the outset that there were many people [other automotive manufacturers] in motorsports. Only four out of all the automobile manufacturers in the world are not involved in racing, Rolls Royce and a couple of others. Then there are the engine builders and people who provide shock absorbers, carburetors, etc. They're all involved in racing as sponsors. One racecar may have a hundred sponsor decals on it, even deodorant and laundry soap decals. So my principal problem was: *How am I going to make an impression on the media that's flooded with so much that they get very selective of what they run and what they don't run.* It was a matter of kicking around the question: *How best can I serve the interests of the media that handled media sports? How do I get them?*

Mr. Preuss' practiced eye quickly identified the problem, which is also his tentative working statement: *How am I going to make an impression on the media that's flooded with so much that they get very selective of what they run and what they don't run?* Nevertheless, he moved cautiously to verify his assumptions that something more than press releases and press kits are needed. The question is: *What?*

Notice how he kept his audience—the media—in mind while formulating his working statement: *How best can I serve the interests of the media that handle media sports?* His overriding purpose was to make the Ford product and logo more memorable than all other products whose logos cover the racecars and walls of the track. His aim to put the Ford logo in the forward line of notice is inherent in his working statement.

He did not have to do any initial research about motorsports. He was already knowledgeable about his product, racecars, and races. Because he did know about these things, he anticipated the scope of the current project and set up an infrastructure to handle some of the field and research work.

> **Preuss:** The first thing we decided this time around was to hire an outside public relations agency to be our arms and legs. I couldn't be at different races and places simultaneously, especially if three or four major events were held the same weekend. We had a veteran motorsports publicist actually form a company for us. He hired a few people; we gave him a budget; our office gave him directions. We had the overall responsibility of being in charge. There weren't any PR firms that specialized in motorsports then and there are only a few today. It takes personnel that know something about cars, drivers and racing to do this work.

Once the infrastructure was in place, practiced procedures came into play. With a previously compiled data file on racecars and drivers, Mr. Preuss knew exactly who to contact to verify his assessment of the problem. But telephone verification was not enough in this case. He double-checked with observations in the field. Notice the questions he generated for his contacts and field observations.

> **Preuss:** Then we had to sit down and determine how we were going to do it. I already knew what I had to know about our racecars: specifications, drivers, race records. First thing was, we were not going to get into routine press releases.
>
> I called some of the news journalists I know and asked: *How many releases are you getting over your desk these days on racing?* They'd say: "They're piling three feet high on my desk."
>
> I knew going in that press releases were going to be a waste of time. This verified it. I also asked: *What kinds of things would you like to see coming in? How can we best help you do your job?* Everybody was doing press kits and that's what most expected.
>
> We then asked ourselves: *What do we have to take to the race tracks with us to use as a handout item?* We took a look around the tracks. Most of these tracks are big complexes with big pressrooms, press boxes. We got some press

credentials and went out and stood around and watched how other people were doing it, noting what kind of material was being passed around in the pressroom. Everybody was falling over one another, putting out news releases to newspapers, magazines, television stations, handing out press kits. There were so many press kits, you couldn't find a place to put yours down.

Journalists are busy taking notes and press kits are too cumbersome for journalists to carry around, so a lot of them were just all over the place. So this confirmed what I knew at the outset, and we decided no press releases, no press kits. We decided we had to have something different, yet had information in it the media could use and wouldn't get in the way of taking notes.

Mr. Preuss noticed that although press kits were abandoned, reporters' notebooks never left their hands. He realized very quickly that the same kind of notebook, with the Ford oval on the cover, with inside pages filled with racing facts and blank pages for taking down notes would also never leave their hands. He has the answer to his main question, but before production can begin, management must approve substitution of a new approach for a traditional one.

Preuss: We came up with a "press notebook." We had to explain to management and get approval from my own Public Affairs management about why we were not going into a press release format, why we thought it would be more effective to do these press notebooks instead of press kits. The press notebook is like a stenographic pad, but narrower, a regular notepad that journalists customarily use. We put all the pertinent information about our teams and drivers in this notebook.

As knowledgeable as Mr. Preuss was about racecars and race drivers, updates were necessary for the press notebook and interviews were arranged with appropriate sources (see chapter 7).

Print News: The Navy Story

Originally, the Ashenfelter-Freedberg team raised several preliminary questions: *How did these kids die? Could their deaths have been prevented? Was the Navy negligent? Was Terry Collum murdered?* Up to this point, the cause of Terry Collum's death and those of the other five seamen remained a mystery. But mounting evidence seemed to indicate the deaths of all six seamen could have been a result of Navy negligence. That research brought the team to the threshold of a tentative working statement: *What kind of treatment did they get?*

Ashenfelter: Well, we sat down and talked about what we wanted to find out and as we found each bit of information in each one of these cases that would lead to raising the next question.

In the case of Jeff Sellers [one of the dead seamen], Sydney [Freedberg] was going through the report and noticed that one of the crewmen down in the berthing compartment where he [Sellers] died had said that they had to call for an emergency medical team at least five times before an emergency team showed up. The initial investigation report that the family got and that they showed Sydney concluded that Jeff Sellers received the best possible medical care. Well, that was just not true. And Collum, he had been on the verge of breaking down. So that got us into the whole arena of: *What kind of treatment did they get?*

Meanwhile, in the other seaman cases, Ms. Freedberg had found similar discrepancies between statements made by witnesses and a family's knowledge of their son's death. All this added to other anomalies Mr. Ashenfelter found in the Collum case. Comparing Navy documents, he noticed that the Navy had never interviewed other prisoners in the brig concerning Collum's mistreatment by prison guards.

Ashenfelter: I wanted to verify the accuracy of the Navy's investigation. It appears that there were five prisoners, witnesses, who were doing exercises with Collum. Only two of them were ever interviewed [noticed in NIS report]. The JAG investigation didn't interview any of the prisoners, just simply took the Marine commandant's word that the brig was run according to the rules and interviewed the Marine guards. The guards said the kid was doing exercises and went over the side of the ship.

In still another document, Mr. Ashenfelter noticed that Seaman Trerice had suffered abuse similar to that experienced by Seaman Collum.

Ashenfelter: . . . his father [Mr. Trerice] had arranged to have a private autopsy done. The outcome was that he [Trerice] hadn't had anything to eat and that he died of heatstroke and a heart attack. We had all these witnesses saying they were exercising the hell out of him on the day that he died, that the temperature out there was pretty high, the humidity was high, and that they were on one of the hottest places you could be on an aircraft carrier, the flight deck.

The team's research and verification effort may seem endless, but each new document during preliminary and primary research was matched against other documents, while checks with witnesses and families raised new questions and the need for additional evidence and verification. All of which led to interviews with key people (see chapter 7).

Print News: The Ford Plant Fire

Once on the scene, Mr. Cain discovered the firefighters had brought the fire under control and that toxicity from the smoke and wind direction were the new concerns of fire officials. He canceled his original perspective about explosions and turned his attention to this revised working statement: *How real is their concern? What's in that smoke?*

Cain: The fire officials were very worried about the toxicity of the smoke. If the wind changed on them, they would be risking death and they were making contingency plans to pull their people back. So the question now was: *How real is their concern and what's in that smoke?*

I'm there when the police chief is making arrangements to try and get some people [the Environmental Research Group] out [on the scene] so they could test the smoke content downwind where the residences were. I was there when they [the Research Group] showed up to find out exactly what the chief wanted.

What happens is that each piece of information that you collect feeds to additional questions. You have to change the order of priorities as events change. *Are they going to save the plant?* Once it's clear we're not going to have wholesale death out of this thing because the fire is being beaten down, and it's clear the plant's not going to be lost, then you can go on to questions like: *What do we really know about the toxicity of those chemicals? What effect, if any, is there likely to be on the people who ate the smoke? How did they save the plant? What steps did they take to avoid spread of the fire? What were the priorities of the firefighters?* There are lots of areas for questions. There's a kind of an A-B-C, almost a conformal logical type of approach. The events and areas that belong to them give you the questions.

Notice Mr. Cain's thinking process, which he called *a conformal logical type of approach*, and his recognition that questions pop up when one takes *events* and *areas* into account. And yet, none of those categories appeared in his mentally framed working statement. They were all unconsciously included in his revised working statement. Notice, too, that on-scene observation and alertness to activities around him generated the kinds of questions he raised to continue the research. He can take these questions to fire and plant officials because he has already done what a reporter must do in such a situation:

Cain: The first thing I did was to find the Saline chief of police and get his okay to stay because if some officers would see me as a reporter and say, "Get out of here," I could say, "No, I've already checked in with the chief."

And although he did interview officials, he also got answers to most of his questions just poking around on his own (see chapter 7).

Broadcast News: The TWA Hijack

For Mr. Meisner, modification of the working statement was not necessary. When it was clear St. Louis residents were among the hostages, the next step was to find out who they were and: *What were they doing there? What was the effect of this on their families?*

> **Meisner:** Now the main question for us was: *Who are the St. Louis people? Also, What were they doing there? What was the effect of this on their families?* We scrambled and got reporters out to different locations where we could get good family reaction regarding the concern people had for their loved ones.
>
> Our first stories aired about 1 hour after we heard about the hijacking. The information was very unclear at that point. We just knew we had a hostage situation and reasonable assurance about the names of the people on the flight. I knew we had to go after the families of these individuals, maybe send some people overseas. Actually we did go to Frankfurt where some of the hostages were released.
>
> At the outset we were merely talking to families of those people who were held hostage and later also went to channels in a couple of other states in the U.S. to talk to other family members and that's something initially we didn't anticipate doing.
>
> We brought in the international and national perspective, of course, but had to ultimately bring it all down to the most common denominator, the St. Louis people and their families.

With first determinations about the St. Louis factor and the decision to enlarge on that with the factor of family effect, interviews with key people soon followed to augment data already obtained from preliminary source contacts (see chapter 7).

Broadcast News: Illegal Use of Public Land

Having verified that drug farmers and survivalists were misusing public lands and recreationers were being threatened, Ms. Timmons began working from a tentative statement that, as it did in the previous case, took the form of two question statements: *How are they threatening the public? What should the public do to protect themselves?*

> **Timmons:** I didn't have any idea in mind for this story other than if this was going on in Michigan it might be a good story. The only reason we ran the story was that it was happening in Michigan. A lot of times we get information of things happening all over the country and we will follow the same process. We will check with Michigan people to see if we have a similar

instance here. If we don't, that would be in national news only and would not concern us and we probably would not do a local story.

After I confirmed there was a story here, the issues became: *Why are these people using public land? Why are they threatening the public?* First, I had to establish if they were using public land for illegal purposes. Then I had to establish if they were threatening the public.

Once it was clear that in both instances the case was true, then you get into: *How are they threatening the public? What should the public do to protect themselves?* If the public wasn't threatened, it would just be information only.

Even after a reality check on the evidence, professional writers perform still another reality check: whether their intended story would interest their audience. They raise a simple question about their working statement that is very much to the point: *So what?* Another common self-inquiry usually supplies the answer: *What does that mean to me?* That was what Ms. Timmons did here.

Timmons: All this verification got into the new methods being used in marijuana growing. We had to bring out the fact that marijuana growers are changing, that they are more sophisticated, that they are becoming agricultural experts, that they are growing a much more potent marijuana in Michigan than they are any place in the world. We got into areas that said: *Yes, people must be careful when they go into the woods.* But we also got into what people should do as precautions when they do go into the woods. It's not just the facts. You have to go a step further and answer the questions: *What can people do to protect themselves? What should they do when confronted? Why are the drug dealers using public lands?* You have to raise these questions. Otherwise, it wouldn't be an important story just to say that marijuana growers are using public land. The obvious answer is: *So what? What does that mean to me?* As a reporter, you always say: *What does that mean to me?* You have to bring it out.

Actually, we did not have a problem with squatters, so that did not relate to the California story. There had been a few instances involving survivalists in Michigan which did relate, so the California people relayed that material to me. And because we had instances of marijuana growers who had threatened some people, we asked them to relay that information to us, too.

It is clear that these professionals take little for granted. They raise questions generated by a working statement, declarative or question, and from there critical thinking and constant self-inquiry guide their movement from one phase of activity to another. Ms. Timmons then continued the process by carrying out some additional research and going on to primary interviews (see chapter 7).

5 Evaluating the Research: General Materials

As you have learned, professional media writers are persistent researchers and they take little of what they see, hear, or read for granted. They raise critical questions about all received data and even evaluate their own determinations. Novices, too, must be critical judges of received data. To help you improve your evaluation skills, this chapter deals with general materials that media writers customarily have to read: reports, documents, professional journal articles, feature news articles, popular magazine articles, books, newsletters, and other similar materials. Unlike data in such references as encyclopedias, directories, fact books, and almanacs, data in general materials require a great deal more scrutiny. In order to communicate accurate information in your own copy, you must be able to distinguish the genuine from the counterfeit. First ask Critical Self-Inquiry 4: *What information fails to stand up to question?* Then follow the line of questioning and the clues to answers provided in this chapter.

CRITICAL READING FOR EFFECTIVE WRITING

Learning how to become a critical reader has side effects. You become a better listener and a better writer. Your ear becomes fine tuned to flaws in verbal messages; you develop a heightened awareness of the needs and expectations of discerning media consumers; the questions you raise to judge information received will guide you when you write. If you fail to raise questions about your own writing, discriminating media consumers will. To avoid challenge, learn how to do the following whether the general material you read (or write) aims to persuade, explain, explore, or report.

- Identify the writer's copy organization.
- Locate the writer's conclusion about the topic/subject under discussion.
- Identify and evaluate evidence given (or not given) for the conclusion.
- Notice violations of clarity, completion, fairness, and balance.

If the the author's argument is flawed in any of these factors, that should raise a yellow flag of caution in your mind against quick acceptance of the author's argument. If the argument collapses on more than one factor, that should raise a red flag, meaning the content is too fragile to support the conclusion.

Some Fundamental Elements of Communication

Words, phrases, and sentences are the reader's only clues to a writer's meaning. How they are used and organized makes the difference between understanding and confusion. The writer who considers the elements a reader must have in order to understand the message usually delivers well-communicated copy. Some of these concern elements introduced in previous chapters. The others are described here and given additional attention in subsequent chapters, but right now you need to know what the necessary elements are. The important ones include the following:

- A statement or question establishing the problem or issue.
- A statement establishing what the writer intends to say about it.
- Historic and/or past background on the problem, issue, or question.
- Current background on the problem, issue, or question.
- Definitions of terms used.
- Reasons, examples, instances, authoritative statements (evidence).
- Documented facts, numbers, charts, graphs, tables (evidence).
- A counterargument, or an "on-the-other-hand" presentation, or recognition of weaknesses in given data, or counterarguments to a stated position (fairness and balance).
- Optional conclusions one could make for the evidence given.
- A summary of the whole and/or a conclusion.

First Clues: Transitions

Aside from basic elements of content, a communication needs transitions. Transitions help the receiver follow the overall organization of the message.

They connect one idea to the next and may appear as a word, phrase, or sentence at the beginning of a paragraph to introduce the idea, or to connect two thoughts within a paragraph, or to signify the end of one idea and movement to the next one. A single idea may run one or more paragraphs and the end of an idea is usually signaled by a conclusion or summary sentence. Transitions transport the reader smoothly from the last point made to a new point in the next sentence, the next paragraph, or series of paragraphs.

When a writer provides a chain link of ideas, it not only reveals the writer's organization, it also produces continuity and a progressive flow of guiding signposts. Look for them, but you may discover they are not always there. Then you have to work that much harder. The examples shown here give you an idea of how transitions can link sentences and paragraphs.

> Without fanfare or legislation the government is orchestrating a quiet *revolution* in how it regulates new medicines. The *revolution* is based on the idea that the sicker people are, the more freedom they should have to try drugs that are not fully tested. (Graham, 1991, p. 34)

Repetition of the word *revolution* serves as a transition from a sentence stating the author's purpose to the next sentence giving a basis for the change.

> In May of 1987 the FDA adopted a *new rule* that under certain conditions allows people with AIDS and other serious or life-threatening illnesses . . . to buy experimental drugs through their doctors one to three years before the formal approval process for the drug has been completed. . . . *But* AIDS activitists remain angry about restrictive conditions on the testing and release of new drugs. First, the FDA must have seen preliminary evidence that the drug is safe and effective. Second, the FDA and drug companies can set limits on who gets it.
>
> *Even so*, the *new rule* departs sharply from previous practices. In the 1970s and early 1980s experimental drugs such as . . . were sometimes available to people who knew how the system worked and had a good doctor at a major medical center. (Graham, 1991, p. 34)

Here you see several transitions. *But* is a short transition to a sentence that reflects a contrasting idea to the idea in the previous sentence. The introductory phrase, *Even so*, links the second paragraph to the first paragraph, whereas the phrase, the *new rule*, reminds the reader what the article is about,and the sentence as a whole acts as an introduction to a new idea: that the FDA has made some adjustments in past policies.

Most producers agree that the personal, targeted approach to pitching stories — especially the top 20 markets — is more effective. But they stress that nationwide satellite delivery is the most cost-effective and sensible approach to getting a client's message out. "After all the money the client spends, it makes good sense to try every possible avenue to get the VNR aired," explains Bahr.

To make producing a VNR most cost effective for clients, suppliers are increasing distribution to cable operators, preparing radio news releases from VNR audiotapes, and using VNR footage in other ways, such as in-flight videos and sales videos. (Shell, 1990, p. 28)

In this case, the introductory phrase in the second paragraph links the conclusion (the last sentence of the first paragraph) to ideas that follow in the second paragraph.

Tracking the Author's Organization

But you cannot always depend on transitions to clue you in on the author's organization of ideas. When they are absent, look for the opening sentences of a piece, first sentences of subsequent paragraphs, and points of evidence given in those paragraphs to support an idea. Together they signal the writer's copy organization, argument, and conclusion. Without them, reading and the evaluation process is a struggle. To begin the evaluation process, ask:

• *What is the writer's organization?*

Words, sentences, phrases, and paragraphs communicate a message when they are organized in an orderly fashion. One of their functions is to convey the writer's intended plan for message presentation. Writers often signal their pattern of explanation in the opening paragraphs. When they do not, they arrange copy in a pattern the reader can follow. Pattern gives a message form and tells the reader what to anticipate. It facilitates reading and the evaluation process. Without such a map, the reader has little notion of the writer's subject/topic or purpose. Such a plan is made quite clear in the opening sentences of this excerpt from a book review:

Ten years as a journalist in Lebanon and Israel taught Thomas L. Friedman two important lessons. "First, when it comes to discussing the Middle East, people go temporarily insane, so if you are planning to talk to an audience of more than two, you'd better have mastered the subject. Second, a Jew who wants to make a career working in or studying about the Middle East will always be a lonely man: he will never be fully accepted or trusted by the Arabs, and he will never be fully accepted or trusted by the Jews."

That last clause will raise some eyebrows and hackles, but Friedman, who *has* [*sic*] mastered his subject, fully documents its accuracy. (Gray, 1989, p. 62)

Even without its obvious transitions, this excerpt clues the reader to the author's copy organization. The first sentence is the writer's statement of the subject and the intent of his topic. It tells the reader that he will discuss journalists in Lebanon and Israel, particularly one journalist and the lessons he learned in that troubled area of the world. The second and third sentences back up the first with quotes from the book defining the learner, the lessons learned, and the teachers. The last sentence is the writer's conclusion, his judgment of the author's expertise and a verification of the author's authority. Having set up the reader's expectations, it is now up to the writer to deliver the evidence for his conclusion. An expression of intent is a promise and represents one measure against which the reader can evaluate whether the writer has fulfilled the promise made.

In the example given, the writer clarifies his intent and conclusion in the opening lines (deductive style). Sometimes the writer will state the intent, but instead of providing the conclusion at the outset, will wait until all the evidence is presented before closing with a conclusion (inductive style). Another pattern can develop when the writer uses an inductive style of organizing paragraphs. That is, this style opens with specific points of evidence related to an idea or issue, closes with a summary of those points, and then ends with a conclusion.

Unfortunately, writers do not always use such clear-cut patterns. This complicates the evaluation process. When the copy appears to be an unorganized jumble, the reader looks elsewhere for clues — to sentences and paragraphs.

In the absence of a clear pattern, look for first or last sentences in a paragraph. A beginning sentence (or sentences) tells the reader the specific point the writer intends to develop in that paragraph. The next sentences support the point made and may continue through several paragraphs. The last sentence (or sentences) summarizes the evidence given and tells the reader the specific point made in the paragraph.

Even when copy organization is obvious, it is a good practice to make a marginal note of the function of certain paragraphs. The notations will help, as well, when the organizational map is missing or for a quick review of the writer's ideas. In any case, following the progression of ideas often reveals the writer's organization, or lack of it. Follow the guidelines given earlier to help you answer the question: *What is the writer's organization?* Whether organization is present or absent, the author must clarify what the message is about.

Identifying the Message

Most reading matter involves some problem, issue or question. Critical readers try to determine whether the writer's message is solid enough to take seriously. Clues to the writer's copy organization are helpful when trying to identify the problem subject/topic and conclusion. Along with the previous question, always ask:

- *What is the problem, issue or question?*
- *What is the writer's conclusion?*

In chapters 2, 3, and 4, you learned how to identify problems, recognize necessary questions and sources, and appreciate the meaning of evidence. Now be advised that conclusions are responses to or summations of the evidence. If at first glance, the organization seems sloppy, or the subject and conclusion are unclear, one recourse is to skim through several pages. Make a note of references made to whatever matters are under discussion, then decide by the frequency of their appearance which is the main subject and topic, which are the minor subjects/topics. Concentrate on the main one, then on the others.

For clues to the conclusion, look for indicators like the following:

- hence, thus, therefore
- obviously, apparently
- indicates that
- suggests that
- it should be clear
- it is not surprising
- the point here is that
- all things considered
- the conclusion to draw is

- it is generally believed
- all the evidence points to
- it is my opinion
- there is no question that
- it is highly probable
- it is most likely that
- in my judgment
- in view of the fact that
- it can be said, therefore

The conclusion will follow these and similar words and phrases. A word of caution—conclusions are not always preceded by indicators. In such instances, be reminded that conclusions are responses and are located near the beginning or end of a piece, or at the close of several paragraphs of argument that are then summed up in a final conclusion at the end.

In sloppy organization the conclusion may be anywhere. In that case, look for the writer's observations (responses to ideas) and for documented evidence and interview information related to them. Identifying the conclusion is crucial to the rest of the evaluation process because everything that follows depends on locating it. When you do find the conclusion, it is a good idea to mark it, or to write it out, because you will need to refer to it as you continue raising evaluation questions.

Look for the Evidence

Professional writers are rational thinkers. They support their observations and conclusions with reasons based on evidence. Evidence is the measure against which a reader determines the worth of a conclusion instead of reacting to it.

When one of your friends makes the statement: *I believe that _____ ,* or *I know that _____ ,* you are prompted to ask: *Why? How do you know?* And the response is: *Because _____ .* What your friend is doing is giving you a reason, opinion or fact for the claim made. It is just as important to ask the same question when you locate an author's conclusion. To evaluate the conclusion always ask:

- *What is the writer's basis for this conclusion?*
- *Are the reasons relevant to the problem discussed?*

When a writer provides evidence to support a conclusion, a main reason is usually given. This is then followed by reasons why the main one was made. In lengthy and complex material, these supporting explanations may be followed by minor items of evidence and these, too, usually have reasons why they were made.

You may also encounter material where the writer arrives at more than one conclusion. Make a note of the additional conclusions and follow the same process of identifying the evidence for each conclusion. Whether there is one conclusion or more, it is important to group the right reasons with the right conclusion.

Many times the reasons of evidence are irrelevant to the conclusion and are given when the writer has few solid supports to offer. You have the right to dismiss irrelevancies, or similar misfits, and to judge the conclusion purely on the relevant and valid reasons given.

When looking for reasons, watch for these words and phrases. They indicate that reasons will follow:

- because, for example
- a little known fact is
- there are several reasons for this
- some of the evidence that
- the factors involved include
- moreover
- the (an accredited group) claims
- furthermore
- in addition
- (name of record) indicates
- consider
- namely
- first (expect more reasons)
- finally

Much written work is not well organized. This makes it difficult to keep track of a conclusion(s) and the reasons, especially if the piece is long and complicated. Reasons for a conclusion may not follow in an orderly manner. They may be scattered throughout the piece. You will have to group reasons together that demonstrate some relationship to the conclusion so their relevancy (or irrelevancy) to the conclusion is easy to see.

Test the validity of a reason by asking: *Yes, but how do you know that?* Or, *Who says so? What qualifies this person to say so?* Then check if the source given is a valid and authentic one. That is, find out if the information comes from a qualified person, a reputable publication, a respected institution, also if it is verifiable, or has been verified and by whom. Test the relevancy of a reason by asking:

- *What does this reason have to do with the problem discussed?*

When a reason tests out and is relevant, take it under consideration for judgment of the whole.

In the instance of lengthy and complex material, a good practice is to mark or label the relevant reasons in the margin, or to make a list of them on a sheet of paper below a notation of the conclusion to which they belong. Aside from making lists of grouped reasons for each conclusion, you could label each conclusion A, B, C, and so on, and then number the reasons for each: A-1, A-2, A-3; B-1, B-2, and so forth. Some readers diagram or chart conclusions and the major and minor reasons that belong to them. Use whatever system works best for you.

Never underestimate the importance of keeping the conclusion(s) in mind while reading. Otherwise relevant reasons, when they are present, will slip away and the writer's false reasoning will trip you.

Where is the conclusion, its reasons, in the following excerpt? Are they relevant? Answer these questions before you read the feedback that follows the excerpt.

Corporate and nonprofit public relations practitioners are increasingly aware that their cooperative efforts benefit both their reputation and profitability. The public relations profession is now a mainstream discipline that helps to relate philanthropic, social and marketing efforts.

Companies realize that reputations, particularly as they relate to key social issues, affect profitability. For example, consumers are making more informed choices regarding purchases. In many cases, issues such as a company's environmental record or stance on such topics as animal rights and education also influence consumer choices. Astute CEOs and their public relations executives realize a company's concern for societal issues can influence competitiveness in the marketplace.

The New York-based Council on Economic Priorities, for example, has sold about 700,000 copies of "Shopping For A Better World." Available since January 1989, it rates the makers of over 1,800 brandname products on 11 issues, including: advancement of women and minorities, animal testing, giving to charity, nuclear power, the environment and involvement in South Africa.

This tie between company policy and social issues is particularly evident with the animal rights movement and the cosmetics industry. For example, People for the Ethical Treatment of Animals (PETA), Rockville, Maryland, launched a program nearly five years ago called the "Caring Consumer Campaign," which provides a free listing of companies that do not use animals for testing product lines. According to Kathy Gaillermo, director of the campaign, the list has grown from a scant 50 to more than 300 companies.

Every month, PETA receives 2,500 requests for the list from consumers who might consider this factor when making their purchasing decisions. Realizing that this issue can affect sales, many companies have started to promote the fact that products are not tested on animals. (Sizemore-Elliot, 1990, p. 26)

The author's first "response" is that there is a growing need for cooperation between manufacturers of products and public relations professionals. The author's reasons: consumers are getting smarter; 700,000 have bought a magazine sold by the Council on Economic Priorities that lists the names of manufacturers who either operate counter to or are sensitive to social issues; some 2,500 pet lovers requested free PETA listings of manufacturers who use animals to test their products.

The reasons are relevant and substantiated, and the author is director of communications at the 70001 Training & Employment Institute, Washington, DC. However, one should double check any author's validity as a titled authority by examining his or her background, reputation in the field, the purpose and service record of the institution he or she represents, and the references from which the author obtained data to see if information was accurately represented. Based on her reasons, this author finally concludes that if developing the corporate image is the role of public relations professionals, then they must act as principal informant to corporate executives about consumer reaction to social issues and how these could affect their marketing efforts.

Faulty Reasoning

A reason may be valid, substantial, and relevant, but unless the conclusion follows logically from the reason, the reason is irrelevant and invalid. In addition, the reason given may be based on an erroneous assumption, or an improbable one. If so, the reason is invalid because it will not support the conclusion. A well-reasoned argument requires not only substantial and relevant reasons, it must also manifest assumptions that are verifiable or highly probable in order to logically link one reason or statement to another and for the conclusion to follow logically from those reasons.

Irrelevancy is an obvious clue to faulty reasoning because the author forces the reader to call on private assumptions about a reason to link it logically to the conclusion. The argument then becomes the reader's and not the writer's point of view.

If you can think of other valid reasons for the conclusion, that is another clue to faulty reasoning. If your reasons vary widely from the writer's, the likelihood of false argument is strong. Again, keeping the conclusion in mind as you read is crucial. Once it and the reasons for it are identified, ask yourself:

- *Do the reasons logically support the conclusion?*
- *What other reasons support the conclusion?*
- *What value preferences or beliefs are embedded in reasons given?*
- *Are assumptions that are embedded in the reasons verifiable, probable?*
- *Does the argument make sense?*

Still another clue to faulty reasoning is the unstated assumption. It is like a private assumption. It is nonlanguage. It assumes you share the writer's sentiments. The danger here is that if the writer's views do match yours, you are inclined to prematurely accept the writer's conclusion. When writers assume readers share the same value preferences or beliefs, they also assume the reasons given represent adequate support for the conclusion, or that no other conclusion may be drawn from the evidence presented. In reality, the supports may have been carefully selected and alternative conclusions may have been deliberately ignored to establish the author's value preference or personal belief.

A *value preference* means one accepts the concept of honesty over dishonesty, or freedom of the press over national security. A *belief* is attachment to an idea or faith in a person. For instance, one may believe capital punishment should be abolished, or that the president will keep the lid on taxes. Value preferences and beliefs are often emotionally charged and motive directed and are easily noticed because they seldom allow for other viewpoints.

One way to detect an unstated assumption is to ask the following questions as the writer moves from reasons to conclusion:

- *What is the author's definition of_____ ?*
- *Does the author assume I share the same values and/or beliefs?*

- *If they are the same, can I set these aside and take on an objective attitude?*
- *What unexpressed reason or evidence weakens or discounts the author's conclusion(s)?*
- *What conclusion(s), other than the one the author gives, is also consistent with reasons/evidence given?*

In the case of unstated assumptions, whether in copy, a conversation, or interview, challenge it by saying: *Yes, what you say may be true. However, you assume* (or, *you overlooked the possibility,* or, *you failed to recognize) that* _____ .

The dispute about abortion rights is a case in point. The pro-life and pro-choice groups select data that support their respective positions and ignore whatever information might weaken their strategy. For example, the anti-abortionists may argue for life under the unstated assumption that the care of unwanted children is the taxpayer's responsibility. Their opponents may argue for state-sponsored abortion under the unstated assumption that abortion is less costly than years of taxpayer dollars to support unwanted children. Notice that each is stating a *value preference*: life over death as opposed to freeing the fetus from a life-long sentence of second-class citizenship, or the belief that abortion is murder as opposed to depriving a woman control over her own body. In any controversy, the critical reader must be alert to the writer's unstated assumptions.

Another way to uncover hidden assumptions is to examine the background of the author. Active religious practitioners are likely to be pro-lifers. A union member will object to corporate union busting. A physician with a successful private practice is likely to oppose socialized medicine. That is not to say all members of these or any other group feel the same way as the rest of the membership. Dissension always exists within groups. The point is, personal values, beliefs, affiliations, and self-interest are motivating forces in any controversy. You need to be aware that such motivations exist and can lead the writer to say or write only what the writer wants you to know.

Still another way to detect unstated assumptions is to play the devil's advocate, that is, play the role of the opposition. This is particularly fruitful if you have researched and read about the issue. If you have not studied the problem, take the attitude of disagreement with the conclusion, especially when you discover your value preferences and beliefs are in agreement with the author's. If you align your biases with the author's, you could forfeit critical thinking to mutual sentimentality. Instead, let your objective responses guide you in playing out the role of the devil's advocate.

INSIST ON CLARITY

The previous sections helped you to understand the basic architecture of a written piece and the means of evaluating evidence for conclusions made. Now you will learn to examine the language used so you can respond to the meaning of ideas presented. One point of examination is *clarity*. Without clarity, accurate understanding is elusive. Its absence obscures meaning and interferes with the reader's willingness to accept the author's reasoning, solid or flawed, and places doubt on the writer's conclusion.

One frequent offense against clarity is *ambiguity*, an imprecise use of language. Although there are many types of ambiguity, three types appear most often: jargon, abstract words, and omission. Look for these ambiguities after asking: *What words and phrases are vague and unclear?*

Jargon.   The first type of ambiguity, jargon, is easily identified because it is a specialized vocabulary and always a source of confusion. It represents the language of those in the same trade, profession, or geographic area. For example, sportswriters, social workers, and astronauts share a specialized language known only to them. Writers using terms used by these and other segments of society are obliged to define their meaning for the rest of the population, or face questions concerning them.

Abstract words.   Another common source of confusion are abstract words such as "justice," "faith," and "freedom." Each one of us has a private understanding of what these kinds of words mean. That is the danger. We carry those meanings to reading material with the assumption that we understand what the author means. Nor does context make the meaning obvious because the reader can carry the same assumptions about abstract words to the context and again mistake the meaning. It is important for the reader to know what meaning the writer intends for abstract words and phrases.

Imprecise language forces the reader to make a choice, usually not the one the writer intends. Furthermore, when readers are forced to make choices, the writer deprives them of the opportunity to form an accurate judgment of the conclusion. The communication link breaks down, the reader begins a private process of selection, and the writer loses the reader's attention. This holds true, as well, for the spoken word.

A writer's conclusion is (or should be) supported by reasons, and both the conclusion and its reasons are important places you, as the reader, should look for ambiguity. Simply remember that when the author fails to clarify unfamiliar and abstract terms in any sentence, including the conclusion or a reason, it is unlikely you will be able to understand the author's intent, or accept all parts of the piece, and possibly its conclusion. The author needs to clarify intended meanings. Look for that clarification. For example, the abstract words given earlier become less abstract when replaced with or supported by these explanations: *justice* (the right to a fair trial by jury), *faith* (unquestioning allegiance to a person, cause or idea), *freedom* (the right to make one's own choices). These explanations may not square with your notion of these abstracts, but if clarified by the writer they tell you the meaning the writer intends for these words.

In the absence of clarifying explanations, look for a definition: *"excellence* is a virtue,"* or, an example: *"excellence* is what Olympic gold medalists represent," or, criteria: *"excellence* is a standard of superiority like the one Olympic judges indicate when they hold up a display card with the number 10 on it."

If a reason is ambiguous, attend to other reasons. If the conclusion is ambiguous, the evaluation process is immediately handicapped. As a critically active reader it is your responsibility to raise the questions that will clarify content, but if ambiguity interferes at too many points, you may decide the material is not reliable enough for further effort.

On the other hand, for a media writer those very ambiguities can become the substance of interview questions or subject matter in copy. Keep ambiguities, or any other weakness discussed here, in mind. They provide data for an enterprise news story, substance for a PR release, or an idea for an ad. With editorial approval, you can become an agent of correction, clarification, or challenge.

For instance, suppose you read a magazine article about a miracle skin cream that erases wrinkles and that the cream was endorsed by a leading dermatologist. The author's representation of "endorsement" is unclear. You check it out and discover your understanding and the author's view of endorsement are two different things. It turns out that the physician is a paid representative of the drug company promoting the skin cream and that some users have experienced skin damage after applying the cream — basis for a news story.

Omissions.   Another source of ambiguity, particularly those concerning one of the W questions (who, what, where, when, why, and how), are omissions of relevant data. Writers often assume that readers will or should understand details related to a subject. Again, they force choice on the reader who may make a wrong choice and misunderstand the message.

Omissions, too, are a good source for interview questions if you intend to interview the errant author or someone else close to the subject/topic problem. You may ask why a particular point or relevant detail was overlooked, or question the conclusion because of the missing data. Omission in a body of information is a serious offense and should be noted.

Glaring omissions appeared recently in a metropolitan newspaper reporting theft in a hospital. The story concerned a hospital janitor who was caught robbing hospitalized children. The story ran for nearly 18 inches and included the basics of a news story, but failed to answer some important questions related to the story: *What did the janitor take from the children? If it was money, how much? Was the loot confined to or did it include comforting toys, other items? What? Why did the janitor, who had no previous record, commit the alleged theft?* The author raised questions in the reader's mind, lost credibility, and misused valuable space.

Sometimes omission is beyond the writer's control. Deadlines often limit an author's freedom to gather and organize all the available information and even when the complete picture is delivered to the editor, air time or space restrictions limit presentation of all the relevant evidence. Also, no writer can know all there is to know about a particular problem even if given unlimited time and space. For example, we may never learn all there is to know about the assassinations of John F. Kennedy and Martin Luther King. Restrictions of time, space, and circumstance aside, writers are obliged to provide readers with as complete a picture of the problem as possible. After that, responsibility for omissions rests with editors who may slice away important content.

Finally, omissions occur when there is a deliberate attempt to present a position or product only in favorable terms. Discovering what has been left out is still another opportunity for an enterprise project. For example, a cereal company claims their product contains all the daily vitamin requirements, but they leave out an important detail. As an ad writer for a competing cereal company, you discover the claim holds up but that one would have to eat multiple helpings before gaining any benefit from the product — springboard for a new ad campaign.

Writers who try to influence the reader present reasons that are consistent with their position and, at first, their logic seems sound enough. They deliberately avoid bringing in any information that might weaken their argument. To defend against this tendency, critical readers should be aware that writers are prone to do this, and that they should not hesitate to ask: *Yes, but if* _____ ? Or, *Yes, but what about* _____ ?

Here's how such inquiries work. A new line of microwave meals is currently on the market. The meals are vacuum packed instead of frozen, and so need no refrigeration. One product was touted as fresh, ready to eat, and void of preservatives. It begged the question: Yes, but if the meals are vacuum packed and not frozen, what keeps them fresh and ready for the microwave? What the advertisement failed to tell the consumer is this: The meals contain anywhere from nearly 600 to almost 1,000 mg. of sodium, a component of a preservative, and amounts to more than is in some canned foods. According to the American Heart Association, Americans consume more sodium than is needed: 3,000 to 5,000 mg. daily; recommended daily levels are 1,100 to 3,000 mg. Although consumption of one of those meals falls within the recommended range, those on restricted salt diets would be well advised to read product labels carefully. More than one high-sodium meal might prove risky for persons watching their intake of salt and other food additives.

The evaluation process becomes a slippery slope with so many types of omissions to look for. Your one major defense is a *questioning attitude*, even toward material that "makes sense." After raising the questions above, make a final test by asking:

- *What necessary elements of information has the writer omitted?* (refer to the list on p. 79).

The habit of probing for missing information avoids quick acceptance of a writer's given conclusion. The habit also trains you to react to gaps in verbal messages and interviews and to search for them in your own copy.

FAIR PRESENTATION

Aside from violations of clarity, a writer can confuse readers by intentionally or unintentionally biasing the reader. That is, the writer forfeits objectivity by injecting emotion, private motive, personal point of view, belief, or assumption into the copy. To detect slanted copy notice the writer's use of words. The language may include hyperbole, subjective adjectives and adverbs, innuendo.

Bias in any form disallows a fair presentation of the information, particularly when a fair and objective account is the reader's expectation. The use of *hyperbole* (an exaggeration) is quite common and easily noticed as in the following sentence. The piece discusses the Japanese-American effort to win retribution from the U. S. government for having confined Japanese-Americans in federal prison camps during World War II. Japanese-Americans were split on the issue of reparations to survivors. Some favored compensation to survivors and their descendants, whereas others felt that demand was an unrealistic burden on American taxpayers and favored the Congressional bill that provided a cash payment of $20,000 only to the survivors.

It may be fatally ironic, then, that this Japanese community, so effective in maintaining its heritage for 40 years, has not maintained its unity on this issue.

The exaggeration displays the author's bias and annoyance that one or the other issue failed to muster full support. Moreover, it is quite unlikely that a cultural heritage that endured prejudice and resentment prior to, during and even after the war in this country would expire because of the lack of unity on a single issue.

The clue to bias in the sentence just given comes through in the adverb, "fatally." But you will find those clues in adjectives as well. An adjective should describe the noun it modifies. An adverb should describe the verb it modifies. And the description should be concrete, a precise description of the noun or verb, not a label that manifests the writer's prejudices, as in this sentence from a review of an autobiography.

> The *ego-centric* [*sic*] analysis revealed the extent to which _____ [name of the personality concerned was removed] was engaged in personal problem-solving than with political matters.

The term, *ego-centric,* and its hyphenation, is a giveaway of the author's personal sentiment about this person. A less cautious reader might be tempted to follow the author's lead and take on the inference intended about this person.

Innuendo is still another form of nonlanguage. It is similar to the kind of inference a biased word like the one just discussed generates, but is less direct. That is, it is an indirect statement implying a meaning, usually in a derogatory sense, rather than expressing meaning concretely. Again, the writer assumes you share the same sentiments and this may be far from true. Even if you find yourself agreeing with the writer, avoid the temptation. It is your job to abstract only objective statements, not subjective ones. See if you can detect the implication in the following. Then ask one of your friends what the innuendo means to them. Chances are it will be different from your understanding.

> The _____ group's [a hard rock music album] way of dealing with serious topics makes these songs more readily acceptable and listenable. On the surface they appear to be silly tunes with no meaning beyond the farcical, literal meanings. Closer analysis shows that each song has an underlying social commentary. Nightmarish circus music would best describe this collection of songs. The bastardization of the music of our youth forces us to disassociate ourselves from the music of our past and reassociate it with the way our world is going.

At first glance, it appears the author is defending the album. But one could detect more than one implication. The adjective "nightmarish" and the sentence with the term "bastardization" in it could mean objection against the defamation of youthful memories, or it could mean the author approves of the way the album shakes us out of our nostalgia. Does the author assume you share the nostalgia or approve of the "bastardization?" The ambiguity suggests a variety of implications. Take your pick, but you should not be forced to choose. Look for another reviewer.

BALANCED PRESENTATION

Balance in copy means the writer has presented as complete a picture of the problem at hand as possible. That is, the writer has answered all the reader's questions, provided more than one viewpoint of the problem and, particularly in uncertain situations, indicated other possibilities or conclusions that could be drawn from the given evidence.

Any exclusion of relevant data produces only part of the picture and a lopsided view of the problem. Such writing mismanagement limits your understanding and as a critical reader you can withhold judgment on the writer's conclusion. Although time and space may have limited the writer's coverage of all the available data, you are entitled to know more than a single side or viewpoint on any matter, and there is always more than one position on any given issue. If the material you read or hear presents only one side of the picture, neglects "on-the-other-hand" information, the writer is asking you to make a decision from an incomplete picture of the problem. Defend against this type of subjective persuasion by insisting on more than than a one-sided view.

Violation of balance is especially obvious in copy where the author's reasons are reasonable and appear sufficient enough to support the conclusion. As with all the other communication flaws just discussed, the writer mistakenly or intentionally ignores relevant reasons that may weaken or contradict the conclusion. One way to avoid being trapped by convincing argument is to anticipate and to look for a balanced presentation. Indicators help. Some of these signposts are:

- however, but
- on the other hand
- the opposite view
- despite all the
- not everyone agrees with
- other groups, however

- another researcher found
- an exception to
- contrary to
- nevertheless, notwithstanding
- this does not hold true when
- disagreement occurs when

Such indicators are not always present and are no substitute for a mind alert to overzealous argument. If you feel you have been shortchanged, it is probably because the writer has presented only the good side of an issue (or only the bad), or argues too well or too fervently on a singular slant.

MAKING DECISIONS ABOUT GENERAL INFORMATION

All matters previously discussed suggest caution against accepting available information too quickly. A seriously flawed piece is reason enough to ignore it. On the other hand, a critical reader does not dismiss material with elements in it that do stand up to question. It is a matter of determining the best in a piece on the basis of the criteria just given. And keep in mind earlier cautions against confirmation and selection bias. If the source is reliable, if the conclusion is clear and holds up under some of the best evidence given, and if the evidence is balanced, relevant to the conclusion and moves logically to it, then even the information that runs counter to your working statement should be included in your collection of reliable data. Set all other information that fails to stand up to question aside, but do not toss it. It may prove valuable as substance for challenge in your own piece or may trigger an idea for an enterprise project.

Even if the conclusion is accepted on the basis of some of the evidence given, note where the evidence collapses. And keep in mind that no conclusion, however well supported, is ever final. Something always develops to change the picture. A conclusion only represents a current status, not a final one.

SUMMARY OF EVALUATION QUESTIONS FOR
GENERAL MATERIALS

Tracking the author's organization:
  • *What is the writer's organization?*

Identifying the message:
  • *What is the problem, issue or question?*
  • *What is the writer's conclusion?*

Look for the evidence:
  • *What is the writer's basis for this conclusion?*
  • *Are the reasons given relevant to the problem discussed?*
  • *What do the reasons have to do with problem discussed?*

Faulty reasoning:
  • *Do the reasons logically support, lead to the conclusion?*
  • *What other reasons support the conclusion?*
  • *What value preferences or beliefs are embedded in reasons given?*
  • *Are assumptions embedded in the reasons verifiable, probable?*
  • *Does the argument make sense?*

- *What is the author's definition of _____ ?*
- *Does the author assume I share the same values and/or beliefs?*
- *If they are the same, can I set these aside and take on an objective attitude?*
- *What unexpressed reason or evidence weakens or discounts the author's conclusion(s)?*
- *What conclusion(s), other than the one the author gives is also consistent with reasons/evidence given?*

Insist on clarity:
- *What words and phrases are vague and unclear?*
- *Are definitions for abstract words provided?*
- *What has the writer omitted or failed to say?*
- *What necessary elements of information has the writer omitted?*

Fair presentation:
- *Does the author project bias, subjectivity?*
- *Does the author express his/her meaning concretely, or use innuendo to imply meaning?*

Balanced presentation:
- *Is the author's presentation slanted, one-sided, or balanced?*

Evaluating general materials takes practice, but it is time well spent because of the benefits that accrue from reading critically. The evaluation process becomes easier with each application until it is virtually automatic. Without thinking about it twice, the practitioner becomes an astute decision maker about received data, develops sensitivity to failures in verbal messages as well as written ones, and learns to avoid similar faults in one's own writing. It all begins with Critical Self-Inquiry 4: *What information fails to stand up to question?*

In the next chapter, you will learn how to evaluate another type of data that today's media writer frequently depends on.

6 Evaluating the Research: Scientific Reports

In chapter 5 you learned about evaluating evidence in general materials. Here, the principal question is also Critical Self-Inquiry 4: *What information fails to stand up to question?* But in this chapter you learn about evaluating empirical research reported in professional journals. To obtain empirical evidence, researchers conduct interviews with people or observe and record the behavior of people or things. Evidence is gathered concerning any one of these elements, transferred into numbers, and conclusions are drawn from the evidence based on quantitative methods of analysis.

Empirical research has many faces: polls and surveys,[1] field studies, experiments, quasi-experiments, and others, plus any hybrids of these. Strategies will differ according to research purpose and funds available to conduct the research. For example, an experiment, usually a controlled type of research, may include a survey. A field study may require the researchers to observe and note group interaction among toddlers in a nursery school and include a survey testing teachers' responses to certain questions. Besides a variety of research designs, empirical studies range across a broad set of research strategies.

Admittedly, explaining the intricacies of empirical research in a single chapter is an ambitious effort, even for our purposes. To begin with, the functions of empirical research are so interdependent that one function cannot be considered without considering its influence on another. That interdependency is one of the complexities of empirical research, but there

---

[1]Many research scientists feel these are so similar in kind that they are used interchangeably in discussions concerning them, and that is how they are regarded in this text.

are others. You will find yourself dealing with reports written in more than one language, the language of empirical research and the language of the discipline in which the research is conducted. Each type of empirical research in any particular discipline—agriculture, chemistry, medicine, economics, and the like—has its own language peculiarities and complexities.

It takes time and experience to understand the principles of empirical procedures in so many different contexts. In fact, whole texts are written about the mysteries of empirical research, sometimes on only one aspect of a specific operation in a research type concerning a single discipline. Moreover, although empirical studies achieve publication (sometimes a test of their worth), researchers are not always the best explainers of their own studies and the written report is often a muddle even for those in the same field of work.

However, your concern here is not so much about the varieties of empirical research or the details concerning their various functions, but about some of the things you should look for and raise questions about when reading a scientific report. There are many other issues related to empirical research, but those discussed here carry a great deal of weight in any evaluation process.

Once you have come to a fair understanding of these issues, seek out a research scientist for verification of your understanding. That expert will point out other important elements related to those you have reviewed. Try to consult with a research scientist who is an authority in the same field of work discussed in the study, or with a research scientist at a private research agency or university research institute who specializes in the discipline discussed. Getting expert opinion is so essential that you will see that recommendation made here more than once. Do not try to handle a scientific report on your own. But before seeing a consultant, evaluate the study by raising the questions introduced in the following pages.

Responsible handling of scientific reports by media writers is extremely important because media writers are the ones who transmit advancements in research science to the general public. Numbers make a powerful impact on the eye and ear, and if these are misrepresented or sensationalized, misreport by a media writer is not only a disservice to the researcher, it is simply journalistic irresponsibility.

Above all, never accept second-hand evaluations. Unfortunately, too many media writers obtain information about research studies from press releases. They are not the best source. A press release rarely gives a full report of the study, only those features the PR writer chooses to disclose. Nor is a news or magazine article a good source because here, too, only select fragments of the study are included for whatever purpose the writer may intend. Play it safe. Read the report in its original form. Check it against results obtained by other researchers who studied the same problem. You will make a better judgment about the study and a PR writer or author's use of study results in general materials. To assist your understanding of the sections to follow, you will find examples throughout this chapter. They serve as illustrations of points under discussion, but no attempt is made to attach them to any particular class or research strategy.

TARGET THE SPONSORS

A good first step is to find out who is underwriting the study and what purpose they had for funding the research. Sponsors of research work are usually foundations, corporations, special interest groups, government agencies, and university personnel. Researchers customarily indicate the sponsoring group on the first or last page of the report or in a footnote at the beginning. If that indication is missing, one way to find out is to ask the researchers directly or to contact the editor of the journal or monograph in which the report appeared.

Foundations sponsor research principally to advance knowledge in a particular discipline, and they award these studies to research institutes at universities or to commercial research agencies. Corporations and special interest groups normally sponsor research for reasons of specific interest to them. Their assignments more often go to commercial research agencies and sometimes to universities.

University research institutes are dedicated to precise and accurate research and report, as are reputable research firms such as Harris and Gallup. You can rely on studies conducted by such commerical agencies, but if you do not know about an agency beforehand, check on them through a university research institute.

If a survey was used as part of the research strategy, try to obtain the questions that were asked of respondents so you can determine if the questions were a true test of the research purpose. For instance, researchers in the employ of a tobacco company could conceivably single out a very select group of smokers and design questions in such a way that the company would then be able to report no one suffered any ill effects from smoking the company's cigarettes.

Find out who is doing the research as well as who is footing the bill. Once the research group is validated, direct all questions to that group, rather than questioning the PR writer or anyone else who wrote about the report. And in the instance of a study sponsored by a corporate body or special interest group, but conducted by an outside research agency, contact persons at that agency and not persons connected with the corporation or special interest group.

Often a research agency produces a well designed and objective study, but the sponsors are inclined to be highly selective about reporting the results. Reputable research firms usually establish an understanding with the sponsor that only a full account of the results will be distributed when the sponsor is contacted for information, or that the sponsor will confer with the agency before giving out a particular result. You cannot always be sure that the understanding will be honored. In instances of political polling, for example, a candidate, or the candidate's staff, will report only those results which cast a favorable light on their effort and will ignore any unfavorable aspects. Or, a corporation will report only those parts of a study supporting the position that their product is well manufactured and will ignore the part that specifies a time period when the product was produced with defects and reached market. It is wise to verify such announcements with the research agency and not the politician or the sponsoring corporation.

Then there are the independents, researchers not attached to a university or reputable research agency. Independents may be funded by some group with a profit motive or an axe to grind, or the researchers may harbor these motives themselves and somehow find the means to underwrite their research. Be wary of these independents. Find out who they are. Find out if they are qualified to conduct such research, if they have done any other research studies in the past and whether reviews published about those studies were favorable or unfavorable. Find out if there is anything in their background that might have motivated this effort and who is supporting the study. With some assistance from a research scientist, you may discover the independent's research methods are sound, indeed, or that they reflect personal biases. Awareness is the key when you are evaluating research reports. Begin with:

- *Who is sponsoring this research?*
- *What is their purpose?*

THE THEORETICAL STATEMENT

The theoretical statement or hypothesis is a probabilistic statement and customarily reflects both the research purpose and the specific problem. That is, researchers theorize that a particular thing is so, but they are not sure, so they conduct an investigation to clarify their belief and to determine, as far as possible, to what extent that belief applies to a majority number as a general condition. They can then determine if they were right, partially right, or off the mark.

If the researchers wanted to study the population of working mothers, they might set up hypotheses such as these: (a) *We believe the stress on working mothers relates to concerns about child-care accommodations while working rather than to job or marital stress.* (b) *We also believe child-care facilities established by the employer relieve that stress and reduce absenteeism among working mothers.*

First and foremost, you should expect to see the researcher's definition of all concepts entertained: *stress, working mothers, concerns, child-care accommodations, job stress, marital stress, child-care facilities, relief, reduction, absenteeism.* You need to know what these terms mean to the researchers, what they are thinking about when they use these concepts and how they intend to measure them. That is: *What do they mean by stress? Is it manifestation of physical problems, poor job performance, irritability, etc., or all of these? What constitutes job stress? Marital stress? What defines the working mother? Are they part-time or full-time working mothers? Day or night shift? In what types of work? Where? Does their definition include single working mothers? In what time period or periods were they studied? What are the child-care concerns of working mothers? What is meant by child-care accommodations? What kind of facilities? Where? How is relief achieved, or not achieved, determined? What is their definition of absenteeism? How is reduction of absenteeism determined? What aspects concerning this particular issue about working mothers should have been explored and were not?*

If these explanations are absent, you will not be able to determine if the researchers have a relevant population of interest that fits their research purpose and theoretical statement. The number of questions you raise about the theroretical statement depends a great deal on the declared purpose of the research. But first make sure you get some answers to these basic questions:

- *What is the theoretical statement?*
- *Are the concepts clearly and fully defined?*

THE POPULATION OF INTEREST

The population of interest is a body of certain people, places, or things about which the researchers hope to establish a generalization. The elements within such a population share similar characteristics: working mothers, teen-agers, voters, high schools, rain forests. The population of interest may be a particular group, or the group and all or some subgroups represented in it. For example, the population of interest may be tenured college professors only, or college professors broken down into subgroups of tenured and untenured professors, broken down further on the basis of private vs. public colleges, location, age, experience, and any number of other divisions.

The population of interest may be Republican and Democratic party voters to the exclusion of other parties, coal miners to the exclusion of all other classes of miners. The population of interest can also be things and places: U. S. urban communities only in certain key cities, art museums in cities with populations of over a certain number, or all U. S. daily metropolitan newspapers, or athletic programs at inner-city schools only and limited to locations in three major cities.

Although the population of interest is normally revealed by the theoretical statement, you still need as complete a picture of the population of interest, including its subgroups, as you ought to get about the concepts in the hypothesis. Otherwise, you will not be able to determine if the concepts in the hypothesis are relevant to the population in question, or if the generalization made applies to that population.

The researchers are obliged to clearly define who or what they are dealing with and must provide a complete description of the distinctive features that separate those people, places, or things from other elements in the rest of the population. You need to know these details because you have to determine not only if the concepts in the hypothesis apply, but also if the sample drawn from the population of interest to test the hypothesis is an appropriate sample for the population of interest concerned. The population of interest, as well as the sample, is the key to evaluating the researcher's findings about the sample and any generalization made about the population of interest. Look for answers to these questions:

- *Who or what is the population of interest?*
- *What characteristics set this group apart from the rest of the population?*
- *Is the population of interest clearly defined?*
- *Are the people, places, or things examined appropriate for the problem examined?*
- *What subgroups were included or omitted and why?*
- *Does the generalization apply to this population of interest? Why? If not, why not?*

PROBABILITY VERSUS NONPROBABILITY STUDIES

Now notice whether the study is probability or nonprobability research. A probability study refers to one in which there is some kind of probability method employed to select the group of people or things the researchers have examined. A nonprobability study means the examined group was selected by some convenient or purposeful method and not by chance.

Where probability methods are conducted, researchers are able to determine a number of important things. Random selection permits differences to appear in the group examined so that certain comparisons can be made. Random selection also allows an estimate of the degree of error in results obtained and, above all, affords researchers the opportunity to generalize about the results. And generalizability is the principal aim of researchers. That is, they hope to infer that the results obtained from a randomly selected sample of people, places, or things probably holds true, as well, for the unexamined portion of the population of interest.

But the strength of any generalization made to the population of interest depends on how large the error estimate in the sample is from true values in the population of interest.[2] Researchers hope their sample estimate is reasonably close to the "true" value in the population of interest because that feature gives heightened interest to results obtained from the sample. If results turn out to be seriously in error, generalizations cannot and should not be made to the population of interest, even if the research is a probability study. For example, suppose you saw two polls that measured the popularity of the president. One reports 54% of the voters support the president, but shows a sampling error of ±15 percentage points and a small sample. The other reports 49% of the voters support the president and shows a much smaller sampling error, ±4 percentage points, and a larger sample. The level of confidence in the results reported by the two polls are quite different. The issue would be whether the first researcher, with such a large sampling error and small sample, could make the statement that the majority of voters support the president.

Probability studies may be either simple or complex. In the instance of the first kind, simple random selection methods are used. That is, each person, place, or thing in the population of interest has an equal chance of being selected. Perhaps the method of probability selection might be choosing the 5th, 7th, or 10th from a list of names or things. Tables of random numbers are commonly available, but not frequently used for probability selection.

Probability selection for complex research strategies are many and varied. For example, researchers may stratify their sample in order to be sure to include subgroups that reflect certain characteristics inherent in the population of interest. It can be confusing if, for example, the subgroups

---

[2]Error estimates are complicated statistical calculations involving a number of concepts including the level of confidence in results obtained, numbers of people or things researched, and other factors. Error estimates and what they mean in the context of other concepts associated with them are matters that should be discussed with a research consultant.

are randomly selected but the sample is not. The study would then fall into the class of nonprobability designs. Degree of randomization and the strategy employed depends a great deal on the purpose of the research. But no matter what their purpose, researchers will use some sort of probability selection in order to generalize results from the sample to the population of interest.

If the study is a nonprobability study, that is, one where the sample was self-selected by the researcher because it was convenient to do so or subjects volunteered to participate, the features just mentioned, including generalizability cannot be achieved. On the other hand, there are instances where nonprobability method is necessarily part of the research strategy. For example, if researchers want to experiment with a medication for high blood pressure, they are limited to selecting only those patients with hypertension. Such a study is customarily conducted under controlled conditions to improve reliability. But, even in these studies, researchers arrange for some method of random selection so that a generalization to other high blood pressure sufferers can be made. In such an instance, random selection might be employed for the group selected to undergo the treatments. Or, random selection might be applied in the administration of certain dosages of the medication. You have to search out these possibilities in complex probability designs.

Without random selection of the elements examined, you may find yourself dealing with a biased study. The Shere Hite (1987) study is an example of nonprobability research and a biased study. Her research appeared in a book entitled, *Hite Report: Women and Love: A Cultural Revolution in Progress*. The author concluded that despite women's liberation and the sexual revolution, women are still psychologically harassed and physically abused by men. Qualified researchers raised many questions about the study. Among other problems, researchers found fault with her ill-defined population of interest and method of selecting her subjects for investigation.

Hite had sent out 100,000 questionnaires to self-selected American women's organizations in 43 states. That sample mainly included women who belonged to organizations such as church and garden clubs who were, according to certain critics, "joiners" and "malcontents," and failed to include other types of American women (Wallis & McDowell, 1987). Self-selection prohibited differences to appear and disallowed estimations of error, as well as generalization. Nevertheless, Hite argued that study results supported her hypothesis that even today's American women are subject to male cruelty (Barol & Brailsford, 1987).

Some reviewers admitted Hite's survey was flawed science, but still credited her for helping women "know they are not alone, she articulates their discontent" (Hochschild, 1987, p. 3). Nevertheless, other reviewers did not take Hite's conclusions seriously and, in fact, found still other evidence of unreliable data (Smith, 1989). The Hite study is a classic example of nonprobability research from which inappropriate generalizations are drawn and attributed to the population of interest.

Another important issue is the value of such a study to other members in the scientific community. A study that is carefully designed, executed, and analyzed according to scientific standards is usually one that can be replicated by other researchers for the purpose of confirming the results of the original study. If the original study is judged unreliable because of questionable design and methods used, then other researchers cannot replicate the study. When other researchers are able to demonstrate results similar to those obtained by the original researcher, more confidence is attached to generalizations made.

If the study involves nonprobability research and a generalization is made to the population of interest, you should regard it as invalid. On the other hand, when the researcher makes no attempt to generalize and suggests, instead, that the research is groundwork for further study, you can represent it, not as a conclusive finding, but as a movement that is going on in that particular area of work. However, that is contingent on how well other features of the research hold up under questioning.

This is not to say that all nonprobability studies are suspect. In fact, some of these do hold up under questioning and have proved useful to their discipline and other researchers. But they do not pretend generalizations to the larger population of interest. In such an instance, take note of the study's points of value, but also note its nongeneralizability.

When evaluating a study, add these questions to those already mentioned:

- *Is this a probability or nonprobability study?*
- *Is there some probability selection method used?*
- *On whom or on what things?*
- *At what point in the strategy?*
- *During what time period or periods was the study administered?*
- *Is generalization to the population of interest justified? Why?*
- *If not, what explanation is given for having conducted a nonprobability study?*

There are a multitude of complexities associated with empirical research reports, but your concern at this point is mainly whether the report you are reading is probability or nonprobability research. Then consider the sample, an issue related to all other issues just mentioned.

THE SAMPLE

A sample is randomly selected from the population of interest because it is simply not cost effective or even feasible to examine all elements in the population of interest: all working mothers, all high schools, all coal miners. The problem of logistics and expense involved would be enormous. So researchers rely on a sample or samples from the population of interest to test a theory and strive to avoid a biased study by employing probability sampling methods. Besides probability selection, the key thing about the sample is whether it truly represents a reasonable facsimile of the population of interest.

Look for a match on basic characteristics between the sample group and the population of interest. Although no sample can ever be a mirror image of the population of interest, it can be a close approximation of it. For example, any sample of a mixed adult population should contain about equal numbers of men and women. If you see a sample and notice that two out of three in the sample are men, or two out of three are women, that is an indication of unequal representation that could have an impact on the concepts under examination and, ultimately, the conclusions made. Anything less than a close approximation to the population of interest is not a representative sample and invites sampling bias.

A representative sample shares characteristics manifest in the population of interest. Suppose an auto manufacturer hires a research agency to explore customer dissatisfaction with a certain new model. This is a special population, so you must look for the link between the population of interest (owners of the new model in question) and the subjects being sampled. If only satisfied owners or only large numbers of owners of the same model produced under different conditions or at different locations than the defective lot were questioned, biased sampling that conceivably could disprove customer complaints occurs. In the Hite case, her sample confirmed her hypothesis, but her sampling method was biased. It was not a representative group and any conclusion the researcher put forth invited challenge.

A sample is also representative if it reflects certain classifications or subgroups in the population of interest. Even though shared characteristics identify the population of interest, a sample or samples selected from that population usually exhibit differences. Voters in presidential elections represent more than one party, more than one race, religion, economic class, or educational group. Rain forests vary in size, area, foliage, and the like. These representative subgroups permit analysis of differences between the various subgroups and report of how those differences relate to the theoretical statement and the total sample.

Suppose you were reading the report of a survey sponsored by a tobacco company for the purpose of researching the consequences of smoking cigarettes. To begin with, the sponsoring group alone should be the first alert against a possibly biased report. It is also important to know the researchers' definition of smokers so you can determine if they stratified to include the appropriate subgroups representative of these subgroups in the population of interest: People who were nonsmokers before the research test and in good or poor health, those who were "once-in-a-while" smokers in good or poor health, long-term smokers in good or poor health, what periods of time they had been smokers, what gender, age, and so on. The differences between these classes of people would have a direct bearing on reported results inferred about them, especially in regard to the theoretical statement and the concepts involved. If only healthy subjects appeared in the sample, or only short-term smokers, such a bias would limit the chance of differences appearing.

In the study of working mothers, representative subgroups might include married working mothers with unemployed mates, married working mothers with employed mates, unmarried working mothers, working mothers separated from their mates, divorced working mothers, and other subgroups of working mothers. Here, differences would illustrate variations between working mothers in two-parent households where the mother is the sole provider and the husband or mate is a "house husband." Also, in this case, subgrouping should illustrate how classes of two-parent groups differ from households with one parent.

If subgroups are overlooked, you would have to know if any assumptions made by the researchers are possible with or without such comparative groups. For example, in a political survey where the subgroups are Democrats, Republicans, and Independents and the purpose is to discover favoritism rendered to either one or the other party's policies, it is necessary to know what percentage of the total sample expressed Democratic leanings and what percentage expressed Republican or Independent tendencies.

When subgroups are named, ask:

- *Do the researchers define the subgroups clearly, fully?*
- *Do they describe differences between them?*
- *Are the groups mutually exclusive?*[3]
- *What representative groups are omitted?*
- *Is it important to know about them? Why?*

In addition, look for explanations of location and locale characteristics as well as time period of the study, particularly when more than one sampling

---

[3]A *mutually exclusive group* may be defined as one in which members belong to a specific group and are not and may not be members of any other group.

area is included in the study. If researchers are looking at the stress problem of working mothers only in the midwest, you need to know where and how variations in those locations influence the hypothesis.

Depending on how the hypothesis is stated, you might also need to know the difference between rural employment in one midwest location as opposed to urban employment in that area and other midwest areas; the differences between rural employment in homes, farms, factories, and the like, as opposed to the types of jobs held by urban mothers. In addition, you would need to know whether working mothers in these locations were studied during the same period of time, or at different time periods (e.g., when school was in and when it was out), and what difference that made. Also, whether those periods were normal periods of employment, what groups were examined in this period as opposed to a depressed period of employment in another location, and what difference that made. If any issue remains unanswered in your mind, you should question whether comparisons made are valid in the absence of the missing information. All these factors go back to a clear statement of who or what is being examined and why, including where and when, followed by a complete description of how, what differences were found, and the impact of these on the total sample.

A representative sample is also one in which numbers in the subgroups are similar in proportion to their numbers in the population of interest. For example, if 25% of all working parents in a particular location are single mothers, then their representative number should be about 25% of the total sample. It is frequently the case that members of the African-American population are underreported in national surveys because African-Americans represent only about 10% of the population nationwide, and very often there are very few of these cases to analyze in some areas. In the instance of a political survey such underreporting would seriously compromise results because, for example, African-Americans tend to vote Democratic.[4]

There is still another factor related to representativeness that has to do with the measurement instrument used to test a theory. These are many and varied. The instrument may be a memory test, a new medication, a questionnaire, or randomly selected records of absenteeism from certain

---

[4]An exit poll conducted by Voter Research and Surveys (VRS) found 22% of African-American voters selected Republican House candidates. The Republican Party and the media hailed this as a shift in African-American voting habits. However, according to analysts at the Joint Center for Political Studies, the 1990 elections showed only a 12.5%-15% shift. Pointing out that the VRS poll demonstrated numerous sampling problems, political analysts at the University of Michigan and others agreed that the movement is minimal and that current evidence fails to warrant a change in the African-American voting profile. For a discussion of this dispute, see Dionne and Morin (1990).

high schools, just some valid method of testing a particular theory. Look for the number of persons from the total who completed the memory test, who took the medication and for how long, who completed and returned the questionnaire, or the number of schools out of the number contacted that released their records.

Researchers express these numbers in terms associated with the type of research strategy used. For example, when a survey questionnaire is used to test a theory, the percentage of completed and returned questionnaires out of the total distributed is presented as the "response rate." In surveys, researchers look for at least a 70% return. This is considered a reliable response rate on which to base a generalization of any findings to the population of interest.

If too few members in the random sample take part in the test, the results are considered unreliable. Low response rate was another weakness researchers found in the Hite study. Despite the number of survey questionnaires mailed (100,000) only 4.5% completed and returned them. That is way below the 70% reliable response standard. Hite's low response rate prompted some reviewers to conclude her results failed to represent the attitudes of other members in her population of interest.

Adequate sample size is still another important factor in representativeness. This is an extremely complex statistical issue that involves still other issues concerning confidence levels and error estimates, all of which take training and experience to understand. Adequate sample size, and all other issues associated with it, is something you can discuss with a research consultant after you have made some of the evaluations suggested here.

This is another piece of information you should look for: baseline or absolute numbers for total sample size, as well total size for whatever subgroups may have been included. You need a comparative base from which to understand researchers' statements about results obtained from the sample, the subgroups, and their relationship to the total sample, the hypothesis and its concepts.

Baseline numbers might have helped in the understanding of this claim: "Four out of five doctors recommend Speedy Pain Relief." The claim begs the questions: *Is this the number of doctors surveyed? Out of what total number of doctors surveyed?* The sample could have totaled only six doctors. You should not be forced to assume that possibly more than five doctors were interviewed out of thousands of doctors in the population.

A great deal of scrutiny, detection, weighing, and balancing goes into the determination of whether research data renders reliable evidence. When reading a research report, first notice who is sponsoring the research. Keeping this in mind, note the purpose of the study, the research issue, and the concepts the researcher is examining. Look for a description of the population of interest, the sample, and how the sample was selected to determine whether you are reviewing probability or nonprobability research. Note the representativeness of the sample based on the issues discussed here.

A more complete list of questions about the sample are included in a summary of all questions raised in this chapter and may be found at the end of the chapter. Once you have tried to answer them, seek clarifications or verify your understanding with a research consultant.

TESTING THE HYPOTHESIS

A weakness in any one of the issues discussed here is reason enough to question the validity of a research study. But if they do stand up to question, there is still another interdependent factor that could weaken the whole structure, the instrument used to test the hypothesis.

It was indicated earlier that instruments are many and varied and the one used depends on what is being examined. However, the questionnaire is one instrument many researchers include as one of several tests of the hypothesis. For this reason, it is the one discussed here. Furthermore, examination of the questionnaire is something you can work on independently of a research consultant, and why you should try to obtain a copy of it before seeing a consultant.

If the researcher has defined the sample and all the concepts related to the hypothesis, these give you a fair base from which to judge whether the questions are a fair test of the theory. So the issue now is:

- *Are the questions really measuring those things?*

Suppose the researchers used a questionnaire for the study concerning working mothers. First review the questions and note which are closed-ended and which are open-ended.[5] The differences between these two types of questions, how they are worded, how they are preceded or followed by

---

[5]A more complete discussion of the differences between closed and open questions is covered in chapter 8. For understanding here, however, simply know that a closed question evokes a specific response such as a "yes," "no," or "don't know." These become predetermined categories for recording responses. An open question is less specific, permits respondents to answer in their own terms, and categories for recording are determined after analyzing the responses. Categories for responses to an open question are more likely to fall to interpretation (or misinterpretation) than a closed question. In such cases, several coders are given the task of coding responses. If they demonstrate at least 70% agreement, the coding of an open question is usually accepted as a fair interpretation. Researchers prefer the questionnaire with more closed-end questions than open-end questions because such a questionnaire takes less time to code and is cost effective.

related questions, all this will have a bearing on your evaluation of them. That is, you need to determine if the questions evoke responses that are a true measure of all concepts included in the stated hypothesis.

In the hypothesis about working mothers, the concepts include job stress, child-care concerns, and the rest. Imagine yourself in the place of a working mother, then ask: *What type of question* (open/closed) *was asked? How was it asked? Does the question evoke a complete, accurate, and unbiased answer? How would I respond?* Then look at all the questions and see whether they seem to be measuring the concepts and the aim of the theoretical statement. At the same time, be on the alert for any question you feel might prejudice a working mother's response to respond unrealistically.

Placement of a question or series of questions within a questionnaire often influences how the respondent answers other questions. So you must notice if any arrangement of questions could influence responses in any way. Also, look at all questions carefully and notice whether they are *leading* or *loaded* questions, *double-barreled* questions, or questions too *ambiguous* to solicit a fair response.

The *leading* or *loaded* question directs the respondent to answer with information the interviewer wants to hear. Or, it may have emotionally charged words in it, or encourage a "yes" or "no" answer, or when prefaced with a suggestive preamble would invoke a biased response because it threatens a respondent's sense of prestige or self-confidence.

Some examples of leading or loaded questions are those you have probably heard many times over on the national news networks and in other interview situations: "Don't you believe. . . ." "However, wouldn't you disagree that . . ." "Wouldn't you say. . . ." "Isn't it true that. . . ."

Without an opportunity to say what one really thinks, the respondent is led by the nose to answer as the interviewer's question suggests. Reluctant to appear ignorant or to displease the interviewer, the respondent follows the interviewer's lead and the response becomes the interviewer's and not the respondent's. The result: false data.

Questions in surveys conducted by reputable pollsters and research scientists are rarely deliberately leading, but they still may be loaded enough to direct the response. When reviewing a questionnaire, look for questions with terms that could play on the respondent's emotions. For example, it might make a great deal of difference whether a question related to China was prefaced with the words "Red" or "Communist" instead of "mainland," or "People's Republic of China." The first two terms might evoke more hostile responses than the last one if attitude toward China was an important aspect of the research.

Another emotionally charged question might be: "Do you favor or oppose sending our surplus wheat to the starving people of XYZ country?" Although a response to either side of this "either-or" question would be legitimate, the word "starving" plays on the respondent's sympathies and the researcher is likely to get more "yes" responses than "no" answers. Even if emotion is absent, a question framed to evoke either a "yes" or "no" answer will generally tend to encourage a "yes" answer.

Sometimes the interviewer will ask a loaded question that churns up other emotions, forcing the respondent to answer defensively. It is called the *social desirability* factor and it usually creeps into questions that challenge some aspect of the respondent's ego: personality, behavior, class status, education, knowledge, personal health, and the like. The outcome is usually a half-truth, an exaggeration, or a false response.

If the question begins with a loaded preamble, the defense mechanism gets an early start, for example, "According to the eminent _____ , ..." Even though a respondent's opinion may differ from that of the eminent authority, the respondent will agree just to avoid appearing ignorant, unpleasant, or offensive.

Preambles do not precede the following questions, but they are still a threat to one's prestige: "How many VCRs do you have in your home?" "Do you own a personal computer?" "Do you read *The New York Times*?" The result: exaggeration. For example, Market Strategies, Inc. (a Southfield, Michigan, research firm that conducted voter opinion surveys during the 1988 Bush Presidential campaign) found that questions such as, "Did you vote?" or "Will you vote?" drew 80% positive responses, whereas in reality only 35% had actually done so (F. Steeper, personal communication, January 1990).

Questions that challenge the respondent's knowledge are leading, as well, because rather than admit ignorance, the respondent will give an answer, informed or not: "As you probably know, the President has recently endorsed deregulation of airline fares. Do you favor or oppose eliminating these controls and possibly increasing inflated fares?"

This question is not only *loaded*, it is also a *double-barreled* question. It is loaded because, first of all, the respondent may not want to admit ignorance about presidential activities, but because of strong feelings about the president, the respondent will answer on the basis of those feelings rather than on the issue of the president's endorsement. In addition, with the words "increasing inflated fares" the interviewer assumes the respondent shares the researcher's views on the consequences of deregulation.

The question is also double-barreled because it contains two questions in one. *Which one should the respondent answer? Should the respondent answer the question concerning deregulation of air fares or that deregulation will increase inflated fares? Which response was accepted for coding and analysis?*

Even words that appear to be innocent carry biases. Following field tests of their questions, Market Strategies removed the word, "President" and the names of presidential candidates from their questionnaire because they found that if respondents had an opinion about Bush policy, they responded to his name and not the issue. Or, when asked about Reagan policy, they responded in agreement or disagreement depending on whether they liked or disliked him (F. Steeper, personal communication, January 1990).

Ambiguous questions are still another type that influence response results in surveys. The researcher can expect to get a variety of responses with such imprecise wording as: "What is your income?" *Does the researcher want to know the respondent's hourly pay, weekly salary, monthly or annual earnings? Does the researcher want to know the sum before or after taxes?* Another vague question is: "How long have you lived here?" *Does the researcher mean at this address, in the neighborhood, in the city, state, region? What does the researcher want to learn?*

Chances are the respondent misreplied if, in your review of the interview questions, you have to ask:

- *What does the researcher mean by this question?*
- *Which question am I expected to answer?*
- *Is the question so emotionally charged that it directs my response?*
- *Would I react defensively if I were in the respondent's place?*
- *Is the question directing my answer?*
- *Does the question evoke a complete and accurate answer?*
- *What necessary information does the question fail to evoke?*
- *Is the questionnaire a true measure of the concepts defined in the theoretical statement?*
- *Is there any reason to believe measurement bias is present?*

A question, or series of questions, in the beginning of a questionnaire may be totally unbiased, but they may influence a question, or questions, when placed toward the end. Market Strategies tested a questionnaire design with this question placed at the end: "Do you intend to vote or not to vote?" They found that after answering other questions concerning voting habits, the tendency was to answer positively. In the final design, the question was placed at the beginning and specific political questions were asked later (F. Steeper, personal communication, January 1990).

The design of a questionnaire depends on the issue or the purpose of the study. For instance, response to an environmental issue may produce more reliable results if the question, "Do you favor expenditures for environmental cleanup?", was placed toward the end and after specific questions about attitudes toward pollution, the environment, environmental responsibility, cost to taxpayers, and the like.

When any one of the conditions reviewed here (biased questionnaire design, biased, double-barreled or ambiguous questions) appear in a questionnaire, or the questionnaire in any way is not a true or complete measure of the issues being examined, reliability of the study is seriously weakened.

FAIR REPORT OF RESULTS

Issues reviewed in previous sections may stand up to question, but now you have to see if the results are completely and fairly reported. Interpretation of results can be misleading. It is important to know whether the results are statistically or substantively significant. A result may be statistically significant, but in reality it may have little meaning in the broad picture of things.

Suppose you were looking at a study of salaries for first-year assistant professors at state universities in a certain area. At one university the starting salary is $30,000 and at another it is $30,500. A difference of $500 may be important to an individual in the normal course of conducting one's daily business, but in a comparison of average starting salaries at these two institutions and the search for a substantively significant statistic, the difference is minimal.

The researchers may not say so, but if they gave all the required numbers, you could figure it out and discover the difference is only 2.5%. The difference is insignificant and should not be characterized by the researchers as a statistically competitive feature of salaries between the two institutions. The issue here is not a matter of whether there is a difference, but whether the difference is just a statistical result or a substantive one. When differences are identified as significantly different, ask:

- *Is this difference substantial enough to make it "significant?"*

Sometimes baseline figures, or absolute numbers, are omitted or it is just not clear what they are. For starters, you need baseline numbers for the total sample. These are usually included, but perhaps not for the subgroups. Or, certain basic information may be missing. Suppose researchers report tests of a product show an increase in durability of 50%. That sounds like an impressive increase. But you do not know out of what. You should be given some reference points. That is, you need to know the standard measure for determining durability in that product and where the product was on that scale to begin with. It could have been at the lowest end of the scale, in which case an increase of 50% is not impressive. If the period of durability originally was a year, a 50% increase is only an additional 6 months. That is not impressive either. You would also have to know the durability of other products in the same class. If even one of these is 2 years and the researcher leaves no clue about this, you should not report the so-called increase until you find out about the durability of other products in the same class.

Here is another example. Suppose results showed that the brakes of a vehicle malfunctioned in less than 2% of all cases. Sounds good. But it would be important to know how many of those vehicles were in use because that total multiplied by the percentage of reported malfunctions might number into thousands of possible malfunctions and injuries.

Researchers should provide baseline numbers and reference points in their research report because those numbers and references allow you to make some determinations about researchers' interpretations of the results. Even if they are provided, reserve your conclusion about their interpretations until you have asked:

- *How well does the discussion of results square with my observations about the study and the numbers given?*
- *Does the discussion of results speak to the theoretical statement and the concepts investigated?*

MAKING DECISIONS ABOUT SCIENTIFIC REPORTS

Include a research study in your collection of data if the evidence stands up to test. Apply the questions, clues, and guidelines given in this chapter, which are summarized at the end of the chapter. Those questions are a test of the relationship between the sponsor, research group, and research purpose. They remind you to notice whether the research is a probability study or otherwise, if the hypothesis and population of interest are clearly and fully defined, if the sample and response rate are fully described and representative of the population of interest. If these check out, the research has much in its favor. But don't stop there.

Notice the test device employed and if any of its aspects raise a question in your mind. See if results are fully described and reported fairly, if conclusions are relevant to the research problem. If weaknesses do appear, no need to eliminate the study. Take note of the study's strengths and, at the same time, consider the weight of their value in light of its weaknesses. You might choose to commend the hypothesis explored and the population of interest sampled, but then challenge the results if you discover bias or ambiguity.

Your next step is to see if any other studies on the same issue either confirm, modify, or disconfirm the one you have reviewed. If disconfirmed, that does not mean you eliminate the study. It does mean either a confirmation or modification of your observations. Along with assurances about your observations from a research consultant, either a confirmed or disconfirmed study gives you another item to add to your collection of data.

Sometimes a flawed study is a media writer's gold mine. The study not only adds to your data for a particular media assignment, it is also cause for an enterprise piece: a news or magazine article, a radio brief, or TV news feature. No matter how carefully a study is conducted, the outcome remains tentative until a series of similar studies confirms the results. As indicated earlier, one of the criteria for reliable evidence in science is whether study results can be precisely replicated, not once, but several times. When reading a research report be aware of the fragile nature of a single study.

Throughout this chapter we have emphasized the importance of critical thinking and repeated the precaution of seeking an expert's judgment about conclusions made in a research report before using it as part of your media piece. Apparently, some media writers did little critical thinking or checking in the following case concerning a medical study conducted in Sweden.

A CASE IN POINT

Earlier, it was suggested that a publication that had won the confidence of its readers served as a fairly good criterion of trust in its content. However, for specialized areas of work such as medicine, finance, agriculture, and the like, the reputation of the publication in which a study is published is sometimes not enough. It is true that editors of highly regarded professional publications screen all submitted studies. Prior to publication, a select review board made up of the researchers' peers, but unknown to them, checks the study and decides whether the study meets certain standards and contributes something of value to the discipline. Still, this stringent defense by a reputable publication is insufficient assurance. Not because either the publication or review board is at fault, but because researchers are not the best translators of their own work, and they write in a language and style known only to those in their field and the editors of a specific journal. Often, the research report is so obscure, even practiced media writers give up in despair and make the mistake of assuming, *Well, if it's published in the _____ results of the study are probably safe to report as they appear.*

Publication does not necessarily mean endorsement by the journal. Editors may publish a study simply to invite discussion or encourage further research. Media writers cannot assume that if a study is published in a prestigious journal, it should be taken at face value.

That was the error of some American writers reporting on an article that appeared in the August 3, 1989, issue of the highly regarded *New England Journal of Medicine*. The article concerned a field study about the risks of breast cancer in postmenopausal women on estrogen therapy. The study involved 23,244 women, 35 years of age or older, in the Uppsala region of Sweden. Some women were placed on estrogen alone, others on both estrogen and another hormone, progestin.

In the *abstract* (a summary that precedes details given in the detailed report), researchers revealed that in the follow-up period at the end of 5-1/2 years, 253 women in the group receiving estrogen alone had developed breast cancer. Compared with "other women in the same region," women in the estrogen only group had a 1.1 "relative risk" of developing breast cancer. For women on combined estrogen and progestin therapy for "extended periods," the "relative risk" was much higher (4.4). Researchers concluded, in the introductory summary, that "long-term" treatment with an estrogen type called *Estradiol* "seems" to be associated with a slightly increased risk of breast cancer, which is not prevented and "may" even be increased by the addition of progestins (Bergkvist, Adami, Persson, Hoover, & Schairer, 1989).

On the surface, this reads convincingly, matter for immediate publication. But in this case, that was the problem. Media writers were too hasty. They ignored the qualified language in the abstract, failed to read the rest of the report or the comments of a reviewer in another section of the journal and, instead, jumped on the study's sensational potential: Women on estrogen therapy risk breast cancer.

A more critically minded writer would have noticed the qualified terms and immediately raised such questions as: *What's meant by "seems" and "may?" What's "long term" mean? What's short term in comparison? What's meant by "relative risk" and the estimates associated with it? What dosage of estrogen and progestin were given to the women who developed breast cancer as opposed to those who did not develop cancer? Is the test device, Estradiol, an estrogen type used by American women?*

Reading further one learns that among long-term patients, the 4.4 "relative risk" figure applies to only 10 women who had been on estrogen and progestin for 6 years and to 23 who had been on estrogen alone for 9 years. The baseline figures for these subgroups are unclear. So is their relationship to the researchers' meaning of "long term." *Even so, are the numbers large enough to warrant a public alarm?* That is a question you could raise with the research consultant, who is likely to tell you they are not.

At the end of the report one learns that *Estradiol*, although commonly used by physicians in Europe, is not the type of estrogen used by physicians in the United States. That information alone is enough to collapse the whole report and deter American media writers from making any association to estrogen users in this country.

This does not mean an announcement about this study should not be made. It does mean care should be taken to make the difference in medication quite clear at the outset, not in the middle or end of a media announcement. And the difference should be made clear before any presentations of estimates are made that, if placed at the outset, could cause unwarranted alarm about a treatment that is not even administered in this country.

Media writers would have noticed all these things if they had read the original and full report, including its discussion section. Here they would have noticed that the researchers give reasons why qualifying terms were used in the abstract. They explain that although their findings showed "relative risks," the number of observations on which their findings were based was "relatively small." Also, that some of their findings could have been due to chance and should be considered against results found by other researchers. In fact, other studies have not shown the same results.

The media writers who made a beeline for their word processors would have known this if they had read the physician's commentary regarding this study elsewhere in the journal. The commentary was written by Dr. Elizabeth Barrett-Connor, a noted gynecologist specializing in postmenopausal problems and a professor of medicine at the University of California, San Diego. She wrote that other studies conducted in this country showed only a slight increase in breast cancer, whereas other studies suggest an estrogen-progestin regimen reduces the risk of breast cancer.

It is also here that one is alerted to weakness in the selection process of the 253 women. Dr. Barrett-Connor pointed out that the only randomized placebo controlled trial of extended hormone replacement and breast cancer risk conducted to date in the United States was with 168 institutionalized women who after 10 years showed no sign of breast cancer. She concluded that in the Swedish study "the data are not conclusive enough to warrant any immediate change in the way we approach hormone replacement [in this country], but they do show the need for additional research" (Barrett-Connor, 1989, p. 320).

Unaware of all this and ignoring the qualifiers at the very outset, some media reports issued the misleading news that American women on extended periods of estrogen or combined estrogen and progestin therapy had a greater risk of developing breast cancer than others without postmenopausal treatment. As a result, alarmed American women scurried to their doctors, and indignant scientists and physicians flooded media phone lines.

The lesson here is: Do not depend on the abstract in a research report to tell you the whole story. Claims of confidence in results could be misleading and details are often omitted. Read the whole report. Read reviewers' comments. Look into what other researchers have found. Use the critical thinking methods suggested, then raise other critical questions related specifically to the study you are reviewing. Check your evaluation with specialists in the discipline and experts in research methods. Above all, do not assume the name of a prestigious journal is a guarantee that you will not misreport its contents.

Dr. Karen D. Bartscht, formerly with the Division of Gynecology at the University of Michigan Medical Center and now in private practice, said:

> What happens as a result of this [the alarm sounded about the Swedish study] is that many American women stop therapy, especially the combined regimen of estrogen and progestin. Other studies have shown this therapy reduces the risk of breast cancer and is beneficial in the prevention of the crippling disease, osteoporosis. It is essential that writers understand the medical information they write about before submitting it for publication to the general public. (personal communication, January 1990)

SUMMARY OF EVALUATION QUESTIONS FOR SCIENTIFIC REPORTS

Target the sponsor:
- *Who is sponsoring the research?*
- *What is their purpose?*

The theoretical statement:
- *What is the theoretical statement?*
- *Are its concepts clearly and fully defined?*

The population of interest:
- *Who or what is the population of interest?*
- *What characteristics set this group apart from the rest of the population?*
- *Is the population of interest clearly defined?*
- *Are the people, places, or things examined appropriate for the problem examined?*
- *What subgroups were included or omitted and why?*
- *Does the generalization apply to this population of interest? Why? If not, why not?*

Probability vs. nonprobability studies:
- *Is this a probability or nonprobability study?*
- *Is there some probability selection method used?*
- *On whom or on what things?*
- *At what point in the research strategy?*
- *During what time period or periods was the study administered?*

- *Is generalization to the population of interest justified? Why?*
- *If not, what explanation is given for having conducted a nonprobability study?*

The sample:
- *How was random selection conducted?*
- *Is it a probability sample? Why? If not, why not?*
- *Is the sample representative of the population of interest?*
- *Is the sample clearly and fully defined in all its characteristics?*
- *Does the sample adequately represent all relevant subgroups in the population of interest?*
- *Are relevant characteristics of the subgroups adequately defined?*
- *Are differences between the subgroups described?*
- *Are the groups mutually exclusive?*
- *Do the researchers provide proportions of the subgroups included?*
- *Are the subgroups in the sample proportionate to their proportion in the population of interest?*
- *What representative groups are omitted that might have been relevant to the research question for this sample?*
- *Why are these groups important to include?*
- *Is the outcome for each group fully described in terms of its relationship to the hypothesis, the total sample?*
- *Does the sample and its subgroups appear to be adequate in size?*
- *Are error estimates given for the sample? For the subgroups?*
- *Was the specified test of the hypothesis fulfilled to the extent that results render reliability, generalizability?*
- *What is the response rate?*
- *Was generalization to the population of interest justified?*
- *If not, what explanation is given?*

Testing the hypothesis:
- *What types of questions* (open/closed) *were asked?*
- *How were they asked?*
- *Do the questions evoke a complete and accurate answer?*
- *How would I have responded?*
- When the question appears to be flawed ask:
  - *What does the researcher mean by this question?*
  - *Which question am I expected to answer?*
  - *Is the question so emotionally charged that it directs my response?*
  - *Would I react defensively if I were in the respondent's place?*
  - *Is the question directing my answer?*
- *What necessary information does the question fail to evoke?*

- *Is there any reason to believe measurement bias is present?*
- *Is the questionnaire a true measure of the concepts defined in the theoretical statement?*

Fair report of results:
- *Is the difference reported as "significant" substantial enough to say it is significant?*
- *How well does the discussion of results square with my observations about the study and the numbers given?*
- *Does the discussion of results speak to the theoretical statement and the concepts investigated?*
- *Are there other studies of this problem?*
- *If so, do they confirm or countermand results found in this study?*

You may not need all these questions for the research report you are reviewing, especially if it is a simple probability study. However, if you are unable to find answers to some of these in a complex probability study, or even a simple one, your frustration is probably well founded. The researcher's explanation may not be clear even to a practiced research consultant. But the point is you now know some of the things a researcher should include in a study even if it is all there but still ambiguous. Furthermore, having reviewed the study carefully, you are now better prepared to raise relevant questions with the research consultant and to understand the consultant's explanations. As importantly, the consultant will appreciate the fact that you did some homework beforehand.

When examining evidence given in general materials or research reports, keep in mind the questions and clues given in chapters 5 and 6 and in each case start with Critical Self-Inquiry 4: *What information fails to stand up to question?*

Critical thinking in media writing begins with basic questions and extends beyond those questions to others. Critical thinking also means that questions and ways to find answers to them in predictable situations develop a mindset for managing new situations. In the remaining chapters you will see how vital it is to have such a mindset when it comes to interviewing and writing.

7 Designing the Interview Plan: It's In Your Collected Data

In the last two chapters you learned how to separate the counterfeit from the genuine in your data. In this chapter you learn how to make the collected research work for you. If you have been thorough and kept complete notes, all the clues to interview questions and sources will be in your data. Give direction to that search with Critical Self-Inquiry 5: *What do I need to ask who about what and how shall I ask it?*

One of the payoffs of having done a solid job of research is that the data you have collected will tell you what to ask who about what. Moreover, having studied the problem and background of prospective interviewees, you will also be able to manage responses you did not expect to get. Knowing almost as much as the respondent, you are equipped to come back with another question that will elicit an adequate response.

Cornelius Ryan, the late journalist and author,[1] once said that no one should ever interview anyone without first knowing 60% of the answers. He advised writers to do their homework because they could be sure that the person they planned to interview had and would be prepared.

William Manchester, another journalist and author, wrote that his first interview with the late President John F. Kennedy lasted nearly 4 hours. The president was generous with his time, Manchester explained, because he recognized the extent of research Manchester had done. One of the questions that came out of Manchester's research was a question no one else

---

[1]Ryan (1920-1974) wrote several bestsellers about World War II, some of which include *A Bridge Too Far*, *The Last Battle*, and *The Longest Day: June 6, 1944*. He also wrote the screenplays for the last two titles.

had ever asked the president. During his research, Manchester noticed that among the appointments President Kennedy had made, 80% were people within a few years of his age. Manchester asked President Kennedy if he was a "generation chauvinist." The president found this amusing enough to repeat in public, giving Manchester an anecdote for his book, *Death of a President: November 20-25, 1963*.

Prepare for interviews, or be prepared for an abrupt end to the interview, Manchester warned. That is what happened to one newspaper journalist who asked former Secretary of Agriculture, Orville Freeman, how he planned to open Eastern Europe's markets to Minnesota milk. Freeman replied that if the journalist had been reading the papers he would have known how he planned to do it. End of interview.

Such moments are especially embarrassing for television or radio broadcasters. Their interview flaws are exposed to a larger audience and because they are locked into air time, the show must go on even when its deflating to a whimper. Jessica Mitford, a journalist and author who exposed the funeral industry's exploitation of grieving survivors in her book, *The American Way of Death*, once said that the worst interviewers are the ones who have no idea as to what they are interviewing you about. A skilled interviewer herself, she recalled hitting rock bottom with an interviewer at a Tulsa, Oklahoma, radio station where the interviewer was supposed to talk about Mitford's book. Just as they went on the air, the interviewer leaned over and whispered, "What is it you've done?" Fizzle-down collapse of a promising interview. It never got off the ground.

Although the interview figures more in the work of newswriters than in the work of PR and ad writers, all mass media writers conduct interviews. They just do so in varying degrees of formality and intensity to achieve different ends. A newswriter, whose purpose is to inform, is often obliged to search out and pursue interviewees with questions they may not want to answer. The relationship between the newswriter and respondent runs in increments from mutual goals to distant poles of purpose. In contrast, PR and advertising writers have ready and willing sources of information in clients, account executives, managers and staff who provide answers without too much pursuit and probing because, as a necessarily cooperative group (usually), they are unified in purpose.

WHAT TO ASK

Interviews are held because there is always a need to fill in gaps, clarify, or update researched data. The important thing is to ask the right interview questions. Because your best source for "right" questions is the data you have collected, read through your research notes. Professional writers say they review their notes not just once, but several times. The point is to internalize those notes until they become part of your mindset. Then review them once more, this time critically. Raise these analytic questions:

- *What research questions on my original list are still unanswered?*
- *What is missing in my data that the media consumer needs to know and is not on my original list?*
- *What information in my data fails to stand up to question?*

To answer the first two conditions, return to the research and make a note of your observations. As you review, check for the third condition and make a note of your assessments. If the information is unavailable in other documents or records after this review, the unanswered questions, missing information, and the third condition all become part of your interview plan.

Also refer to your working and alternative statements. Reviewing your main purpose and re-reading the working statement and its alternative(s), help you identify the gaps and weaknesses in the data you do have. Those gaps and weaknesses create reason for interview questions. Avoid composing questions just for the sake of having a long list of of them. You will be running around in circles and wasting a lot of precious time. Let your careful review direct you toward raising *relevant* interview questions. Relevant questions tell your interviewee that you have done your home- work, and because you reflect this preparation you are more likely to evoke interest and accurate responses, your ultimate aim as the interviewer. If irrelevant questions or questions you could have answered with research creep into your interview plan, you run the risk of antagonizing your interviewee, or having the interview cut short, perhaps even terminated.

Too many zero questions are asked too often by interviewers and the only thing such questions evoke is a zero answer. In the aftermath of the Iran-contra arms scandal, a news broadcaster asked then President Reagan, "Mr. President, are you going to give Congress the facts about Iran, or are you gonna stonewall like the Democrats charge?" Reagan ignored the question and returned the innuendo with a zero answer, "Never talk about a no-hitter 'til it's over." The broadcaster replied that Reagan's answer was not much of a response. The news person's question illustrates so well that what you ask is what you get.

For relevant questions, notice areas in your information that collapse under scrutiny. It is important to do this, even with evaluated data, because certain parts of a piece you accepted as reasonable may still contain missing or unsubstantiated elements. Or, there may be some differences in fact between two or more different documents that are generally considered reliable. Or, there may be some differences in conclusions made in two or more reports or references on the same matter. None of these situations negate your data. They do raise the need for further research either in source materials and/or through interviews.

In the process of studying your notes, look for points of information that need *clarification, amplification, explanation,* and/or *verification.* In short, as you review your data, look for information that fails to stand up to question. Use these analytic questions to help you make those discoveries:

1. *What information is*
   — *incomplete?*
   — *controversial?*
   — *contradictory?*
   — *inconsistent?*
   — *ambiguous?*
2. *What information indicates*
   — *possible error?*
   — *consensus?*
   — *a trend or pattern?*
   — *a relationship?*
   — *a contrast?*
   — *similarities?*
3. *What information needs*
   — *defining?*
   — *updating?*
   — *the latest related development?*

Any one of these may need clarification, amplification, explanation, or verification. Those needs become the structural underpinnings of your interview question. The following definitions will help you identify those needs.

Incomplete: Something is missing, a who, what, where, when, why or how, or an explanation, definition, or statement of evidence, or a point(s) of evidence.

Controversial/contradictory: One authority disputes the findings of another authority. A respondent claims another respondent is not telling the truth. Two documents on the same matter differ in content.

Inconsistent: An authority contradicts him or herself within a single document, or claims one thing in one record that fails to agree with content in another record on the same or related matter. Two documents hold inconsistent data on a person, event, issue, finding, explanation, or conclusion.

Ambiguous: A statement, record, or explanation is unclear, vague, inadequate, incomplete, or embedded with arguable assumptions, values, beliefs.

Possible error: Omissions, misplaced entries in records, erroneous placement of numbers in columns that seem greater or lesser than others listed, missing entries of numbers, dates, names, descriptions, and the like, in documents, or misplacement of these or other items in categories where they do not belong or fail to correspond to other entries listed.

Consensus: Documents, records, and/or statements confirm an event, detail, issue, finding, statement, explanation, or conclusion.

Trend/pattern: A series of behaviors, incidents, statements, and the like, repeat themselves in a similar manner over a period of time.

Relationship: A particular factor, event, or behavior that has some connection to the nature or function of another factor, event, or behavior.

Contrast: Differences between two or more, or a class of things, statements, beliefs, events, persons, and the like.

Similarities: Two or more, or a class of things, statements, and the like, share the same characteristics.

Definition: Use of a term or phrase fails to correspond with your understanding, assuming you have first checked with the dictionary.

Update: Someone has the most recent knowledge of an event or subject matter that is not yet generally known or available in a published document or record.

Latest development: An event(s) that has just occurred or a fact(s) just revealed and not yet published, but adds to your collection of published events or facts.

Once the analytic question is articulated, the objective of the interview question becomes apparent. That objective will suggest how the interview question should be structured. The hypothetical examples in the following section explain how this works.

WHAT TO ASK ABOUT WHAT

Knowing what to ask is one part of interview planning. What to ask about what is still another part. These examples illustrate how detecting flaws in gathered data can reveal the needed question.

News/Magazine

- *Incomplete data*—Respondent: Contact person listed in a press release from ABC Research Institute.

Q: Request for missing data. *A press release from your institute reveals that coffee brewed from a specially grown bean eliminates the need for chemical removal of caffeine, but no further explanation is given. For instance, what is the name of this bean?*

Keep the doors open for follow-up questions and continued probing. The most effective way to do this is to *anticipate* the response and plan your next questions based on possible types of responses. For example, the respondent gives the name of the bean. These questions, one at a time, could follow:

Q: Request for clarification, amplification, explanation. *How was this bean developed to be caffeine free? Where is it grown? Who developed the bean?*

Or, the respondent may say that the bean is a processed product developed from a certain mix of natural grains and other additives. In which case, you would ask:

Q: *What types of grains are in the mix? How are they blended to develop a caffeine-free bean? What additives are included in the grind? Who produces this coffee for the consumer? Where can a consumer get it? How much does a pound of it cost?*

Keep in mind that responses to each of these follow-up questions may prompt other follow-up questions. The important thing is to listen carefully and react as if you were the media consumer.

- *Controversial/contradictory data* — Respondent: Authority on plastics, or a representative of a highway safety institute.

Q: Request for verification. *The XYZ Mfg. Co. has patented a dent-proof, crack-proof plastic for producing automobile bodies, but Dr. Jameson of Superior University claims the plastic will not remain dent-free or crack-free after a series of continued impacts. What is your response to this?*

In this case, the respondent may agree or disagree, or give a qualified answer. The operative technique is a follow-up question: *Please explain why you agree (disagree) with Dr. Jameson.* Listen carefully to the qualified answer. The response may be: *Well, the plastic is dent-proof and crack-proof; however, Dr. Jameson is also correct because* _____ . If the reason is technical and difficult to understand, don't be shy, say: *Could you expand on that a little?* Then translate it in layman's language and ask for confirmation of your understanding. Or say: *That may be difficult for my audience to understand. Please tell me what you mean by* _____ . Then repeat the explanation and ask for confirmation.

- *Consensus data* — Respondent: Nutritionist at a hospital, university or government public health department.

Q: Request for explanation. *Physicians are recommending reduced intake of fatty food. Their patients seem to agree because the industry has responded with low-fat products in the marketplace. But how does a consumer determine if the fat content listed on the label lives up to the food producer's claim that the product is a low-fat food?*

You can anticipate a lot of unfamiliar terms in this response, as well. In which case, you ask for definitions of each and use follow-ups such as why those ingredients are good or bad, in what amounts they are beneficial or harmful, how they support or defeat the food producer's claim of a low fat product, and what foods can be substituted that are more beneficial because they contain much lower fat content.

Public Relations

- *Ambiguous data* — Respondent: Mechanic in an automobile manufacturing company.

Q: Request for clarification. *Some of our customers are complaining that their gears shift into the rear drive position when placed in park position. I've read some of our manuals on how gears work, but it's not clear to me how use can cause such shift failures. I'd appreciate it if you would clarify this for me.*

Ask for clarifications and definitions at any point in this response, even ask for a demonstration on a model of the gear mechanism.

- *Inconsistent data* — Respondent: Same person.

Notice that the complaint comes from some, not all, customers. Still, the complaint is important and must be investigated. Your question should be something like the following:

Q: Request for explanation. *Why would shift failure occur in the cars of some owners and not in others?*

The mechanic's response here could then lead to investigations into any area of the manufacturing process and/or observations of the production line operation.

- *Possible error data* — Respondents: Persons responsible for keeping the records in question.

Q: Request for explanation. *I notice that figures by Customer Relations differ with those of Quality Management concerning the number of returns expected on our recall of the CX2 model. What is your explanation for differences in the estimate?*

Advertising

- *Trend/relationship data* — Respondent: Ad agency librarian, public library, or research agency.[2]

Q: Request for amplification. *According to Consumer's Forum there's a trend in car purchases by working women at younger and younger ages. What data are available concerning the average age of a working woman's first new car purchase?*

Suppose the data indicate the average age of first car purchase for working women is 21. Anticipate the media consumer who might say: "So what? I'm 26 and been working since I was 18, and even though I've got a good job now, I still can't afford to buy a new car."

A logical follow-up in your interview plan would be a relationship type question. Can you think of one? Was it something like this?

Q: *What is the relationship of age and income to the kind of car working women purchase as their first car?*

- *Similarities/differences data* — Respondent: Ad agency nutritionist, librarian, or account executive. The writer's job ticket[3] just might have this and other information on it. If not, the respondents mentioned here should be able to tell you.

---

[2]Some agencies hire an outside research firm to investigate market trends or to test a product or commercial.

[3]A job ticket is a form on which information concerning a product and client expectations are entered. Ad writers are usually up on facts concerning the products they write about, but they will, nevertheless, conduct research and interviews on matters involving certain specific requests made on the job ticket.

Q: Request for amplification. *Our product is low in fat content. Our competitor makes the same claim, but their food label fails to indicate types of fat used. Do we know what types of fat the competitor's product contains?*

The answer will be either yes or no. What would be a good follow-up plan? Did you anticipate questions along these lines?

(If yes). *What are they? How is our use of fats better than theirs?*

(If no). *Why are the fat types used in our product more beneficial than those used in similar low-fat products?*

These examples illustrate how questions concerning flaws in the data convert into interview questions. Note that the mode of critical analysis is the same across all types of mass media, and that gaps and weaknesses in the data direct the nature of the question. Moreover, the questions may be quite simplistic and direct queries such as the following hypotheticals:

- Omission: *Personnel records on one of our employees is missing. How come?*
- Clarification: *What is the significance of this entry?*
- Amplification: *Please tell me a little more about what you know about this.*
- Explanation: *I don't understand how these two records could differ so much on the same matter. Why do they differ at all?*
- Verification: *Dr. Jones says, _____ . What is your response to this?*

Both the direct and less direct approaches apply, as well, to questions regarding *definition, update,* and *latest development.* For example:

- Definition: *I know what _____ means in your field of work, but I'm not sure what is meant by _____ .*
- Update: *A 1987 report by the Bridge Engineers of America indicates that more than half of this country's river bridges are unsafe for motor vehicle crossing. What recent data are available on the decay of river bridges?*
- Latest: *We know that _____ , and that _____ , but what is the latest development in this situation?*

WHEN TO STOP

The previous discussion may suggest the need for long lists of interview questions — not so. The discussion indicates possibilities. Moreover, if your research is solid and you are well versed in it, you need not have any more questions than are necessary to make your knowledge complete for writing. This means no more than a few main questions of a general nature and a handful of objective questions for any one respondent, and often some of the same questions may be asked of more than one respondent for the purpose of corroboration. End your list of questions when your data have exhausted reasons for raising them. Just be prepared for follow-up questions during the interview.

It is often recommended that an interview should last no more than 40 minutes, whether it is a telephone or one-on-one session. A study sponsored by the Bureau of Social Science Research tested the quality level of responses with a 60-minute one-on-one interview as opposed to a 20-minute one-on-one with the same main questions in both questionnaires. Length of interview had no apparent effect on the quality of response in the longer interview that had more subquestions. The study was done for the Federal Housing Administration at the request of the Office of Statistical Standards of the Bureau of the Budget because the Bureau believed more than 30 minutes was too great a burden on the respondent. It turned out in this case that length of time was not a burden (Cannell, 1985a).

Scientists at the Institute for Social Research, University of Michigan, have found that the length of an interview tends to be guided by the interest of the respondent in the topic. They learned that if the topic and its questions interest the respondent, the respondent gives longer responses and the interview lasts longer (Cannell, Miller, & Oksenberg, 1981). This was Manchester's experience with President Kennedy. The President was so intrigued that a prearranged hour interview stretched into 4 hours.

If you feel the respondent is comfortable about the topic and the time, let the respondent go on. Some interesting information usually develops during these extended periods. But if the respondent seems anxious to keep to the prearranged time, be sure you get all your questions answered. If not, make arrangements for another interview period before leaving.

WHO TO ASK

Beyond serving as the source for interview questions, your data are also a source for identifying appropriate respondents. If a piece in your data collection appears reasonable on the whole, but contains a fact, entry, or statement that fails to stand up to question, your first likely interview sources are those who authored the document or statement, or persons who have some connection with either the document or statement. To verify the document's content, or the author's statement, or to obtain another point of view, use the same piece for clues to other documents and persons in the same field who are knowledgeable about the subject. Authors invariably name the sources of their supportive evidence and sometimes those who have another point of view.

If the piece fails to provide any of these clues, it is still useful because the evidence itself will suggest a related group or association that persons in the same field usually join. These groups and associations fill a range from the serious to the sublime: American Psychiatric Association, Mothers Against Drunk Drivers, Resort Timesharing Council. A university or public library will have directories of these groups and associations where names, addresses, and phone numbers are listed. If there is a government agency related to the matter at hand, it is another source.

The authors of a document, their references to authoritative figures, authorities in the same field listed in directories, and personnel at related associations listed in directories and the phone book, are all sources where you will find persons to interview and with whom you can verify or challenge the information you have collected. There is every likelihood, as well, that a document or author's report was sponsored by a particular group, association, research organization, or institute. They are usually mentioned on the title page, in the acknowledgments, or in a footnote. A representative from any one of these collectives also becomes a lead for possible interviewees.

In the rare instance that a group or association does not exist for the subject area you are working on, the material you are reviewing is still a source for clues. It may suggest the type of private institute or organization where there are appropriate persons who can provide answers. Then there are professors at universities who are experts on the subject in question. Again, the university or public library can provide leads to private institutes or groups, and the public information office of a university can direct you to the appropriate department and professor.

Do not overlook government departments and agencies. Sometimes these sources turn out to be your first contacts. Other times they may supplement your private sources and vice versa. Either the telephone directory or library will yield leads on the most appropriate government sources. Libraries usually have directories published by city, state, and federal governments, and they will also have manuals explaining the function of government departments and agencies. If your library does not have them, inquire at a city, state, or federal office for permission to use their references.

When you hit a blind alley, remember to ask the question introduced in chapter 4: *Where can I find* (or *who can provide me with*) *this information?* That simple question uncovers more leads than any other.

In assembling your list of interviewees for any question, select the most appropriate source. This means you want someone who is knowledgeable about the subject content of your particular question and is, as well, a reliable source. Above all, be prepared to explain why you want to interview a particular respondent. Without a good reason to give up valuable time to answer your questions, the candidate may just say, "Sorry, I'm tied up." Test your choice of respondents by asking yourself these critical thinking questions:

- *Who is the most knowledgeable and reliable person to answer this question?*
- *What is my purpose in interviewing this person for this question?*
- *What do I know about this interviewee?*

If your first interviewee choice fails to stand up to question, look for another candidate. Your time is as precious as anyone else's. Do not waste it.

SAFETY IN NUMBERS

A precautionary note: Never count on one respondent to answer an important question. Include at least two or three respondents for the same questions in your interview plan. In highly questionable situations, or on controversial issues, you might even need to plan on more. Beyond corroboration in documents and records, corroboration between authorities and respondents is the writer's means of obtaining verification of information that has either been published or stated. Perhaps you noticed corroboration was a characteristic and repetitive feature of preliminary work by professional media writers interviewed in earlier chapters. You will find that corroboration again is a feature in the interviews at end of this chapter.

Planning what you will ask who about what helps that verification process. An interview plan with a line-up of appropriate respondents on any one issue can also encourage a reluctant respondent to agree to an interview. For example, suppose you want to ask the director of a public service agency why tax-supported public services have not been delivered, and the agency director says, "Nothing doing." If you have lined up an appointment with the head of another agency to whom the director is responsible, say so, and that you also want the director's side of the story. Maybe you will win agreement, maybe not. But chances are that the reluctant director will want the opportunity to voice a few words, if not now, at least after you have talked to the other agency head. Use of such a tactic, however, might not have been possible if you had not planned on interviewing the agency head.

Earlier you learned that comparison of documents and records is one way of validating the data in them. Corroboration of statements from several interview respondents is still another means of verifying information given. Neither function should be overlooked.

SUMMARY OF SELF-INQUIRIES ABOUT INTERVIEW PLANS

What to ask:
- *What research questions on my original list are still unanswered?*
- *What is missing in my data that the media consumer needs to know and is not on my original list?*
- *What information in my data fails to stand up to question?*

Who to ask:
- *Who is the most knowledgeable and reliable person to answer this question?*
- *What is my purpose in interviewing this person for this question?*
- *What do I know about this interviewee?*

You now have an idea of the basic questions for an interview, but before making your list and assigning respondents to them, reserve further planning until you learn more about *how* to ask those questions, and that is the second part of the discussion related to Critical Self-Inquiry 5: *What do I need to ask who about what and how shall I ask it?*

In the next chapter you will learn how to structure what you want to ask so that the question evokes a productive response from your interviewee. But first take note of how advertising professionals describe the function of interviewing in their medium, and the questions these professionals raise and with whom. Also, note the questions the other media writers raise for their specific sources, and how a few of them who faced hostile respondents handled the situation.

*   *   *

Discussion in this chapter mainly concerned what to ask who about what. What you will see here is how professionals raise questions with appropriate respondents and what some had to do to manage reluctant interviewees. But temporarily set aside attention to that for a quick briefing on how some procedures in advertising, mainly interviewing, are at the same time similar to and different from other mediums.

Advertising writing constitutes a great deal more than just producing a print or broadcast ad. As in PR, the advertising writer is expected to be a versatile performer. A copywriter may be asked to contribute to a major campaign or write a flyer, a 4x8 brochure, a direct mail or specialty item promotion, even a product or consumer manual. A copywriter may be assigned to various types of client accounts: manufacturers of consumer products or mechanical or electronic parts, wholesalers or retailers of these products, food producers, educational and religious groups, organizations who provide consumer, sales agent or industrial services, and the list goes on.

No one can possibly know all there is to know about all products, all clients. Nevertheless, at one time or another you will be faced with the problem of dealing with a product or service you know nothing about.

That is not as overwhelming as it seems. Like news and PR writers, advertising writers have consciously or unconsciously found a private support system—the right strategy and right questions to guide them through whatever writing challenge comes their way.

However, as suggested earlier, advertising writers rarely conduct field research or hold formal interviews. Those functions are carried out by the agency research department or a hired research agency. Researchers are trained to study the market, field test a campaign idea or the product; they perform the functions of research and interviewing for the ad agency.

But that does not mean copywriters never raise questions with appropriate sources or never use reference or research materials. Not by a long shot. It is just that they have some ready data at the outset and, depending on the assignment, augment it with additional research and informal interviews, as you will notice quickly enough from the following interviews. The first interview demonstrates the evolution of a campaign idea, and the second describes the evolution of a TV spot once the campaign theme is established. The narrative on these and the other six professionals resumes in chapters 11 and 12 where all explain how they managed the data collected to produce their written assignment.

You will also find two additional interviews in Appendices B and C. One represents an entirely different type of advertising production—a consumer education video—and the other is an interview with a former advertising writer who demonstrates the opportunities available to seasoned mass media writers who choose to move into free-lance work.

* * *

HOW THE PROFESSIONALS DO IT

Designing the Interview Plan and Conducting the Interview

Advertising: The Pizza Campaign

Mathew Thornton

Mathew Thornton, is one of the principal creative directors for Hummingbird Productions, which has its headquarters in Nashville, Tennessee, with satellite offices in New York, Chicago, and Detroit. At Hummingbird, Mr. Thornton specializes in composing music and lyrics and directing production of commercials for the company's national accounts, some of which include Pepsi Cola, McDonald's, Wrigley's Gum, Shell Oil, Chrysler Corp., and Radio Shack.

The following interview took place in March 1989, when Mr. Thornton was vice-president of Creative Services at Group 243, Ann Arbor, Michigan. Finalization of merger negotiations with the Ross Roy Group in Troy, Michigan (a suburb of Detroit), was under way at the time and in 1991 Mr. Thornton chose to join Hummingbird Productions.

Here Mr. Thornton described how he and his staff at Group 243 developed a basic campaign for Domino's Pizza that eventually led to a broad-based marketing effort nationwide. The campaign included local and national distribution of advertising in all areas of mass media: placement of print ads in magazines and newspapers, spot broadcasts with local and network radio and TV stations, a direct-mail program, and a public relations program to establish the client's public image.

During the first 5 years of the campaign, Domino's share of the market increased from 12% to 20%. In addition, the promotion generated a massive market for consumer premium items such as T-shirts, toys, knick-knacks, and the like. Some of these carried the familiar animated character, "The Noid," which proved to be the catalyst that sustained the success of the initial Domino's Pizza campaign. Later Mr. Thornton described how "The Noid" character emerged from systematic strategy and critical thinking, a process that Mr. Thornton explained as *all pretty logical*.

Media writers rarely plunge headlong into a project without first surveying the field and the opposition. Advertising writers are no exception and that is precisely the precaution Mr. Thornton took before going to the drawing board and before setting up even a tentative working statement. He explained the precaution as wanting to *take the temperature* of the market. That is, he and his staff wanted to find out about pizza consumer likes and dislikes, reasons why the consumer bought one pizza over another, or switched around.

Once research agencies test the market and first questions are answered, a more definitive portrait of the pizza consumer emerges. The creative staff has already done its preliminary work — learning about the client and the product from in-house and client files. The research surveys make up the rest of the knowledge base for the creative staff, as does information obtained from informal interviews.

Notice Mr. Thornton's recognition of the problem: *We had to identify the public's perception about Domino's delivered pizza, and we had to get a better competitive edge.*

Thornton: At the time we took on the Domino's account [in 1984, before Group 243 became part of Ross Roy], Domino's Pizza was the only pizza company that delivered. Now many more fast food vendors in the industry deliver. There was a public perception out there about delivered pizza that we didn't know much about at the time. And Domino's was the underdog in the industry, competing with pizza houses like Pizza Hut and Little Caesar's.

So we started out with two major problems. We had to identify the public's perception about Domino's delivered pizza, and we had to get a better competitive edge. We had a pretty good idea of what we were up against.

The activities involving backgrounding and research moved into motion, but they did not involve the copywriter. Research work was turned over to in-house researchers as well as outside researchers. Notice the kinds of interview questions consumers were asked. Also, notice how the research produced a working statement, provided a profile of consumer attitude about delivered pizza, and altered the client's and agency's former perceptions about the product: *Delivery is great, nice and convenient, but the pizza is not as good as when I buy it in the pizza parlor and, besides, the box top sticks to the pizza.* Answers from consumer interview questions provided the working statement and built the staff's creative bank.

Thornton: Our practice at Group 243 is that whenever we embark on a campaign for a client, we do some research. We kind of take the temperature of the water out there, metaphorically speaking, by talking to consumers. We ask such questions as: *What do you think about the product? What is your* *image of it? What is your notion of its price?* Just everything to find out how we might best sell the product to the consumer.

Group 243 has what we call focus group research. This might involve mall intercepts, that is, stopping shoppers at the malls and just asking them these questions. We also do a tracking study that involves a lot of telephone call-backs to customers. It's quite an extensive research program that we help them set up just to find out what people are thinking about Domino's and their pizza product.

Actually, we had three groups of people working on the first market research. We have our in-house market research group. They worked with the market research group at Domino's Pizza, and we also hired a particular market research vendor to do a particular job, for example, to interview the focus groups, and another to do the competitive market, etc. We wanted to see what dynamic we could pull out of all this.

We chose about five or six areas across the U.S., one in Kansas, one in the Southeast, one in the Northeast, the Northwest, West, etc., just spread it out across the country. We asked: *What do you think of delivered pizza? What's important to you about pizza?* And they told us: "Hot, yes, that's very important, also, to have a choice of toppings."

Then we asked a lot about delivery, and we found out some specific things at this time. People felt, in general, that a delivered pizza was not as good as having it in the restaurant. That was the conclusion drawn from a massive amount of research.

To put it on the line: *Delivery is great, nice, and convenient, but the pizza is not as good as when I buy it in the pizza parlor and, besides, the box top sticks to the pizza.* So now we knew what we had to attack. Going in, we didn't expect that delivered pizza was regarded not as good as the one in the pizza parlor. You need to have a real good picture of who you are talking to in order to talk to them in the language that will best sell your product.

The research did not stop with consumer interviews. It continued with studies of the competitive market and this added to the knowledge base that Mr. Thornton, in the previous comment, called the source for the inherent advertising *dynamic.* Only a few of the market research questions are given here, but notice the few that are mentioned and the answers they provided.

Thornton: But that was only one aspect of our market research. We had little marketing weight, that is, how often you're in print or on TV and how many impressions you can get out there. We were a small player in that arena at that time, and Domino's Pizza didn't have as much money to spend on a national level as our major competitor Pizza Hut, or most of the other fast-food companies. Whatever we had to do we had to really make a big bang. But because we didn't know how much public awareness of Domino's pizza there was out there, we had to know how much of a big bang we had to make. So we did competitive research as well as consumer research.

We wanted to know: *What is our competitors' scope of advertising? How many people know about Domino's Pizza in the U.S.? What percentage of the people are aware of the product? What percentage of the people have tried it? What percentage of the people were repeat customers?, and so on.*

What we found was that we were spending only half as much as Pizza Hut, and an eighth as much, or less, as McDonald's. All of them were trying to get the same people to buy their products. We also tracked consumer awareness of Domino's Pizza. I think at the time people's awareness was less than 50 percent, so that was another problem we had to attack.

Of course, this consumer and market research never ends. Over the years we've had the Domino's account, we've kept a close watch on consumer awareness and attitude change in order to make appropriate adaptations in the advertising.

At this point, the creative staff has a completed preliminary study of the client's product and a reading on the *temperature of the water out there.* Mr. Thornton's staff then moved on all this information to produce a creative campaign theme (in chapters 11 and 12).

Advertising: The TV Spot Ad

Anne Gahagan

Anne Gahagan is a senior writer with the W. B. Doner advertising agency, Southfield, Michigan, another Detroit suburb. One of the top national ad agencies, the Doner agency serves such clients as BP Oil International, BF Goodrich Tires, Chiquita Brands International, and numerous other local, national, and international accounts.

In this interview, Ms. Gahagan explained the process that follows a creative director's effort to identify a substantive base for a campaign idea. Her job was to come up with some ideas for a 30-second TV spot, and her description illustrates the teamwork that characterizes the nature of mass media production in advertising agencies.

Keep in mind that research on tests of the product, consumer preferences, and market climate have been completed, including the writer's own preliminary study of the client and the product. All this provided Ms. Gahagan with an initial base of information.

The assignment identified the ad problem and together with previous research established, as Ms. Gahagan indicated, a basis from which to begin creative work: *Basically, we have a fair overview of the product and what they put into it from the job ticket, what we have to deal with here.* Aside from data on the product, the job ticket also included market and product test information and requests made by the client. It is this background material the writer reviews and studies before other procedures take place. Inherent in that job ticket information, however, is a suggestion of what the working statement might contain: the taste reactions of consumers, the tested ingredients that set this product apart from all others like it, and the client's personal preference for something humorous.

Ms. Gahagan explained an assignment like this typically takes about 3 to 4 months before production begins. Also, that deadlines depend on the project and that timeliness is also a factor. If, for some reason of timeliness, the ad had to air immediately, pressure would be on to get the assignment out faster. On the other hand, she pointed out, projects of some magnitude require extended schedules.

In her comments here notice, particularly, Ms. Gahagan's understanding of the kinds of questions that had to be raised in order to obtain the information that now appears on the job ticket. At the request of the ad agency, product and client names are omitted in the following responses.

Gahagan: When I was hired in at Doner, I was placed in a particular group. At Doner every group has a list of certain clients that the writer is responsible for. I happened to be in the group that included [the client]. At the time, there were two writers and two art directors in the group. I typically work with one of the art directors and usually there are six on a creative team: two writers, two art directors and two supervisors.

The client had requested television ideas for a new product, a country-style [product type] they had come up with. Having dealt with the client before—they tend to have a certain style in mind—we knew with [client] they'd want something humorous but very human, so we kept to that idea.

I read what the account people gave us as far as information and background [pretest results, client requests, other data]. They usually prepare what's called a job ticket for us and that usually outlines the basic concept of the job, some of the things that the client wants and certain strategies that they recommend for selling.

We determined from the materials we were given about what kind of questions were asked of the focus groups. We'd say: *The focus group moderator must have asked such questions as . . . .* For example, we could tell they must have asked people how they would describe the texture of [product name], how they would describe its taste. So we had that to work with. They do a lot of testing as far as giving people the product to try and having them describe the taste, that kind of thing. Basically, we have a fair overview of the product and what they [the client] put into it from the job ticket, what we have to deal with here.

Very often, results from field research are not enough. The writer is obliged to conduct research, as well. Results from field research may raise questions that need answers and, as you know, answers are usually available in in-house files and libraries, or other appropriate references. Any other questions are normally raised during informal interviews with the account executive, sometimes with researchers who conducted the surveys. In this case, the client's kitchen staff also answered some questions for the writers.

> **Gahagan**: Since the assignment revolved around a country recipe theme, we wanted to know if, indeed, the product came from a true country source, and I think the answer to that was that it came from several different recipes.
>
> We asked: *Where the recipe came from, what groups or areas it may have come from, how they got it.* We also found out about this woman who tests recipes in their test kitchen [the client's kitchen], and we asked questions about that [the product was found to be an adaptation of several traditional country recipes from various rural areas].
>
> If there was information we had some question about, we'd ask [the account executive]. Sometimes they [the account group/client] don't specify whether this particular item of information should be spelled out in the commercial, or if it's something for us to know as overview. So we ask: *Do they* [the client] *want us to say specifically that this is the flavor? Or, do they want this or other points about taste made?* A lot of times these questions aren't answered until we come up with something and the client sees it and says: *What we really wanted was to emphasize this in it.*

Ms. Gahagan's questioning attitude continued right to the point of creating the product, during, and even after the creative work had been completed (in chapters 11 and 12). You will find this holds true for all the media writers.

Print News: The Navy Story

Like all mass media writers, newswriters must be alert to weaknesses in the collected data that call for additional probing through interviewing. This was especially true for the Ashenfelter-Freedberg team. When they found what Mr. Ashenfelter called "telltale signs" in the Judge Advocate General's report that Seaman Collum had been severely mistreated (see chapter 3), that initiated interview questions with other seamen who had been with Collum when he leaped overboard to escape further punishment. He found the names of the seamen in the Naval Investigative Service (NIS) report and was able to locate three of them who had witnessed Collum's

leap. Responses obtained from these witnesses provided key information
the investigative team used in their final report.

> **Ashenfelter**: I tried to track down the five brig prisoners to see what they had
> to say, to prove they weren't interviewed for the JAG investigation. I got hold
> of three [Rogers, Off, and Augustyn]. I interviewed these three guys
> separately and gave them all the same questions: *I understand you were there
> that day, what happened? What kind of exercises were you doing that day?
> Did the Marines mistreat you? Did they ever hit you?* I just went through a
> whole series of questions.

Mr. Ashenfelter soon learned that Seaman Collum had suffered abuse
similar to that experienced by Seaman Trerice. But notice he did not face
the opposition until he and Ms. Freedberg explored and verified the details
concerning the deaths of all the Navy seamen.

> **Ashenfelter**: Without knowing of the other's report, Rogers, Off, and
> Augustyn corroborated one another's stories, and what they told me dove-
> tailed completely with what the other two prisoners told the NIS investigators,
> but what they [NIS investigators] didn't delve into was the treatment in the
> brig. That whole area wasn't probed at all, and all I had to go on was what
> these three guys told me, and I corroborated that with what Collum had told
> the legal officer who had visited him the night before he went over the side.
> He [Collum] told the legal officer that the Marines had refused to give him
> drinking water and that corroborated with what Rogers, Off, and Augustyn
> were telling me.
>
> After we got the investigation report, after we retraced as many of the
> witnesses as we could that were quoted in the report, I then called the captain
> of the ship [the Ranger], and I asked him about it [the Collum incident]. I also
> called Collum's commanding officer and asked him some questions about
> Collum's death.
>
> What I was investigating was what the investigators in the Collum case really
> didn't investigate and that was abuse in the brig. But we weren't sure we just
> had six aberrant cases [Collum and the five deaths] or whether this really was
> a widespread problem. Sydney [Freedberg], meanwhile, is getting the run-
> around [from Navy officials] on her five cases. We can't get to the bottom of
> these cases. *What are we going to do?*

The team found an answer to their question—a survey, interviews with
families of the dead seamen. The team also found that a previously
researched document proved valuable in that effort. The survey provided
reliability power to the whole body of data thus far collected and filled holes
due to Navy failure or reluctance to release important records.

Unlike the type of survey conducted under the strict standards of an empirical study, this survey is an exploratory investigation and simply represents interviews held with a select group of people—families of servicemen who died while in the service of their country during peacetime. Results of that survey apply to only those related to that loss, but they are, nevertheless, valid because they are to the point of this particular problem.

Ashenfelter: We suspected it [Marine guard abuse, Navy secrecy] was widespread and wanted to try to verify how widespread this whole thing was. Together we decided [the editors and the team] we had to do a survey of other families that lost kids. So we asked the Navy to give us a list of how many people died last year in the Navy and they said, "Well, we're not going to tell you."

We thought of the cruise books. If we could find out where they kept the cruise books, we could get all the names we wanted. One of the public information officers on one of the carriers we had interviewed on something else told us that they always sent a copy of the cruise books to Washington. So while I was in Washington picking up the Collum investigation report, I had asked one of the people there, "Who's in charge of the cruise books?" Got a typical runaround. So I asked his secretary and she took me to a guy and he said that they had sent them over to the Navy archives, a big warehouse-type library at the Washington shipyards. I grabbed a cab and went over there and picked out all the cruise books I could find during the last 5-year period, went back to Detroit with something like 125 names from all these ships.

We wrote up a list and a FOIA request to the Navy for death certificates on all 125 of these kids because we wanted the next of kin. Well, the Navy said they'd give us the death certificates but not the next of kin. Then they said, "We'll give you the names but not where they live." So we negotiated for 2 more days. Thoroughly exasperated, I said, "Just give me the hometowns."

We got a couple of people in the office to start calling all these families. Out of 125, we got hold of about 75 families. We figured that maybe 15% of those families would say they weren't satisfied with the way the Navy gave information. It turned out to be 75% of the 75 families. We didn't have any proof that the Navy was lying to the families. What we had was these families who said the Navy knew more than they were telling. I don't think we would have had anything without that survey. That survey really, really gave strength to the point we were making.

We knew when we called each of these people [the 75 families] what we wanted to ask them. We frequently read out the questions and then as we interviewed we ticked off the questions. [Re the survey questionnnaire] . . . there was just a list of about six questions: *What did they know about their kid's death? Were they satisfied with the way they got the body back? Was the body sent back in a timely manner? Were they satisfied with the Navy's funeral arrangements?* After we called a couple of families, we decided that [questions about the body] was causing more alarm than what we needed to find out about. We simply wanted to get a feeling from these families: *What did they know about their kid's death? Were they satisfied with the information the Navy was giving?*

The team's research and verification effort prepared them for interviews with the opposition — the military. Here is what Mr. Ashenfelter said about interviewing these officials.

Ashenfelter: On real sensitive guys, like the captain of the ship, the commanding officer, we knew we were going to get only one shot at them. We knew we had to have all the right questions and had to ask all the questions we had because they'd never answer any more phone calls. The sailors [the witnesses] had nothing to lose by talking to us so we called them back a number of times.

And when the team faced obstruction to their requests for official documents, this is how they got around it.

Ashenfelter: As I explained, we were getting the runaround from the Navy. We had asked them: *What is the procedure we use to request the reports if we have parents' written authorization to look at the investigation reports?* They said, "You don't have to use the FOIA, just send us a request and the family's authorization letter." It was like a month and under FOIA they have 10 days to respond. So we called them back. They said, "You didn't use the FOIA so we're not going to give you the information."

We sat down and just wrote a long appeal letter to the Secretary of Defense explaining all the different ways we got the runaround and I quoted the law [FOIA]. In the Collum case, they sent us the investigation report. They had taken out the social security numbers when they censored this stuff. They had it marked out with magic marker. I took the report up to our Art Department and asked if they knew what type of solvent would remove magic marker. They gave me some stuff and it worked well enough to lift off enough of the magic marker to read the sailor names [the witnesses] and their ID numbers. Then we called a FOIA officer at the records center in St. Louis, gave him the list of social security numbers and he told us where they were holding records on these guys. So that's how we were able to reach the witnesses in the Collum case. The cruise books, that was another way we got around attempts to frustrate us.

With research, interviews, and verifications completed, the team then faced the task of putting this mass of collected data into a form that projected the tragedy of the seamen's deaths and the way their families were deceived about the circumstances surrounding the deaths (in chapters 11 and 12).

Print News: The Ford Plant Fire

When assigned to a story where there is constant change, the newswriter has little time to make studied comparisons or draft formal lists of questions and sources. You either respond quickly to the requirements of the moment or the information eludes you. As it is, there is little time to even write down one's observations. Mr. Cain's response to fast changing events in the Ford plant fire is characteristic of this type of news coverage. Here again you will see resourcefulness in action. If interview candidates are unable or refuse to cooperate, a little bit of ingenuity will give you what you need.

If you remember, the priority of questioning moved from loss of plant property and employee lives to the issue of toxins in the volume of smoke filling the atmosphere. Here is what Mr. Cain said about his response to that change and the nature of interviewing in a tense situation.

Cain: Once on the scene you begin to go through a second order of priority, observing and talking to key people. I wanted to describe what was happening, and at the same time try to seek out those people around the event. It's important to get to them very fast and on the scene because people in the midst of a crisis will say what's precisely on their minds, with what they are having to do. People after a crisis will say what they're supposed to say.

I knew I had to see the senior police official, the one who would direct security for the plant, also the senior fire official who was fighting the fire. I knew that at some point there would be somebody from the State Police Fire Marshall's office. I'd have to get hold of the plant manager or other responsible supervisors. That's sort of who counts.

The fire could spread through the plant and I knew huge storage supplies of plastic were stored inside.

Thinking about the modified working statement, Mr. Cain anticipated information he might possibly need to write a report he is already juggling around in his mind. Even though the fury of the fire's first moments had subsided, Mr. Cain refrained from interrupting officials' work with questions about the toxins. Instead, he relied on his own resourcefulness to obtain the data he believed might prove useful.

Cain: There are a lot of things you can get on your own without asking anyone [questions about the toxins]. As soon as I had some time [after it was clear the fire was under control] I went into the plant, because I knew where the plastics were. I went through all these bales from Monsanto and everything else that was stacked against the wall on the other side of the fire, and I simply wrote down the chemical content of every bale of plastic I saw in there, to give me a basis of saying—had the wind changed and these guys couldn't control the fire—this was the potential, what they would have been up against.

I could of asked some official, but he could have turned me off, so I simply walked into the plant to find out for myself. One of the real frustrations was Bill Treml didn't get in and I couldn't get to him. I didn't know where our photographers were and there was no phone that I could go to without risking being ejected. So I was completely on my own. I didn't know what anybody else was doing. I was unable to coordinate with the rest of the staff.

But that coordination was possible after the excitement was over and everyone returned to the newsroom. It was then simply a matter of matching notes to validate and verify data each team member had gathered in the field before writing the story (see chapters 11 and 12).

Broadcast News: The TWA Hijack

The stress involved in getting out a breaking news story is not much different for broadcast newswriters. As in print news, the assignment is rushed, mostly done on the run, but can be handled easily enough, especially if you are practiced at knowing who to ask about what. Mr. Meisner called that refinement a "gut feeling." In reality, it is the gradual development of systematic work habits that cultivates that gut feeling and secures the confidence interviewing demands.

> **Meisner**: Just being a journalist, just being in the business, you get a gut feeling of who it is you need to talk to and what you need to ask. It's generally not something you sit down and make a list and say, "On a story like this, these are the ten people I have to talk to." There are stories like that. This wasn't one of them.
>
> But I did give a great deal of thought to my questions. When you're dealing with families who are distraught, it's stressful for them, and you like to put a lot of thought into your questions. And certainly when you're talking to official types you like to put a lot of thought into it because you might not have a second opportunity to ask questions. I wanted them [officials] to give me status reports on where the crises stood. From the families, I wanted to get an idea of what it was they were going through.

Although Mr. Meisner checked information as he received it, that was not the end of validations and verifications. The management in New York also kept an eye on him.

> **Meisner**: You check everything you can. Some things you can't. For example, if you're talking to a Nabih Berri in the Middle East, thousands of miles away, and he claims the hostage release is imminent, there's no one close to the

hostages to verify it with. He's working in conjunction with Syrian officials. The Syrian officials aren't necessarily commenting.

But you have to check, because there's always someone checking on you. When the *Today* show heard I had talked to Nabih Berri—we had actually scooped our own network—they questioned whether or not we really talked to him. Of course, the proof I had that I had talked to him was that we had recorded the interview on audiotape. There are two important things in this business—be first and be right. The most important is being right. If you're first and wrong, you have nothing, because if you're wrong, you have no credibility. You've got zero.

And this is what Mr. Meisner had to say about fielding questions with cooperative and uncooperative respondents:

Meisner: The government was very unhelpful. I simply circumvented them. Any time there's a plane crash, any time you have a hostage situation, they give very little information to the families under the guise they don't want false information to get out. I did have a source in the government who was very helpful. You have to circumvent the people who are stonewalling you.

Reports of the hostage situation were broadcast nightly on the evening news, including key interviews with families, officials, and finally the released hostages. It was from these brief newscasts that the hour-long documentary on prime time was edited and aired (see chapters 11 and 12).

Broadcast News: Illegal Use of Public Land

The data from California and preliminary research contributed some of the background for Ms. Timmons' story, but her primary source provided the principal data and interview possibilities for the Michigan story. Notice how Ms. Timmons finally located her key interviewee. It is apparent that trail to an authoritative source would never have materialized had she not asked earlier contacts: *Who can provide me with this information?* Notice, too, her extended check on the validity of that interviewee's information.

Timmons: For this story, I selected my initial interview subjects through recommendations. I started with the Bureau of Land Management in Washington. They referred me to someone else who was a regional person with the Bureau of Land Management, and they referred me to other Federal agencies and state agencies. I started with the Bureau of Land Management because they were the baseline source used in the California report.

But my primary interview was with the Michigan police lieutenant in charge of "Operation Hemp" in Michigan. I just thought about: *What was the most important information I needed for the story?* In other words, the who, what, where, when, and why, and he answered all of those. And then I expanded on each of those questions to be more specific.

Since he was the one in charge of the hemp program here in Michigan, he was well informed of different instances in Michigan that would relate to the things happening in California, this so-called "terror in the woods." He also had the specifics I needed, a lot of facts and a lot of figures to do with Michigan as far as how much marijuana was being grown, how many growers there were, how much was confiscated, how much was eradicated. And then he also had information on the different booby traps [devices used to cause injury] that were, perhaps, being used by survivalists, or by the marijuana growers. He had a lot of documents about marijuana growth, marijuana eradication, and the number of marijuana arrests. His office had compiled all this information, that is, the Michigan State Police in cooperation with the Dept. of Natural Resources, because it was a combined effort, and I should also say, the Sheriff's Dept., because they all worked together. It was a local, state and federal team working together [to get at the facts].

I checked all this by checking other agencies to see if I would get the same information, and I did. I checked with the Michigan State Police Dept., Dept. of Natural Resources, Dept. of Agriculture, the Justice Dept., others, and I basically got the same information.

I had pre-interviewed the Michigan State Police and all the other people by telephone, but at the point where I'm going to do the actual [primary] interview, I take the cameraman and the cameraman does the interview along with me and then any other visuals we may need we shoot at that time.

Ms. Timmons later explained how all this was finally pulled together and written (in chapters 11 and 12).

Public Relations: The Converted Ambulance Crisis

When the Ford management told Mr. Snearly to "push hard for the data," he did. It is always a good idea to inform department heads of management's attitude so that you can assure yourself of their cooperation. Unless informed, they and their staff may be reluctant to share the needed data they regard as exclusive to that department. In this case, Mr. Snearly informed his contacts about the *risks* involved in keeping *facts and figures* under wraps and the *benefits* of disclosing important information.

Snearly: I had to discuss this [obtaining data] with our people, told them what the risks and benefits were. Sometimes I had to tell them: *We have to have facts and figures because if you say, no comment, they'll* [the media] *figure we're either stupid that we don't know, or sinister because we're covering up something.* My standard, our standard, is to be straightforward and candid with questions the media poses.

We went to the engineers involved and asked: *What do you think is happening here?* They explained it to us in a lot of engineering terms, and we said: *We're not engineers and we're not talking to engineers. How can we get this across in a simple way?*

We needed something that simplified it quite a bit, but sort of made a lasting image. What it came down to, what our engineers were telling us, was that one element was missing [compliance with Ford's conversion recommendations]. It's like a three-legged stool. If one leg is missing, the whole thing collapses. We later used that image in our first presentation.

We had a lot of other questions. I basically laid out all the skeptical questions I was getting [from the media and others] for the people in charge of the recall, the service engineers, division managers. I'd say: *Wait a minute, you say there's no defect in this chassis, but look here's television footage of a burning chassis. How can you say there's nothing wrong when there's a fire?*

Responses to these and other questions, along with other collected data, provided Mr. Snearly with a body of data that became the source of conclusions about the problem and presentation to the media (see chapters 11 and 12).

Public Relations: The Motorsports Promotion

Once Mr. Preuss received approval for the press notebook, the next step was to get updated information on race drivers and their race cars for inclusion in the notebook, because that is the data media people would be looking for in the press notebook. The questions and interview sources for answers were an obvious matter for Mr. Preuss who is knowledgeable about sports car performance and the people who maintain and drive them in competitive races.

Preuss: Anything about the cars came from what we call Special Vehicle Operations [an in-house department that farms out most of the engineering work for the various race teams and provides technical assistance and monitors how Ford supported teams are doing]. The race teams [part of the Special Vehicles department] are our best source of the most current information.

The idea of the press notebook was that people could pick up these notepads at the racetrack, have some pertinent information in them, and have something to take their notes down on. We gave information on the wheelbase, the weight, the length of the cars, the horsepower of the engine, the race schedules, standings of drivers, our [Ford] race standings, championship point standings of other manufacturers. We had to keep our audience in mind [the media], figure out what they needed, what they would look for. We gave them bios [biographies] on the drivers, the type of car each drove, their records, quotes from the drivers, specifics about the cars. The homework goes on all the time. The press notebook turned out to be very valuable. It has been copied by a lot of people and now everybody's got press notebooks.

Mr. Preuss also instructed the outside PR agency to interview the racecar drivers after the race.

Preuss: Agency people were told to ask such questions as: *What happened in turn #4 when you kind of lost it? What problems did you encounter? Why were you going that slow, or that fast?*

At the end of the day, sheets of quotes were handed out to members of the media in the pressroom, plus any other information that happened with Ford cars during that day's activities. The whole idea was to keep the Ford oval before the eyes of the media in every way possible. The idea of a press notebook did that and so did all the side products. Yet, Mr. Preuss pointed out in his next narrative, the job did not end there (in chapters 11 and 12).

In the two chapters that follow, you will learn how to frame productive questions (chapter 8) and how to conduct an interview (chapter 9).

8 Designing the Interview Plan: The Secret is in the Asking

Your interview plan will be incomplete unless you give a great deal of thought to how you design your interview questions. For some complex assignments, experienced writers write out their questions before an interview. For less complex ones, they may just formulate questions in their heads on the way to the interview. But before they get to that stage of skill, they have learned through trial and error which questions work and which questions will not. That is how one TV sportswriter learned his lesson. After a Detroit Pistons basketball game, he asked star player John Salley: *Were you "on" tonight?* Salley's reply: *On what? You mean was I on drugs or something?*

Salley probably guessed what the sportswriter was asking, but why should he guess? It was the writer's responsibility to structure that question in such a way that neither Salley nor the TV audience would mistake the interviewer's meaning. Salley may have been making a joke of it, as is his habit in such situations, but in the wake of publicity about drugs and sports, Salley's challenge was justified. To help you learn what professional writers have learned through experience, and what behavioral science researchers have discovered about question structure, this chapter concentrates on the last portion of Critical Self-Inquiry 5: *What do I need to ask who about what and how shall I ask it?* . . . namely, the design of productive, unbiased interview questions.

HOW TO ASK

The literature of behavioral science includes a vast number of systematically conducted studies related to structuring productive interview questions. The

151

literature of mass media is scant in comparison. Much of it chronicles the personal experiences of writers and concerns the general subject of interviewing rather than question design.[1]

In contrast, literature on interviewing in the behavioral sciences is rich in replicated studies by researchers who have systematically tested interview questions to learn what does and does not work. The problem, however, is that conclusions reached are mainly tentative, principally because replication may be similar in some aspects, but not all. For example, levels of respondent capability vary, settings cannot always be duplicated, question delivery varies with the interviewer, and response behavior changes as the subject matter changes. All have an effect on replication results. Nevertheless, if one takes these conditions into account and notes what works most often under similar circumstances, the literature of behavioral science serves as an alternative source for mass media writers who seek tested methods of question formation.

COMMON GROUND

It is true that media interviews vary widely from survey research interviews. Nevertheless, these two dissimilar groups strive toward a common goal: They both seek informed and accurate information. Researchers conduct surveys to canvas large numbers of people for an aggregate representation of human behavior, knowledge, or thought concerning a particular issue, event, or problem. So do media writers, except they canvas smaller numbers of people for specific responses from particular persons regarding their knowledge and thought on a particular issue, event, or problem, or regarding their behavior, or the behavior of others.

Researchers build a single questionnaire for large numbers of people and instruct interviewers on how to administer it, either in person or by telephone. Writers build different lists of questions for different individuals and conduct unrehearsed interviews in person or by phone. However, it is now common practice even among news, PR, and advertising writers to augment their research data and interview information with data gathered from groups of people, and they do so for any number of reasons in the manner of researchers with a single questionnaire (e.g., the survey conducted by the Ashenfelter-Freedberg team described in chapter 7).

The discussion in this chapter concerns tested techniques of question design that have received fairly wide acceptance in the behavioral sciences.

---

[1]For one of the few texts by a journalist based on personal experience that also devotes some attention to question formation, see Metzler (1977).

They are presented here so that you can understand why these techniques work, an understanding media professionals learned by trial and error.

Speak Like the Rest of Us

Interview questions are usually designed by educated persons who ask questions about topics they already know a great deal about. Although they may cast these questions for people who are also well informed, both researchers and professional media writers urge use of the spoken language most commonly used by English-speaking persons. This means finding synonyms for jaw-breaking and elevated words. It means translating jargon, slang, or idioms used by people in a particular geographical or cultural area into universally used words. And it means substituting plainer words for special terms used by people in a particular field of work.

Why use *maladroit* when *clumsy* will do? Why say *forthwith* when *immediately* says the same thing? Social workers have a habit of saying, "We *interfaced* with Group One," when they are really talking about having *met* with Group One. If you use unfamiliar words, chances are your respondent will respond in kind and those responses will creep into your copy to confuse the message receiver. If you do use substitutions and respondents still choose to answer with unfamiliar words, ask for definitions. Even though you may know their dictionary definition, you need to understand the user's understanding of such words.

The whole point is to talk to respondents on their level, to speak a mutually familiar language, and to be casual and at ease so the respondent can be at ease as well. The interview should be as natural as possible and reflect the characteristics of conversational exchange. The major difference, of course, is that although the respondent is the key figure, you are in charge and you are the one asking all the questions.

Words and Meanings

Question designers are urged to use not only familiar language and simple words, but also unbiased and specific ones. This is sound advice. However, for interview questions that advice may not be enough. First and foremost, have a clear idea of *why* you are asking the question. Then be mindful of how words, despite your intended meaning, take on a life of their own in the context of a question, even familiar, simple, and specific words.

Familiar words with clear-cut denotative meanings may be too general, or may be misunderstood when used in an unfamiliar way, or connote another meaning for a particular respondent. Stanley L. Payne, author of the classic work on interview questions, *The Art of Asking Questions* (over 10 printings since 1951), demonstrated what happens when question purpose is vague and how a familiar word with a specific meaning deteriorates into generality and ambiguity when used in an unfamiliar way.

A questionnaire on the subject of household disenfectants was mailed to a national sample of housewives. One of the questions asked what *household disenfectants* were used in home cleaning. Ammonia is a common household disenfectant that most housewives keep in supply, yet only 1% of the respondents reported using ammonia. Payne explained that the question failed to conjure up the image of an ammonia container because housewives recall housekeeping products in terms of their specific uses. The question was reworded in a later survey, this time with sharper focus on the objective. Housewives were asked about *bottled disenfectants, antiseptics,* and *bleaches.* Of the housewives, 40% reported they had ammonia on hand. Expansion on the phrase, *household disinfectants* and addition of the word *bottled* provided cues and stimulated housewives' visual memory to evoke a more complete image of household cleaning agents (Payne, 1951, p. 13).

Frames of reference also provide cues and can mean the difference between understanding and confusion. However, the frame of reference must contain words with commonly held meanings. On occasion, a particular word in a frame may not be one that the respondent ordinarily uses. For example, the words *family* and *neighborhood*, although familiar words, can conjure up different meanings in different minds. For some, *family* means only immediate members. For others it includes extended family members and distant relatives. *Neighborhood* is another one of those elastic words. A design technique survey researchers use to avoid this problem, is to say: *By family I mean _____ .*

Words have a way of changing meaning and drawing different interpretations even in matching contexts. Payne illustrated this with the following questions. Both questions posed the same issue, but different words produced different results:

Do you think the United States should <u>allow</u> public speeches against democracy?

Do you think the United States should <u>forbid</u> public speeches against democracy?

This is what happened:

First question		Second Question	
Should allow	21%	Should not forbid	39%
Should not allow	62%	Should forbid	46%
No opinion	17%	No opinion	15%

The word *forbid* seemed undemocratic, but *allow* suggested that the United States should encourage such speeches. Payne said, "People are more ready to say that something should not be allowed than to say that it should be forbidden. It is always safer to offer both choices to avoid the assumptions implicit in giving just one choice" (p. 57). It would have been interesting, Payne added, to see the results of a question restructured this way: *Do you think the United States should allow or forbid public speeches against democracy.*

Never underestimate the power of words, even such words as *a* and *the*. In one of her experiments, Elizabeth Loftus (1974), professor of psychology, University of Washington, and an authority on eyewitness testimony, asked 100 student subjects to watch the film of a multiple-car accident. Half of the subjects were asked:

Did you see the broken headlight?

Others were asked:

Did you see a broken headlight?

Those who answered the question with *the* in it reported "yes" more often than those who answered the question with *a* in it. The *a* witnesses were more likely to respond, *I don't know.* Loftus explained that although both words are articles, receivers assume an object exists when *the* is used. The article *a* carries no such assumption.

In another Loftus experiment, again with films of automobile accidents, witnesses were asked:

About how fast were the automobiles going when they hit each other?

Other witnesses were asked the same question with these words substituted for *hit: smashed, collided, bumped,* and *contacted.*

All the words denote two objects coming together, yet they imply different speeds and force of contact. Subjects who were asked the question with the word *smashed* gave the highest speed estimates. Those asked the question with *collided, bumped*, and *hit* gave progressively decreasing speed estimates. *Contacted* drew the lowest estimate (Loftus, 1979).

Each one of these words evoked a different reaction in the minds of the respondents. They demonstrate how easily words used in a question can blur an eyewitness' memory of the actual incident. Your sensitivity to the power of words in a context will improve respondent understanding of the question being asked.

Relevance to Mass Media Writers.   These few examples should heighten your awareness of how even the most simple, specific, and familiar words change their colors in a context and influence visual memory. Keep in mind that words in a sentence or question trigger images, sometimes incomplete or inaccurate ones that lead to misinterpretations. The lesson here:

- Have a clear idea of why the question is being asked.
- Make certain you are asking the best person for an answer.
- Consider who is being asked and appreciate what words that receiver needs to hear in order to grasp the true picture and fulfill the question's objective.
- Understand the power of words and their fluidity in a context.

More examples would demonstrate still other "black holes" that words can sweep you into, but it all comes down to being a critical thinker about a designed question before taking flight with it.

Payne and others remind us there are no hard and fast rules about selecting the "right" words or structuring them in the "right" context. However, all suggest that question designers act as vigilant custodians of the words they do use. Payne (1951) recommended frequent reliance on dictionary definitions to test the denotative and connotative meanings of a word in the context of a designed question. That is a start, but don't stop there. Apply critical thinking. Analyze the questions you design. Ask yourself:

- *What exactly do I want this respondent to tell me?*
- *Would this respondent have the answer?*
- *What answer might this respondent give?*
- *What words may be unfamiliar, too general or ambiguous, or imply connotations that could defeat the purpose of the question or might trigger the wrong images in this respondent's mind?*
- *What word adjustments and clarifications are needed to improve contextual meaning in order to project the purpose of this question?*

Beyond dealing with the slippery power of words, you will want to design a question that is crisp enough to remember, but clear enough to stimulate the memory and evoke a complete and accurate response.

Question Length and Type

An issue closely related to question wording is question length. A common precaution is to design brief questions, keeping words down to about 20 or less (Payne, 1951). This is also good advice. However, in some instances clarity should take priority over brevity.

One way to achieve brevity at the outset is to *limit a question to one concept, issue, or meaning.* If you have more than one concept per question, researchers warn, it is an indication that you have lost sight of the question's objective and will not know which concept the respondent is referring to or answering (Cannell & Kahn, 1968; Labow, 1980; Payne, 1951).

Furthermore, if you give a respondent too many tasks to deal with, you can expect an unproductive interview. In other words, the respondent will say, *Which question do you want answered?* Or, *Whadya mean?* Or, *Forget it.*

Assuming your question has a *single* concept, your aim is to now design a *clear, understandable* question. Length in that instance becomes a matter of careful decision. Extra words, even redundancy, may be necessary to jog the respondent's memory for complete and accurate recall.

Researchers Sudman and Bradburn (1982, pp. 65-68) compared a long and short form of behavior questions. They found that longer questions provided memory cues which acted as a means of aided recall:

Short: *Did you ever drink, even once, wine or champagne?*

(If yes)   *We are especially interested in recent times. Have you drunk any wine or champagne in the past year?*

Long: *Wines have become increasingly popular in this country over the last few years; by wines, we mean liqueurs, cordials, sherries, and similar drinks, as well as table wines, sparkling wines, and champagne. Did you ever drink, even once, wine or champagne?*

(If yes)   *You might have drunk wine to build your appetite before dinner, to accompany dinner, to celebrate some occasion, to enjoy a party, or for some other reason. Have you drunk any wine or champagne in the last year?*

Cues of possible settings and occasions reminded respondents of their use of wine. In addition, the longer question took more time to deliver, which gave respondents more time to think, more time to spend on the memory task.

Matarazzo, Wiens, Saslow, Dunham, and Voas (1964) found this to be true with astronauts. When questioned about their flight experiences, astronauts gave more detailed responses to longer questions than to short ones.

There is some evidence that long questions draw more complete responses even on threatening type questions. Bradburn and Sudman (1981) experimented with both short and long questions concerning individual gambling and sex habits. They found high threat questions with 30 or more words evoked more complete reporting than the same high threat questions with fewer words.

In addition, researchers at the Institute for Social Research (ISR), University of Michigan, found that response length also depends on what and how a question is asked. They discovered over a series of studies that respondents recall and respond well when a topic is of concern or interest to them and when they are prepared for the question in a nondirective way (Cannell et al., 1981).

Adding words, however, for the sake of encouraging a lengthy response is of little value. Words are added when there is reason for length. That is, when it is necessary to prepare the respondent for the question, to reassure or put the respondent at ease, or to clarify the question. In some cases, it may be necessary to do all these in combination.

Experienced Washington correspondents follow this practice at White House press conferences. They explain why they are asking the question, preface the question with a few words about its importance, and tell the respondent they are now going to ask the question. Here is a fictional example of that technique:

> *Mr. _____ , legislation for cleanup of the Great Lakes was passed by both houses of Congress six months ago and since then nothing has been done to implement that legislation. People who live in the area have voiced protests against the delay. My question is: When will implementation of this legislation begin?*

Together these techniques put the respondent in a mindset for accurate and complete response. And if the topic also interests the respondent, you could experience a very productive interview.

Relevance to Mass Media Writers.   Whether the question concerns an attitude belief, behavior, or account of an experience, determination of question length depends on:

- Use of a single concept, issue, or meaning.
- How much detail you need from the respondent.
- How much detail is necessary to clarify the issue and ensure that the respondent understands your purpose, your question, and the importance of the topic.
- Whether aided recall is necessary.

The foregoing discussion clearly suggests serious consideration of the question in relation to information required and the person who will answer it. The ultimate aim is to keep the number of words down to a minimum, but not at the cost of clarity, understanding, and a complete response. Continue analysis of the questions you are designing. Rely on these self-inquiries:

- *Does my question contain more than one concept, issue, or meaning?*
- *Does this question require a frame of reference? If so, does the question adequately prepare the respondent?*
- *Is the issue or event recent enough for the respondent to recall the information needed?*
- *What cues must I provide to aid recall?*
- *Is the respondent concerned enough or interested enough in the issue or event to give a complete and accurate answer?*
- *If not, what words and phrases are needed to impress question importance on the respondent, to arouse interest, and/or to aid recall?*

Question design is a matter of reflective thought about what you need, who can deliver, and how you can get it from that person. Ask yourself the critical questions listed here to reach a decision.

Question Form and Sequence

Questions are designed in different shapes and sequences. They may be:

- Open or closed.
- Indirect or direct.
- Funnel or inverted funnel.
- Primary or primary with secondary sub-questions.
- General (subjective/opinion) or specific (objective/factual).

Open questions are general questions. They are asked to draw an opinion, an explanation, or a description of an experience and elicit extended subjective responses.

Closed questions are more direct and specific. They are asked to evoke factual, objective information and elicit shorter responses.

An *indirect* question asks a series of fairly restricted questions to ease the respondent into the main question at the end, and this question may be open or closed. Or, it asks a series of restricted questions to obtain responses that will indicate the respondent's attitude or behavior. The *indirect* question has the characteristics of an inverted funnel question. In contrast, the *direct* question asks the primary question at the outset.

A *funnel sequence* is a series of "filter" type questions. That is, questions in a funnel sequence move from general to specific, from a broad plane of unrestricted general questions or statements to successively restricted ones that narrow down to a precise objective in an open or closed question.

An *inverted funnel sequence* is also a series of "filter" type questions, but is the reverse of the funnel sequence. It starts with specific questions that progress successively into general questions and ends with a precise objective, usually an open question, sometimes a closed question.

A *primary* question is a main question. It is the interviewer's primary objective and may be the only question that is asked. Another way of getting to the primary objective is through a series of introductory statements, or *secondary* or *subquestions*. Similar in form to the "filter" question, the design may be used when the interviewer needs to:

- Ease the respondent into the primary question which may be too sensitive for direct questioning.
- Gather secondary information related to the primary question.
- Stimulate recall on the primary question through related subquestions.

Here are examples of question designs:

Open Question

Recent events in Eastern Europe have brought about remarkable changes in Poland, East Germany, Czechoslovakia, Hungary, Bulgaria, and the Soviet Union. In most instances, the Soviet leader, Mikhail Gorbachev, has encouraged popular efforts for democratic election procedures. What is your opinion about the popular effort in these countries?

Characteristics.   This is a long attitude (belief) question with lots of memory cues in substatements that precede the primary objective at the end of this open question. In this respect it is a "filter" question with a funnel sequence. The statements move from general to specific and, in the process, cue the respondent. The technique permits the respondent time to think before the open question at the end is asked. This kind of question also provides a context, that is, a point of reference, for the respondent. A shorter version of the same question might be something like the following question:

Open Question

What is your opinion about recent popular attempts in Eastern European countries to achieve democratic elections?

Characteristics. This is also a general question meant to draw a subjective response concerning one's opinion about an event. However, there is no preface, no sequence of memory cues in this one. The question is a short primary question, is more direct, but it assumes the respondent is informed about the 1989 political upheavals in Eastern Europe.

Closed Questions

- *When did you lose your job?* (Reply: June 6).
- *Do you have a hunting license?* (Reply: No).
- *How many incidents of product tampering were reported?* (Reply: 12).
- *What natural fragrance is in this soap?* (Reply: Wild heather).
- *Have you gone to the movies lately?* (If yes) *Do you remember seeing any commercials about passenger cars?* (If yes) *What manufacturing companies advertised their passenger cars in these commercials?*

Characteristics. The first four questions are direct, primary questions with no relationship to one another. These closed questions have a single objective and evoke specific and factual answers. Each question in the last item is a closed question, as well, but together they belong to a related unit leading to the primary objective—to discover the memory value of a film commercial promoting a passenger car. As a unit they make up a "filter" question with an inverted funnel sequence because the sequence moves from narrow to less narrow questions. Each objective question eliminates the uninformed respondent and prepares the informed respondent for the last closed question at the end. For additional information and another primary objective, the same series could have ended with an open question immediately after the final closed question: *What sort of feeling did the commercial leave with you?*

Indirect Question

- *How long have you been out of work?* (Reply: 2 years).
- *Have you ever been out of work before?*
- (If yes) *What did you do then?*
- (If no) *Has any member of your immediate family ever been out of work?*
- (If yes) *What was the impact on you then?*
- *Have you tried to get work?*
- (If no) *Why not?*
- (If yes) *Have you had any offers?*

- *How are you able to pay your bills?*
- *What has been the effect on your family?*
- *What are some of the things you've had to give up?*

Characteristics.   Each one of these questions appears to be a direct and primary question. They are really a series of secondary and indirect questions. The effort is to understand the impact of unemployment on well-being without having to ask that hurtful question. This particular indirect is a long one. Indirects may be shorter to accommodate time allowed and to reduce stress on the respondent. A somewhat expanded series may be necessary in instances of high threat questions. For example, respondents coping with the trauma of trying to get a job without result may have difficulty explaining the bad luck of unemployment. A series of questions gets to the same objective with more restraint than a direct question: *How does it feel to be out of a job?* All you might get is: *Well, how would you feel! It's demoralizing, that's what!*

There is little conclusive evidence that any one of these designs holds superiority over the other. Both open and closed, direct and indirect questions have their advantages and disadvantages as do the other types (Converse & Presser, 1986). Researchers prefer closed questions over open questions mainly because brief answers facilitate interviewing as well as coding and analysis of data. Open questions extend interview time and increase the interviewer's data organization and analytic effort. Still, survey researchers believe open questions have their place and that holds true for media interviews, as well, especially when time is limited to ask about everything in specific detail. In fact, it is often the case that the respondent fills in many of those details during the course of answering an open question, eliminating the need to raise any planned objective questions.

Relevance to Mass Media Writers.   Determination of when to use what type of question on whom and in what mix is not easy, but neither is it impossible. Just remember, the same principal that applied to other issues, applies here. Use the type of question and in any mix that achieves the objective of your question. Rely on the "rules" of language recommended so far:

- Know the objective of your question.
- Let the type of question form and sequence fit the objective.
- Use universally understood language.
- Use simple, specific, familiar words.
- Expand on their denotations and connotations when ambiguity is suspected.

- Avoid use of words that suggest reactions you do not intend, either by themselves or when attached to other words.
- Provide memory aids for retrieval where necessary.
- Provide specific frames of reference where necessary.

To help you make these determinations, use critical thinking to help you reach a decision:

- *Why am I asking this question?*
- *Is my respondent informed about this matter?*
- *What question type and design (open, closed, funnel, etc.) will achieve the objective of this question with this respondent and evoke an adequate and accurate response?*
- *Do I use simple, unbiased, and precise words to achieve that objective?*

Keep the guidelines given here and others that follow in mind. Test your interview questions. Use the critical thinking techniques suggested in this chapter.

Options and Balance

Another "rule" about question structure concerns imbalance. An imbalanced question is one that ignores an opposite option and thus directs the response and sets up automatic bias. Notice the imbalance in the following questions:[2]

Are you in favor of the death penalty for persons convicted of murder?
Is this PR approach acceptable in your view?
Are you in agreement with our campaign plan?

Research experiments indicate that if a respondent suffers from "acquiescence tendency" (the habit of agreeing in order to avoid confrontation or being disagreeable), these questions give the respondent little choice other than to say, *Yes.*

Correction is simply a matter of letting the respondent know it is okay to disagree:

---

[2]Italicized questions in this chapter concerning subjects related to the death penalty and gun permits may be found in Schuman and Presser (1981, chapter 7).

Do you favor or oppose the death penalty for persons convicted of murder?
Is this PR approach acceptable or not acceptable in your view?
Do you agree or disagree with our campaign plan?

Balancing a question may have little impact on a respondent who feels the interviewer expects agreement, but as the designer of questions you have an obligation to remove any trace of bias from your question. This may be especially important with a respondent who has had limited schooling. Researchers Converse and Presser (1986) found a relationship between acquiescence tendency and education. Those with inadequate education tended to agree more often than those who had been substantially trained.

Another form of imbalance and bias is a question that provides choice but gives the respondent little opportunity to consider a counterargument. That's what this question does:

Would you favor or oppose a law which would require a person to obtain a police permit before he could buy a gun?

Again, correction is a matter of structuring a fair question by providing choice. The revised question is balanced, but this one allows a counterargument as well:

Would you favor a law which would require a person to obtain a police permit before he could buy a gun, or do you think such a law would interfere too much with the right of citizens to own guns?

Interestingly, in this particular test, Schuman and Presser (1981) found some response difference between the two forms, but the longer version added a dimension absent in the shorter version: Registration interferes with citizens' rights.

	Favor	Opposed	Interfered
Disagree option:	71.7%	28.3%	
Counterargument:	67.3%		32.7%

The point is to avoid the error and risk of designing a biased and imbalanced question. Offer the respondent the opportunity to disagree, to say, no, and/or to consider an alternative side of the issue.

Relevance to Mass Media Writers.   Providing choice in interview questions is just as important in news, public relations, and advertising as it is in behavioral science. No responsible interviewer chooses to lead the respondent by the nose, yet it is an easy trap unless the questioner is aware of the human tendency toward bias.

Acquiescence tendency in respondents may not be as great a problem in news, PR, and advertising work as it is in research work. In the main, media writers work with learned, informed persons who are quick to disagree or offer a counterargument even when those options are missing. Still, this does not cancel your obligation to insert those options in your question no matter who receives the question, including the informed respondent. Otherwise, the respondent will quickly recognize your bias, or your ignorance, and may choose to criticize your lack of interviewing expertise.

The Five Ws and How

General/subjective questions were given a great deal of attention in this chapter because of their inherent ambiguities and complexities. That does not mean specific/objective questions are less important. The flexibility of words and other factors discussed here apply, as well, to objective questions. However, biases and ambiguities are not as obscure in objective questions as they are in subjective ones. For either objective or subjective questions, rely on journalism's masters of inquiry, the *who, what, where, when, why,* and *how* questions. They get to the point.

Notice most of the example questions throughout this book, particularly those for short deadline assignments in chapter 4, begin with one of the W questions. And perhaps you noticed most of the questions media professionals mentioned in their comments began with one of the W questions.

Ask *who,* you will get a name; ask *what,* you will get a specific; ask *where,* you will get a place; ask *when,* you will get a time; ask *why,* you will get a reason; ask *how,* you will get a description.

However, if you ask: *Do you know who that is? Will you tell me how this mechanism works? Could you tell me what's in this product?,* you will probably get what you asked for, a *yes* or *no.* This does not mean you should never ask yes/no questions. In their place, they are required. But, if you want a substantive answer and prefer not to chance a *yes* or *no,* ask a substantive question.

The W questions are just as useful for general/subjective questions: *What is your opinion about _____? Why do you believe that's true? How did you decide that was the case?* And do not overlook *why* and *how* questions for probes and follow-ups that are discussed here.

Multiples, Multiple Items, Probes, and Follow-Ups

As you already know, a question may include a series of questions organized in different ways to achieve the primary objective. These are called "multiples." A single objective may also be worded two or three different ways and asked of the same respondent at different points in the questionnaire. These are called "multiple items." The purpose of using multiple items is to test the consistency of the respondent's answer to what is essentially the same question. If all answers match, the multiple items are a fair index that the response is valid.

Multiples and multiple items are used because an interviewer can never be sure how adequately the respondent will answer the question's objective. If, in a series of questions, the respondent grasps the purpose of the primary question, the interviewer gains some assurance that the message got through. If after having asked the same question several times in different ways, the respondent gives answers that appear to be a reasonable match, the interviewer has some assurance the response is accurate and reliable. If there is a serious mismatch, the response should be questioned.

Multiples and multiple items are applied to both attitude and factual questions. In fact, success of a question may depend on use of either one of these techniques because a single question may not achieve the purpose of adequate and accurate response.

To design multiples for attitude/belief questions, Kahn and Cannell (1957) recommend a series of closed questions, or an open question with probes or follow-up questions, or a combination of these. If a closed series is chosen, the funnel sequence is a useful design. For example:

Who should legislate the abortion issue, the state or federal government?
Do you think the state (or federal) goverment should legalize abortion?
(If no, use a follow-up) *Why not?*
(If yes) *Some people say legalized abortion is legalized murder, others say without legalized abortion taxpayers will be taxed to support unwanted children. What is your opinion?*

Do you think this campaign strategy has merit or not?
(If no) *Why not?*
(If yes, use a probe) *What do you think are its strongest points?*
(Followed by other probes) *What do you think are its weakest points?*
What do you suggest we do to improve those areas?

Or, in the event of a controversy:

External affairs feels the campaign strategy is weak on consumer satisfaction and too heavy on causes. Marketing feels just the reverse. What is your response to the strategy?

An alternative way to explore attitudes and beliefs is to begin with an open question. If the respondent fails to give an adequate answer, reinforce with probes and follow-ups (similar to an inverted funnel sequence). For example:

What is your attitude about men getting their hair permanented?

Respondents will answer in any number of ways. Some will tell you precisely how they feel and give detailed and specific reasons for their opinion. Others will be vague. A few probes will help this type of respondent verbalize until you get an answer to your question:

(If answer is) *In a way, it's kinda of feminine, but I guess it's okay.*
Q: *What do you mean when you say it's feminine?"* (probe).
A: *Well, it's not what men do ordinarily to their hair.*
Q: *What do you think men ordinarily do to their hair?* (probe).
A: *They just get it cut every once in a while. That's about it, no fuss or muss.*
Q: *I see. Please give me an example of what you think is feminine.* (follow-up).
A: *Well, women go to beauty shops, wear makeup, fussy stuff like that.*
Q: *Do you favor or oppose the practice by men to have their hair permanented?*

Besides multiples for complex questions, multiple items on a single complex issue is also good practice. Schuman and Presser (1981) found that working with a single item on important issues is risky. They recommend more than two items to avoid unpredictable influences of question form, words, and context.

The short and long versions of the question on gun control are multiple items on the same issue. The longer version not only added another dimension to the response, interference with citizens' rights, it also confirmed responses on the first item.

Relevance to Mass Media Writers.   It is generally not practical to ask multiples or multiple items on everything. Limitations of time as well as respondent energy are always considerations. You will need to decide which questions can be asked without having to ease the respondent into the primary question through a series of introductory objective questions, and you will need to decide which questions need multiples to verify respondent consistency. These decisions usually apply to attitude questions and to objective questions when there are no records against which to check the response. Again, rely on the guidelines given and ask the analytic questions in this chapter to help you make decisions.

Probes and follow-ups are a different matter. No decisions necessary here. Just anticipate that you will need them, especially for open questions, and prepare them in advance. Do not assume that respondents will be spontaneous. It is better to assume that they may be shy, reluctant, or evasive, or that their memories may need prodding. A standby of probes and follow-ups manages respondents who are unexpectedly a disappointment.

Never assume, however, that a probe or follow-up is legitimate license to prod a reluctant respondent by being directive. Your probes and follow-ups must be as unbiased as your questions. There is little point in leading the respondent your way when your objective is to learn what the respondent knows or thinks. Researchers recommend only enough prodding to jog the respondent's memory. They suggest that a question requiring too much probing often ends in directive probes from a frustrated interviewer (Cannell & Kahn, 1968; Cannell et al., 1981). There may also be something wrong with the question. A common strategy is to rephrase the question without changing its objective or meaning and to ask it again immediately or in another place during the interview.

Types of probes depend a great deal on the objective of the question, but just to give you more of an idea of what is considered a "neutral" or nondirective probe, here is a list of them:[3]

- *Please tell me more about your thinking on that.*
- *What are other reasons why you feel that way?*
- *You've explained how _____ , but please expand on that a little more.*
- *What do you think?*
- *What do you mean?*
- *How do you mean that?*
- *Which is closer to the way you feel?* (in the event of options).
- Repeat the question or part of the question.
- Rephrase the question without changing its objective or meaning.
- Pause and allow the respondent time to think.

Neutral probes usually work best with general questions, but for specific questions, you may have to use some other techniques. For example, many women are reluctant to reveal their age. In such a case, you might ask if they are within a particular age group, 16-20, 21-29, 30-39, 40-49, and so on. Also, people remember incidents better if given a time frame: *How many house robberies have occurred in your neighborhood since July 4th?*

---

[3]This list is adapted and augmented from a number of probes recommended by researchers at the Survey Research Center, Institute for Social Research, University of Michigan, Ann Arbor, Michigan. Portions of the list may be found in Beed and Stimson (1985, p. 55).

You cannot use probes with any question. For example, if you have to find out if someone was involved in misappropriation of public money, a direct question would be resented, or denied, and probes would not work. A more practical solution is to use a question design containing a series of questions that gets to the heart of the matter indirectly.

ORDER OF QUESTIONS

Beyond constructing each question carefully, the success of your interview rests, as well, on the order in which those questions are placed. One of the issues here is whether the flow of questions should move from general to specific questions or vice versa. That decision depends a great deal on the nature of the questions and the interviewer's purpose. For example, in interviews concerning health or personal habits, sensitive questions are customarily placed toward the end of a questionnaire. Another issue is whether the order of the questions could possibly bias a response on any one question. The best defense against that trap is to be aware of that possibility.

As a general guide, some researchers recommend that topics within a questionnaire be arranged ". . . to make the total interview experience as meaningful as possible, to give it a beginning, a middle and an end" (Cannell & Kahn, 1968, p. 571). In this sense, order also means unity in the questionnaire itself.

To achieve such unity of form, other researchers (Sudman & Bradburn, 1982) suggested a simple preliminary procedure. They recommended putting each question on a separate sheet of paper or an index card. After decision is reached on which questions should be included, questions are shuffled and moved around until the best order is found. "Best" order meaning the questionnaire should have a logical flow, but that no question(s) placed before another should influence an answer to the following question. Remember the order problem Market Strategies found in their questionnaire design for the Bush Presidential campaign (chapter 6)? "Best" order guides the respondent through questions comfortably and in an unbiased, nonthreatening manner and, at the same time, fulfills the purpose of the interview.

Many researchers and media writers agree that an interview should begin with easy, salient, nonthreatening and relevant questions and gradually increase in difficulty. Usually, starting with a general question and moving toward more specific ones minimizes the chance of response errors and gives respondents opportunity for spontaneous response. Opportunity, in turn, communicates to the respondent that he or she is the key figure in the transaction and not the interviewer. Starting with a few general questions also gives the respondent time to reflect and think about the specifics as the interview continues. Objective questions placed toward the end are likely to illicit more accurate responses and sensitive questions seem to be less threatening.

This strategy is by no means a sure-fire guarantee of success. Schuman and Presser (1981) found there are still some problems with respondents who underreport (memory failure) and problems with respondents who overreport (exaggerated response) even when the questions follow a fair order. Their research tentatively suggests that respondents who misreport share certain common characteristics. Reluctant to disappoint the interviewer, misreporters respond, informed or not (social desirability effect). The well educated and those with high interest in the question topic or issue tend to overreport.

One way around misreports, particularly on objective questions, is to check received information against data in your research notes. If your research is lacking, go back to the references and make a check against the records.

Another dimension of question order concerns transitions. Converse and Presser (1986) recommended a "sensible arrangement" of questions to begin with because logical order contributes more than flooding the questionnaire with transitions. They suggested simple transitions at each major topic change, or something more elegant:

- *Now I'm going to ask you some questions about* _____ .
- *Now I have some questions on* _____ .
- *Let's turn to some questions concerning* _____ .

The whole point of a transition is to give the respondent a signal that you are moving into another topic, allowing the respondent to shift gears in preparation for the change.

Relevance to Mass Media Writers.   Clearly, organizing whatever questions you may have is a matter of ordering them in a logical way so that your presentation gets to the heart of the matter without offending or biasing your particular respondent. For example, suppose you have a mix of general and specific questions and some of these, whether general or specific, are of a sensitive nature, questions that might embarrass or enrage the respondent. Rather than risk having the phone slammed in your ear, or the respondent walking out on you, save the touchy questions for last (Mitford, 1979).

Suppose you had some objective questions that seemed more important than the few general questions on your list, it might be better to get the specific questions answered first, as long as they were not of a threatening kind. Suppose you had some general and objective questions, all of them important, ask the general ones first because very often the respondent will answer some of your objective questions in the course of answering the general ones. If by the end of the interview some objective questions are left unanswered, ask them at that time. Try the technique of putting questions down on separate sheets of paper or index cards to organize your questions. Shuffling and rearranging them around will give you a feel for researchers' meanings of logical order and unity of form.

PRETESTING QUESTIONS

Researchers commonly pretest their questionnaires before conducting the actual interviews. It is not usual practice in mass media work. The Ashenfelter-Freedberg team had a pretest of sorts. Following first interviews with families of the dead seamen (chapter 7), they soon discovered flaws in one of their survey questions. Pretests in media work are more often conducted by researchers who conduct surveys for news, public relations, and advertising organizations. They pretest questionnaires with a small sample of respondents before launching a full-scale survey or market research program. Whether the pretest is conducted by a researcher or, on occasion, by a media writer, the purpose of the pretest is to learn:

- Whether planned questions will realize the question's objective.
- If the questions are understood or need rewording, restructuring, probes, follow-ups, or rearranging.
- If certain questions are too difficult or embarrasing.
- If the questionnaire places unrealistic demands on the respondent.
- How the respondent reacts to an advertisement or new product, in the instance of market research or focus group survey.
- How response and/or behavioral reactions to questions vary across respondents.
- How well various interviewers delivered the questions and/or managed the interview.

Although these matters are of more concern to the survey researcher than to the media writer, information concerning them may, for any number of reasons, be of great value to media writers, as it was in the instance of the Navy story.[4]

---

[4]A useful document concerning question pretests is a study by Cannell, Kalton, Oksenberg, and Bischoping (1989).

No matter how carefully a question is structured, only a pretest will reveal whether major revisions are necessary, or if the interviewer needs to correct delivery or personal mannerisms. Sometimes several pretests may be required before a workable series of questions is obtained.

If pretesting seems like a lot of work for what should be intuitive management, consider the findings of one researcher (Belson, 1981). In several experiments, the researcher discovered that the meaning investigators intended for many questions was not the meaning respondents understood. In addition, respondents often failed to hear every word of the question or failed to understand the concepts. Sometimes, when a respondent found it difficult to answer a question, the tendency was to modify the question in such a way as to be able to answer it more easily. For example, *im* in the word *impartial* got lost and the respondent only heard *partial*. The word *impartial* may have been an unfamiliar word for the respondent so that only its familiar portion, *partial* was heard, or the interviewer may have failed to deliver the word clearly. Converse and Presser (1986) believe these mishaps occur because respondents think they have heard the question correctly, or they transform questions into structures that are meaningful to them as they strain for understanding to answer the question.

If you do conduct a pretest, it is helpful to know that it need not include all the planned questions, perhaps only important objective and general ones. Nor, is it necessary to pretest with dozens of people. Colleagues and family members are usually willing to oblige, and they are close enough in kind to the people the newswriter, for example, would be interviewing. The PR and advertising writer might do the same for exploratory purposes on some project. To evaluate such a pretest, look for:[5]

- A question you had to repeat.
- A question that was misinterpreted.
- A question that was hard for you to say.
- A question that evoked a frown, look of puzzlement, or discomfort.
- A question that caused a phone respondent to pause, gasp, or falter.
- Points where the respondent seemed bored, tired, or disinterested.
- Points in the questioning that seemed to drag.
- Plus any other reactions you noticed in the course of the pretest.

Even though you may have taken great pains with a question, a pretest will reveal some surprising information about how people hear questions and assume unintended meanings, or how you have handled the questions and/or the interview. You will then appreciate the value of taking time to pretest questions before going to an actual interview.

---

[5]This list was adapted and augmented from recommendations made by Converse and Presser (1986, p. 72).

REALIZATIONS AND CERTAINTIES

The few techniques revealed here are only part of the complexities involved in structuring productive questions. But these few are some of the important ones and will help you develop an awareness of their importance, especially in media work. After all, the business of media is asking questions, in and out of interview situations.

Perhaps you feel that no matter how you structure an interview question, there is every chance it will be misunderstood. If so, you are right. On the other hand, that possibility does not negate your responsibility to design a question with all the critical attention it demands.

Perhaps you have the sense that question design is an odd mix of artful approach and systematically based findings, most of which are inconclusive, at best. If so, you are right again. Question design is not yet a science, but neither is it all just art. Davis (1964) pointed out that if question design is seen as an art, it is more like architecture than sculpture or painting. This suggests that, like architecture where there is reliance on tested guidelines for durable materials, sound structure, and compatible design, there is also need for reliance on tested guidelines when designing questions. Although these guidelines are not set in stone, they represent fairly certain reference points by which question designers can measure their structural handiwork.

If nothing else, the guidelines given in this chapter will raise your awareness of the complexities involved in question design. Refer to the following checklist to test your interview questions:

SUMMARY OF EVALUATION QUERIES FOR INTERVIEW QUESTIONS

How to ask and words and meanings:
- *What exactly do I want this respondent to tell me?*
- *What are the facts and/or details I need to know about this issue or event from this respondent?*
- *Would this respondent have the answer?*
- *What answer might this respondent give?*
- *Do I use simple, precise, unbiased words to achieve the question's objective?*
- *What words may be unfamiliar, too general or ambiguous, or imply connotations that could defeat the purpose of the question or might trigger the wrong images in this respondent's mind?*
- *What word adjustments and clarifications are needed to improve contextual meaning in order to project the purpose of this question?*

Question length and type:
- *Does my question contain more than one concept, issue, or meaning?*
- *Does this question require a frame of reference? If so, does the question adequately prepare the respondent?*
- *Is the issue or event recent enough for the respondent to recall the information needed?*
- *What cues must I provide to aid recall?*
- *Is the respondent concerned enough or interested enough in the issue or event to give a complete and accurate answer?*
- *If not, what words and phrases are needed to impress question importance on the respondent, to arouse interest, and/or to aid recall?*

Question form and sequence:
- *What question type and design (open, closed, funnel, etc.) will achieve the objective of this question with this respondent and evoke an adequate and accurate response?*

Options and balance:
- *Does my question permit optional choice in agree/disagree questions?*
- *Does my question permit a counterargument?*

Five Ws and how:
- *Do my questions begin with one of the W or how words?*

Multiple items, probes, and follow-ups:
- *Does any question call for a multiple item?*
- *Does any question design call for probes, follow-ups?*

Order of questions:
- *Does my questionnaire guide the respondent through questions comfortably and in an unbiased, non-directive manner and, at the same time, fulfill the interview purpose?*
- *Do I provide an appropriate transition between question subjects?*

These critical self-inquiries will remind you that a question is more than just a statement that ends in a question mark. Before structuring interview questions ask Critical Self-Inquiry 5: *What do I need to ask who about what and how shall I ask it?*

Having a set of solid questions is part of planning the interview. Getting the interview and managing it are the next steps in the interview function of your operational strategy, and those are the topics of discussion in the next chapter.

9 Conducting the Interview

This is where research and verification pay off again. Because you have researched the problem, verified the data, internalized it, and are now armed with thoughtfully designed questions, you will be able to recognize errors and inadequacies in respondents' answers. Moreover, you will be able to play off the research to keep the respondent on track. Research goes a long way, but you cannot depend on research entirely. Interviews must be held to obtain:

- Current information about the problem.
- Verification or clarification of what you already know.
- Explanations about contradictions, mismatches, controversies, gaps, etc., in the data.
- Comments from respondents concerning their solutions for or attitudes and opinions about the problem.
- A measurement for evaluating response validity.

Chapters 7 and 8 covered the first four items. The last one is the focus of this chapter and concerns conducting the interview in a manner that defends against failure. To ensure at least a minimum of success:

- Know the research data well enough to recognize invalidity (incomplete, inadequate, less-than-truth responses).
- Rely on tested interview techniques that provide some measurement for anticipating invalidity and counteracting with correctives.

Discussion here concerns getting ready for the interview and conducting it in a manner to reduce the failure factor. That is, you review the data once more in order to manage the interview, and as you listen to the respondent you will know what to do next when this question runs through your mind: *How complete, how true is this respondent's information?*

To prepare for skillful management of an interview, rely on Critical Self-Inquiry 6: *What data, prepared questions, and interview techniques must I review in order to identify inadequate and/or inaccurate responses and to raise impromptu questions?*

Professional media writers say they review everything, not once or twice, but several times. They read and reread the data until it is thoroughly internalized. Only then, they say, are respondents' inaccuracies, deceptions, or equivocations heard.

Once you feel you have a handle on the data, review the questions scheduled for a particular respondent. Go over those portions of the data that relate to the questions. Try to imagine both positive and negative ways the respondent might answer. Then mentally prepare or write down probes and follow-up questions to induce an adequate answer. Think about some answers that might not square with your information, or would elicit a challenge. Then fall back on related and other data to phrase a question to overcome the discrepancy. For reassurance, add these to your interview plan in case these expectancies materialize. To effect this process, try an internal dialogue like this (regarding the hypothetical concerning industrial waste discharges into the Great Lakes):

If the respondent says, "But we've had no discharge violations issued against us," then I'll just refer to _____ , and ask, "How do you explain the fact that records of the State Environmental Agency show 22 counts of violation against your company this year alone?" If the answer is that the records are wrong, I'll refer to other records that agree with state documents and ask why there's so much discrepancy between company records and all these other documents.

The object is to know your collected research well enough to respond competently to anomalies and incompletes in information you are trying to get. Rehearse probes and follow-ups. Then during the interview keep the interaction going until you score. If all this sounds like a sparring match, sometimes it is. Newswriters often face some tough customers. PR writers occasionally experience confrontations with the press. Advertising writers, too, have their moments of conflict. Although interviews in advertising are relatively informal and agency personnel are usually cooperative, there are tense moments when interview skills help sell an idea to the editor, artist, or account executive and, in some instances, to the client. The goal is to be knowledgeable, frank, and courteous, not argumentive in either word or tone.

WHAT "TO INTERVIEW" MEANS

The encounter does not have to be a sparring match, not if you know your stuff and know how to get around obstacles. Then it becomes less combative and more a game of skill. And that is how we will look at the interview process in this chapter, as a game of skill with all its features: players, rules, fouls, remedies, and rewards.

Unfortunately, in mass media agreed upon "rules" or standards by which to judge a successful interview do not exist. Of course, there are personal accounts by professional writers. These are always interesting and insightful, but novices need more specific rules to play the game of interviewing. Even though replicated studies of interviews conducted by mass media writers are rare, such work concerning the techniques of survey interviewing do exist in the literature of social and behavioral science.

However, the means and ends of interviewing vary in different areas of life. For example, the medical interview between doctor and patient is not the same as the job interview between employer and candidate. Nor does the journalistic interview resemble either situation or the interview between survey researcher and respondent. Still, these and other similar interview settings have several things in common: The interviewer is the information seeker; the respondent is the information giver; all interviewers have to deal with difficult respondents.

For example, in doctor-patient interviews, patients want to disclose their personal medical history so the doctor can diagnose their illness, but some patients are unable to recall dates, incidents, past medications, and similar medical data. The job candidate wants to reveal all positive qualifications necessary to land the job, but may withhold information about a drinking problem. The survey respondent, who agrees to be interviewed, usually tries to answer the question, but is subject to memory lapse. The newswriter faces hostile respondents whose every intention is to conceal information. The PR and advertising writer may occasionally confront hostility and concealment for any number of reasons.

For media writers and any other interviewer, preparation is the key. The media writer must know almost as much as the respondent and have a fair idea of how much the respondent is able to disclose. Thus, the commonality among all these interview situations is that interviewers aim to elicit what the respondent does know, and that is where all these situations, particularly the journalistic interview, can benefit from relevant literature in the social and behavioral sciences.

Characteristics of the Interview

Some psychologists look at the interview as a game of skill between two people (Higgins, McCann, & Fondacaro, 1982). In a sense, the analogy is an apt one. The interview is an exchange between two people that has many characteristics of the game: specific roles, rules, designated areas of play, goal achievement strategies, fouls, recoveries, and rewards.

However, in a media interview, instead of just one winner and one loser, there can be two winners or two losers. There are two winners when the game ends satisfactorily for both parties, mainly because the interviewer was able to evoke adequate answers from a shy, confused, or reluctant respondent. There are two losers when either the initiator of the game (the interviewer) or the receiver (the interviewee) violates the rules, or the interviewer is unable to draw out the respondent.

Moreover, media writers should not play the game of communication to win or "defeat" the interviewee. Where athletes use standardized strategies to prevent their opponent from scoring and winning, media writers use tested strategies to help respondents achieve the mutual reward of a successful interview. The media writer's aim is, or should be, to play an "even game"; that is, to fill in the gaps left by research and to produce a winning result for both parties in the communication game. Keeping these differences in mind, the comparison of interviews to a game is a useful analogy for the similarities that are present.

In a somewhat different vein, social scientists view interviewing in less dramatic terms: The interview is a conversation for the purpose of obtaining information. Survey scientists add still another dimension: The interview is also a means of measurement (Cannell & Kahn, 1968). That is more easily done in science research than in media work. But measurement is not beyond the reach of novice writers if they know something about the standards of interviewing and making judgments about it.

For our purposes, the game analogy fits definitions in both social and behavioral science so that we can now talk about two players who have particular roles and learn about rules in order to recognize when violations are made and what amends are appropriate. Roles, rules, and recoveries also contain the clues necessary for measuring the quality of the play. So begin your understanding of the game by learning the responsibilities of the players.

Roles and Rules

It is the interviewer's place to initiate the game, to encourage accurate and full responses, and to listen carefully and use remedial techniques if the response is inadequate, inaccurate, or evasive. The basic role of the respondent is to receive and answer the question as completely and accurately as possible. The interaction continues, but it is always the interviewer who acts as initiator and keeps the action moving.

The literature of cognitive science makes both initiator and receiver responsible for an "even game." That is, communicators should (Higgins, 1981, p. 348):

- Take the recipient's characteristics into account.
- Convey the truth as they see it.
- Try to be understood (to be coherent and comprehensible).
- Give neither too much nor too little information.
- Produce a message that is appropriate to their communicative intent or purpose.

You learned about the means to apply these principles in chapters 7 and 8, so let's assume you have met these rules of the game. For their part, message recipients should (Higgins, 1981, p. 348):

- Take the communicator's characteristics into account.
- Determine the communicative intent or purpose.
- Take the context and circumstances into account.
- Pay attention to the message and be prepared to receive it.
- Try to understand the message.
- When possible, provide feedback to the communicator concerning interpretation or understanding of the message.

It would be nice if respondents met these criteria of communication, but even the author of the rules admits respondents may live up to only a portion, or none, of these criteria. After examining the results of many experiments concerning response adequacy, survey scientists are now inclined to place principal burden for an evenly played game on the initiator. Interviewers are, therefore, not only initiators, they are also vigilant evaluators of the game and responsible for correctives to assist the receiver. Although survey scientists generally agree with cognitive psychologists about the rules for communicators, they see the role of the receiver as purely voluntary. The communicator is at the whim and fancy of the recipient. To save the communicator from being either manipulative or a "willy-nilly" interviewer, social scientists at the Institute for Social Research (ISR) add that communicators should also:[1]

- Describe the purpose of the interview in terms likely to be meaningful to the respondent.
- Treat the respondent with a reasonable amount of warmth and interest.
- Indicate directly and approvingly those responses that are relevant and complete.
- Let the respondent know when the response is irrelevant or fragmentary.

Aside from roles and rules, interview setting and method of communication are also important elements in the communication. That is, on whose grounds the game should be played, in what setting, and whether the interview is to be conducted face-to-face or by telephone. These details should be settled before the interview takes place.

The Place

For the media game, the receiver's home base is usually the best location. The interviewer has an opportunity to observe the receiver's environment, to note personal objects of interest, choices in surroundings, including people. All these are clues to personality and values. Such information is important for newswriters, sometimes for PR and advertising writers. For example, an advertising writer may want to know whether a client is a traditionalist or nonconformist in order to meld assignment requirements and client preferences together. Observation of office decor and certain personals added to the established design is a window on some of those preferences.

But not all interviews can be held at the preferred location. Newswriters catch respondents on the run. PR and advertising writers often conduct informal interviews in office hallways, over lunch, or during a coffee break. So the field of play is wherever the respondent agrees to conduct the game. The same holds true for the method of communication.

Face-to-face interviews allow observation of facial and body expressions and permit more opportunities for interviewer evaluation and correction than do phone interviews. Again, a one-on-one is not always possible and the telephone is a fair substitute, especially when time is a factor. But because you are asking respondents to give up a chunk of their valuable

---

[1]This list represents an adaptation and distillation of recommendations which may be found in Cannell and Kahn (1968); Cannell et al. (1981); and Kahn and Cannell (1957).

time, allow them to make the choice. Compliance to respondent needs may prove to be a deciding factor in whether you are able to schedule an interview.

Depending on what you need and when, a phone session is no less effective than a one-on-one session. Survey researcher Dillman (1978) has found that both face-to-face and phone interviews score fairly evenly on dimensions such as response rate and response adequacy. However, Dillman is quick to say that this does not mean they are "equal," only that each vehicle has as many advantages and disadvantages as the other.

Dillman's studies were done some time ago and there is some evidence that survey researchers today are having difficulty with scheduling willing respondents for either face-to-face or phone interviews. Escalating crime rates, invasion of privacy by phone solicitors, and the like, appear to be part of the reason for phone interview refusals (Cannell, 1985b). That trend may not apply to media writers in every instance, but it is a factor to consider if respondents other than familiar contacts are interviewed. The unavoidable fact is that the final decision is a mutually subjective one controlled mainly by the needs of the assignment, time limitation, and often cost.

Scheduling the Interview

Because decisions about the location of the interview and the means of communication depend on mutual decision, with first choices given to the respondent to encourage consent, try to reach the prospective respondent personally. You may be sidetracked by a secretary. In either case, follow a procedure similar to the one introduced in chapter 3 and repeated here:

- Give your name and whom you represent.
- Explain why you want the interview.
- Give reasons why you contacted this person and for what purpose.
- Give the candidate an idea of how much time the interview will consume.
- Allow choice of several places (respondent's home court first) and the means.

Suppose you were working on the project concerning pollution in the Great Lakes and wanted to schedule an appointment with one of the state senators who wrote the Great Lakes Clean Water Bill, Your phone request might be something as formal or less formal than this:

Senator _____, my name is _____, I'm a reporter with the _____ news agency. We're planning on doing a story concerning pollution in the Great Lakes. Because you're one of the authors of amendments to the Clean Water bill, we felt you'd want to respond to recent lobbying by _____ Industries to block your efforts. The interview would take take no more than 20 minutes. Could we arrange to meet in your office at your convenience before the end of the week? Or, if you prefer, I could ask you some questions now.

You will either get a future appointment for an office or phone session, an interview at the time of your call, or a turn down. If the latter, don't let go, say:

I understand, but is there someone else you could refer me to?

If you get a substitute name (which you should check out before contacting that person) say:

If I have a question that only you can clarify, may I call you again regarding it?

If you get a flat turn down, don't get mad, say:

I see. My intention is to talk to Mr. _____ at _____ Industries. I'll get back to you after that and perhaps you'd like to schedule an appointment at that time.

Different words for different situations, but the format and general routine works across the board for news, PR, and advertising writers. The point is, you try to get the respondent you want, but if that does not work, get a reasonable replacement from the refuser, and if that does not work, don't get testy, just work around the reluctant candidate and get another appropriate contact.

Rehearsals and Equipment

It cannot be said too often, for an even win you must be prepared to play well. Partners in a game expect top performance from the other participant. Partners in an interview expect as much from one another. In either case, preparation is the key. You may rightfully say that you have researched your subject thoroughly, know who you need to talk to, and thought out carefully phrased questions, what more? Review and rehearse. If your reaction is: "What! Review my notes again?" Yes, again.

Let me remind you, media writers review their work over and over. So do artists. Mel Gibson, the Australian actor who made a hit in American action movies, recently took on a more serious role in the movie version of

Hamlet. During a television interview in which Barbara Walters probed into both Gibson's professional and personal life, Walters asked Gibson how many times he had read Shakespeare's difficult play. Gibson answered that he had read and studied it carefully up to 30 times and could recite on call any one of Hamlet's speaking parts from memory. When asked to select one, Gibson easily drew four lines from the middle of one of Hamlet's long soliloquies addressed to his mother, the queen. But in this instance, Gibson directed the selected lines to Walters which he apparently felt were appropriate in the context of this interview:

> O most pernicious woman!
> O villain, villain, smiling, damned villain!
> My tables, — met it is I set it down,
> That one may smile, and smile, and be a villain. (Act I, Scene V, lines 105-108)

Gibson delivered the lines in the spirit of poking fun at a persistent interviewer and Walters accepted them in the same spirit. Of course, your interview is not a Shakespearean drama, but the point here is that if you intend to perform well, on demand, and appropriately in any situation, review and rehearse. So, before leaving for the interview:

- Review the data.
- Review, once more, areas of research related to questions planned.
- Practice delivery of questions prepared for the scheduled respondent.
- Rehearse techniques designed to overcome anticipated holes in responses.

Delivery means practicing out loud so you can hear the places that need emphasis, inflection, and rhythmic phrasing. Internalization and rehearsal prepare you for the construction of:

- Substantive follow-up questions for unpredictable responses.
- Nondirective, but content-related probes to activate respondents' unexpected memory lapses.
- Appropriate statements and questions to contradictions and other responses that fail to square with the research.
- Knowledgeable comments about information given by respondents which demonstrate agreement with other research sources and where it serves the purpose of encouraging respondents to continue the exchange.

Moreover, review work contributes to crisp, knowledge-based delivery, reinforces your competence as a communicator, and reassures the respondent that you know what you are talking about. Because you have done your homework, the respondent, in most instances, is motivated to meet the objective of questions asked. You may also discover that the respondent wants to continue the interview beyond the agreed upon time. The general mood after such a session is one of exhilaration for both participants. It is the occasion when there are two winners and that is the mutual reward.

Aside from reviewing your research and questions, be prepared to take notes and to tape. Gather your tools and check to see if they work before the interview takes place. If you do tape, face-to-face or via the phone, you are obliged to ask the respondent's permission. Taping ensures against noting respondent messages erroneously. On the other hand, audio recorders are unreliable and taking hand notes as a backup is a safeguard against mechanical failure. Furthermore, the fact that you are taking notes reassures respondents that points made by them are getting across. Portable word processors are popular with their users, but chances of mechanical failure are just as high, so is the risk of misplacement or theft. In any case, do take hand notes.

If the respondent talks faster than you can write, use some delay tactics. Hold up your hand to indicate need for a slow down. Or, even when you understand the explanation, but want to catch up, say: *I'm not sure I understand what you mean, Mr. _____ . Please clarify that for me.* Then continue noting as the respondent goes on.

A final point about preparation is dress. Attribution theory in social psychology declares that in some personal encounters individuals recall impressions of appearance and behavior of the other party more easily than they recall content of the encounter (Schneider, Hastorf, & Ellsworth, 1979; Snyder, 1981a, 1981b). Whether inappropriate dress has a negative effect on the respondent is not known, but studies do suggest any interviewer can fall victim to a poor first impression by dressing inappropriately. More often, it is the subject of the question and not the interviewer that seems to influence respondents' answers (Bradburn & Sudman, 1981; Hagenaars & Heinen, 1982). Play it safe. Consider the interview setting, respondent, and question subject to determine the level of conservatism or informalism necessary and dress accordingly.

TECHNIQUES OF THE SKILLED INTERVIEWER

Individual interviewers have their own ideas about what constitutes interviewing skill. However, in systematic experiments to test response adequacy, survey scientists have found that at least three principal factors must figure in the effort to obtain complete and accurate responses: cognition, accessibility, and motivation.

In replicated studies with thousands of respondents, ISR researchers found underreporting was related to elapsed time between the reported event and the interview, salience of topic and events under question, and respondents' perceptions of the social desirability of their responses to question subject matter. It should be no surprise to anyone that details of events fade in the memory, that respondents do not respond well to subjects of little interest to them, or that they are reluctant to talk about subjects that could diminish their image or reputation. But having had some confirmation of the common wisdom, researchers were now able to go on and learn how to encourage a confused or reluctant respondent. Ongoing experiments led ISR researchers (Cannell & Kahn, 1968; Cannell et al., 1981) to conclude that a successful interview results when the interviewer is able to (a) create a comfortable interview *climate*, (b) stimulate *cognition* of the objective, (c) provide *accessibility* to an adequate and accurate response, and (d) *motivate* response. Here's how it works. The interviewer:

- Opens the interview with an appropriate introduction or "warm-up" (climate, cognition, motivation).
- Explains reasons for conducting the interview (climate, cognition, motivation).
- Obtains commitment for effort from the respondent (climate, cognition, motivation).
- Creates a task-oriented rather than a socially oriented mood and supplies necessary instructions (climate, accessibility, cognition, motivation).
- Delivers questions slowly and with proper phrasing and inflection, necessary context and memory aids (accessibility, cognition, motivation).
- Provides reinforcement and feedback (accessibility, cognition, motivation).

Relevance to Mass Media Writers. These characteristics of a successful interview are examined in the sections that follow. They are presented as a means of assisting respondents who cannot or do not choose to play the respondent's role. The standards given come from studies in survey techniques and are useful as a measure of what systematic study has shown works with difficult respondents. Survey researchers encounter the same kind of people as media writers do and, despite the differences between them, they share a similar purpose: to elicit adequate and accurate information.

Opening Protocol

Participants in any game cannot be expected to play well without first being informed about the rules of the game. The same concept applies to interviewing. However, in mass media, there are no standard rules, including those that concern opening rituals Most media writers have learned the rules by trial and error, or bumbling willy-nilly through the game of give-and-take. After testing various methods of approach over a number of years with thousands of respondents, ISR researchers (Cannell & Kahn, 1968; Cannell et al., 1981) concluded that response quality is heightened if interviewers follow a protocol for the interview by recognizing the participant, setting a tone of legitimacy for the interview, providing assurances of protection, and then defining what is expected of that person. You can follow those recommendations by opening the interview in the following sequence:

1. Interviewer identifies him or herself.
2. Establishes the legitimacy and value of the interview to the respondent.
3. Explains the process by which the respondent was chosen.
4. Explains what protection the respondent can expect.
5. Explains what is expected of the respondent (instructions)

Relevance to Mass Media Writers.   This protocol corresponds fairly closely to suggestions made earlier about scheduling the interview. Such a routine sets the stage, establishes interview relevancy and role expectations, and gives the respondent an opportunity to warm up for the task ahead. Coming into the presence of the respondent, you acknowledge the respondent, re-introduce yourself and re-establish your legitimacy by repeating the name of the organization you represent, the reasons why this respondent was chosen and why you are there.

Of course, you choose respondents, not by any random process, but with considerable thought and reliance on their willingness to participate. Nevertheless, you offer respondents protection when you seek permission to tape and/or to quote. By repeating the purpose of the interview and explaining the contribution you feel respondents are able to make, you are instructing them about their responsibilities to the game. At the same time, you are introducing the "rules" and providing appropriate warm-up time so respondents can perform well.

How might an opening protocol sound like in a journalistic setting? For a **newswriter**, perhaps something like this:

Good morning Senator _____ . *I'm* _____ *from* _____ *and I appreciate having this opportunity to talk to you. Do you have any objection to having this interview taped?* (answers yes or no).

Also, please let me know when you do not wish a comment attributed to you, otherwise everything said will go on the record. Does this meet with your approval? (introduction, permission, offer of protection).

Because you're one of the authors of the amendments to the Clean Water Bill, I'm sure you understand we're anxious to hear your comments about the recent campaign launched against your effort by _____ Industries. (legitimacy and value of interview).

The questions I will ask you involve two major issues in their campaign. One issue concerns their claim that they never exceed their waste quota, and the other is that the bill singles out their company and ignores other companies (instructions, frame of reference).

Let me begin with the first issue by asking: _____ ? (transition).

For a **public relations** writer:

Hi Stan. I'm _____ from the Consumer Service Division of Customer Relations. Thanks very much for seeing me. If you agree, I'd like to tape in order to get this down accurately. Is that okay? I don't believe I'll need to attribute any of this to you, but in case I do, do you have any objection to that? Now, you've followed development and production of the XL 200 from its first design stage to final production, so I hope you can help us with this. You know we've been getting some complaints about gear slippage on the XL 200 and that's what I want to talk to you about. If you would answer the questions as specifically and completely as possible, it will help me understand this problem better. The complaint we hear most is that _____ . Why _____ ?

For an **advertising** writer:

Note: Advertising writers rarely interview with persons other than their editor, artist, and account executive. No formal introductions are needed for such contacts because most problems are ironed out during team meetings. However, in large agencies with test kitchens, research libraries, and similar in-house departments, an editor or account executive will recommend further digging with such sources. Or, they will recommend an interview with outside researchers who worked on a survey concerning test runs of a product or focus groups that had tested a projected TV commercial, etc. In such instances, the opening protocol might be something like this:

Hello, Ms. _____ , I'm _____ of _____ . Thanks for taking the time to talk to me. I want to be sure to get this down accurately so is it okay if I tape? It's not likely we'll need to use your agency's name, but in case the client wants to reference your agency as the research group, would you have any objection to that? What I want to discuss are the results of the market research your company did on the _____ . My questions will refer specifically to the data on _____ . I'm just a novice with research reports, so if you would please answer questions with precise and complete information a layperson like myself can understand, I'd appreciate it. For example, I'm not sure what you mean when you say "_____." Was that a function of _____ or of _____ ?

Essentially, the opening protocol is a means of setting the mood for the game by providing the respondent with an appropriate frame of reference from which to play out his or her particular role. Without getting too familiar, acknowledging the respondent and expressing thanks for relinquishing precious time provides just enough rapport in the opening protocol to establish the tone for a task-oriented encounter. In addition, instructions cue the respondent on the type of information and performance required. These along with respondent agreement about conditions of the interview establish a respondent's willingness to live up to the task.

Instructions are not necessarily confined to the opening protocol. They can accompany a change in the topic or an instruction may be phrased to fit the need of a particular question. For example, to help respondents think of total time spent watching TV the night before, an instruction would ask the respondent to think of each program viewed that night, and if an exact date is required of a question, the respondent is instructed to give an exact date.

Commitment, too, is an important element. Obtaining permission to interview and quote is one thing, but obtaining commitment is quite another. Commitment means the interviewee agrees to perform a specific task. In the case of some sensitive or difficult problem, you may simply ask for overt agreement that the respondent try very hard to answer questions completely and accurately. For instance, a respondent may find it difficult to answer questions about such topics as sex, personal health, job loss, or charges of negligence. You might begin by saying: *I know this is not easy for you, but just take your time and answer as honestly and completely as you can.* Or, in the case where some product is still under test, or an issue is still unresolved, you might preface your questions by saying: *I realize you don't have all the answers yet, but please try to tell me as much as you can about _____.*

Sociologists have found that commitment induces goal-related activity even in instances that would otherwise discourage effort, and the principle of commitment is frequently used as a theoretical concept of predictive behavior in the literature of social psychology (Aronson, 1980).

The success of the interview may depend entirely on the opening protocol. In fact, survey scientists have found that when this formality is ignored, response faults are common, a matter covered in the sections that follow.

The Issue of Rapport

Before leaving the subject of opening protocol, reference to the controversial issue of rapport should be made. As discussed in earlier chapters, most professional writers encourage a conversational manner and small talk. Those who know about interpersonal relationships recommend the same (Brady, 1976; Donaldson, 1979; Higgins, Kuiper, & Olson, 1981; Mitford, 1979; Walters, 1970). The small talk may include mention of the respondent's personal interests, family members, achievements, or an unfortunate incident, and the like. The rationale for this is that personalized treatment will evoke disclosure.

Rapport is a central concept in many studies, either as a desirable tactic to achieve cooperation, or as a criterion of the degree of mutual purpose achieved. However, other researchers have extensively documented the concept of rapport as too ambiguous to be of any value (Hagenaars & Heinen, 1982). And ISR researchers have found personalized interaction has its limits (Henson, Cannell, & Lawson, 1973).

They conducted experiments to learn whether a personal interactive style was necessary and if respondents performed as well in a task-oriented interview. They worked with a sample of persons who had suffered bodily injury in an automobile accident which had occurred within a 3-year period of the study. Half the sample was given a rapport-type interview. Interviewers made personal references, displayed positiveness, smiled, nodded, and made supportive comments. The other half was interviewed stressing interview goals. No socializing was permitted by the task-oriented interviewers.

The results showed no difference in completeness, but the task-oriented group reported more accurate accounts of the accident and their injuries. After the experiment, respondents from both groups were asked about their reactions to the interview. Those in the rapport group were somewhat more likely to report that they felt comfortable responding because the interviewer was businesslike, yet supportive, and because the interaction was managed professionally and revolved around the topic. However, neither group expressed negative feelings about one or the other treatment. Based on these findings, the researchers abandoned a rapport style that became too familiar and initiated techniques akin to the rapport techniques previously outlined, but within the bounds of a businesslike approach. They focused, instead, on performance of the response task rather than on a personalized approach.

Relevance to Mass Media Writers.   Busy people appreciate a businesslike manner. And because a task-oriented interview encourages accuracy, that approach will probably serve the information seeker's objectives more satisfactorily than a chatty one. Besides, even the person who has time to spare is neither flattered nor fooled by manipulative tactics. A little may be alright, but too much is likely to sour the respondent and sow doubts about the interviewer's professionalism. The point is to know your interviewee well enough to indicate you are aware of who you are talking to. Also, that you have done your homework on both the respondent and the problem at hand. That kind of management will help you avoid stepping over the line of professionalism into intimacy. This does not mean the interviewer should be cold and detached. In fact, one can be friendly, courteous, conversational, make a few comments that will interest the respondent, and still focus on a task-oriented interview. But, none of the former elements should outweigh the latter.

Interviewer Fouls and Remedies

Much of survey research indicates that response errors occur mainly because of fouls committed by interviewers, and that most errors stem from bad questions, failure in the opening protocol, absence of nondirective probes, lack of feedback, or poor delivery.

ISR researchers studied the encouragement effect of simple verbal reinforcements such as *uh-huh, hmmm, all right, I see, that's useful, good, we're interested in details like these*, and after a difficult question, *thanks, we appreciate your effort*. Although studies since the 1950s and 1960s demonstrated verbal reinforcement encourages verbalization, ISR researchers wanted to see if reinforcement was a source of interview bias. They also tested feedback that indicates to the respondent that a better answer is needed (sometimes referred to as "negative" feedback): *You answered that quickly. Could you think about it again? That's only two things, can you think of two more?* Or, *Let's look at this once more. Tell me why* _____ . The researchers found these types of feedback tell the respondent that you are not accepting everything just said and a better answer is required. Their experiment included instructions and feedback (both positive and negative), also probes after responses to feedback cues: *Was there anything else?*

After multiple studies over a period of time with more than 2,000 respondents, ISR researchers (Cannell, Fowler, & Marquis, 1968; Cannell et al., 1981; Marquis & Cannell, 1969) concluded that interviewers obtain more complete and accurate reporting when using a standard of approach that includes an opening protocol, instructions, commitment, probes, and feedback.

Relevance to Mass Media Writers.   If these recommendations suggest structure to you, you got it right. But that does not mean you handle the structure in a militant way. With the right words in the right places, a businesslike approach, friendly voice, and nonevaluative manner, such an interview can become quite informal and conversational. How does one do that?

- Consider the objectives and fashion the words to suit the question and the respondent's needs.
- Exercise sensitivity to the respondent's apparent position of being questioned, the effort required and the difficulties involved.
- Refer to the examples in this chapter and chapters 7 and 8 and substitute the interview situation related to the assignment you have in mind, then rehearse it.

Pace, Voice, and Summaries

Questions delivered at machine-gun speed and a voice that sounds like sandpaper are two other factors that can reduce response quality despite appropriate preparation and approach. Observation of interviewer styles at ISR revealed that nearly all interviewers went through questions, probes, and feedback too quickly. The end result was an atmosphere of urgency and impersonality. So interviewers were trained to ask questions slowly and with proper phrasing and inflection. The recommended pace was an average of two words per second. Interviewers were also trained to pause before a probe, giving respondents time to internalize the question and find an answer as they flicked through their mental filing systems (Cannell et al., 1981).

The time it takes for a respondent to carry out this cognitive process is still another reason why the interviewer must try to stick to the facts in the question and avoid irrelevancies. Respondents may not be able to eliminate those irrelevancies from the basics and you risk getting a response you did not want.

Regarding voice, are you receptive to a shrill, high-pitched tone or a middle-range and pleasant tone? Then why speak in a voice that would scare off your mother? Is your attention maintained by a montone or a voice with some variation in it? Then why sound like a robot? Would you cooperate with a person who delivered a hostile challenge or a challenge that projected understanding that another answer might be possible? Even though you verified your information, why get testy and assume the respondent is dead wrong? Further verification may prove the respondent was dead wrong, but verification may also prove the respondent had a point.

The technique of summary is an additional aid to the receiver and often works in favor of the initiator, as well. At each transitional point, it is a good tactic to review what has been covered before going on to the next body of questions. This gives the respondent some feedback on whether you have received responses accurately. If you have not understood a response, corrections can take place at the time of review. A summary also serves to remind the respondent about information originally overlooked. A summarization might sound something like this:

Mr. _____, we've just discussed the problem of _____ and you've explained that _____. Also that _____. Is there anything else you'd like to add? (If yes, note it; if no:) *Then let me continue with some questions concerning _____.*

In studies conducted at ISR, researchers found that feedback of this kind as well as others discussed below improved both adequacy and accuracy of responses (Cannell et al., 1981).

Relevance to Mass Media Writers. Preparation, correctives, pace, delivery, and summaries do not guarantee satisfactory results. They just reduce the possibility of failure. Interviewing is uncertain and unstable and requires constant balancing if the objective is to end in an "even play." So don't throw in the towel just yet. Keep at it. Skillfully managed techniques can improve the game. Just remember, even competent interviewers commit fouls and so do receivers. In either case, it is the interviewer who restores equilibrium by executing remedies for fouls played on either side of the field of play.

Interviewee Fouls and Remedies

The interviewer can also "lose" because of fouls commited by the interviewee: resistance, suppression of information or misinformation to protect self-esteem (social desirability), anxiety, and lapses of attention and memory. We have already discussed remedies for a few of these:

- Thoughtfully designed questions.
- Carefully worded questions.
- Frames of reference and other techniques to aid recall.
- Re-establishing interview purpose, respondent role, and commitment.
- Sensitivity to the respondent and offering both positive and negative feedback.
- Follow-ups and nondirective probes.

Resistance is a frequent foul, especially in news work, even after the respondent commits to the task. Threatening topics stir up resisting forces too powerful for the respondent to overcome. The interviewer must then either restore equilibrium or accept the respondent's refusal to continue. One way to restore balance is to call on motivational techniques touched upon earlier:

- Contribution of the interview to the goals of the respondent.
- Contribution of the respondent to solution of a problem.
- Gratification derived from making such a contribution.
- Satisfaction derived from the interview as an interpersonal experience.

Another approach is to postpone the question to a later time in the interview. The relationship with the respondent may need a little more time to develop in order to reduce the respondent's anxiety level.

You learned earlier that anxiety is usually a function of the question topic. Sometimes the respondent feels a sense of inadequacy. It happens even with the most knowledgeable people. A great deal of evidence demonstrates that shyness, self-esteem, and lack of communication skills are significantly associated to apprehension and a chronic tendency to avoid or devalue oral communication. One study indicates communication anxiety is also due to expectations of negative outcomes due to inability to identify or engage in behaviors that would bring about desired results (Greene & Sparks, 1983).

Inattention is another receiver problem. Although there is a lack of agreement about what constitutes listening, cognitive psychologists believe listeners have no more than a 10-20 minute attention span. Also, that attentiveness and recall ability are directly related to the importance of the topic to the respondent (Bostrom, Ray, & Coyle, 1989).

The importance and recency of a topic is a pivotal factor in respondent attentiveness. Respondents are even more attentive if the topic somehow touches their own lives. Yet, this feature cannot always be cranked into every question, so the best defense against the respondent's inattention is to listen carefully to each answer. If the respondent fails to meet the question's objective, the initiator should repeat the question: *I see, but I'm interested in* _____ .

The same tactic can be used on the respondent who gets off the track, the one who goes on and on about everything and forgets to answer the question: *That's interesting, however,* (then repeat the question, but this time rephrase it in another way).

Relevance to Mass Media Writers. The possibility of a respondent's negative perceptions of an interview situation make the correctives mentioned here all the more important, including other techniques such as the opening protocol, use of instructions, frames of reference, nondirective probes, and feedback. Even when the respondent is qualified to provide the expected information, the very position of being the one in the the spotlight, is enough to render an articulate person speechless. If the subject matter is sensitive, threatening, or difficult to explain, remove some of the tension by acknowledging these may be difficult questions to answer, but together you and the respondent will try to make sense out of the whole thing. It is the initiator's job to let the respondent know the objective is to get at the facts and not to evaluate or embarrass the respondent.

Topic salience seems to be a prevailing operative that influences respondent attention, and that is no less true in mass media settings. Salience, not only of the topic content itself, but how the overall subject or general issue affects or relates to the respondent. Again, an important motivator is the opening protocol. The initiator's best opportunity to legitimize the purpose of the interview in terms that make it important to the respondent is at the very outset with the opening protocol. Instructions, too, add meaning to interview purpose. And respondent commitment compels attentiveness to fulfill the promise made as long as the interviewer continues to demonstrate the promise of protection. Furthermore, reinforcement and feedback serve to pull a faltering respondent back into the action.

As remedial as these techniques appear to be, there is always the chance that the eager interviewer may become so earnest that initiator behavior borders on bias and manipulation, even offensiveness. The only way the initiator can retreat from these traps is to be aware of the degree and nature of the intervention and to conduct self-censure on personal eagerness.

Aside from the possibility of bias or offense, correctives, no matter how adeptly applied, may not work because of a respondent whose every intention is to withhold information, deceive or equivocate.

Trick Plays and Countermoves

It may not be possible to draw out a reluctant respondent, elicit truth, or compel a direct answer. It is possible, however, to know when such trick plays interfere with an even game. A good barometer is your research— what the records say. If the respondent's information fails to square with documented data, the information given falls under question. A backup measure to documented evidence is information obtained from other appropriate and responsible respondents. If their information confirms the record, questionable responses from a trick player are subject to legitimate challenge.

Newswriters are up against this breed of respondent more often than PR or advertising writers, but there are occasions when they, too, face trick plays. For example, departments within a corporation are sometimes highly competitive with one another and one department may be reluctant to release its records to another, or offer information it fears might diminish the department's image. Here again, it is a matter of stressing the importance of the project, not only to the company at large, but especially to the particular department involved, and assuring the ones concerned that the job can be done without fracturing anyone's image.

But how are tough respondents managed when evidence does show their answers are invalid? If invalidity (mainly a response that turns out to be less than true), is apparent during the interview, or discovered after it, handle it directly. Confront the respondent with it, not as an intimidating prosecuting attorney, but as one who has hit a snag in the data and wants to clear up the confusion. This is a hypotheticial example, but a newswriter might say:

Mr. _____, you mentioned earlier that the state singled out your company as the primary source of toxic waste pollution in the Great Lakes and that your company denies this charge. Yet not only state records, but records of other environmental interest groups indicate that _____ Industries discharged the highest percentage of toxic chemicals into the Lakes between 1984 and 1989. I don't understand why there's such a wide difference in judgment. Please explain this to me.

You may get a straight answer, or one like this: *They're wrong.*

Countermove: *Please explain why you think so.* You may get an explanation, for example, about differences in assessment procedures.

Countermove: Then you match procedures under which each group's studies were conducted and arrive at a reasonable conclusion about who is closest to the "truth."

Or, you might get an answer like this:

We don't have to explain anything and we have no further comment.

Countermove: *It's not that you have to explain, Mr. _____, but this issue is as important to _____ Industries as it is to the public it serves. Your opponents have had their say. I'm sure you'd want your company's viewpoint represented, as well. This is your opportunity to make it known.*

The respondent may still say: *No comment.*

Countermove: All you can do is to ask someone else in the company. If that fails, use other appropriate sources and report that the company denied the allegations and had no further comment. This may be the best return you can expect from a respondent who refuses to play by the rules.

Notice that countermoves focus on salience of the issue to the respondent and probing until an adequate answer is obtained. Alternative countermoves include saving the question until a later portion in the interview, and if that fails, the next move is to talk to another respondent. The same strategies apply not only to newswriters, but to PR and advertising writers as well.

Another kind of trick player is the equivocator. This type is similar to the respondent who talks and talks but never answers the question. However, the equivocator skirts around the question with every intention of avoiding a straight answer.

Countermove: *I see, but that doesn't answer the question which is _____ ?*

Equivocators never give up. Neither should you.

Countermove: *Perhaps you didn't understand the question which was _____ ?*

Avoidance tactic again?

Countermove: *Let me rephrase the question: _____ ?*

When all else fails, drop the question temporarily and return to it at some other point in the interview, but use different words. You may never get a straight answer from an equivocator. In that case, you report what you were able to get and let the message receiver decide about the respondent's veracity.

Trick players are fairly easy to single out. Some, but not all, send out signals that suggest deceit. Researchers at UCLA (Mehrabian, 1972) conducted a series of studies with hundreds of respondents in an effort to detect differences between deceivers and truthtellers. They found that those who deceived preferred distanced positions from the interviewer, exhibited more pleasant and fewer facial expressions, fewer gestures, head nods, and leg movements than nondeceivers. The researchers concluded that deceivers had a high degree of control on their deceptions, whereas truthtellers were characteristically more animated when responding. Deceivers also talked less, talked slower, made more speech errors, and smiled more than nondeceivers.

Since then other researchers have found similar results. Deceivers showed greater control over their nonverbal behaviors, even when prodded for answers. They played a cool game to demonstrate confidence and truthfulness. Truthtellers were less poker faced and demonstrated many more facial expressions and bodily gestures. And when prodded, they showed many more nonverbal behaviors. They squirmed, winced, and gestured in an effort to respond truthfully (Buller, Comstock, & Aune, 1989).

Although these conclusions may account for deception in whatever form (composure, hesitation, anxiety, and so on), they do not help the interviewer overcome the problem. ISR researchers admit deception is a tough one to detect and that it is not easy to draw out a reluctant interviewee. They have found, however, that if respondents hesitate or say they cannot respond, often the interviewer is able to find out why by asking questions prefaced with a supportive statement, for example: *I can understand why you would have trouble with this question. Let's talk about it a little more.* Then an appropriate question related to the situation is asked. The aim is to behave as if the respondent is a truthteller and then let your probes and questions politely convey doubt about the response given. Deceivers are quick to pick up on initiator displeasure and they bias their responses to please the initiator or become more defensive, negative and aloof. Nevertheless, there is little harm in trying the remedies suggested here. They could prove fruitful.

Relevance to Mass Media Writers.   Countermoves on tough players remain constant across all areas of media work, whether the interview is carried out for a news, magazine, PR, or advertising assignment. Interview techniques remain constant, as well, across all types of players, the cooperative and reluctant, the inept and clever: courtesy, initial protocol, persuasion about interview salience, instructions, probes, follow-up questions, feedback, and remedies.

Specifically, the countermoves on receivers, especially the tricky ones, include:

- Emphasizing salience of the task.
- Acting as if the receiver is a truthteller.
- Letting the probes, follow-ups, and feedback reflect your doubt.
- Repeating and rephrasing the avoided question.
- Checking response validity against the documented evidence.
- Using other appropriate sources as another check.
- Using other appropriate sources in the event of uncooperativeness.

Like professional sports games, interviews involve moves and countermoves. Also like professional sports games, they end with specific closing procedures.

Closing Protocol

Before closing the interview, make a quick review of your notes and see if all your questions were covered, and if you need clarification of a date, spelling of a name, or any point made. Then ask what survey scientists call the "bushel-basket" question. Ask: *Is there anything else you would like to add?* You could get your best information at this moment, sometimes even information the respondent had suppressed earlier. Another pre-closure technique is an appeal to the respondent as an informed person: *Is there anyone else you think I ought to talk to about this?* Leads like this can start a very rewarding chain reaction of additional sources.

If you have everything you need, begin the closure process by asking the "open-door"question: *If there are any clarifications I may need, could I contact you again?* Leave the path clear in case you do need to call back regarding given information or some new and related data on which the respondent is qualified to comment.

Then give the respondent evidence of your satisfaction and gratitude for giving up precious time, especially if the game was an "even play." Something along the lines of: *Thank you, Mr./Ms. _____. This information will be very useful, and I appreciate having had the opportunity to talk with you.* Shake hands and say goodbye. If the exchange was less than satisfying, try not to convey your frustration. You may have to call on this respondent again some time. Keep an even demeanor and say something like this: *Thank you, Mr./Ms. _____. These were difficult questions, but I appreciate your willingness to see me.* Shake the person's hand anyway and say goodbye. The point is to leave on good terms.

When You Get Back

Check your notes. If they are an illegible scrawl, transcribe them immediately while their meanings are still fresh in your mind. Transcribe, as well, the notes you have about the respondent's surroundings, environment, and nonverbal behavior. Nonverbal behavior could easily be misinterpreted, so move with caution, particularly if you do not know the person well. If you are well acquainted, then nonverbal behavior could be a clue to attitude and could add color to your copy. Above all, guard against personal bias and jumping to conclusions about any of the nonverbal clues. Let the concrete evidence speak for itself. If you have taped, transcribe immediately. Any questions? Call back immediately, while the interview is still fresh in the respondent's mind.

You may not use all your notes. It does not matter. Transcribing notes imprints the content on your mind. The process helps you sift relevancy from irrelevancy, note redundacies, and identify items that need comparison with the research or verification with other sources. Transcription helps the mind distill the interview down to its essence and allows you to evaluate your interview style at the same time.

Do review your transcribed notes, and if you have recorded, listen to the style of your interview. Reading your notes and listening to the tape helps you detect the holes in both your content and your style. When ISR researchers tried to learn about factors that would improve respondent performance, they also learned that interviewers needed training to perform the correctives effectively. In tests to measure the difference between the trained and untrained interviewer, findings demonstrated more and improved responses in interviews conducted by trained interviewers as opposed to those conducted by untrained interviewers (Cannell et al., 1981; see also Hagenaars & Heinen, 1982).

Researchers at the New South Wales Division (Australia) of the Market Research Society agree that trained interviewers improve interview results. One of their studies asked respondents about their reactions to interviewers who had conducted a product survey for a marketing agency. Of the sample of 87 buyers, more than 1 in 3 (39%) expressed misgivings about interviewer skill. Their findings showed that 1 in 4 respondents (28%) complained about interviewers' substandard performance, 1 in 5 (22%) doubted their objectivity and lack of bias, and 14% were concerned about fictitious responses given and interviewers' lack of ability to perceive them. The researchers concluded it was glaringly obvious that the marketing agency had to train and provide skilled interviewers (Korbel & Bell, 1985).

Relevance to Mass Media Writers.   Transcribe and digest your interview notes. Compare responses against your research data. Double check with other appropriate sources. Review and measure your own performance against results obtained. Ask yourself these questions:

- *What question failed in its objective? Why?*
- *What questions hit the mark? Why?*
- *Was my opening protocol effective? If not, why not?*
- *Did I deliver questions clearly, in a pleasant voice, at a reasonable pace?*
- *Did I project knowledge or ignorance about the subject matter?*
- *Did I probe sufficiently or was I overbearing?*
- *Did I try the question again? If not, why not?*
- *Were my probes effective? If not, why not?*
- *Did I ask enough follow-ups? If not where did I fail to do so?*
- *Which memory techniques failed? Why?*
- *Were my feedbacks sufficient, effective? If not, why not?*
- *Were transitions satisfactory? If not, why not?*
- *Did I use summary feedbacks periodically to check my understanding of the response?*
- *At what point did I misunderstand the respondent? Why?*
- *If some of my countermoves did not work, why did they fail?*
- *Did I check my notes carefully before leaving and ask pre-closure questions?*
- *Did I end on an amiable note?*

Professional athletes prime themselves for an upcoming game by observing videotapes of past performances. Self-evaluation of your interview style can do the same for you. Do not underestimate your role as initiator and balancing artist. Your performance can mean the difference between an even game or a bust.

SUMMARY OF INTERVIEWING TECHNIQUES

Scheduling the interview:
- Give your name and whom you represent.
- Explain why you want the interview.
- Give reasons why you contacted this person and for what purpose.
- Give the candidate an idea of how much time the interview will consume.
- Allow choice of several places (respondent's home court first) and the means.

Before leaving for the interview:
- Review the data.
- Review, once more, areas of research related to questions planned.
- Practice delivery of questions prepared for the scheduled respondent.
- Rehearse techniques designed to overcome anticipated holes in responses.

Rehearsals prepare you for:
- Substantive follow-up questions to unpredictable responses.
- Nondirective, but content-related probes in order to activate respondents' unexpected memory lapses.
- Appropriate statements and questions to contradictions and other responses that fail to square with the research.
- Knowledgeable comments about information given by respondents that demonstrate agreement (disagreement) with other research sources and where it serves the purpose of encouraging respondents to continue the exchange.

The skilled interviewer:
- Opens the interview with an appropriate introduction or "warm-up" (climate, cognition, motivation).

- Explains reasons for conducting the interview (climate, cognition, motivation).
- Obtains commitment for effort from the respondent (climate, cognition, motivation).
- Creates a task-oriented rather than a socially oriented mood and supplies necessary instructions (climate, accessibility, cognition, motivation).
- Delivers questions slowly and with proper phrasing and inflection, necessary context and memory aids (accessibility, cognition, motivation).
- Provides reinforcement and feedback (accessibility, cognition, motivation).
- Considers the objectives and fashions the words to suit the question and the respondent's needs.
- Exercises sensitivity to the respondent's apparent position of being questioned, the effort required and the difficulties involved.
- Adopts a reasonable rate of speech and pleasant tone of voice.
- Structures thoughtfully designed and carefully worded questions.
- Provides frames of reference and other techniques to aid recall.
- Closes on an amiable note.

Countermoves for respondent failures:
- Emphasize salience of the task.
- Contribution of the interview to the goals of the respondent.
- Gratification derived from making such a contribution.
- Contribution of the respondent to solution of a problem.
- Act as if the receiver is a truthteller.
- Let the probes, follow-ups and feedback reflect your doubt.
- Repeat and rephrase the avoided question.
- Check response validity against the documented evidence.
- Use other appropriate sources as another check.
- Use other appropriate sources in the event of uncooperativeness.

When you get back:
- Examine your interview performance (apply the self-inquiries listed on p. 200).

Begin the process of preparing for the interview with the recommendations made in chapters 7-8 and to conduct the interview ask Critical Self-Inquiry 6: *What data, prepared questions, and interview techniques must I review in order to identify inadequate and/or inaccurate responses and to raise impromptu questions?*

The preparation is important because you will need at least a minimum of success with your interviews to add credence to your research and to have a substantial body of data to organize and analyze, topics for discussion in the following chapters.

10 Organizing and Coding the Data: Getting Ready for Analysis

Once you have gathered your data, you will need to organize your notes for effective analysis. Organize by dividing your notes into relevant categories that facilitate fact-driven analysis and sound conclusions. Each category should be labeled, that is, coded for ease of reference during analysis. The object is to capture a global view of the facts commanded by logic of the data rather than by writer whim. The point is to ensure that verified facts reveal the meaning inherent in the whole and to avert biased conclusions. But first it may be useful to review what you have learned to do so far.

STATING THE PROBLEM

Critical Self-Inquiry 1: *What is the problem, issue, or question?* You began with an assignment or curiosity about something that identified the problem requiring preliminary research.

BACKGROUNDING AND RESEARCHING THE PROBLEM

Critical Self-Inquiry 2: *What information has been and/or is currently documented and known by whom?* The assignment or your own curiosity generated preliminary questions that you researched. Preliminary research gave you a background of the problem and also revealed appropriate sources of whom you made initial inquiries.

Critical Self-Inquiry 3: *What is the working statement?* You were then able to formulate productive working and alternative statements and continue further (primary) research.

Critical Self-Inquiry 4: *What information fails to stand up to question?* Before accepting received information from either preliminary or primary research, you evaluated and verified the data. Before calling on interview sources found in either the preliminary or primary stages of research, you verified their status (validity) and reputation (reliability) and tried to learn something about them as persons.

DESIGNING THE INTERVIEW PLAN

Critical Self-Inquiry 5: *What do I need to ask who about what and how shall I ask it?* Because research fulfills only part of the required information, you reviewed the collected data to check for confirmations/contradictions, omissions, gaps, ambiguities, any item that carried little consensus or failed to stand up to question. If checks in references failed to provide correctives to these, you designed a plan to interview a balanced group of appropriate sources who could provide the necessary data. Then you designed a series of relevant, clearly worded, and unbiased questions to evoke adequate and accurate response.

CONDUCTING THE INTERVIEW

Critical Self-Inquiry 6: *What data, prepared questions, and interview techniques must I review in order to identify inadequate and/or inaccurate responses, and to raise impromptu questions?* To prepare for interviews, you reviewed the data again, internalizing the information in order to catch inadequate and inaccurate answers, to prime yourself for impromptu questions and follow-ups, and to know when to probe. You followed the conventions of a skilled interviewer and played the game of communication to the satisfaction of both yourself and the respondent.

Now you are ready for that part of the strategy when you put pieces of the puzzle together so you can describe the picture it reveals, whether that picture is an outcome of work for a news, magazine, broadcast, PR, or advertising assignment.

ORGANIZING AND CODING THE DATA

Critical Self-Inquiry 7: *What are the units of information in the collected data?*

Cleaning Up the Data

It is time now to organize, that is, cleanup your data and reduce the mass of details so you can see the overall picture. You did some house cleaning before conducting your interviews. That is, you verified your research data, filled in omissions, resolved discrepancies, and so on. You also internalized that information in order to recognize and remedy inaccuracies or omissions in interview responses. But the cleanup process continues even after the interviews.

As you learned earlier, not all fouls committed by the respondent can be corrected during an interview. Some have to be remedied after the fact. To do this, repeat the crucial question about your researched data again, this time in reference to the interviews: *What interview information fails to stand up to question?* Then take these steps:

- Make sure you have not made errors in your research notes concerning the evidence or misunderstood a respondent.
- Match your personal record of the interview data against the documented evidence.
- Match interview information given by one respondent against information given by other respondents. *Who's on the outer fringes of generally acknowledged information? Why?*
- Verify the match or mismatch of these controversies against the documented evidence.
- Supplement this work with calls to old and/or new sources to validate the matches or mismatches. *Any agreements? Any differences? Why? Any recent developments? When did they occur? Who's involved? How come? Any consequences? Any predictions?*

The Final Cleanup

The task of coding is often facilitated if the whole body of information is reviewed once more to eliminate irrelevancies and to note what is informative, interesting, memorable, and has stood the test of questioning. However, be on guard. This operation opens up many opportunities for biased selection, unless you, as always, make an earnest effort to maintain a defense against such temptations. Especially keep in mind the meaning of relevancy—pro and con data associated with the working and alternative statements collected during research and interviews, plus any new data.

Mark those items that, in your unbiased judgment, deserve to be coded for further consideration. You will find that you have collected a lot more information than you will be able to use. Never mind. The effort has served its purpose. The extra information gives you a measure against which you will be able to separate the relevant from irrelevant, interesting from dull, informative from noninformative, items that stand up to question from items that do not.

Reducing the Data

Assuming all your data are now validated and verified, cleaned up and up-to-date, you are now well prepared to do what professional media writers do to abstract meaning from a mass of disconnected, but substantial data items. They reduce it further. You reduced your data when you gave it the final cleanup. That is, you eliminated the irrelevant, dull, uninformative, and weak information. But now you reduce it once more in another way.

Media writers do this by noticing which of the remaining pieces share similar characteristics or attributes. These labeled units of information then become a network of solid information. The network, as a whole, then takes on the potential of revealing something more than each of the parts by themselves display. It is true that coding is still another reconstruction of the data that opens even more doors to biased choices. But if you have accumulated solid evidence and defended against biased choices thus far, there is every reason to believe your defense will be as strong at this point. Besides, final coding is a cognitive process that allows you to make the leap from uncertainty to reasoned enlightenment, from routine thinking to disciplined original thinking, from specific facts to valuable insight.

You are prepared for this cognitive process because you have reviewed the data often enough so that it is now part of your mindset. You may find yourself mulling over all the puzzle's pieces even when you are not focusing on the effort. Unconsciously, you will be able to fit related pieces together and units of manageable data will fall into place because the specifics are now familiar items in your mind.

The discussion here concerns the task of coding, but it also deals with analysis and decision about the meaning inherent in the data. These three functions are closely related internal processes, even overlapping, yet each one makes a specific and important contribution to the whole process of abstracting understanding from the data. In order to appreciate the complex cognitive process involved and the relationship of the three functions, we look at each operation separately — coding in this chapter, analysis and decision in the next.

THE CODING PROCESS

Coding is a matter of recognizing the shared attributes of a wide variety of information items and grouping these under category names, letters, or numbers to signify they belong together as units of information that are different from other groups of information with shared characteristics.

Grouping data items is much like the cognitive process of making sense out of external stimuli, that is, fitting specific items into organized frames of reference, or schemas,[1] in your mind. The pieces of information you have collected are also external stimuli waiting to be organized into a meaningful structure. However, now you will transfer that mental filing system to paper for the purpose of analyzing the whole body of data. If you followed suggestions made in chapters 3 and 4, you have already organized, or precoded, your research and interview notes under subject/topic categories. But modifications in the working and alternative statements, additional research and interview information, may call for modified categories or adding new categories to those you already have. If you did not precode, you can still postcode, that is, organize your collected and verified data now that it is all in.

Simple projects may require just a mental arrangement of the facts, projects of intermediate breadth and depth may require only postcoding. More complex projects often require both precoding and postcoding. Whatever level of coding is used, data are meaningless if left as disjointed pieces. Karen Elliott House made that clear when she described the news work that earned her a Pulitzer Prize in 1984. She was then assistant foreign editor at *The Wall Street Journal* and she told a public audience that writing stories on the Middle East was like putting together a 1,000-piece jigsaw puzzle. That is, the pieces by themselves made little sense until the appropriate pieces were linked together to reveal the story inherent in the whole.[2] The observation is no less true for PR and advertising writers and others who have discovered the merit of thinking in an organized manner.

Coding Methods

Methods of handling coded data for analysis vary within and between disciplines. For example, researchers in social science assign numbers to

---

[1] British psychologist F. C. Bartlett, coined the word *schema* in 1932 saying then that he never liked the label and preferred *organized setting* instead. Nevertheless, he continued using the term, *schema*, and psychologists since have followed suit. Bartlett defined *schema* as an "active organization of past reactions" on which we depend to respond to similar and new stimuli (Bartlett, 1977, p. 201). *Schema* is akin to a "frame of reference," that is, people set up memory files to organize stimuli reception and/or experiences concerning objects, events, persons, and the like. Then that memory file becomes a frame of reference in an organized, compartmentalized system and is retrievable when activated by similar stimuli or experiences.

[2] In 1989 Ms. House was promoted to foreign editor at *The Wall Street Journal*. Today she is vice-president of the International Group for Dow Jones & Co., Inc., the parent organization of *The Wall Street Journal*.

single information items. Families of related items are then lumped together under numbered categories of information and fed into a computer programmed for the appropriate and standardized entry of the data.

During analysis, the numeric and electronic method of data entry simplifies recognition of data frequencies, relationships, correlations, deviations, and significant or insignificant differences. Numbered items and categories are keyed to descriptions of the data with corresponding numbers recorded in a "codebook." Analysis by the researcher is controlled by standardized techniques for uniformity of approach.

Media writers, however, do not assign numbers to single items or grouped data, nor do any standardized methods of coding exist. The absence of standards leaves any analytic process in media work open to free choice and, therefore, open to question. However, the usual practice is to lump items under name categories that may or may not be alphabetized or numbered. Then on a complex assignment the writer might do a final coding and post these on to a summary sheet for a global view of the data. Again, the possibility of biased selection during lumping or posting lurks in the background. The principal defense is vigilance against it.

One more precaution: If you lump too many items together, you may find yourself grouping similiar as well as near similar items under a single category. Sometimes those near similar items may require a category of their own in order to detect differences or links between units of information during analysis. It is always better to have a manageable set of categories, that is, not too many categories. On the other hand, if there is a distinct dissimilarity in an item or group of items, a feature that could make a difference during analysis, split the existing category and make another unit for the item or items with the distinctively dissimilar feature. This works the other way around, too. If you have made too many categories, combine the ones that share close similarities.

Not every media writer bothers to lump or even post data in such an organized manner. A seasoned professional may keep only a few notes and store everything else in mind. Some simply gather related research and interview notes and file these in labeled manila folders. Instead of posting on to summary sheets, they read and reread the data, mark relevant areas with a check mark, highlight them with a felt marker, or underline them. Then they review the marked portions to determine what the data suggests.

On certain rush assignments, these expedients may be all there is time for. On more complex matters, however, media writers do keep a more elaborate system of notations. Some organize notes in spiral tablets and reserve a separate tablet for each anticipated subject category (precoding). Others fill ring binders with indexed sections and keep adding notations and categories as necessary throughout the life of the project (precoding and postcoding). Still others keep research and interview notes on 5x7 index cards, shuffle them around looking for an order, or trends, or patterns, or post them on a wall to get an overview visual of the data. A few post or chart the categorized data from their file folders, tablets, or ring binders and then study the units of data for relationships, patterns, agreements, disagreements, gaps, discrepancies, anomalies, and the like.

A common method today is the split-screen device on a word processor. All data are entered into the computer, either from hand notes or notes entered into a portable computer. All the specific items are listed on one side of the monitor. Related items are identified and then moved around and grouped into subject categories. The other side of the split-screen is reserved for the category label or summary description that identifies a particular family of data. Analysis follows from the screen or from a printout. A software program that allows electronic categorization and summarization is another convenient method of organizing and coding data.

Because media writers do not have the advantage of a standardized method, any one of the more disciplined schemes mentioned here may work for you, or you may think of a better one. There is no "appropriate" method. In fact, the most appropriate method is suggested by the data itself. The way to detect what organization the data suggests is to follow the coding guidelines provided in this chapter. That is:

- Organize similar data items together.
- Let the nature of the grouped data suggest the name under which that group should be to categorized.
- Let the coded (categorized) data suggest how the body of catego-rized data should be posted in an appropriate summary for analysis.

A more elaborate coding system may be required if the project is of broad scope and depth, especially if the project promises continuation or appli-cation to related assignments in the future. By no means do any of these suggestions ensure correct coding and accurate analysis. Human error is always a problem even with machine-fed data. No matter what the process or method, it still takes attentiveness to the data and vigilance against bias.

Value of Coding Data

Disciplined thinkers code data in order to work through problems and to manage complex issues. Conclusions inferred by the data are then more easily and accurately noted and stated. In many instances, the findings can be related to other knowledge (Babbie, 1983; Selltiz, Wrightsman, & Cook, 1976; Wimmer & Dominick, 1983).

It is easy to understand that if you organize several groups of related facts together, the task of analyzing the attributes of a single group and detecting differences between several groups is greatly simplified. It is also easy to understand how coding permits inference and conclusion, or what psychologist J. S. Bruner (1957) called "going beyond the information given." That is, from the "presence of a thing and a relation one immediately educes another thing" (p. 41). In some of his first experiments, Bruner and his associates presented young students with jumbled letters of words and found that spellers who had learned the general code, or structural system, for English words could infer the correct arrangement of the letters on fewer trials than those who learned to spell by rote, some of whom could not even make the attempt.

Rand Corporation researchers (Hayes-Roth & Thorndyke, 1979) also found that structure facilitated integration of related facts to permit formation of new ideas from separately acquired facts. For one experiment, the researchers presented subjects with pairs of related facts embedded in three meaningful stories. Then through both a sentence completion and matching test researchers evaluated subject recall ability. Because of the structure provided by the stories, subjects were able to remember related as well as unique occurrences of the facts.

In another experiment by the same researchers, subjects were asked to identify true and false information given in three structured stories. True items were defined as those supported by facts given in the stories. Still another test asked subjects to indicate which inferences followed logically from several facts that preceded it. Results from both tests showed that subjects used factual data in the stories to identify the correct information and draw accurate conclusions (Hayes-Roth & Thorndyke, 1979).

These studies suggest that schema formation and inference are data-driven organizations of the mind, a factor that Norman (1979) also found held true in his cognitive psychology experiments at the University of California. Several of these involved testing subjects with nonsense words, incomplete sentences, and partially obscured words. In one experiment, subjects were asked to identify words on an intricately designed background that obscured parts of the letters. Subjects were still able to infer the correct words from given portions of the letters. These results and results from similar experiments prompted Norman to conclude that a schema formation is confirmed when sufficient supporting evidence for it exists. Also, that when more than one schema is available, the schema chosen is the one with the strongest evidence for best fit.

Coding Traps

Although these experiments support the notion that data-driven organization is a human cognitive capability, coded systems can be a major source of bias and subjectivity. After conducting an extensive series of experiments at the Hebrew University, Jerusalem, psychologists Tversky and Kahneman (1974) found that people used three procedures to categorize and predict. Instead of utilizing base-rate information (factual data), people relied on *representativeness*, *availability*, and *anchoring*.

Representativeness: People tend to classify persons by using impressionistic categories rather than the person's true attributes. For example, given the description, "John is a meek and tidy soul who likes order in his life," people classified John as a librarian rather than a salesman and ignored the base-rate information regarding the absolute numbers of librarians versus salesmen that exist in the population.

Availability: People judge frequency or probability on the basis of relative comfort with which instances or associations are brought to mind.

Anchoring: People make estimates that are biased toward initially held personal values (a human tendency discussed in earlier chapters).

A great deal of systematic study concerning first impulses supports the Tversky-Kahneman studies (e. g., Aronson, 1980; Dutta & Kanungo, 1975; Nisbett & Ross, 1980). In fact, bias can go beyond these habits in its avoidance of factual data and succumb to such extremes as prejudice. Zajonc (1980), psychologist and director of the Institute for Social Research at the University of Michigan, found that affect had a powerful influence on cognitive encoding. In one experiment that asked subjects to make discriminations on the basis of like-dislike choices, Zajonc found significant evidence that judgment is entirely under the influence of affective factors without the participation of cognitive processes. The affect factors included such "hot" impulses as perceptual defense, subliminal perception, and mood. These rose to the surface first before "cooler" and less affective impulses. Perceptual defense, for example, is voluntary closure against new data that could correct a distorted view of a stimulus, be it a person, idea, or information item. It begins at the moment of perception and ends only at the end of the cognitive process (Erdelyi, 1974).

Psychologists Taylor and Crocker (1981) also found other liabilities with schematic processing. Pointing to numerous experiments designed to detect biases, they concluded that schematic processing can result in much information loss. Cognitive error occurs at the point of selectivity during recall when substitute schemas are inserted, or when ambiguous data misdirects interpretation. Selection of the wrong schema, Taylor and Crocker observed, is the stuff of which comedy is made, particularly in literature. They noted, for example, that Goldsmith's classic comedy, *She*

Stoops to Conquer, is built around mistaken identities and erroneously defined situations.

The human tendency to embrace a correct schema too enthusiastically is still another source of cognitive error and results in what Taylor and Crocker called an "illusory database." This means that in taking too fast a hold on a schema, one bases an inference on information that is not really present in the stimulus. Instead of selecting schemas based on data in the stimulus, perceivers add their own assumptions to the stimuli that then become indistinguishable from the original data.

In spite of the liabilities of schematic processing, Taylor and Crocker recognized the tension that exists between the human tendency to biases and the equally human necessity to invoke schemas. They concluded that its drawbacks aside, schema formation ultimately serves to organize and place order on the whirl of stimuli surrounding us.

Relevance to Mass Media Writers.   Taylor and Crocker offered no simple solutions that would bring more weight on the side of schematic processing. Still, they and others suggest that the natural function of schema formation, and by implication the coding process, requires unwavering attention to attributes in the stimulus if one is to avoid the traps of bias and snap judgments.

Some answers appear in the studies reviewed here. For example, note the differences between them. Studies that showed subjects' ability to stick to original facts were conducted under laboratory conditions where subjects were highly motivated to fulfill the demands of tests and, in some cases, prompted by prior instructions. Other studies were designed to catch the unsuspecting subject off guard. These subjects responded spontaneously rather than reflectively, and they did not have the advantage of prior instructions. The manner in which these studies were conducted suggests that subjects are driven by the data when motivated and directed to do so. When motivation and direction are absent, "hot" impulses predominate and the result is distortion and information loss. The point seems to be that if one is motivated to arrive at a considered judgment and is encouraged by instruction to do so, one can direct focused attention on the data. It is possible, then, to avoid subjective coding if one honors an *inner instruction*, a self-directed motivation to permit the objective data to identify and name the categories for a coding scheme. To accomplish this, first tell yourself you will permit only the verified evidence to direct organization of your data, then be honest about it. Ask yourself:

- *Where do my interests, values, beliefs, or assumptions interfere with the objective or opinion items collected?*

- *Have I allowed "hot" impulses to blur my vision of the data?*
- *Where have I failed to take full account of all factors concerning the working or alternative statements, or other information not antici- pated by these statements?*
- *What are the units of information suggested by the data?*
- *What category labels are suggested by the data for those units?*

Coding is a common and useful practice among professional media writers. It can be just as useful for the novice provided defense against bias remains at the forefront of the coder's mind.

Coding Readiness

If coding is a human need to arrange order out of chaos, then it is important to understand whether that drive rises out of a vacuum or out of some content. Bruner (1964) believes it is the latter. He acknowledged the human capacity to move from stimulus cues to data-driven categories and that this synthesis is a silent, even unconscious behavior, but he also found that the process is dependent on previously encoded data. Following a series of extensive recognition experiments, he and his associates concluded that this inner-directed impetus originates not only from a reservoir of previously encoded information, but that four necessary antecedents precede sche- matic processing: *set, need, degree of training,* and *diversity of training.*

Bruner defined *set* as learned experience and knowledge that, in turn, determine the degree to which one is equipped with coding systems to permit going beyond them in order to deal with new situations.

Need is an impelling drive and the degree of its strength determines to what extent one is motivated in a new situation to go beyond the information insightfully. Highly motivated persons may overshoot the information given and make wild inferences, whereas the weakly motivated will undershoot the available data and miss detection of any inference at all. Bruner recommended "mid-level motivation." This type of motivation is neither too weak nor too enthusiastic. It is, instead, generated by curiosity for stimulus-based clues that, in turn, lead to accurate inference or conclusion.

Degree of training simply refers to the level of mastery one has achieved in grasping the specifics of the situation to permit discovery of a global or higher-order generic code.

Diversity of training means exposure to more than one or two exemplars. Bruner explained that children, for example, classify varieties of dogs and cats after first encoding the language for "dog" and "cat" and that they learn the concept of differences between them when shown several illustrations of varied types of dogs and cats.

Following these antecedents and observations that fit stimuli in a new situation, an "emptying" process occurs. That is, cues from old coding systems are abstracted and combined then emptied into an invented or created category to structure a new code in the system. This then permits additional predictions for other new stimulus situations. It is this silent process of recognizing cues, fitting by association, combining, and inventing that Bruner found is the seat of human creative energy.

Bruner is not alone. His findings reflect the experential observation of many newswriters. For example, Bob Baker, journalist and author of *Newsthinking*, believes newsthinking is an "intense examination of those moments in which you make your facts fall into place. . . . where the genius of great writers — their creativity, their imagination, their willingness to take risks — unfolds. Much of it is subconscious, but most of it is also structured." He continued:

> The reporter or book author or magazine essayist you admire may appear to be an artist who launches his impulses from a deep, mysterious font, but in fact he is producing his mastery in a laboratory. With the sophistication of a scientist, he has built and refined a complex set of thought strategies, a system in which nothing is left to chance, where each sentence and paragraph is automatically and rigorously tested. (Baker, 1981, pp. 1-2)

Relevance to Mass Media Writers. That the cognitive process is a complex system is probably not news to anyone, but some understanding of how information is encoded and combined to create new systems may help you appreciate the importance of depending on data-based cues to arrive at new predictions, ideas, decisions, or conclusions. Systematically researched studies of cognitive processing make it clear that a mental reservoir void of content cannot produce answers to problems, questions, or anything else. And Bruner made it plain that mid-level motivation directs attention to cues in the stimulus and away from the misdirection of "hot impulses." Still, this should not obscure the likelihood that even such motivation may be overruled by schemas in one's reservoir that defeat the purpose of accurate inference. As Taylor and Crocker pointed out, tension is always present between bias and evidence, and mid-level motivation demands as much defense against defeat as any other function in the whole process.

In the last analysis, it is still evidence, data management, and vigilance against bias that brings you to the brink of inspired writing. If you thought talent alone was the source of creativity, the research reviewed here and the observations of Karen Elliot House and Bob Baker should tell you that the source of inspired writing has its origin in 99% perspiration. The 1%, often mistaken for other special attributes, is what inventor Thomas Edison called "inspiration." Inspiration may be defined as a point of insight or discovery that rises spontaneously from 99% solid thinking and disciplined work habits. Make no mistake, even the endowed must fill the well with substantive content before they can draw something of value out of it. Keep Bruner's antecedents to cognitive processing in mind and do the following to fill your reservoir.

- Generate curiosity concerning the assignment.
- Learn the terms and expressions concerning your project that are new to you.
- Evaluate, validate, verify, and internalize numerous and varied views in the research and background data.
- Evaluate, validate, verify, and internalize numerous and varied views in the interview data.
- Review the data frequently.
- Study the similarities and differences in specific data items for the purpose of organizing and coding the data.
- Maintain an inner instruction to stick to facts in the data when organizing and coding.
- Maintain a mid-level threshold of curiosity, rather than "hot" impulse or its opposite, disinterest.

Before jumping to any conclusions about what your data says, first determine how well you have achieved the antecedents. Ask yourself:

- *What factors in backgrounding, research, evaluation, or verification are vague in my mind?*
- *What content related to categories in the working and alternative statements are still unclear?*
- *What interview data have I failed to digest thoroughly?*
- *What similarities, differences in specific data items have I ignored?*
- *Where have I made errors in notations, or in grouping of specific items?*
- *What unfounded assumptions have I made?*
- *What relevant data have I failed to include?*

If data are missing, inaccurate, still ambiguous, or unverified, go back to the research and/or interview sources and fill in, correct, and clarify. Assuming you have fulfilled the conditions for coding readiness, you still need to know how to distinguish related items of specific data for grouping into categories.

Coding Cues

A great deal of controversy surrounds the means by which we recognize cues in the stimulus to determine what it is and where it belongs. Cognitive psychologists Gibson and Gibson (1955), for example, differ from Bruner in that the former argue that it is detection of differences between stimuli that triggers perception of stimulus attributes. But studies since the Gibson experiments appear to put the weight of consensus in Bruner's camp who proposed association precedes differentiation (Bruner, 1964; also see Hayes-Roth & Thorndyke, 1979; Norman, 1979; Taylor & Crocker, 1981).

The mind keeps a tight hold on the secrets of its energies and whether association or differentiation comes first or last may be a moot point. One thing is clear, however, experience with a stimulus is necessary for identification and discrimination of its attributes. Even the Gibsons found that frequency of exposure to a stimulus event enriches learning about it and refines the discrimination process (another argument for frequent data reviews). In one of their experiments, they tested three groups of subjects: 12 adults, 10 children aged 8-1/2 to 12 years, and 10 others aged 6 to 8. Subjects were shown a scribble, followed by a series of scribbles indistinguishable from the original one, and then a series of scribbles that could be distinguished from the original. They found that the original stimulus was at first indistinguishable from scribbles in either series and ended by being distinguishable from the whole class of scribbles. That is, after several trials through the stimulus items, subjects became more and more specific about distinguishing cues. Adults, understandably, scored better on fewer trials than the intermediate group and the intermediate group scored better on fewer trials than the younger group, some of whom had more difficulty than others in their group.

The point about internalizing the data with frequent reviews is made here again only because experience with the stimulus items in the data seems to have a significant influence on whether you will be able to notice the similarities in families of data and then the differences that distinguish them from other families of data. As importantly, experience with the data will alert you to some cues you may have overlooked due to the mechanisms of perceptual defense.

Given that background, we can now turn to Bruner's propositions (1964) concerning the sequential properties of perception that direct one's attention to similarities and differences:

1. "Perception is a decision process."
   Bruner called this the beginning of "primitive categorization," a silent and unconscious function. He explained with these illustra-

tions: a particular object is a snake and not a fallen branch because of the snake's particular attributes or properties which, by agreement, we have classified as "snake" and the incomplete word L*VE in the context MEN L*VE WOMEN is LOVE and not LIVE.

2. "The decision process involves the utilization of discriminatory cues, as do all decisions."

That is, the properties of the stimulus make it possible to distinguish those properties for placement into the most appropriate category. "Properties" are those that are required of a particular stimulus. He called this stage the "cue search," which he felt should really be called "clues." This cue or clue check, whichever you prefer, is followed by a "confirmation check" to verify the associative function before a "gating" process sets in. "Gating" closes out stimuli irrelevant to the confirming process.

3. "The cue utilization process involves the process of inference."

This occurs when cue searching is "severely" reduced, incongruencies to original properties are "gated out" and categorization is completed. Bruner defined a category as a "set of specifications regarding what stimuli events will be grouped as equivalent."

Bruner explained that the extent of perceptual accuracy depends on the degree of previous learning. The more inappropriate the perceptual readiness, the more inaccurate the categorization process will be.

Relevance to Mass Media Writers. Perceptual readiness and the perceptual process is as applicable to data categorization in media work as it is in the perception and categorization of objects and events in the environment. One notes similarities and differences between data items in the same way as similarities and differences are perceived between external stimuli. The difference, of course, is that in this instance the stimuli you are looking at are items of information you organize and code simultaneously in mind and on paper (or via the computer).

SUMMARY GUIDE FOR ORGANIZING, CODING DATA

Check, clean up the data:
- Make sure you have not made errors in your research notes concerning the evidence or misunderstood a respondent.
- Match your personal record of the interview data against the documented evidence.
- Match interview information given by one respondent against

information given by other respondents. *Who's on the outer fringes of generally acknowledged information? Why?*
- Verify the match or mismatch of these controversies against the documented evidence.
- Supplement this work with calls to old and/or new sources to validate the matches or mismatches. *Any agreements? Any differences? Why? Any recent developments? When did they occur? Who's involved? How come? Any consequences? Any predictions?*

Coding readiness:
- Generate curiosity concerning the assignment.
- Learn the terms and expressions concerning your project that are new to you.
- Evaluate, validate, verify, and internalize numerous and varied views in the research and background data.
- Evaluate, validate, verify, and internalize numerous and varied views in the interview data.
- Review the data frequently.
- Study the similarities and differences in specific data items for the purpose of organizing and coding the data.
- Maintain an inner instruction to stick to facts in the data when organizing and coding.
- Maintain a mid-level threshold of curiosity, rather than "hot" impulse or its opposite, disinterest.

Achieved coding readiness? Better ask:
- *What factors in backgrounding, research, evaluation, or verification are vague in my mind?*
- *What content related to categories in the working and alternative statements are still unclear?*
- *What interview data have I failed to digest thoroughly?*
- *What similarities, differences in specific data items have I ignored?*
- *Where have I made errors in notations, or in grouping of specific items?*
- *What unfounded assumptions or biased judgments have I made?*
- *What relevant data have I failed to include?*

Organizing, coding the data:
- Organize similar data items together.
- Let the nature of the grouped data suggest the name under which that group should be categorized.

- Let the coded (categorized) data suggest how the body of categorized data should be posted in an appropriate summary for analysis.

In the next chapter, you will learn how cognitive principles of categorization facilitate data analysis. However, the important question to raise when you do categorize is Critical Self-Inquiry 7: *What are the units of information in the collected data?*

11 Analyzing the Data: Making Sense of It All

Once you have identified the units of information that belong together and separated them into an organized and coded arrangement of some kind, the meaning in that network of information comes to light. To make that happen, ask Critical Self-Inquiry 8: *Where are the similarities, differences, anomalies, gaps, and unknowns; where are the agreements, disagreements, or conflicts; where are the links indicating relationships, correlations, patterns, or trends; where does the weight and importance of evidence fall and why?*

MEANING OF ANALYSIS

You will not find all these conditions in one body of information. They only represent what could be present. Furthermore, there may be other points that lend themselves to examination that may not be listed in the above inquiry. The point is to notice opportunities for comparison, contrast, connection, and to question anything that does not add up.

Before getting into the discussion on analysis, it is important to first understand what analysis is and how it occurs. Above all, accurate analysis depends primarily on how well you have covered the ground in previous stages, beginning with stating the problem, raising questions, getting answers from varieties of research and interview sources, validating those sources, evaluating, verifying and filling holes in the data, and then breaking down the mass of data into manageable parts. It also depends on how well you have been directed by the facts and not your personal biases throughout the various stages of the strategy, especially where selection and evaluation play a significant role up to and including the coding process. In short, accurate analysis depends on whether you have a "representative" and substantiated sample of coded data to analyze. And that holds true not only for media work, it also holds true for any task that requires critical thinking.

Assuming, then, that the prerequisites have been met, we can now take a look at the meaning of "to analyze." The dictionary definition describes analysis as the activity of "separating a thing, idea, etc., into its parts so as to find out its nature, proportion, function, interrelationship, etc." That is what you did when you coded your data. But there is more to analysis than breaking a whole into its separate and related parts.

In the analysis of metal ore, for example, an accurate assay depends first on procuring a representative sample of the ore in question. Because distribution of an ore's components is rarely uniform, not one, but several samples are obtained, crushed and mixed together, and then the final mass is assayed. To assay is to measure and analyze the mass to determine the nature, proportion, or purity of the components. The outcome is then reported to interested parties.

In the analysis of a chemical, a chemist breaks it down into its various elements, combines and mixes it with other substances to note the changes that occur. The changes that take place when substances react with one another are then described by the chemist in the form of an equation and this along with other studied conclusions are announced in a formal report.

The work of metallurgy and chemistry is far more complicated than these examples suggest. However, the point is that a representative sample along with the analytic function of breakdown, combination, observation, and report of the outcome is similar in kind to the analytic function carried out by researchers in the social and behavorial sciences. Like the metallurgist or chemist, they take a representative mass of data (the numbers accumulated on explored concepts), break it down into combinations of related parts, and then examine it to see where most of the evidence falls. In their observations, they note the changes that occur and, more often than not, can identify the reasons why the changes occurred. It is from such an analysis that they synthesize their findings (the equation) and arrive at a conclusion (the summed result of factors in the equation).

Professional media writers do much the same. To illustrate how all the above applies to mass media work and what a synthesis statement might look like, here is how news or PR writers might brief their supervisors on how they reached a conclusion:

We know there's a flaw in 15% of the SXL gear mechanisms produced last year. And documents tell us that most of those cars were produced during the summer months when the pattern of attendance showed increased absenteeism during those months. Other records show that some police arrests for drug pushing and use were made on the premises and that two of those arrests involved foremen assigned to the SXL line. We've talked to people on the line who reported minor accidents and who complained that supervision was lacking. A majority of these people took time off during the period we're looking at. Others simply didn't show up.

These facts together indicate that quality may have dipped during those summer months due to fewer people on the job and lack of supervisory checks on the line (the equation).

This may or may not be the answer. But before publication, we need to see if it's corroborated, or ruled out, by other information. Otherwise, that's what our current information tells us (the conclusion).

Note: This is only meant to exemplify the kind of thinking and activity that precedes actual presentation of a public announcement and is not in reference to any occurrence or object in reality. The same applies to the next example.

An ad writer might say the following at an agency group meeting about strategy planning for the next campaign:

The competition claims their product has less calorie content than ours. However nutritionists say where one low-calorie product is lower in calories, but higher in fat, it's better to choose the one with less fat and higher calories.

Our low-cal product contains 290 calories because there's a larger portion of nourishing food in it, but the important point is that it contains much less fat. The competition's calorie count is 275, contains a much smaller portion of nourishing food and has 15% more fat in it than ours. And nutritionists tell us that's not a good choice for someone trying to loose fat because the important thing is the quality of the calories. Furthermore, the American Heart Association recommends that one's daily fat intake should be less than and no more than 30% of total calories taken that day (equation).

Yes, their product has fewer calories, but the consumer's best choice is the low-cal product with the lowest fat content, and that's our product. The evidence tells us that less calories is not always better (conclusion).

In fact, I'd suggest that "Less Is Not Always Better" stand as one of our themes for the next campaign.

All this information for these writers came from thoughtfully collected, verified, and coded data reduced further in the final analysis to an equation and conclusion in a formal report for supervisory clearance to move ahead on a project. During analysis, those parts carrying the most weight and volume of evidence relevant to the problem were combined to see if changes occurred such as relationships, correlations, trends, patterns, and the like. As in the sciences, that operation and description of it made the once obscure equation and conclusion obvious. Together they express a synthesis statement revealed by the mass of data itself and not by the arbitrary hand of a beserk chemist or a sloppy media writer.

The illustrations provided here may give you a better sense of how closely the stages of organizing, coding, analysis, and conclusion are so intertwined that it is sometimes difficult to understand how each is a separate and unique thinking function and that one stage of thinking must be completed before the next one can take place. Analysis and synthesis are functions of logical and data-driven reasoning, the end product of systematic habit, bias-free methods, critical self-inquiry, and the source of creativity.

THE MYSTERIOUS DOMAIN: THINKING

Logic and *reasoning* are abstract terms to describe unseen inner workings of the mind. But the process of analysis becomes less mysterious when named and studied as the human process of schematic thinking. So now we can say that analyzing a stimulus is to note its similarities and differences for identification and storage in memory or in a written record. In memory and/or on record, the stored information becomes an associative base of knowledge, especially when one is exposed to new and unfamiliar stimuli.

Much of the research on schematic, or cognitive thought processes, describes thinking as a natural and human attribute, available to all, but used to its full potential by only a numbered few. The research discussed here is the work of F. C. Bartlett, a cognitive scientist who influenced many of today's cognitive scientists.

In 1958 Barlett published his classic text, *Thinking: An Experimental and Social Study*. The book grew out of all his previous experimental work on remembering, first published in 1932 in another classic text entitled, *Remembering: A Study in Experimental and Social Psychology*, and reprinted at least a dozen times since then. Bartlett conducted most of his work while a professor of experimental psychology at the University of Cambridge, England. He systematically studied the performance of large numbers of students over a period of some 20 years to arrive at his observations about the processes of thinking.

Throughout his text on thinking, Bartlett was cautious about making any final conclusions about his findings, but given what you already know about critical thinking and the work of other cognitive psychologists who followed him, you may find some merit in Bartlett's contributions. You may also develop a greater appreciation of how unique are the functions of coding, analysis, and conclusion, yet so interdependent on one another.

Thinking, Bartlett wrote in his book, is a skill. He likened it to a physical skill because he found that thinking and various types of bodily skill share the same performance properties, that is, characteristics such as "timing," "halts," a "point of no return," and "direction" (Bartlett, 1958, pp. 14-19).

Bartlett found that "Every kind of bodily skill is based upon evidence picked up directly or indirectly from the environment, and used for the attempted achievement of whatever issue may be required at the time of the performance" (p. 11). He subsequently defined thinking as ". . . . an extension of evidence, in line with the evidence and in such a manner as to fill up gaps in the evidence," and that this is "done by moving through a succession of interconnected steps" (pp. 20, 75), the momentum for which, Bartlett later suggested, comes from raising self-inquiries, particularly in instances where few directional clues are provided for the task at hand. These "steps," described in sections throughout the book, were found to include:

1. Abstraction of a "rule of direction" afforded by the evidence.
2. "Transfer" from the given information to filling the gap with information suggested by the evidence.
3. Reliance on the rule of direction and "intuition" or "guesses" when some of the information is missing.
4. Corrective measures on errors made and noticed (which proved to hold true in only a few cases among subjects tested).
5. Then on to the "terminus" or completion of the gap.

Bartlett's subjects mainly worked on tests that gradually increased in complexity and involved missing numbers in a series, incomplete figures, words missing in sentences, and the like. Behavior on these tests demonstrated performances characteristic of a bodily skill and indicated, as well, how the skill of thinking was performed when minimum to maximum evidence was present. The analytic ways subjects handled evidence with these problems are described here. The first terms in italics are Bartlett's. Although Bartlett's words and thoughts are sustained in the following descriptions, they represent a greatly distilled and partly paraphrased version of his research on these three subjects. Other italics were added to emphasize certain portions of his explanation:

1. *Interpolation* [to insert]. There is a *minimal* amount of information below which nobody can fill a gap in the same way as others. Introduction of a rule of direction based on the evidence occurs when instructions or information increase. *As more evidence is presented*, so does the facility to fill a gap. Some persons fill gaps more quickly with fewer instructions or information than others who require more direction and information.

2. *Extrapolation* [to estimate or determine]. These precedents are necessary in making the appropriate *transfer* from given evidence to filling the gap: recognition of the directional properties of evidence, recognition depends on selection of the appropriate items followed by a search for all points of agreement and difference in the items, the latter being easier to locate than the former, and finally, a further selection of the largest number of points of agreement. A thinking person then responds to these items as *linked* together in *some combination* to reach a decision, or *terminus*, and filling of the gap.

3. *Evidence in disguise*. Thinking at times may have to deal with evidence in disguise. That is, evidence needed is present, but the items have to be seen in a different way and then rearranged for *leaps* into insightful understanding. So that thinking goes beyond something which is there. It is the use of information about something present, to get somewhere else.

It is clear that gaps in the information are more easily seen and filled (interpolation) when there is maximum information and adequate instruction. Notice, too, that "links" (extrapolation) between dominating units in "some combination" of data eliminate other possibilities in the range of data so that arrival at a "terminus" point progresses as certain links overrule others. Keep in mind that links can occur not only between units of information, they can occur within a single unit of information.

Analytic thinking is particularly evident in the instance of minimum clues (evidence in disguise). In such cases, Bartlett said what happens is a search for relationships between two related items or units, and added that sometimes evidence outside the data is brought to bear on the data at hand. An example of this is the first illustration given earlier on how a media writer might analyze a single piece of data (consumer complaints on the SXL 200) along with information outside the data at hand: Attendance records were reviewed and absenteeism was noted during the period of high consumer complaints; other records showed drug arrests occurred at the same time; both records matched a period of worker accidents and complaints about supervisory laxity and the period of inferior manufacturing.

"Evidence in diguise" does not necessarily have to be a house record. That data could be an object in the environment, an overheard conversation, a magazine article, a personal experience. Suddenly a previously hidden link or piece of evidence connected to the information already known becomes quite obvious.[1]

Connections like these lead to a discovery or a plausible conclusion about

---

[1]Reports of scientific advances illustrate this avenue to discovery. See, for example, Ghislen (1963) and Watson (1968).

the problem at hand, if progress to "terminus" is made on the strength of empirical evidence previously accumulated, coded and, in most cases, noted as highest in importance and number. Bartlett found that when thinking covers a wider temporal range and descriptive variability of evidence, the criterion of importance tends to outweigh that of number. For Bartlett "importance" in this context means "those features in evidence which, remaining constant, can be applied in a sequence so that a terminal point becomes more and more clear and more and more uniformly and definitely determined as the sequence proceeds" (Bartlett, 1958, p. 87).

Only routine experience with the evidence affords the opportunity to "fill a gap," to "transfer" the given clues over to solution or, in the case of disguised evidence, to make the "leap" from given evidence to evidence unmasked. That leap is described by Bartlett as the discovery of learning that the objective evidence has properties of its own not immediately apparent in its specific parts. However, he made it clear that these processes are highly dependent on selection and arrangement of evidence. Also, that it is a mistake for anyone to believe that the process is purely intellectual rather than a skill. Bartlett said thinking is possible only if precedents occur in a sequential development and continue to exercise an influence.

In short, insight and discovery are possible only after prior conscientious accumulation and internalization of bias-free, verified, and orderly arrangement of relevant data, and only if that arrangement is sustained by the evidence. "Filling the gap," making a "transfer," or making the "leap" then becomes a matter of skill, that is, being able to recognize the predominate and connected factors that make up the equation and suggest a plausible conclusion.

Bartlett reminded us that although the features he described for dealing with evidence are necessary if thinking is to take place, the features by themselves do not guarantee that thinking will actually occur. He explained that before fill-ins, "transfers," and "leaps" can occur, a state of "perceptual readiness," a mindset of preparedness and attentiveness to the task at hand, must be present, a position with which Bruner (1964) concurred. Then that readiness must be sustained, otherwise obstacles to evidence such as distraction, fatigue, or personal interests and values will interfere with thinking and the appropriate fill-in, "transfer," or "leap."

All this should sound some familiar chords in your mind. Much of it suggests several things you have already read about in this text concerning readying one's mind for analysis and decision. As a reminder, here is a review of that information:

- One of the antecedents to thinking is to build a mental reservoir of relevant content in order to receive data concerning the new stimulus situation at hand.

- Self-motivation and self-direction are necessary ingredients to move-ment through the steps of thinking.
- Self-control on one's biases, such as an "inner instruction," assists accurate selection and arrangement of evidence based on attention to only those properties that belong to the stimuli encountered.
- Connections and distances between units of information are seen when such links are based on evidence rather than arbitrary choices.
- Exposure to mounting varieties of relevant (or "important") evi-dence and experience with it facilitates fill-ins and "transfers" and finally the "leap" from routine thought process to discovery and conclusion.

Traps in the Analytic Process

The opportunities for error and bias are just as numerous during analysis as they are at any other time during a writer's movement from selection of references and interviewees to evaluation and selection of specific items for coding. The rules for avoiding the pits of error and bias are just as valid here as at any other point. Regarding the traps and defenses against them, refresh your memory by referring to the pertinent research studies already examined on previous pages regarding "representativeness," "availability," "anchoring," "hot impulses," and "illusory database." Then after your first go-around with analysis, ask yourself these questions:

- *Where do my interests, values, beliefs, or assumptions interfere with my observations about relationships, correlations, patterns, anom-alies, etc.?*
- *What units of data have I failed to include in these observations?*
- *Is biased observation interfering with an appropriate fill-in, "trans-fer"?*
- *Is bias interfering with a "leap" to discovery?*
- *If these errors are present, what data must be reinstated to correct omissions to prevent another erroneous analysis and false conclu-sion, particularly in the instance of "evidence in disguise"?*

Types of Thinkers: "Everyday," Scientific, and Creative

The type of thinker who puts the mind through rigorous effort is rare, Bartlett (1958) found. That does not mean the skill is beyond human ability. Far from it. Because thinking is a human attribute, it is there for use if one chooses to develop it and to do so until it becomes a refined art. Once learned, it is like riding a bicycle, you never forget how to do it.

The type of thinking Bartlett described is characteristic, he concluded, of such disciplined thinkers as scientists (1958, chapters 7, 8). The person who chooses to fall back on the error of bias is the one who moves in the direction of "hot impulses," attempts to influence by assertion, and jumps to conclusions that satisfy personal needs and drives. This mode of thought is characteristic of the type Bartlett called the "everyday" thinker (chapter 9).

It is the scientific *and* creative type that Bartlett identified as the "original" thinker. This type passes through the "steps" of thinking, attends to the evidence, uses characteristic means of dealing with the evidence, corrects lapses into error before jumping to conclusions, and fills gaps that command assent. At the same time, the original thinker opens up and fills other gaps left unnoticed by others.

Creative in this context does not necessarily include the artist. Bartlett put the artist in a class apart from either the everyday or scientific thinker (chapter 10). On the other hand, Bartlett saw no reason why an artist as a creative type could not share in other modes of thought, or why others could not share the artist's mode. To illustrate how the mix and match could occur, he described the common ground on which all thinkers stand. They start from items of evidence that direct interpolation, extrapolation, and reinterpretation where the evidence is disguised. Like the scientist, and unlike the everyday thinker, an artist never accepts things as they appear, nor does the artist make generalizations. Also like the scientist, the artist's preparation for work moves in sequential steps that lead to recognition and filling of a gap in the medium of the artist's expertise.

The singular difference between scientist and artist, Bartlett said, is this: Where a scientist opens up many more gaps than the one filled, the artist ends on a more final note of closure. As an illustration, Bartlett eluded to the case of a novelist. As the novelist's story develops, so do the possibilities of a likely ending increase. Each chapter is both a closing point and a new direction. There are surprises along the way, yet each new direction carries with it an increasing sense that only one outcome is possible. All along, the feeling is: Of all the things that have happened, what will happen next? Then everything comes together so neatly that the reader must agree with the author that the given ending is the only possible conclusion: "This is what must happen. This alone is satisfying" (p. 191). This does not account for the typical surprise ending, but it is still illustrative of the difference Bartlett intended.

Artists, Bartlett pointed out, sometimes behave like everyday thinkers. That is, they may be biased in the direction of certain artistic conventions inherited from their social backgrounds or associations. However, although dominated by convention, the truly creative artist cannot use the convention in its standardized form and, instead, passes beyond it, similar to what

Bruner chose to call, "going beyond the information given," and applies the convention in a manner unique to that artist.

Of course, media writers do not figure in Bartlett's scheme. However, they could easily place among any one of Bartlett's types of thinkers. Depending on how the writer chooses to produce copy, a media writer might place as an "everyday" thinker, or a scientific thinker and disciplined artist.

Relevance to Mass Media Writers.   Earlier in this text, attention was directed to the similarity between a scientist's approach to systematic study and a professional writer's management of mass media projects. Bartlett's 20-year study, continued in one way or another by others who followed him, now gives us a fair idea of the source of that similarity. The work behavior of scientists and media writers is a manifestation of similar thinking processes. That does not mean the journalistic and scientific thinker are precisely alike. It does mean that the professional and creative media writer is obviously not the everyday thinker. The question is, if professional media writers are thinkers as disciplined and creative as scientists, then why do they not share status with those who produce work in a disciplined manner?

One among many plausible answers is that, unlike the work of scientists, media work methods are not uniformly agreed upon and, therefore, they remain uncodified (e.g., see Webb & Salancik, 1966). Most of it is accomplished intuitively or by trial and error. Consequently, neither universally accepted standards for entry into the field or established measures by which to judge a media writer's work exist. This situation, in turn, reduces opportunity for developing a reliable body of literature concerning media work procedures which can be debated and advanced as they are in scientific circles. If this leaves media writers out in the cold, it is not necessarily true that they fail to share the work characteristics of scientists and disciplined artists.

Another answer to this dilemma is that although professional media writers manifest the characteristics of scientists, the connection is not easily made because they also share the characteristics of disciplined artists. As Bartlett pointed out, creative artists never take things at face value. Neither do professional media writers. They, like disciplined artists, work sequentially, always directed by the evidence until they reach the final stage. After that, all thinking leads inevitably to an obvious "terminus."

But here is where the mass media writer shares a characteristic that belongs only to the scientist and still another characteristic that belongs only to the creative artist. If the scientist fills a gap and indicates other areas that still require answers and if, unlike the scientist, the artist fills a gap with a more final statement, the media writer at times fills a gap while pointing out those areas that still require answers. At other times, the media writer, like the artist novelist, fills a gap with more finality.

These characteristics manifest themselves everywhere in news, PR, and advertising work. For example, in news work the report of a house fire of known cause may come to a final note of closure, while in complex news stories, reporting the story of corruption in government may continue through a week-long series or go on for months. The same holds true in PR and advertising. PR announcements about a defective product may go on for several weeks, whereas announcement about a new chairman of the board is reported in a single press release. Ivory Soap has used its familiar advertising theme, "99-44/100% pure" for decades and has done so to the present time. Although confined by the conventions of the medium in which the statement has appeared, the statement itself has generated seemingly endless new creations on the basic theme. On the other hand, many ads are one-time presentations never read or heard about again.

If the scientist uses the conventions of science research and report, but goes one step beyond the given evidence to insight, and the artist remains within the conventions of literature or art, yet also goes one step beyond to insight to display the evidence with a presentation which is uniquely that of the artist's, so does the media writer remain within the conventions of a disciplined strategy to offer insight, but with a presentation that, like the artist, is the writer's alone.

Whether one chooses to classify media writers as scientific or artistic may be an arguable matter. One thing it is possible to say is that professionally oriented writers manifest the analytic characteristics of both the scientific and disciplined artistic thinker, and because both are typified by Bartlett as original and creative thinkers whose work behaviors are controlled and methodical, we can, at the very least, say the same about the disciplined media writer. The bottom line is this: *What do you want to be, an everyday media writer, or a professional one?*

Value of Scientific/Creative Thinking

As you have seen, the two predominate features of process and thinking are sequence and critical inquiry of self and the evidence. Unless one step is completed, it is quite obvious another cannot take place. If a step is taken out of sequence, flaws in strategic process and thought will quickly appear. Moreover, analytic connections to accurate resolution and creative thinking are at once disengaged. That is, if you believe you have passed through all the steps and find you still cannot move on to resolution or creative thinking, you have probably made an error somewhere. Perhaps you failed to raise the appropriate self-inquiry, or failed to get all questions answered, lost interest at some point, did not review the data well enough for coding, misplaced or left out an item during coding, overlooked a contributing factor to the analysis, or just made some wrong interpolations or extrapolations. Get back on track, correct the error and re-engage with the train of thought to "terminus."

The choice is yours. If you choose to be an everyday thinker, take the easy way out. Avoid going through all the sequential steps in the strategy. Forget about defending against personal bias. Never mind about raising critical questions. But, if you want to be an original and creative thinker, act like a professional media writer and work at it.

A "SCHEMATIC" FOR ANALYSIS

Part of your effort will include an analysis of the data. On short deadline assignments, whether they are for print or broadcast, the bits and pieces of information are grouped, compared, contrasted, connected, and weighed in the mind. In some cases, all this is done on the run. Time does not always allow for a systematic array of the data on paper. Usually there is only enough time to review and mentally integrate your coded data. On medium or long deadline assignments, however, the volume of information bits and pieces is usually massive and the relationships between them are not easily managed in the mind. It is too easy to mistake one's personal bias as "intuition" and to draw the wrong conclusion.

When the data are weighty and complicated, final review of the data usually requires some type of systematic arrangement, a visual *schematic*, that is, an outline, diagram, or chart. It is a preliminary plan that permits you to see relevant bits and pieces as a whole just as you would notice the separate images in a painting or photograph. That array of information may vary from assignment to assignment, or you may hit upon a schematic you find is useful for more than one assignment. If you cannot think of a plan, use the schematic shown in Fig. 11.1 as a starter model.

This schematic is for a moderately complex news story, but writers in TV, PR, and advertising could do the same with a similar assignment. A TV writer might draft a scenario from such a schematic; a PR writer could use it as a base to map a campaign; an advertising writer might find it generates ideas for a series of ads or a single storyboard (a series of sketches with captions that tell a connected story).

Let's suppose the data in the schematic represents information you have collected for the Great Lakes assignment, and that you have displayed relevant items from that collection in this schematic. In this case, you used categories for the schematic from pre-coded and post-coded labeled sections in your data book. Or, perhaps, you used categories from a collection of files under those labels, a series of notebooks, or however you may have chosen to pre-code and post-code data for your assignment. Using those category names, you set up a table with vertical columns (could have also made a schematic using horizontal sections or entered category heads on separate pages using a word processor). Then you plugged in brief reminders of relevant, informative, and verified items from each labeled unit in your data collection. Next, you absorbed the array as a whole, then studied each fact in each column or section and understood what that unit of evidence covered and how it related to the assignment you are working on. You took another look at the specific items within that unit to see if any relationships or differences existed between them and to see where the weight and importance of connecting evidence fell within that single unit. You might even have made a summary statement of what you believed that unit of information communicated.

Then you repeated the procedure with each additional unit of information and looked for any patterns, trends, similarities, differences, gaps, or anomalies between the units presented. Finally, and with the working and alternative statements in mind, you noted where the weight and importance of the connecting evidence fell in the overall set of units and wrote down what you decided were the predominating facts. The evidence either confirmed, negated, or modified your working statement. But before making any final decisions, you checked back through your original data records and asked yourself:

- *Have I omitted or overlooked evidence which carries more weight than the evidence I've considered?*
- *Have I ignored important evidence because it interferes with what I want to believe?*
- *Does the evidence support the relationships, differences, etc., I've noted?*
- *Does the evidence support the patterns, trends, relationships, etc., I've observed between the units of evidence?*

Finally, you allow your review of itemized facts settle in your mind and let the mind mull through the fragments of evidence. Assuming you set bias aside in your selection of data items, saw things as the evidence indicated, you then permitted the appropriate equation and conclusion come to mind.

Although there are numerous variables involved here, the assignment itself was only moderately complex and could be classified as a medium deadline assignment. Let's take each column at a time. The first simply is a series of background information on the Great Lakes and the interesting factor here is that the area has the highest concentration of industry on the continent. This suggests the vulnerability of the Great Lakes to pollution discharge effects; also, the depths of the Great Lakes prevent quick

Great Lakes	Toxic waste	Threat/Wildlife	Threat/Humans	Controls/Violaters	Prognosis/Solutions	Conflicts
95,000 sq. miles long	century-long uncontrolled dumping -- 362 contaminants, 24 hazardous	whitefish in plentiful supply, but industry is depressed due to pollution scare	cautions on sport fish consumption	IJC 1909 water treaty w/Canada	L. Erie, Clinton River revived --Ellis	GL a "chemical soup"-- child-bearing women should avoid eating sport fish --Bannister
formed by Arctic glaciers	42 "hot spots," 5 to be remedial test areas	tumors, ulcers on bullheads, advisories on trout, others	DNR: of 700 species fish, 1 of 4 unsafe to consume	1972 Clean Water Act, updated 1978	Congress names GL as nat'l lab	
bordered by 8 states, Ontario	fish/wildlife most obvious indicators of polluted water	small fish feed on contaminated organisms in lake bed, older fish feed on younger ones, in water longer, are more contaminated; poisoned food chain affects other wildlife	studies find defects in babies of women on diet of sport fish	EPA, DNR, FDA & health dept. controls in 8 jurisdictions, Ontario, have greatly improved GL waters	Bush proposes $82 mil in '91 / not enough --Washington research	abide by fish consumption guides --Westin
		whitefish not contaminated to extent of other species because not a predator species			not enough --US Conservation Foundation	sound fish preparation is key --Ogilevsky
only MI nearly surrounded by GL	trouble toxics: PCB, DDT, PAH, mercury, chlordane, dieldrin		study finds cancer risk for humans on sport fish diet	jurisdictions had fish sampling programs by '82	it's starting point --Ellis	need uniform, stricter standards --Moran
holds 1/5 earth's fresh water	20 mil gals PCB produced since '29, 60% in use, 5% only destroyed	crossed bills in fish-feeding cormorants, terns; low repro.	family vacation plans disrupted by beach closing	'90 GL Critical Programs Act	NWF fights to ban 70 toxins	uniform standards could create pbms --French
is largest inland body of water in world	major problem: pre-regulation discharges still in sediment of lake bed where food chain begins	bald eagle reproduction low	Detroit resident gets intestinal infection after swimming in L. St. Clair	major problem: discharges before '72 (lead, mercury, chlor-alkali, PCB) still appear in lake sediment	researchers find way to degrade PCB; not yet proven	IJC declares GL water quality at risk, recommends stricter controls, uniform standards

(see data book for GL turnover rates; length, depth, width)	air deposition a major pollution source --Roberts	toxins found in otter, mink	up to 60 L. Mich. beaches closed between '82-85, some reopened; no further data at this time; no data on other GL	most large industries comply w/ regulations; warnings issued after some accidental discharges; smaller ones are problem, but minimal	public needs to get into act --Ellis
area growth began w/4 canals built between 1799-1959	photographer develops film in L. Ontario	300 plant and animal species threatened	closings not good water quality indicators, too many variables --McIntyre	5 industries issued warning; laundromat chain gets $1/2 mil fine	
area has highest concentration of industry on continent	unknown source pts: land runoff from pesticide-fed farmlands, lawns; buried waste	zebra mussels another threat; attach themselves to fish, any object --Lenz		need more staff to monitor industries to avoid violations before the fact, even if "minimal" --Axelrod	
40 industries in SE MI alone	bacteria from untreated sewage gets into lakes after rainstorms			notable improvements in water quality in past two decades --Daniels	
over 35 mil live in GL area	MI alone pours 16-10 bil gals sewage yearly into lakes			Wetlands Protection Act keeps wetlands out of developers' hands --Ellis	

FIG. 11.1.   A "schematic" model for analysis.

235

turnover, that is, it takes some of the lakes hundreds of years to flush themselves out and renew their waters.

Clearly the predominate factor in the second column is that this dumping went on for a century or more before controls were established and that discharges from those years still remain in the lake bed where fish feed and contamination in the food chain begins (Column 3). But discharges are only part of the problem. The Great Lakes are waste baskets for pollution from many other sources, as well (Column 2). Column 3 tells us our working statement about whitefish does not hold up and requires replacement. A suggestion for a replacement appears in the fourth column, that is, the contaminated food chain carries potential health risks to human life.

Successful elimination of the deadly sea lamprey holds some hope of getting rid of another nuisance, the zebra mussel, but control experiments are still in the test stage (Column 3). The item on the oppressed fishing industry is interesting (Column 3), but you have learned commercial fish are safe for consumption because they are marketed under government health standards; sport fish are the problem, as data in several columns indicate.

Controls established in the 1970s have helped improve water quality (Column 5), but some observers want tighter controls and the International Joint Commission (IJC, Column 7) agrees. Others want violaters caught before the fact, not after, and a great deal of unsettled argument between government and business surrounds this issue (Column 5). However, except for a few infractions, industry seems to be cooperating with regulations (Column 5). Although new efforts to save the Great Lakes have been initiated, the cost of remediation goes up faster than government implementation of remedial programs get off the ground (Column 6). That is another suggestion for a new working statement, but you also note that your data are thin in this regard, so you decide to put this one on the back burner for now. No one would argue with the observations in the last column about the quality of the Great Lakes.

In terms of a pattern, it seems that no sooner one pollution problem is corrected, another crops up to multiply past offenses to the Great Lakes and plague remediation efforts. The evidence now in hand seems to fall on the fact that toxic contamination in the Great Lakes has reached such proportions that human life is threatened as well as the fish and wildlife. In the next section, you will see how these fragments make up the equation and conclusion in a final synthesis statement.

Perhaps you feel you understand the meaning of analysis and what it takes to analyze collected data, but still experience difficulty in noting relationships, differences, the weight of the evidence, or the connections between them. You may not have internalized your data well enough. Or, you may just need practice noticing and connecting. Try looking at the items again.

It might also help if you looked on a single item as a "vignette," a set of related items within a unit, or a complete unit of data as a family of "vignettes." Abelson, a cognitive scientist, defines a vignette as a visual image of an event, or a "picture plus a caption." Each vignette is an episode in memory. Vignettes are then linked together to make up a "script," which is a "coherently linked chain of vignettes." If a single vignette is a "picture plus caption, a chain is metaphorically a cartoon strip, a sequence of panels telling a story" (Abelson, 1976, p. 34).

In cognitive science, "scripts" are meant to signify learned experiences stored in memory to guide a person's behavior in familiar and unfamiliar social situations. Nevertheless, if scripting helps you in your efforts to analyze coded data, there is little reason why you should not use the device. Furthermore, instead of thinking about a script as a cartoon strip, it might be easier for you to visualize scripting as a scenario for a TV project, or what writers in electronic media call a "storyboard," a series of sketches with captions that tell a connected story based on the given data. Visualizing a script from a series of vignettes may just open up some doors for you.

DRAWING A CONCLUSION (THE FINAL STATMENT)

Critical Self-Inquiry 9: *What is the statement inherent in and manifested by the body of verified and evaluated data?* This may sound difficult. It isn't. You should have confidence in the work you have accomplished thus far. You have gone through all the experiental maneuvers necessary to etch the data in your mind: research, validations, verifications, and data review; interview questions and review; interviews, verifications, and review; then organization, coding, and analysis. You are "perceptually ready" because the data are so ingrained in your mind, the fragments that make up the equation will fall into place and direct your attention to the concluding statement. Read on. The next sections may help you better understand this naturally human capability is within your reach.

FROM ANALYSIS TO CONCLUSION

You have learned how coded data is broken down and reduced and how this operation facilitates analysis, either in the mind or with a schematic. Also, you now know that analysis is a thought process and that such thinking is a skill performed by systematic thinkers who stick to the evidence. Furthermore, you know that it is this tactic that directs one to the appropriate conclusion, discovery, or insight, or as Bartlett called it, the "terminus." At times, in the case of "disguised evidence," the conclusion is a "leap," or a "step beyond the information given." Keep in mind, however, that the "step beyond" is guided by reference points in the evidence, so that any conclusion that results from such a leap is based on validated, verified information and is, therefore, plausible.

THE WORKING STATEMENT REVISITED

The procedure outlined here gives you an idea of how that process works. Once you have reached a conclusion, articulate it. It could be in a form similar to the examples on pp. 222–223. Or, it could be a statement of no more than one or two sentences. It is at this point that you learn with certainty whether your original working statement, or its alternative, held up under the evidence, was disconfirmed and completely changed, or simply modified. Whatever the result, the important factor is the articulated conclusion, the sum total of the known facts to date.

What the Final Statement Is and Is Not

Essentially, the conclusion represents your internal synthesis of the given information. No matter how you do it, via a schematic or in your head, the conclusion takes on form and expression when you articulate it as a statement. The statement itself stands as an announcement which you submit as true, as true as anyone can get to the truth at the present time. In short, the statement is a declaration of the current state of affairs concerning the problem you have explored. You transform a synthesis of the data (the conclusion) into a final statement because it can provide you with a starting point from which to develop a news or magazine story, a press release or PR campaign, a single ad or a campaign series of ads.

You should be aware, however, that the statement is not a prophecy, prediction, or assertion. It is not the lead for a news or magazine article; it is not the PR theme or advertising slogan. Rather, the statement serves as the creative seed for these and often translates easily, sometimes directly, into an effective lead, or substantive PR or advertising campaign idea.

Notice the equations and concluding statements and the differences between them in the examples on pp. 222–223. The first statement reads: *These facts together indicate that quality may have dipped during those summer months due to fewer people on the job and lack of supervisory checks on the line.* The statement makes a declaration, but it is inconclusive. It stands as a possible explanation for substandard production during a certain period of time. The statement is neither a claim nor assertion, prediction or prophecy. Although the facts by themselves can be substantiated, the links between them are inferred. Further investigation may strengthen the links or throw an even wider spotlight on the problem. At the moment, however, the evidence suggests that the above factors may have been the source of substandard production. Meanwhile, the newswriter can report the coincidence of absenteeism and supervisory laxity, write a full story about these factors and include the sentiments of consumers, company, and union spokespersons concerning the product lot in question. The magazine writer can do as much, but depending on the magazine, might want to include the history of such incidents elsewhere, what was done about these, or any other aspect the editor would expect to see. The PR writer can announce the possible connection between the facts and the substandard production for the period involved and, perhaps, explain what the company intends to do about supervisory management.

In the second case, the evidence is more conclusive. What is known is that nutritionists agree that fat intake is a priority issue in a healthy diet. And, that the competition's product has 15% more fat in it than the house product. The equation provides a more conclusive synthesis statement: *The facts indicate that we should concentrate on the theme of less fat, and that fewer calories are not always better.* This is an instance when the final statement also lends itself to a campaign theme idea, *Less Is Not Always Better.*

In regard to the story on Great Lakes pollution, you now know that Great Lakes whitefish is not in danger of extinction and is, in fact, one of the most abundant species, mainly because it is low on the food chain and not a predator species. Whitefish feed on shrimp and other small organisms least exposed to contamination. Furthermore, pollutants in the water penetrate into the flesh of some fish species, instead of settling in the skin, which can be removed before cooking. The latter type is marketable and whitefish is one of these.

Your notes show a few cases of discharge violations, but that most companies abide by the rules or make amends after state warnings. Only a few have resorted to litigation and those cases are still pending. In addition, you have some data on beaching closings, but records are available only on Lake Michigan and closings there have diminished in number since 1985. Moreover, jurisdictions near the other lakes did not submit reports on beach closings, and you have learned that beach closings are not the best indicators of persistent pollution in the Great Lakes. So your notes on discharge violations and beach closings will have little bearing on your synthesis statement.

Stories on the tug-of-war between government and business and the argument about stricter standards have been done by others, so these also can be set aside until something new develops. But something else you have learned is that many commercial fisheries have closed shop, partly because reports about polluted waters reduced the market demand for Great Lakes fish, including whitefish. Retail food managers refuse to stock Great Lakes fish even though fish caught for commercial purposes, unlike sport fish, must stand the test of government standards before going to retail markets.

Of course, the information about whitefish cancels out everything you thought was true about whitefish—no harm done. But, you still have to write a feature story. You know you cannot use the impaired fisheries as a topic. That is going to need a lot more investigation, but that does not mean you forget about the topic. Instead, you put it on the back burner and use it as an enterprise project for another time, and you hold on to notes you have already collected on it, including those concerning Great Lakes whitefish. You also keep an eye on discharge violations and pending litigations, beach closings, progress with the PCB experiment, control of zebra mussels, and whether the government is moving on stricter standards and remediation plans for the Great Lakes.

What you do have for the feature you have to write is that despite improvements in water quality over the past two decades, the signs of harm to those who consume Great Lakes sport fish are now more evident. Although there are many natural nuisances, like the zebra mussel and bacteria from untreated sewage after rainstorms, these are within human control. The weight and importance of connecting evidence points to chemical contaminants as the source of persistent and growing potential harm. Century-long dumping before regulations restricted industrial discharges, together with toxic deposits from land runoffs and air currents, all these have transformed the Great Lakes into a reservoir of toxic pollutants, contaminating a food chain that starts with fish and wildlife and ends on the dinner tables of sport fishing enthusiasts.

You, therefore, replace your original working statement with one that conditions indicate is the story at the present time. That is, you work from verified pieces of evidence at hand putting together an equation that reveals the picture, spells out the data-driven conclusion and, at the same time, articulates a synthesis statement that might say something like this:

Remedial action over the past twenty years has improved Great Lakes water quality. However, residue from decades of uncontrolled industrial discharges have left traces of hazardous contaminants in the water and lake bed. Although industrial discharges are now under control and the IJC has recommended stricter government standards, other problems such as pollutants carried by air currents have found a home in the Great Lakes and hamper restoration efforts (equation).

The legacy today is poisoned fish, defective wildlife, and a contaminated food chain that carries the potential of generational damage to human life, particularly for consumers of sport fish. The once pristine Great Lakes are reservoirs of toxic waste and may remain so for some time (conclusion).

Above all else, this chapter should make the tight interrelationship of coding, analysis, conclusion, and the final statement abundantly clear. Also, it should be clear how important it is to collect complete, accurate, balanced, and unbiased evidence during the research and interview stages in preparation for these functions. The coding process depends on it. Analysis stands or falls on the merit of the coding process. The validity of the conclusion relies on every function that precedes it. And the impact of your presentation in the form of copy depends on the validity of the final statement.

Let's assume now that you have done everything necessary to analyze the data, draw a conclusion, and articulate a synthesis statement. You are now ready to give shape and life to that statement in the form of a creative presentation, whether it is for a news story, PR release, or advertisement.

If, however, you have come to this point on an assignment of your own and are still unable to formulate a statement, the reasons may be the same as those given earlier. Review your research and interview notes. Go back over the critical questions listed throughout this chapter and determine where you may have strayed from making further progress.

Perhaps you lumped too many similar items together. Perhaps there is a significant difference in one or more of those items that disqualifies listing them in the same unit of information. If so, use the procedure that was suggested earlier. Split that category and create a separate and appropriate unit of information for those items which show a distinctively different feature from other similiar items in that category. The new unit may help you see certain things in your second analysis that you overlooked before.

Maybe you have so many categories that similarities and differences between units are blurred. Lump items that share a majority of similar features into a single unit so that a predominating feature or features are revealed. Differences between units will become evident. The weight of the pros and cons will become more distinct.

Perhaps you feel there is nothing wrong with your data organization, but you still cannot draw a conclusion. Review and internalize the details in each unit. Understand the summary meaning of each unit. Compare the units. Notice where the weight and importance of the evidence falls. A second and even third look often triggers notice of something that escaped your attention the first time around. Or, cultivate the vignette technique.

If you are still having difficulty, put the material aside for a few days. Give yourself some time to turn the evidence around in your mind. More often than not, the synthesis you need is there and will suddenly occur to you. If this does not happen, discuss your problem with someone. Perhaps you are so close to the material that the clues escape you. Another eye on the evidence often helps clear your vision.

The Final Payoff

If all these stages, returns, modifications, and repetitions seem like a long and tedious route to the final payoff, the writing, remember that 99% routine work is the source of 1% inspiration. Remember, too, that every function you have been introduced to thus far, including thinking, is a "skill" and skill improves with practice.

Although Bartlett defined only thinking as a skill, other researchers after him have discovered that other human functions, as well, can be perfected to a point where they become automatic. For example, a British computer scientist (Sharples, 1985), has found that writing is a systematic and constraint-influenced process which contains the elements of generating (finding something to write about), planning, selecting, verifying and, finally, transforming thoughts on to paper or a keyboard; that these skills improve with practice over time and with maturity. But he cautioned that no one should make the mistake of believing that the process is a direct route to actual writing. It is, rather, an antecedent which is both recursive and repetitive (Sharples, 1985).

In short, each media assignment becomes less and less overwhelming and the road to writing becomes smoother and easier in due time. It is why seasoned writers seem to produce their work effortlessly and why novices, in the beginning, falter, produce slowly, and frequently wish they had chosen another line of work. All the pain quickly disappears, however, when the novice wins that first byline or draws accolades for a successful PR project or ad.

SUMMARY GUIDE FOR ANALYZING DATA

When analyzing coded data, ask:
- *Have I omitted or overlooked evidence which carries more weight than the evidence I've considered?*
- *Have I ignored important evidence because it interferes with what I want to believe?*
- *Does the evidence support the relationships, differences, etc., I've noted?*
- *Does the evidence support the patterns, trends, relationships, etc., I've observed between the units of evidence?*

To avoid traps of bias during analysis, ask:
- *Where do my interests, values, beliefs, or assumptions interfere with my observations about relationships, correlations, patterns, anomalies, etc.?*

- *What units of data have I failed to include in these observations?*
- *Is biased observation interfering with an appropriate fill-in, "transfer"?*
- *Is bias interfering with a "leap" to discovery?*
- *If these errors are present, what data must be reinstated to correct omissions to prevent another erroneous analysis and false conclusion, particularly in the instance of "evidence in disguise"?*

If you have performed all previous stages in a systematic and "constrained" manner, namely, under the discipline of a strategy and the habit of raising critical questions, the final stages will fall into place. Expedite those functions by first asking Critical Self-Inquiry 8: *Where are the similarities, differences, anomalies, gaps, and unknowns; where are the agreements, disagreements, or conflicts; where are the links indicating relationships, correlations, patterns, or trends; where does the weight and importance of evidence fall and why?*

Next, ask Critical Self-Inquiry 9: *What is the statement inherent in and manifested by the body of verified and evaluated data?* The final payoff, writing, then becomes a source of great satisfaction. The next chapter tells you how to make the final payoff work for you, but first read how the professionals interviewed in this text, organized, coded, and analyzed their collected data.

* * *

HOW THE PROFESSIONALS DO IT

Organizing, Coding, and Analyzing the Data

Discussions in this and the previous chapter suggest that the functions of organizing, coding, and analyzing the data and arriving at a conclusion are closely related, often occur simultaneously and sometimes trigger a presentation idea. The reality of this may come through a little more clearly in the following comments from professionals introduced in previous chapters.

Characteristically, these and other writers interviewed were hard put to describe the thought processes that led them to their final conclusion, nor could they easily describe how their presentation ideas suddenly popped into their minds.

But having read chapter 10 and this chapter, perhaps now you can see that systematic procedure, critical self-inquiry, "perceptual readiness," "mid-level motivation," and "scientific/creative" thinking, all have a great deal to do with formulating a presentation idea that stands up to question. How the elusive functions of organization, coding, analysis, and conclusion synchronize data in your mind to serve your creative drive may remain a mystery, but for you they may be a bit less mysterious because you have learned something about these activities. As importantly, you have learned they make up a human capability that is within your reach.

Print News: The Navy Story

Here is how Ms. Freedberg and Mr. Ashenfelter handled the organization, coding, and analysis of their story and arrived at a conclusion which led to an approach for stories on five of the seamen and a unique presentation idea for Mr. Ashenfelter's story on Seaman Collum. Note how he organized and thought about his data, a process that became the recognition point of *what the stories were*. The presentation idea, he said, occurred to him *suddenly*. But that, as you now know, is principally because he had internalized the organized/analyzed evidence so well.

> **Ashenfelter:** Before writing up the stories, we generally outlined what we had, and I think we had one session together where we just sat down together and talked about the key things we wanted to get into each story and based on that we both did some general outlines covering the main points. We knew at that point what the stories were, what we were going to write about. We knew what the bottom lines were in both [Trerice and Collum] stories. We just did not know how we were going to present it.
>
> I didn't know what was going to be the first section of the [Collum] story. I didn't know what was going to be the last section. I just started running through my notes and the investigation report and putting things into the computer terminal, things that I wanted to write about. I found the things that I thought were the most interesting, things that the witnesses had to say, what happened the day before, what occurred in the brig, what conditions were like in the brig, then what happened the day he [Collum] went over the side, the moments leading up to it, who the family is and how they feel about all this.
>
> I ended up dropping some stuff. We had more than we could have ever gotten into the paper. Then suddenly it occurred to me that the way I wanted to tell that story was with those italicized dividers on different stages leading up to his death, and what people saw, and then tell those components of the story. Then we just sat down and started trying to write it. It took us, I think, two weeks to write those first two stories [on Trerice and Collum]

Note that the writing took only a brief period of time compared to the months of effort that preceded it. In chapter 12 Mr. Ashenfelter and the others tell more about how they finally put their work on paper for publication. Although this reference appears after each of the following segments, it is important to read the contents of chapter 12 first before referring to "How the Professionals Do It" in the last section of chapter 12. What the professionals were able to say and what they could not explain will have more meaning for you.

Print News: The Ford Plant Fire

Even though Mr. Cain had little time to formally pre-organize his notes, he did keep a time-ordered arrangement of observed events and other data. He later post-organized and coded his data using the same chronological order, explaining that he orders and files notes on most of his stories in the same chronological manner. In another comment, Cain said he kept his chronologically ordered notes sometimes for weeks, months, and even years because they often provided valuable background data for stories that turned up concerning the same subjects, people, or events.

In his comments here, it is evident Mr. Cain's habit of self-inquiry influenced the organizing, coding, and analysis of his data which, in this case, he does on the run. He later explained that when he got back to the office, he verified his data with others who were on the scene. In his comment below, notice that he does not allow his original beliefs about the fire and the toxicity problem interfere with his conclusion.

> Cain: I went through my notes, read them all the way through once, then went back with a marker and underlined those things that looked like they were reasonable elements of the story worth writing about and talking about. A lot of the material was redundant. So if you've got three or four people saying basically the same thing, making the same observation, you look for who was the the most credible person. I tried to capture the best quotes and the best picture of each of the different aspects of the story. I wanted to give the reader a feeling that they were there.
>
> I recognized the first domain of the story, threat from the chemicals. So I try to bring up all the pieces of information that I've got on that. Then: *How great a threat was it or wasn't it?* Just asking questions of myself.
>
> Seven miles from the plant there were these huge jet black clouds with orange flames going right up through hundreds of feet in the air. There were some loud booms going off. Those turned out to be paint cans. My expectation was much greater than the final result. It [the fire] turned out to be much smaller than I thought. The final test results showed a much lower level of toxicity.

In chapter 12, Mr. Cain describes how he put his story together for presentation.

Broadcast News: The TWA Hijack

Mr. Meisner explained that the news documentary about the TWA hijacking was produced from a long tape (an unedited tape) of the 30-odd nightly newscasts that he and his staff had edited, sometimes from Boston, most of the time at St. Louis.

Although unaware of it at the time, Mr. Meisner later realized that all the time he was editing the nightly newscasts and putting together the long tape, he was, at the same time, organizing, coding, and analyzing his material. Notice his criteria for selecting the parts for those tapes: *compelling but informational, solid information, entertaining, interesting*.

Mr. Meisner knew he wanted to produce stories that tied the international incident to St. Louis people and said that focus for the final project took shape only after work on the short tapes captured the overall drama of the situation. The stability of his working statement guided that process and, in this case, was part of the final conclusion for presentation: a creatively compelling, but informational presentation of a shocking international incident and its dramatic relationship to St. Louis victims and their families.

> **Meisner**: Most scripts were written in St. Louis, except in cases where we had our people in Germany, or where we had our people in Boston. We shot, reviewed the tape, wrote the script and edited from those locations. For example [on the long tape], when we were in Boston and interviewed the couple together, we did two hours worth of interviews knowing we also had to turn around a one-hour special that night in St. Louis [after the 6 o'clock news].
>
> We started doing the interviews at 2:30 in the afternoon, trying to make tape available, as well, for airing in St. Louis at 6 p.m. We had one advantage. Boston's in the Eastern time zone. St. Louis is in the Central, an hour behind Boston time. We went back to our affiliate station in Boston, wrote and edited a package [a video and sound tape] and sent it to St. Louis for airing at six. Then we fed a long [unedited] tape and sent that to St. Louis probably about 7:30 p.m. where it was written for the one-hour show aired that night at 9 p.m. We were able to prevail on Tom Brokaw [NBC network anchorman] to cut in on that one. I picked the best interviews for the script and suggested these to a producer handling the story back in St. Louis. I look for compelling, but informational ones. What we're doing today, more than just journalism, we're giving solid information as well as news, but we're also giving it in an entertaining, interesting fashion. Because if it's not interesting people are going to turn off the TV. The hijack was a shocking incident in itself, that much more for the people involved. From the start, our focus was on the St. Louis passengers, and we needed to get all these aspects into the nightly broadcasts and then into the prime time show.

For more about Mr. Meisner's documentary, see chapter 12.

Broadcast News: The Illegal Use of Public Land

In Ms. Timmons' account of how she organized her data, notice that she managed several functions at once. With audience always in mind, she based data organization, coding, and analysis on data that are *important, relevant*. She relied on *facts, information*, and *interesting* data that stand up to question. Keeping the data in mind, she simultaneously analyzed, synthesized, and visualized both the visual and textual presentation of her story.

> **Timmons**: When the interviewing was done, I compiled all the information, reviewed it to pull out the interviews that were the most informative, that is, the ones that would pertain particularly to the public, that the public would grasp the most information from.
>
> I looked for the facts, the most important ones, that I was trying to make the public aware of. And, again, it goes back to the facts: *There is a problem on public land. So if you are going to use public lands, you should be aware of this problem, and here's what you can do if you're confronted with it.* I couldn't use all the information I had, but I did use quotes from my initial interviews. Among those interviews, my primary interview with the State Police lieutenant in charge of Michigan's "Operation Hemp" was the most relevant.
>
> I usually start with a copy script, but I use that in unison with a visual script. I had the Michigan information and visuals of Michigan woods, and along with that I used the video available from California where they had different interviews with hikers and campers who had actually been shot at. I just tried to get as much relevant, interesting information into it as I could and not run over the time allotted for the story. This particular serial documentary ran in two-minute segments three nights a week during the 11 o'clock news hour, so there was no room for irrelevancies.

Ms. Timmons raised questions up to the very last and discovered she had to return to a previous step for additional information. Notice the thinking related to that piece of information. Notice, too, that at certain points in the overall procedure, she has informed her editor about her progress and provides an outline for his inputs before completing the final script.

> **Timmons**: Because I tape record everything, I can check on myself to make sure I'm not passing incorrect information because I'm quoting different experts. Then I have a means to rely on if any of that information is

questioned. There are no holes because I stick to the facts and I have to make sure I have all the information beforehand.

If I discover, as I'm reviewing or writing, that something is missing, I call back for more information. For example, as I was writing this script, I needed to know how many acres of public land there are in Michigan. I noticed that I was talking about Michigan land and didn't have a context for it. That is, I didn't have the number of acres, and I knew the viewer would say: *How many acres?* Then you have to put the answer in perspective. If there are only three acres of public land, then it's not very important. If there are 20 million acres of public land that people can use, where drug growers can hide, then it's important. The news director checked with me to see how the story was developing, and then once I'm into editing, I give him the information, on the basis of the story, in an outline before the story is aired.

Once the problem of land misuse in Michigan was established, ensuing research provided data that prompted modification and enlargement of the working statement. That is, although squatters were not a problem in Michigan, hostile drug farmers and survivalists were and that data suggested defense precautions for unwary recreationers were in order. That data provided Ms. Timmons with her final statement and set the focus of her feature story for each of the three broadcast segments which are described in chapter 12.

Public Relations: The Converted Ambulance Crisis

After research, including interviews, Mr. Snearly *found* and finally *concluded* that *a combination of factors* was causing the ambulance fires. He pointed to the evidence, the equation for that conclusion and, at the same time, summarized its ultimate meaning.

Snearly: We fairly rapidly concluded that we couldn't find one single defect in the chassis that we sold. We found it was a combination of factors that was causing the fuel system to have excess pressure and heat, and that was causing the fires. There are about 40-50 converters [the companies that convert the Ford chassis into an ambulance].

A lot of them [the converter companies] were doing things that were inappropriate like rerouting fuel lines and exhaust systems. Also, in some cases, the vehicles were being poorly maintained [by the ambulance companies that bought the converted vans] and, in a lot of cases, run excessively in a severe usage pattern. Another factor was the volatility of fuel which has increased dramatically in recent years. As lead has been removed from the fuel, refineries have been replacing it with additives like butane to make it [the vehicle] run better and give it more power. That tends to evaporate more rapidly at lower temperatures and causes pressure problems. But regardless of how it was happening, they were our vehicles and they were catching fire.

The major PR campaign begins with a recall effort directed, on Mr. Snearly's suggestion, by the National Highway Traffic Safety Administration (NHTSA). He also conducted another briefing that extended beyond PR staffers. Other personnel needed to know the facts in the case and how to handle themselves when bombarded with questions or complaints from the media, or any other quarter.

Snearly: Once we had the information, we called in our regional field managers and our broadcast news people [Ford World Headquarters has its own video production facility within the Public Affairs Department] and held a day-long seminar on what the problem was. I wanted our people to understand the problem and to know what to say if they had an incident in their area.

We initiated the recall announcement and developed some footage that showed what the modifications were and taped interviews with our executives and handed these videos out to television stations.

The basic message was what I called, at the time, the three-legged stool [the final statement and presentation idea].The idea was that this is a complicated problem and the only way it could be solved was for Ford, the third-party manufacturers, and the ambulance operators in combination doing their part. We used this idea and the information in my records for the background paper [given to managers and PR staff] and for press releases, and I'd pull out my Q&A file when the media or anybody called me. We also incorporated a lot of this information in a news brief that goes out to Ford executives each month to update their knowledge of what's going on.

When we made the announcement that we were going to make it an official NHTSA safety recall under their registered regulations, we had a seven-city satellite hookup and had Helen Petrauskas, Ford vice-president of Environmental and Safety Engineering, announce it from Washington. This gave reporters in those cities where the incidents occurred a chance to talk to our people in Washington along with the Washington press corps.

In chapter 12, Mr. Snearly describes how the initial presentation had to be modified to accommodate unexpected reaction to the final statement and presentation of it.

Public Relations: The Motorsports Promotion

For Mr. Preuss research and field work triggered a spontaneous solution to the immediate problem of substituting press kits with a new idea. Formal organization and analysis were reflexive functions for this experienced writer. Although press kits were filled with information sportswriters needed, Mr. Preuss noticed these were soon put aside. He also noticed reporter's notebooks never left reporters' hands. Doing some associative thinking, as Bruner and Bartlett described it, he suddenly realized that the same kind of notebook, with the Ford oval on the cover of it, some blank pages for notes, and other pages filled with racing facts would also never leave their hands. That was the conclusion drawn from tested data which was then tossed about in the practiced mind of Mr. Preuss. Once management approvals were obtained, the notebook was produced as well as other product promotions. For more on presentation of the press notebook, see chapter 12.

Advertising: The Pizza Campaign

The research is in, and now the creative group begins work on shaping a creative campaign idea. Note that the self-inquiries never stop. Mr. Thornton used the terms *mapping* and *interpretation* for organization-coding-analysis-conclusion, but that is what happened next, a synthesis that he described as *all pretty logical*. Take special note of the last statement in this excerpt.

Thornton: It's all pretty logical. We had defined the problem. We had the research. We had a few people sitting around in a room. We said: *Okay, what's the research telling us? Delivered pizza isn't as good.*

We started looking at the individual lines of the research, the verbatim items we got from the people in the focus groups, etc. *Why isn't it good? Oh, when it's delivered, it's cold. When it's delivered it could be stuck to the top of the box, or it could be late, or they could have wrong toppings on it.*

So we start mapping each one of these and made a particular interpretation of all the data which boiled down to the question: *Is delivered pizza as good as pizza served in the restaurant? Well yes, it is, because Domino's pizza is different. Domino's pizza is always hot. It's delivered in a special hot box. It's never late. Domino's pizza is delivered in 30 minutes, or less. Domino's pizza isn't stuck to the top of the box. It's got a special box and delivered carefully on the way.*

We had to convince people that Domino's pizza is different because we do all these things. That led to a strategy that we called, for our own purposes: *The Domino's Pizza Difference* [final statement and presentation idea] It's a theme, the main idea to give to the creative group and say: *Here's what you want to communicate. It's the direction the research indicates.* The real creativity is later in the process.

Even though controlled procedures have produced reliable conclusions, it is necessary to find out if the creative conclusion is going to be understood and remembered by the audience—the pizza consumer.

Thornton: We wanted to validate *The Domino's Difference* concept. We put a couple of test [video] commercials together. What we did then was a copy testing of the idea. We used focus groups in malls and hired a company to do the copy testing. They get people in one-at-a-time, or in a group, and they [the subjects] watch a reel of commericals. Your commercial is in there and then they'll [the research group] ask them questions afterwards: *Did you remember it? Who was it for? What was the main idea? What was it about? What were they trying to say? Did it look good? Did it make you want to buy the product?* The Domino's Difference proved to be a valid theme.

Now the creative functions move into place, but not without controls and supervisory checks on the artistic imagination. As in news and PR, controls in advertising are self-administered (Bartlett's definition of the scientific/ creative thinker). More checks on individual creativity emerge during team conferences. At the same time, each member knows and is further guided by the expectations of their account executive and the client. Preliminary presentations to the client reflect all these controls.

Thornton: At that point we had another creative pow-wow, all the creative people at Group 243. Their job was to fill in this theme idea with some advertising. Lots of ideas were flying around. Choosing five or six of these for development becomes both a logical and political process. Although research solves the problem on paper, you also have to please the people [the client] that are running the campaign. They have to be behind it. It's more than just writing ads.

I'll just talk about two of the ideas we developed. In one campaign plan, a guy comes out in a white coat with a pizza box in his hand and says: *I've just taken this pizza out of the oven, and I'm putting it in this pizza box* [Domino's insulated delivery box]. He takes the temperature and it's 200 degrees. Then he says: *Now I'm putting it in this freezer.* After a time lapse, he takes it out of the freezer, takes the temperature again and it's still hot. So he says: *You see Domino's pizza is always delivered hot and oven-fresh.* And at the end when he arrives with the pizza, he says: *That's the Domino's Difference.* We could do a promotion like that on each one of these line items that came out of the focus group research.

Another approach was the Noid campaign. That was a creative idea. The Noid was developed to symbolize all the consumer concerns we found out about in the research, lumped together in one character figure. If your pizza's cold, the Noid did it. If it's stuck to the inside of the box cover, the Noid did it. If there's anything wrong, the Noid did it. All these circumstances would happen to a pizza delivered by some other fast-food company. But Domino's pizza avoids all that. We avoid the Noid, and you get your pizza hot, fast and oven perfect.

Group 243 put about five or six campaigns together and presented these to Domino's marketing people and to the Domino's franchise people and said: *Here's what the survey research showed, here's what the copy-testing showed, and here's ways we could use the strategy, the Domino's Pizza Difference.* The Noid campaign was one of these, but actually they liked three or four out of the whole group.

In chapter 12, Mr. Thornton describes how the campaign idea was finally formalized for public presentation and became the catalyst that put Domino's Pizza in the forefront, first with the national and then the international market.

Advertising: The TV Spot Ad

With findings from the research agency and her own collection of information, Ms. Gahagan then approached the job of pulling it all together to come up with an idea for the TV spot. Her method of organizing, coding, and analysis is informal but grounded in well reviewed and internalized data so that she was then able to *come up with some ideas*. Notice her choice of inspirational material, external to the data—visuals and recipes—but still relevant to this particular assignment and in keeping with the customary practice of Bartlett's scientific/creative thinkers.

In chapter 12 she defines her criteria for creative selection as data that are relevant, informative, interesting, substantiated, and have memory value— familiar sounds you have heard before. Here she introduced another criterion, *funny*, which is appropriate in this case because it speaks to the client's preference for something humorous.

Gahagan: Before I do the script—I don't have any formal approach—I just put all my notes in a manila folder under the name of the assignment. Sometimes I'll go back and separate things, if there's a lot, but there isn't that much information on any one project that can't be pulled out and gone through.

I just review and digest the information, get a general overview of the material and come up with some ideas. A lot of times I do visual research for ideas. In this particular case, it was searching for different looks, different areas of the country, kinds of countries. I might look at anything from a photography annual, which has all kinds of stock photography, to recipes. This is an integral part of the final spot [that is, part of the data file]. To me that's just what you do. That was part of the feel for the first spot, where there was really more effort put into coming up with an original storyline that was interesting and funny. It's a matter of remembering [the material] and looking for it [the creative idea].

Once members of the creative team digest the assembled data, they meet and put their ideas forward on the conference table. Ideas are examined, evaluated, and decisions are made. Notice, in this case, the writers visualize *vignettes* in their search for ideas. And, again, these final activities (informal organization, review, analysis, visualizations) are all simultaneous activities that lead to a presentation idea, a process Ms. Gahagan, in chapter 12, admits she cannot explain.

Gahagan: When we work on something like this, we usually just talk among ourselves and come up with some [visual] ideas saying: *Let's say we're in a country fair.* We just talk among ourselves and set up the scene as to what's going on, what this little vignette or story would be that goes on in the spot, then we decide what does the job best.

The first thing that's written down is the script. And then we go in and do a storyboard after that. What I mean by a script is that we usually work with paper that's divided with a description of the video on the left and the other half page is what's going on in the audio portion, and that's what we work with before we get to the point of actually having an artist sit down and do the storyboard.

When team members complete their analysis and decide on the best direction to take, preliminary work on presentation ideas begins, which is described in the next chapter.

12 Presenting and Writing the Copy: Putting It All Together

The imagination imitates. It is the critical spirit that creates.
—Oscar Wilde, *Intentions.*

Let's assume you have just completed a methodical investigation of a media writing problem and arrived at a data-driven conclusion. Now you need to give voice to what you have uncovered. Rely on your support system: a final statement that crystallizes your view of the problem and stands up to question, an organized set of relevant and verified information from validated sources that reflects thorough, unbiased coverage to assure writing accuracy, and a detailed set of notes for development and impact. In this chapter you learn how to transform this support system into appealing and comprehensible media copy.

To put the process on "go," start by asking the first of three questions crucial at this point in the strategy. Answer the first one and the next two develop naturally because they become part of the first process. All that follows makes this more clear.

Critical Self-Inquiry 10: *What appropriate and effective presentation ideas are manifest in the synthesis statement?*

Critical Self-Inquiry 11: *What organization of the copy will render a clear and balanced elaboration of the synthesis statement and its presentation?*

Critical Self-Inquiry 12: *What information for elaboration is relevant, informative, interesting, provides a thorough and balanced account, and stands up to question?*

With a solid support system as an underpinning, you should be able to answer these questions quickly. But if you are stumped, especially by the first two, that's okay. It is normal. The aches and pains of presentation and development are common ailments, even for experienced writers. Besides, there is a remedy: visual thinking and visualization.

VISUALIZE TO MATERIALIZE

Whether you realize it or not, you performed several functions of visual thinking and visualization when you practiced critical thinking, because while you were evaluating, you were also creating. But not all educators see critical and creative thinking as an interactive function. Some prefer to see the two functions as distinctive in certain respects. Still others agree with most psychologists that the two functions complement one another. For example, during the process of coding and analysis, critical thinking can operate simultaneously with creative thinking. Sometimes, even as data are verified and validated, visualization of data-driven information begins to materialize. At other times one or the other thought form operates as a contributing force on the other (Marzano et al., 1988).

This describes the complementary nature of creative thinking, but it is not a formal definition of visual thinking and visualization. For such an explanation, one must turn to the world of art because mass media has no agreed upon definitions for those terms. In the art world, *visual thinking* is defined as the process of organizing mental images around shapes, lines, colors, textures, and compositions, whereas *visualization* is the process of graphically (photos) or pictorially (sketches, diagrams, drawings, paintings, etc.) representing objects, concepts, or feelings (Wileman, 1980, p. 13).

Although neither definition accounts for the operational transfer of images into words, both indicate that visual reproduction of mental images is possible. The first definition describes an inherent dimension of visual thinking—reasoning, an internal process. Visualization suggests that internal processes of reasoning can be externalized as objects in reality.

The German philosopher Schopenhauer, on the other hand, declared that self-instruction, or reasoning, fails to accompany information processing. Arnheim (1969), author of the classic work, *Visual Thinking*, and professor emeritus, Harvard University, Center for the Visual Arts, takes another view. He believes that the two functions, receiving information and reasoning, separate neatly in theory, but not in practice. Arnheim demonstrated how perception at the subconscious level contributes to thought through imagery (visual thinking) and determined that thought without imagery would be incomrephensible. Visual thinking, Arnheim concluded, pervades all human activity. Without the capacity to imagine (to form mental images of persons, places, notions, or ideas) the world would be void of any creative objects (visualizations such as paintings, artifacts, sculptures, buildings, the written word).

Visualization and Creativity

The creative impulse to imagine is not exclusive to the realm of fine art, architecture, or mass media. Medicine, too, illustrates Arnheim's conclusion about the pervasivenes of imagery in our everyday lives. By means of a technique called "biofeedback," a creative idea in itself,[1] physicians treat stressed and even terminally ill patients. Stressed patients imagine serene landscapes and comforting scenes; diseased patients imagine internal "widgets" devouring cancer-producing cells; mentally disturbed patients, unable to articulate the horrors locked in their minds, visualize the inexplicable in scribbled letters or fantastic paintings. Listen to people talking and you will hear: "Look at it from my point of view," "You have to see the big picture in this," "I have an idea how to do that," or "Here's the way I see it."

Those pedestrian phrases may sound simplistic, but even the most complex scientific discoveries materialized from simple visualizations: words or symbols noted on blackboard or paper, sketches drawn on any surface available, representative models constructed from cardboard, metal pins, polystyrene foam, Lego kits, and the like.

Recalling the thinking that preceded his discovery of the DNA structure, molecular biologist J. D. Watson wrote (1968, p. 184) that one important idea "came while I was drawing the fused rings of adenine on paper" (Fig. 12.1), from which he later designed a three-dimensional model to show his colleagues (Fig. 12.2). One of them scoffed at the makeshift model. However, after Watson won the Nobel prize for physiology and medicine,[2] the challenger had a change of heart about visualizations of complex scientific images, and Watson observed, ". . . our past hooting about model-building represented a serious approach to science, not the easy resort of slackers who wanted to avoid the hard work necessitated by an honest scientific career" (Watson, 1968, p. 212).

Value of Visualization

The point here is that you, too, can compose an image in your mind about what you discovered during your investigation of the topic problem. If you

---

[1]Biofeedback, introduced in the early 1970s, is a method of learning how to control one's bodily functions by monitoring one's own brain waves, blood pressure, degree of muscle tension, etc.

[2]Watson shared the 1962 Nobel prize with two other science researchers, F. H. Crick and M. H. F. Wilkins, who had worked on the DNA project with Watson to uncover the mysteries of genetic structure.

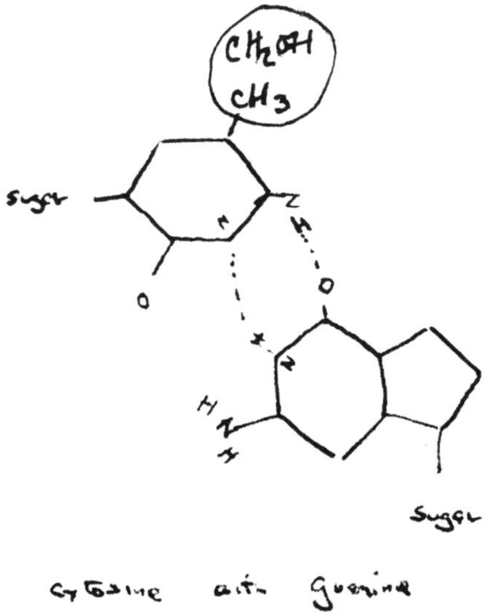

FIG. 12.1   Sketch that inspired Watson's double helix model. Courtesy of Cold Spring Harbor Laboratory Archives.

see the image in your mind, you can reproduce what you see with the tools of the writer – words on paper.

Scholars and educators of critical thinking know that a litany of facts plants only sterile seeds in the minds of students. They found that in order to touch the mind of the information receiver, the sender must stimulate the visual sense of the receiver with whatever tools of visualization may be appropriate (Stice, 1987). Words are the writer's means of reaching receivers' senses, and the narrative form is one way the writer impresses the big picture on receivers' minds.

If you felt our earlier connection of the term *narrative* to nonfiction writing excluded mass media, consider this. By definition, all mass media products, no matter in what medium they are marketed, tell a story. There is a reason for that. A well-structured narrative has unity, parts that add up to a meaningful whole. Together, structure and unity transfer an unmistakable energy – memory value.

Cognitive psychologists have known for some time that recall of a story is directly related to its structure. Rumelhart (1980) formalized the structure of the narrative based on schemata theory and identified it as the "grammar" of story telling. In its simplest form, the story "grammar" opens on a protagonist with a problem and the remainder of the story is a description of the protagonist's problem-solving behavior toward a goal that must be satisfied. Some stories unfold in several episodes and sometimes with different protagonists. The goal is resolution of the problem. Sometimes the story ends happily, sometimes not.

Earlier and in line with this view of story structure, Mandler (1978) used

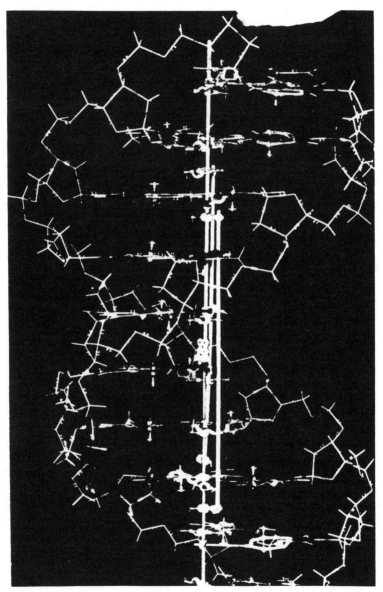

FIG. 12.2. Original demonstration model of the double helix. Courtesy of Cold Spring Harbor Laboratory Archives.

story "grammar" to test recall quality in 96 subjects, ranging in ages from 7 to 19 years and included second-, fourth-, sixth-grade, and college students. Each subject listened to four two-episode stories appropriate to age level. Some subjects listened to stories where two problems, two solution attempts, two outcomes, and two endings had been rearranged to create an interleaved version. Others listened to a standard story of one problem, one attempt, and so on. Twenty-four hours later, subjects were asked to recall everything they could remember from the stories. Adults understandably showed equally good recall of both types. Fourth and sixth graders were also good at recalling the standard type, but had trouble with the interleaved version. Second graders had the most difficulty. What is interesting about this experiment is that the given input order proved to be subordinate to subjects' dependence on the structural order characteristic of narrative form. This proved to be the case even when stories were presented in an unusual interleaved fashion; subjects in retrieval efforts reverted to the basic structure of the story schema, that is, its "grammar."

Mandler readily admitted that people use retrieval methods other than story structure. Adults, for example, show greater flexibility than children using alternate retrieval methods. However, she found reliance on known structure in retrieval so ingrained, even in children, that she concluded people have great difficulty recalling in other ways (Mandler & DeForest, 1979). Similar results had been found in a study by Thornkyke (1977).

In the absence of structures such as narrative form, researchers at the University of Michigan (Reitman & Rueter, 1980) found subjects reverted to an alternate method, for example, association. Working with college-age adults and using a technique of detecting an associative order called an "ordered tree," researchers found subjects were impelled to use any underlying association to aid them, even when words were given from many different starting points. The impulse to use an underlying order led to creation of structure when it was absent, which is actually what a mesage receiver will do if the media writer fails to provide structure in a communication.

Relevance to Mass Media Writers. The visual process creates order out of disorder. Whether that order is a story "grammar" or some other construct, media consumers deserve order in the messages presented to them. If the writer does not provide structure, something with a beginning, middle, and end, media consumers will create their own. The risk is creation of inaccurate order, one that displaces the writer's intended meaning derived from substantiated data. Or, the receiver may not be able to make any sense of the message at all.

Professional writers feel compelled to order their material, and although the forms for creative order provide many choices, the narrative form is a centuries-old style of communicating messages. As science has shown, and ancient Greek and Roman wisdom long ago determined, narratives of human events have memory value. Yet, not until recently has nonfiction been heralded as reflecting the vitality of the narrative and its visualization techniques (Allen, 1983; Blundell, 1986; Feasley, 1985).

Plot and other narrative features are absent in nonfiction. But some of the tags of narrative form that are present include not only structure, but also scene, character, dialogue, description, voice, mood, tone, pace, rhythm, anecdote, analogy, simile, metaphor, and other literary techniques.

In the next few sections you will find a number of ways to activate your mind to think visually for order and other elements in your message. You may use one or several of these methods in combination, or the ones offered may lead to a method of your own making.

If one visualization approach works well with one assignment, you may find the need to try another approach for another type of assignment. It is like medicine. When the body no longer responds to the therapeutic of one medication, the physician changes the prescription. The important thing is to act on the methods suggested, or to continue the analogy, to take the medicine, listen to internal messages, and see if the prescribed medication works. If not, try another prescription.

You will discover that performing one or several of the methods suggested, or one of your own, shifts the mind into high gear. Ideas emerge; bits and pieces combine to create an external unity uniquely your own. That is the essence of creativity. Unlike fiction, however, creativity in mass media must have its base in verifiable data.

If this explanation about visual thinking, visualization, and narrative form seems a roundabout way of getting into the nitty-gritty of "putting it all together," refresh your memory with the Arnheim quote at the start of this text:

> *Without any idea of what sort of process is at work, how is one to comprehend why certain conditions enhance understanding whereas others hamper it? And how is one to discover the best methods of training the mind for its profession?*

Before continuing with visualization processes, it is important to point out that other means of visualization are available to the media writer aside from word pictures and the narrative form. Media writers often work alongside artists when mapping out special visualization schemes. Many of those schemes bear little resemblance to narrative form. Part of the presentation may be in narrative style, but many parts are organized in other ways for quick visual pickup. For example, Fig. 12.3 is a visual of the facts behind one news report. The sketch and bulleted items in the copy attract reader attention and render additional memory value to the story.

Mutual-fund primer

Start with basics in choosing a fund

By John Waggoner
USA TODAY

Investing in mutual funds is easy, but you still need to do your homework.

Mutual funds pool money from thousands of investors. As one of those investors, you're buying a slice of a professionally managed, diversified portfolio of stocks, bonds or money-market securities — sometimes a mixture of all three. You generally can buy or sell fund shares any time. The funds' track records and convenience have made them one of the USA's most popular investments: One family in four has a mutual-fund account.

First, decide what type of fund to buy. If you want:

▶ Safety and income, buy a money-market fund.

▶ Income and the chance of some capital appreciation — profit from an increase in the price of the securities — buy a bond fund.

▶ Capital appreciation, buy a stock fund.

You can get a broker or financial adviser to help you choose a fund, but you'll pay a sales charge, or load. The load can be as much as 8.5% of the amount you're investing, so the advice needs to be good. Say you invest $1,000. The 8.5% load means that only $915 goes to work for you. The fund would have to gain 9.3% in the first year just to turn that $915 back into $1,000 so you could break even.

Many funds don't charge a load. Some charge low loads of 1% to 4% of your investment. Others charge a sales fee when you sell shares. Yet others charge 12b-1 fees, taken out of your account annually to defray advertising costs. Some use combinations of sales charges, redemption fees and 12b-1 fees.

If you're going without advice, stick with a pure no-load fund — one that doesn't charge an entry, exit or 12b-1 fee. If you're a novice, you probably should use one of the large no-load fund companies such as Vanguard in Valley Forge, Pa.; T. Rowe Price in Baltimore; or Twentieth Century in Kansas City, Mo.

Now call for prospectuses of the funds that interest you. Nearly all funds have toll-free numbers. If you don't have a fund company's toll-free number, you can call the toll-free directory at 1-800-555-1212.

You should look for four items in the prospectus, says Sheldon Jacobs, editor of The No-Load Mutual Fund Investor:

▶ The fund's "statement of objective." That's where the fund tells you what it will do with your money. It also will tell you whether the managers keep the fund fully invested in stocks or try to time the market by moving money in and out of stocks, bonds and money-market securities.

▶ The fee table. The lower the fees, the better.

▶ The per-share charges. This part of the prospectus tells you what percentage of a fund's share price goes for management expenses. Try to find a stock fund with an annual per-share charge of 1.85% or less. For bond funds, look for a per-share charge of 1.35% or less, Jacobs says.

▶ Minimum investment. This gives the smallest amount the fund will let you invest at first and the minimum amount for additional investments.

Next, look at performance. Prospectuses will give you the fund's performance for several time periods. Don't just look for a fund with a spectacular performance in the past year or two. Look for one that has done well for three to five years or longer. Most of the guides listed at right provide comparisons of performance.

You're almost ready to invest. Before you do, however, be sure that your fund will be as easy to sell as it is to buy. If you're buying a stock or bond fund, ask about the rules on switching money from that fund to the company's money-market fund. You should be able to transfer the money by telephone.

Because most money-market funds let you write checks, it's smart to set up a money-fund account with the same company as your stock or bond fund. Then, if you want to get your money out of a stock or bond fund in a hurry, you can phone to switch it to the money fund, then write a check.

Investing in mutual funds is simpler than managing your own portfolio of individual stocks and bonds, but it helps to know the basics. Here, a primer on mutual fund investing and the three types of mutual funds.

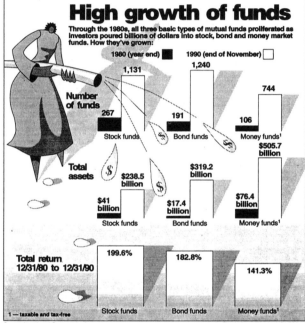

High growth of funds

Through the 1980s, all three basic types of mutual funds proliferated as investors poured billions of dollars into stock, bond and money market funds. How they've grown:

1980 (year end) ■   1990 (end of November) □

Number of funds

	Stock funds	Bond funds	Money funds[1]
1980	267	191	106
1990	1,131	1,240	744

Total assets

	Stock funds	Bond funds	Money funds[1]
1980	$41 billion	$17.4 billion	$76.4 billion
1990	$238.5 billion	$319.2 billion	$505.7 billion

Total return 12/31/80 to 12/31/90

Stock funds	Bond funds	Money funds[1]
199.6%	182.8%	141.3%

1 — taxable and tax-free

Source: Investment Company Institute

By Elys McLean-Ibrahim, USA TODAY

FIG. 12.3. A visual representation of news copy. Copyright © 1991, *USA Today* (January 28). Reprinted with permission.

261

Although the example illustrates how a newspaper might support a story with visuals, other mediums use a variety of other visual aids that serve the same purpose. For example, a complex tax issue presented on TV may be visualized in the form of a flow chart, a pie diagram, or boxed data highlighted with different colors. The purpose, no matter what the medium, is to give the recipient a condensed, yet complete, account of the facts for easy comprehension. However, the attention here is not on art, but on words and the story form. Whether the story is straightforwardly told or imaginatively introduced, writers look for words and a form that stimulates the visual sense of their audience and instills memory value.

Attention is placed on the narrative here only as a starting point. In the main, initial focus on narrative form helps novice writers grasp the technique of presentation and elaboration. With practice, they eventually develop a presentation mode that reflects the dictates of the data yet is uniquely their own.

Where the Process Begins

The visual process begins by mulling things over for a while, then drafting and rejecting one possibility after another until your gut feeling tells you you have hit on the right one. All that activity stems from one focused source of thought, the conclusion you have drawn from the data and summarized in a synthesis statement.

Just remember, a presentation idea is related to but not the same as your synthesis statement. That statement helps you recognize a presentation idea when you see it. Yes, the statement in the advertising example in chapter 11 did provide a campaign theme, but you cannot always count on instant creativity.

If the idea does not occur spontaneously, you may have to go "outside" the data to get one. Sometimes a specific word, phrase, or sentence in the synthesis statement, or the complete statement itself associated with some external can trigger a presentation idea. That external could be an object, place, incident, person or persons, a former time or place, a memorable quote or scene, a picture, concept, or feeling. Or, the idea may come from something as close as your data or "schematic," an item that you associate with some element in the statement. Directed by the statement and its associations, you think in images dictated by the facts. Those data-driven images hold a presentation idea. Selecting an appropriate image, you will suddenly see it translates into a presentation format as well as words that become your opening line(s), PR premise, or campaign theme—words that are true to the data and not personal whim or wild fantasy.

With the presentation idea in mind, visualize its development as you would an architectural design. The idea gives direction to your copy and lends *visual structure* to it, one that draws the eye to a beginning, middle, and end. See this outer design as a place within which you can fill all spaces with appropriate details to make up an architectural order true to the outer design and, in the overall, implants its message on receiver memory.

Some would call such form an "organic" structure. That is true, it is. But this is merely a label and, like most labels, it is easily misunderstood. Besides, labels invite artificiality, inflexibility. They rule out the dictates of the known data and deny opportunity for creativity. Forget about labels. Let your unconscious mind give creative form to the evidence at hand. Conscious expression of it will follow naturally. The German philosopher Nietzsche once wrote, "Every extension of knowledge arises from making conscious the unconscious."

If you think you are still drawing a blank on self-inquiry 10 (recognizing an idea), you are kidding yourself. Imagination is your rightful inheritance. Claim it. The presentation idea is in your mind. You have stored the content for the idea, written a statement about it. It is there. Retrieve it.

Directing you to act, however, is not the same as describing how to switch on your imagination, a shrouded place the humanistic psychologist Maslow (1962) located in the unconscious mind and describes as the seat of "primary creativeness" (p. 95). Like Arnheim and Nietzsche, Maslow claimed the imagination as the most human of endowments from which no person can escape. In fact, he believes, "In the healthy person who creates, I find that he has somehow managed a fusion and a synthesis of . . . both the conscious and the unconscious . . . " (p. 99). In short, for Maslow complete mental health means being available to yourself at all levels of thinking, from the evidentiary to the creative.

Where the Ideas Are

Clues to presentation ideas are, indeed, inside you, but they are also all around you. As already suggested, the first place to look is your synthesis statement. More often than not, the idea will come spontaneously if you have performed all preceding steps of the strategy fully and internalized the material thoroughly, and if you understand how the unconscious mind works on your conscious and creative behalf.

Earlier you learned that the process of information collection, organization, and analysis were both perceptual and cognitive. That is, one must notice (perception) in order to file things away mentally for efficient retrieval (cognition), but one must also determine correct use of stored information in appropriate situations (cognition), and how to transform stored information into new formulations to accommodate a unique situation (metacognition).

Cognitive psychologists Lindsay and Norman (1977) believe, along with others, that these functions are both data-driven and conceptually driven. That is, what is perceived by the eye, ear, taste, smell, and touch is data-driven. Things perceived by the senses are given possible interpretations that are conceptually driven and according to previously learned verbal expressions, observations, training, and experiences. Lindsay and Norman found, as did Bartlett, Bruner, Arnheim, Maslow, and others, that perception and cognition occur together, each function contributing something to the other to reach a conclusion about the input.

You have already experienced that tandem thought process. It may have taken some time to arrive at the final conclusion, but, according to Lindsay and Norman, that is a characteristic difference between the conscious and subconscious modes of thought. It is also illustrative of the incubation period necessary to form the connective bridge between the conscious and subconscious modes. Lindsay and Norman (1977) found, "The solution sometimes arrives far after the initial phase of work, sometimes quite unexpectedly, accompanied by such statements as 'it just popped into my head — I hadn't thought about that problem for months'" (p. 591).

A presentation idea occurs to you in much the same way as you arrived at a conclusion. Unconsciously, higher level mental processes, metacognitive thinking, went to work combining pieces of evidence, and in a moment of discovery you came upon an insightful conclusion from the data at hand. The same processes go to work for the presentation idea. It is the triumphant moment when you are able to say, "Aha! I've got it!"

Turn Up the Speed

One way to drive the imagination is to first think about your *audience* and *who* they are (chapter 1). It helps to have a definitive profile of your audience. Sometimes media organizations will have their research departments or agencies do this for members of their staff. Most media writers have a general idea about their audience, but if you need to crystallize your vision of these amorphous figures try to get answers to:

- *What are their needs, gripes, aspirations, disappointments, habits?*
- *What leisure activities do they engage in?*
- *What kind of work do they do?*
- *Are they men, women, married, divorced, single, with or without children, families, or are they children, pre-teens, teens, under 30, middle-aged, senior citizens?*
- *Do they belong to a specific class of people: artists, economists, scientists, blue collars, teachers, manufacturers, consumers, lawyers, taxpayers, voters, jobless, etc.?*
- *What will my particular audience need or want to know about this story at the very outset?*

Members of your audience number among one or more of these. If these questions are insufficient, continue asking questions until you have a clear vision of your message receivers. After zeroing in on who you are talking to, stir up your mind some more. This time do it in an entirely different way. Set your work aside for a while. Creative writers often move outside the context of their work for an idea. They change their environment or activity. Do the same. Move your work space, change your chair, take a snooze, leave your work space, talk to the postman, go to a museum, weed the garden, ride a bike, take a walk, visit an aquarium or botanical garden, go to a concert. Give your subconscious time to build a bridge to your conscious mind.

During one of those changes, something you see, overhear, feel, or experience will somehow strike an association or contrast to the writing project at hand. Sometimes an idea even pops into mind as you dream or wake from a deep sleep. If the synthesis statement, audience profile, or a change of scene fail to trigger an idea for you, the next best initiators are also external to the problem itself, but closer to home and, at first glance, often distant from any connection to your particular problem statement.

These triggers might include looking through newspapers, magazines, photographic catalogs, books of photographer's photo collections, a photo album, yearbook, etc. Or, just observe and listen to things and people around you. Put your senses to work to receive. If none of these methods work, here's another way to generate answers to self-inquiries 10 and 11.

Making the Unseen Visible

You know that visualization means to represent a mental image in such a way that it may be seen. The degree of image clarity ranges from vague to clear, some vivid enough to be cast into words. The important thing is to *begin* and the number of ways to make the elusive image more visible are as infinite as they are in art. No one way is the best way. But if you are stumped for a presentation idea sometimes you can make the unseen visible by organizing details of the data you intend to use. The word "begin" is important here because as you integrate and organize, you will find yourself visualizing some of the details. You might get a presentation idea at this point. And because you know your data so well, you will recognize the right idea and know where adjustments in your organization are necessary. Here's a list of ways you could get started. Try one that suits you best. If one fails to work, try another. In fact, each assignment you do in any medium may require a different starting device. Rely on this list or develop one of your own. Above all, begin.

- Get out a pencil and paper and draw doodles, sketches, shapes.
- Write down random words or lists of words.

- Make flow charts of the events in your data and the people associated with them. Use a chronological order, or an order where the tension increases or decreases with each event or introduction of a person.
- Draw connecting circles or squares. See these as units of information. Plug in the major points that belong together inside each unit. Place a headline over each to signify the content inside. Prioritize the units later. Look at units and details within. This helps crystallize images you felt were there but could not quite see.
- Make link-node diagrams and label them.

The point is to warm up to your work. Let your subconscious mind rise to the surface by activating conscious movements. You may not refer to your rough sketch again, or you may use it as a creative foundation. Just going through some motions will generate images for a presentation idea and, at the same time, order the copy material in your mind. Here are some more ideas:

- Sketch a storyboard of the sequential and known events and the people associated with them. Write captions for each. Or, just sketch images that pop into your mind. See which ones are related to known events and people, then put them in a sequential order.
- Write down sentences, anything that comes to mind, even headlines. Look at them and think about what they say. *What do they seem to tell you? Will they say the same thing to the receiver?* If not, rewrite them.
- Many authors and film writers use index cards to write down significant facts, incidents and effects, person descriptions and actions, effects of those actions, turning points in the action, changes of pace and place and why, etc. Then they post the cards on the wall or a board, take a look at them, change them around to improve order in terms of logical sequence, heightening suspense, or dramatic effect. Subject titles and ideas for opening and closing scenes often emerge from such an effort. It is the wordsmith's way of visualizing an organization of the copy for a complex news story, TV storyboard, a series of ads, a feature film, or video script.
- Compose a crude outline. Put your synthesis statement at the top of your paper. List all the major points that must be included. Prioritize them later.
- Compose a more formal outline: I. First major point (either a topic phrase or complete sentence), supporting point A, subpoints (1), (2), etc.; supporting point B, subpoints (1), (2), etc.; II. Second major point, etc.

You will find any number of outline types listed in textbooks: chronological, analogical, causal, and others. Some textbooks may even assign certain types of outlines to certain types of writing: chronological for profiles, analogical for informational copy, causal for position pieces, and so on. Again, these are merely labels and as classifications they are sometimes helpful. But novice writers strive so hard to comply with convention that the content and what it suggests are all but forgotten. Permit elaboration of the copy to flow from both your presentation idea and the data behind it.

If you feel the idea and the story it holds is bursting inside you, waiting to be written, and all you need is an informal plan of what you must now do, follow that inclination. The type of plan does not matter much. That you have something in mind that is true to the statement, tells you where to begin, how to develop the story and how to end it, that's what matters. In fact, once you get started, you may revise your original plan for a better one. But starting out with a presentation idea contributes to writing that important beginning, middle, and end.

Story Shapes

Visualization not only materializes mental images and provides structure, it renders a natural shape to your story. So you will find no recommended shapes here, not for news, PR, or ad writers. It is counterproductive to think in terms of predetermined shapes. Illustrations of shapes in textbooks help novice newswriters, for example, to see some of the more common types of news forms such as the "pyramid" (suspended interest story), "inverted pyramid" (all important facts at the top narrowing down to unimportant information) and there are others.[3]

The point is to be directed, not by some predetermined form, but by the content. Permit the content to dictate the story shape. Attempting to accommodate artificialty preempts the creative impluse.

Every media project, whether it is a news or magazine article, PR, or ad piece, carries its own distinctive message, its own form for presentation. You discovered that when you analyzed and synthesized your data into a conclusion and final statement. The message you uncovered is singularly distinctive of the verified data you collected and none other. You should

---

[3]The pyramid form at one time served the purpose of fitting edited copy on a page when stories were manually set in lead by linotype operators. If the type did not fit, the only way the lead could be cut was from the bottom. But today writers use word processors and can determine story length precisely. Typesetting no longer involves lead type. These days typesetting is a photographic process and the type is on paper. If the copy does need cutting, it can be sliced out anywhere with a knife. The idea of adhering to a set form such as the pyramid shape is artificial and outdated.

first hear its unique sound rather than thinking beforehand about established forms. You might be squeezing a unique body of information into the wrong ready-made mold. If it happens to fall into one of these after the fact, that's fine. At least you began from data-driven data. Data generated the presentation idea and now that you have organized the details, its unique message will also shape your copy. All this is such a closely knit mental process that the movement from visualization to composition becomes so integrated that the writer hardly notices the transition after a few trial runs.

GETTING DOWN TO BUSINESS

Let's assume you have a presentation idea, know your audience and how to develop the idea, but the opening lines still will not come. You think you are an insensitive clod, dead cold. You're not. Scan your synthesis statement. Focus on each word, phrase or sentence in it. Try to visualize the associative meaning behind any one of these and link those meanings to what you know about your audience.

Then start writing. Write anything that comes to mind, related or unrelated. Gradually move toward working on those opening lines. Read what you wrote. It may not make sense at first. But if you have done the ground work, you will be so steeped in your material, you will see what is wrong. Try again. Keep writing those first lines until you know they are just right, that is, reflect both the essence of your synthesis statement and the presentation idea you wish to project.

Nothing is better for active thinking than action itself. And for any type of writer, media or otherwise, nothing is more important than the opening lines of your piece. As one media professional put it, "You have only 10 seconds to live." If you can hold the reader or listener with the first few lines, you can pull them into the next paragraph, to listen to the next lines, to keep them fastened to your story.

The Beginning of It All: The Opener

It is important to realize that the opening lines are the product of visual thinking about a statement that stands up to question, no reckless choices here. Visual thinking based on verified data works whether the approach is straightforward, serious, humorous, or, as they are in some TV commercials, visual fantasy. Let's look at the synthesis statement about Great Lakes pollution:

Remedial action over the past twenty years has improved Great Lakes water quality. However, residue from decades of uncontrolled industrial dis-

charges have left traces of hazardous contaminants in the water and lake bed. Although industrial discharges are now under control and the IJC has recommended stricter government standards, other problems such as pollutants carried by air currents have found a home in the Great Lakes and hamper restoration efforts (equation).

The legacy today is poisoned fish, defective wildlife, and a contaminated food chain that carries the potential of generational damage to human life, particularly for consumers of sport fish. The once pristine Great Lakes are reservoirs of toxic waste and may remain so for some time (conclusion).

There are a number of alternatives here that permit several creative opportunities for a presentation idea and opening line(s). Depending on what you and your editor agree on, any one of the following will work because you have the data to support them: (a) current government curbs on Great Lakes pollution inadequate; (b) restoration of Great Lakes cannot keep up with multiple pollution problems; (c) toxic pollutants in the Great Lakes have contaminated a food chain that starts with fish and wildlife and ends on the dinner tables of sport fishing enthusiasts.

Suppose you and your editor decide to address media consumers' immediate needs and select the last point. The examples here illustrate how this might develop creatively. That does not mean the other two points are forgotten. Rather, they are woven into the body of the story as additional information to support the issue of continuing pollution in the Great Lakes.

Suppose you also had an appropriate case incident in your collection of notes that you could visualize and conveyed the concept in the third alternative. Let's say that the case concerned a family accustomed to vacationing near the Great Lakes, but is now vacationing elsewhere because their favorite beach was closed by the state department of public health. You might visualize it all as a family prepared to swim and fish but stopped short by a pollution warning posted near the beach. That would be one presentation idea, a source for an opening line(s), and a way of introducing the concept embodied in the third alternative. With such an idea and a visual image of that family in mind, a print news feature might begin with this picture, but keep in mind that the incident, visual, place, sources, and data are purely hypothetical.

News

Dixon—Every summer for two weeks in August the George Wells family vacations close to the shores of Lake Michigan near Dixon. This August they stopped short of the waterline. A posted sign warned, "No swimming. No fishing." Dead fish and deformed waterfowl along the sandy shore explained the prohibitive words.

If projections by some government and private environmental agencies hold true, it may be some time before the Wells family is able to return to their favorite recreation area to either swim or fish. The number of damaged water life on Lake Michigan shores near here has increased nearly 35% within the past year, according to Duncan Nelson, PhD, an environmental scientist with the Wildlife Conservation Committee.

Nelson does not expect speedy correction of Great Lakes pollution. The Tri-State Water Protection Agency merely warns industrial polluters, he said, while toxic waste discharged into the Great Lakes takes its toll. "It's having a regressive impact on Michigan's wildlife population." Nelson heads a team of researchers who have studied pollution effects on the state's wildlife for the past 10 years.

Notice the features here:

- Description makes this brief anecdote a vivid word picture.
- The picture of a family at the beach is a scene with which your audience can identify.
- Description not only sets the scene, it also presents the problem and permits an easy transition into the introduction that follows.
- Key words in the introduction raise reader expectations for development the writer must meet.
- Details of facts to be enlarged upon are incorporated in the introduction.
- The visual is supported by data.

The writer's grounding in the data and subsequent synthesis statement coupled with visual thinking compelled those lines. Furthermore, accuracy of vision would not have been possible without all the 99% perspiration that preceded it. So the 1% may be called inspiration, but the whole process is more like 100% perspiration in conjunction with critical and creative thinking. Nevertheless, you should still feel the same sense of triumph you felt when you discovered your conclusion, the presentation idea, and now the crucial opening lines.

To continue with the same opener in another medium, a TV feature might open with a graphic black and white image of lifeless birds and dead fish along the shore, and no people in sight. The only activity, the only sound, is the motion of waves sweeping over the shoreline and washing over dead fish and weak waterfowl on the edge. A warning sign prohibiting swimming and fishing also is seen.

TV

Voice-over: People used to swim here. Wildlife was abundant. Not any more. Today, swimming is banned . . . the fish are unfit for human consumption . . . and deformed birds dot the shoreline.

Still another video opening might be a scene showing a red-hot cast over the entire screen. Silhouetted figures of two adults and two children with sand pails in hand appear, almost imperceptible through the haze. They walk toward the shoreline, pause a moment in the midst of faintly visible dead fish and lifeless birds. With the same voice-over, we see the family turn and walk away.

A radio broadcast could use the same visual and open with lines similar to those in the news story. The aim in radio is to recreate the sense of being there that visuals provide. Words recreate a scene, an emotion for the listener. Special effects recreate sounds, a mood or tone. Against such a background, and if the words are delivered well, the impact can be just as poignant as a TV broadcast. Slight adjustments in the print news story are adapted for radio. Some words are eliminated for a more punchy delivery, others are rearranged, a few are added for visual impact.

Radio

Announcer: The George Wells family always vacations near the shores of Lake Michigan. On their last visit . . . to the shoreline near Dixon . . . they saw a scene that made them turn away . . . dead fish and deformed birds marked the beaches . . . posted warnings gave notice of toxic pollution . . . no swimming, no fishing allowed. The Wells family hasn't been back since.

Understand that the chosen approach for the opener does not mean you forget about other main factors in the story. The facts behind the conclusion become part of the whole story. These are incorporated at appropriate places in the development, the middle of the story. So all the evidence you have collected and evaluated is utilized to support the synthesis statement and imagery the opening lines imprint on the receiver's mind.

To continue with more illustrations of the same opener in other mediums, a press release by an environmentalist group might dispense with a consumer-focused opener and begin, instead, with an image of neglected ownership. That image could be projected by using a familiar phrase, followed by the straightforward introduction used in the print news story above.

Press Release

Dixon — Is anyone watching the store? Duncan Nelson, PhD, an environmental scientist for the Wildlife Conservation Committee, wants to know. The number of diseased water life lining Lake Michigan's shores near Dixon has increased nearly 35% within the past year, Nelson told 200 members of Citizen's Watch at their annual meeting here today.

Nelson does not expect speedy correction of Great Lakes pollution. The Tri-State Water Protection Agency, he said, merely warns industrial polluters while toxic waste discharged into the Great Lakes takes its toll. "It's having a regressive impact on Michigan's wildlife population." Nelson heads a team of researchers who have studied pollution effects on the state's wildlife for the past 10 years.

As in the news story, the sentences after the opening line capsulize important information in this hypothetical story: who, what, where, when, and how Nelson evaluates the problem and with what authority he does so. A different approach with the same facts. The opening paragraph also could have been written by a news reporter after covering a press conference, a magazine writer to open a feature story, a TV or radio writer. Perhaps this is another way the latter two may have handled it:

TV

Announcer: It may be some time before people can return to this beach. Swimming is banned. The fish and wildlife are contaminated. Within the past year . . . on just one 20-mile strip along the shore near Dixon . . . researchers found the numbers of diseased fish and nearshore birds had increased by nearly 35% . . . damaged by toxic waste . . . and Dr. Duncan Nelson, an environmental scientist with the Wildlife Conservation Committee, is not optimistic.

Dr. Nelson: Frankly, I don't expect speedy correction of Great Lakes pollution. The Tri-State Water Protection Agency merely warns industrial polluters while toxic poisons discharged into the Great Lakes takes its toll. We've been studying this problem for the past 10 years. It's having a regressive impact on Michigan's wildlife.

Radio

Announcer: Within the past year . . . on just one 20-mile strip along Lake Michigan near Dixon . . . researchers found the numbers of diseased wildlife had increased by nearly 35% . . . contaminated by toxic industrial waste. People can't swim or fish there anymore. Dead fish and deformed birds mark the beaches. Here's Dr. Duncan Nelson . . . environmental scientist for the Wildlife Conservation Committee . . . to tell us more.

Dr. Nelson: Frankly, I don't expect speedy correction of Great Lakes pollution. The Tri-State Water Protection Agency merely warns industrial polluters while toxic poisons discharged into the Great Lakes takes its toll.

We've been studying this problem for the past 10 years. It's having a regressive impact on Michigan's wildlife population.

The examples illustrate the adaptability of the same facts, words, and image to more than one medium and demonstrate several additional points:

- A presentation idea, or visual, can open with no more than a 5- to 10-word sentence.
- An introduction to the problem with answers to all necessary W questions follows quickly after the opener.
- The introduction presents explanatory facts related to the presentation idea in concise and specific terms.
- Opening lines and introduction set the stage for development of the story.
- Opener, introduction, and development, no matter what the approach, are supported by data.

Notice, too, that the presentation idea, as in a narrative, establishes the *problem,* sets the *scene* and *mood,* and all are justified by the factual introduction. The *tone* in the press release is suggested in the beginning. It is meant to project the joint sentiment, the *voice* of the Wildlife Preserves Committee and Nelson. However, the tone in the news article will be balanced. It will present a balanced set of facts researched beyond those voiced by Nelson and permit other voices to be heard. The tone and voice of the magazine article will be the same as the news piece, unless written for a magazine with a certain editorial bent. And the tone and voice of the radio and TV feature will also duplicate the balance in the news article.

Advertising

A print advertisement by the environmental group, Citizen's Watch, might show the same opening graphic as the first or second TV broadcast with this headline: *People and Wildlife Used to Live Here.* The next lines written in the informal style of ad copy read:

Swimmers can't swim here. Fishing is banned, too. It's not a healthy place for man, fish or bird.

Within the past year . . . along just one 20-mile strip of this Lake Michigan shore . . . research teams found the numbers of contaminated fish and fish-eating birds had increased by nearly 35%.

The Tri-State Water Protection Agency merely warns industrial polluters while toxic waste discharged into the Great Lakes takes its toll. "It's having a regressive impact on Michigan's wildlife." That's the prediction of Duncan Nelson, PhD, an environmental scientist with the Wildlife Conservation

Committee. He heads a team of researchers who have studied pollution effects on the state's wildlife for the past 10 years.

As with the press release, although the intent here is to persuade, the information, scene, mood, and tone is always justified by the facts. Everything that follows will support the image the ad creates. Unlike the news, magazine, or TV piece, only the voice of the sponsoring group, Citizen's Watch, is heard here.

The writer of TV ads holds some advantage over the print or radio ad writer. Today's technology permits the TV ad writer greater visual flexibility with such techniques as animation, claymation, stop motion, special effects, futuristic fantasies, and a variety of other visual tricks. However, the spoken words even in these wild visualizations usually stick to the facts. Unless, of course, exaggerations are admitted by the sponsor of the ad. For example, in a recent campaign the spokesperson for Izuzu vehicles deliberately stretched the truth, but the viewer was never led to believe the exaggeration was to be taken seriously. The treatment was handled in good fun, amused the viewer, and placed the real facts, delivered by other spokespersons, on a level the viewer could accept.

When All Else Fails

But what if imagery or externals do not work for you, or what if you are stuck with an uninspiring statement, here's another way out of the hole. Suppose our Great Lakes data did show a reduction in the whitefish population and faced extinction. Your synthesis statement might be as bland as this hypothetical: *Environmentalists predict extinction of Great Lakes whitefish within the next 5 years.*

You might conjure up some images even from this statement. But suppose you can't. Perhaps just seeing a list of starter techniques will help. The following list represents only a few possibilities and is not an exhaustive list. Try any one of them. If the list works for you, use it.

1. Powerful scene description.
2. A question.
3. The direct statement.
4. The conflict or tension statement.
5. The shocking statement.
6. A direct address to the recipient.
7. A quote
   (a) from an interviewee.
   (b) from a famous person.
   (c) from a known saying but giving it a twist, a pun.

8. Character and dialogue.
9. Anecdote (brief account of a happening, often an amusing one).
10. Analogy (a comparison between things that are otherwise unlike).

These can operate separately or in combination. The news, TV, and radio examples given here combined characteristics 1, 9, and 4. The press release example combined characteristics 6, 2, 3, and 4. The ad example illustrates most of the characteristics that appeared in all the other examples. Keep in mind that the list applies, as well, to a media piece that has some sunshine in it. Our subject/topic happens to concern a fearsome environmental problem. An upbeat approach would be ludicrous, unless you were writing about environmental improvements funded by the state, a corporation, or undertaken by volunteer citizen groups. Here are more illustrations of the above listing:

3 and 5: If predictions about the Great Lakes fishing industry hold true, at least 1,200 fishermen in the area will lose their jobs this year.

6: You may never be able to eat the fish you catch. Especially if it's Michigan's most sought after delicacy — Great Lakes whitefish.

7: "We're doing everything humanly possible." That's what _____ , director of the Tri-State Clean Water Bureau, said when asked about the mounting numbers of diseased Great Lakes whitefish.

7 and 5: They said it couldn't happen here. It has.

8, 10, and 5: "Good morning, Mr. Mathews. Got any Great Lakes whitefish?"

"Sorry, Mrs. Jones. None available this week. Maybe next week."

That brief scenario will repeat itself like a broken record. Shoppers may never find Great Lakes whitefish in the markets again.

Lists of opening types have never done much for me or, as I later learned, for others in the media profession. Possible combinations of them are easily overlooked and how they apply in all mediums goes unnoticed.

But, all minds are not the same. Perhaps the multiple technique of knowing your audience, relying on your synthesis statement, drafting a visualization from it, turning to externals, writing out trial openers, any or all of these combined with a list like the one given here and its examples may put you on track. But try not to be "type cast" by labels, classes, lists, or predetermined forms. Think visually with the synthesis statement in mind. Let the data stir your creative impulse, not the convention.

Having said all this about creative openers, it is also necessary to say that dramatic or catch-phrase openers are not absolutes in news, broadcast, or PR writing, although in advertising that is most always the case. A news, magazine, PR, or TV news feature can be quite straightforward. With the appropriate words, such an opener performs all the functions of the creative opener. It establishes the problem and tells the media consumer what to expect in the body of the story. What it often lacks is mood and tone, memory value, and the opportunity to end on an effective close. For example, a straightforward opener for the news story might be:

News

Dixon — Contaminated water life marking the shoreline near Dixon has increased nearly 35% within the past year, Dr. Duncan Nelson, an environmental scientist with the Wildlife Conservation Committee, told 200 members of Citizen's Watch at their annual meeting here today.

Nelson does not see speedy correction of Great Lakes pollution. The Tri-State Water Protection Agency, he said, merely warns industrial polluters while toxic waste discharged into the Great Lakes takes its toll. "It's having a regressive impact on the wildlife." Nelson heads a team of researchers who have studied the effects of pollution on the state's wildlife for the past 10 years.

It depends on the climate in your publishing house. Do the editors prefer the straightforward over the creative? It is up to you to find out and follow suit. Usually, you will be told it does not matter as long as you pull in the media consumer, maintain interest, keep within space and time limitations, and write a piece that stands up to question. Now let's talk about closings before going on to middles.

The Unifying Closure: The Ending

Nothing is more disturbing to a reader or listener than to be left without a finish on a story. In psychology, it is referred to as violating the principle of "closure." That principle is one of the main tenets of Gestalt theory developed by German psychologist Max Wertheimer (1880-1943) and carried on by Wolfgang Kohler and Kurt Koffka. Their writings became popular source references on Gestalt psychology.

In simple terms, "closure" is the human tendency to expect completion even in incomplete visual figures. When closure is missing, the reader's or listener's tendency is to invent a completion even though the invented closure may be incorrect, as are the second images in each of the sketches in Fig. 12.4.

Absence of closure and *proofreader's error* share one common characteristic. They invite perceptual assumption. A person overlooks a mispelled word and, instead, imposes voluntary closure on the word perceiving it as

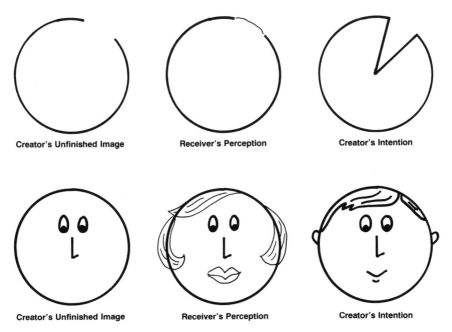

FIG. 12.4.   The drive for closure.

complete and correct.[4] Like the proofreader, someone reading or listening to a story is likely to impose a private notion of completion when closure is absent. Chances are it will be incorrect.

The Alfred Hitchcock movie classic, *The Birds*, illustrates the absence of closure. The movie was based on Daphne DuMaurier's short story, *The Birds*, but bears no resemblance to it beyond the concept of birds invading a small town and attacking its residents. Hitchcock commissioned several movie writers to write scenarios using this concept. One was about an elderly woman who would not give up her home and land to town developers. If they moved her out, she said, she would call the birds. No one paid any attention to her; the developers destroyed her home; she called the birds; the birds beseiged the developers; they begged for mercy and promised to restore her house and land for the price of relief. She agreed; the birds disappeared; she moved back into her rebuilt home on her restored land. Hitchcock did not like the scenario and opted for another which became the basis for the movie (D. Hensley, personal communication, 1989, Toledo, Ohio, Writer's Conference). But the rejected scenario has the dramatic quality of structure and unity: problem-incident-consequence-remedy-resolution.

---

[4]The word "mispelled" is misspelled in this sentence.

In the movie, a visitor comes into town; the birds appear and attack the townspeople; the visitor leaves; the birds remain behind. We never know why they were there in the first place, and we never know what happened to the birds or the townspeople after the visitor leaves. We are left with unanswered questions: *Well? What was the problem? Did the birds leave or not? What's the point?* The moviegoer conjures up private assumptions. The irresolute mystery may pass for dramatic suspense in the movies, but it is damaging if such questions remain unanswered in nonfictional writing. For examples of story closure, let's return to the openings illustrated earlier.

A data-driven closure on the news story about the Wells family might be another word picture of the family at a beach declared safe for bathing and located elsewhere in the state.

News

This year the Wells family spent their August vacation near an inland lake away from Great Lakes' shores. The water is safe for swimmers. Fishing is permitted and the catch is safe to eat.

For the TV feature, the first and second version could close on the same family, clearly visible, at an inland beach. Voice-over could repeat words similar to those used in the news story. Or, the inland lake scene could be shown but instead of closing with the voice-over, one of the children in the scene begins the closure with a question.

TV

Emily (turning to her father): "Daddy, will we ever go back to the big lake again?"

Voice-over (as father draws child to him): If the EPA holds to present control standards, that may not be possible for Emily . . . or for anyone.

The close on the radio feature might eliminate the reference to Emily in the announcer's lines.

Radio

Announcer: If the EPA holds to present control standards, the Wells family may never be able to enjoy their favorite beach again . . . nor will anyone else. Thank you, Dr. Nelson, for joining us today. Hope you'll have better news for us next time. And if you want to support the effort to save the Great

Lakes, here's a number you can call for more information _____ .
That's _____ . Join us again tomorrow, same time, right here on
WWW-AM.

The close on the PR release, or any narrative, could be an answer to the
opening question based on facts in the data or, in the absence of a
data-driven answer, another question, or a quote.

Press Release

If pollution laws are said to be adequate and those responsible claim they are
abiding by them, why are the numbers of dead and poisoned wildlife
increasing?

The close on the ad might be:

Print Ad

Don't let this happen to the largest body of inland seas in the world.
Write to your congressmen today. They represent you. Make that representation work for you.

When Closure Is Not Closure

If your story fizzles out or stops dead at the end of a page, that is not
closure. If your story ends with a summary, it may look like closure, but it
is merely a repetition of what you have already given the receiver and
redundancy is tiresome. Leave summaries to scholars and, alas, authors of
textbooks.

A biased ending is unfair. It tells the receiver to ignore the facts and
accept the writer's viewpoint: *Obviously, Mr. Jones' solution is no solution
at all.*

An unrelated ending tells the receiver you did not know where you were
going in the first place. If you begin by talking about pollution in the Great
Lakes and end up talking about pollution in Boston harbor, you have lost
focus and missed an opportunity to achieve the unity of good form. What
you have produced is a structure without a backdoor exit to memory value.
The goal is not to be didactic or tell the receiver what to think, rather, to
come full circle and make a connection with the beginning. Like
summaries, leave commands up to kings, generals and, uh, yes, authors of
texts.

If thinking about endings before developing the middle seems odd, it isn't. You have an opener and an introduction. You know the content they must deliver. The end is a natural outcome even before the middle is developed, or it most assuredly will be before the last paragraph. So work on the ending now or, if you prefer, wait until after completing the middle. Moreover, if you think of a better end even after pre-arranging one, nothing should stop you from changing your first version.

Breaking stories customarily lack closures because most of the important elements of the story are placed at the top and in the middle portion. This gives editors the opportunity to cut out sections near the end if space is limited. Feature newswriters, however, often include a closure. This does not prevent editors from chopping away, but they usually leave parts significant to the opening, middle, and end untouched. For example, an editor will ordinarily keep hands off of a closure that ends with a statement or an announcement of what the receiver could expect to learn shortly about a particular problem or event. Or, the editor may reposition that type of closure somewhere higher in the copy. If editors do cut away middle parts and even the closure, space or air time may have called for slicing. Still, it is your job to present a unified piece. This holds true, as well, for PR and ad writers.

Now that you have some idea about how to answer self-inquiries 10 and 11, go on to Critical Self-Inquiry 12: *What information for elaboration is relevant, informative, interesting, provides a thorough and balanced account, and stands up to question?*

HEART OF THE MATTER: THE MIDDLE

The middle is simply a natural movement from opener and introduction to elaboration of same. That should prove little problem for the writer equalized by a balanced support system: detailed records plus an organized set of notes, synthesis statement, and now an opener and introduction. The opener and introduction represent a guiding compass. Together, they will steer you away from the siren call of interesting, substantial, but irrelevant information. So will the synthesis statement. Use it as a guide to development possibilities related to your opener and introduction and to keep within the boundaries of your field of writing. If you stray from your opener, introduction, and bounded data field, you will lose unity as well as the receiver's interest.

To maintain a steady course, keep statement, opener, and introduction within easy reference view. Use them to pull those facts from your data pool that meet the criteria of relevancy, informativeness, audience interest, thoroughness, and balance. Because the data have previously been validated and verified, all will stand up to question. However, directives such as these are meaningless unless the novice can see how they work. The example here illustrates the function of elaboration in a print news feature story, a function that applies, as well, to other forms of media.

Let's assume you are a freelance writer, and an editor has asked for about 3,500 words on a feature concerning the impact of Great Lakes pollution. You might write a main piece similar to the one shown here, plus two sidebars to fill out the assignment.

The main piece uses the hypothetical opener used in the examples above. Except for the opening incident, facts and events for the main piece and the sidebars are based in reality and came from various sources: encyclopedias, almanacs, government documents, newsletters and releases, professional journal articles, and personal communication with several environmental and government agency authorities. Titles of government agencies, references, and scientific sources, also are based in reality, but the names of persons and quotes by them are fictional and any resemblance to anyone living having expressed similar statements is coincidental.

Notice how the development moves from just a few key words in the introductory paragraphs of the main story, how the copy answers anticipated reader questions, and how numbers and dates are inserted with other information the reader may look for. Notice, too, the short paragraphs, subheads, and bulleted items. If these devices are compatible with the publisher's general style and form, provide them. The sidebars include historical background on the Great Lakes and a summary of pollution effects on wildlife. Editors invite sidebars because they provide additional information without lengthening the main piece.

It is quite likely that either the editor, or you as the freelancer, would also add photos or artwork. But assuming their absence, the devices suggested earlier are a few of the techniques available to print newswriters. They break up solid blocks of copy and help the reader follow the line of copy progression. The editor may have other intentions, but having some devices to work with always helps.

It is important to say that the example does not stand as a representative model for all feature stories. Each subject, event, or issue with its particular set of data for a specific audience will command its own creative style. However, whether the story is short or long, the logic of development follows a similar progression. It is one of the few constants in the course of putting information together, but only after you have taken your cues from what the data has told you to incorporate in your opening paragraphs can that process begin. It is also conceivable that another writer would have a different creative impulse with the same data than the one you see here, but again, the development process remains the same and that is the point of the following example.

POLLUTION PLAGUES THE ONCE GREAT LAKES

Opener

What's this story
about?

Dixon—Every summer for two weeks in August the George Wells family vacations close to the shores of Lake Michigan near Dixon. This August they stopped short of the waterline. A posted sign warned, "No swimming. No fishing." Dead fish and deformed waterfowl along the sandy shore explained the prohibitive words. Chances are the Wells family may not be able to return to these shores for some time.

Introduction

Is local area an
isolated case?

The polluted shore near Dixon is not an isolated case. The buildup of chemicals and other contaminants in the lakes permitted Toronto photographer Pierre Lyon to develop photo negatives in Lake Ontario. Fuel oils and paints contain some of the same chemicals used in modern photofinishing, Lyon explained. Other water samples he had drawn produced no negatives. "The water from the beach, for instance, was so full of pollutants that it ate the emulsion off my film."

Contaminants in the Great Lakes have reached such crisis proportions that the Great Lakes Water Quality Board has identified 42 "hot spots" along the 95,000 square-mile shoreline of the waterway.

Context

How long has
polluting been
going on?

How bad is the
pollution?

So what's this
mean to me?

While controls on toxic emissions in the 1970s brought about improved water conditions, restoration of the Great Lakes to their once pristine clarity seems out of reach. Aside from the residue left from century-long dumping of toxic substances, contaminants find their way to the Great Lakes basin on air currents from such distant places as South America and Asia.

The legacy today is spoiled fish, damaged nearshore wildlife, and a weakened food chain that could disrupt human life as well as recreational plans.

Middle

How has contam-
ination disrupted
human life?

Recent studies point to the growing plague of pollution. In 1985, research by a group of Michigan State University and Wayne State University scientists revealed evidence of adverse effects in humans. Several hundred babies of mothers who had ingested a steady diet of Lake Michigan sport fish (two to three meals a month for at least six years) were compared to babies of mothers whose diet contained no contaminated fish. The babies of mothers who had eaten contaminated fish had smaller head sizes, lower birth weights, and were less coordinated.

Late recognition

How come polluting was allowed to begin with?

Who's watching the store now?

Detection of pollution in the Great Lakes was slow in coming and efforts to control random dumping did not fall into place until the late 1960s. Independent jurisdictions were established in areas bordering the five Great Lakes and commissioned as monitors of Great Lakes water quality. Located in Indiana, Illinois, Wisconsin, Minnesota, Michigan, Ohio, Pennsylvania, New York, and the Canadian province of Ontario, these jurisdictions also keep a close watch on the fish and wildlife, the most obvious indicators of pollutants in the water.

Sport fish especially command their scrutiny. Under Food and Drug Administration (FDA) guidelines, bureaus within the jurisdictions check for contaminants in fish drawn from Lakes Michigan, Superior, Huron, Erie, Ontario, and their tributary waters. Unlike Great Lakes fish sold in retail markets, sport fish escape government inspection standards. However, state departments of health in the jurisdictions publish advisories on which sport fish are safe to consume.

Are any GL fish safe to eat?

Which GL are monitored?

In one of their most recent advisories, the Michigan Department of Public Health (MDPH) warned pregnant women and women intending to bear children against eating certain species of sport fish: carp, catfish, walleye, perch, or pike anywhere from 10-20″ long, or trout more than 30″ long.

Those advisories were based on fish catches showing high levels of such toxic pollutants as:

What exactly is in the sport fish?

- PCB (polychlorinated biphenyls found in hydraulic fluids, banned in the 1970s).
- DDT (a pesticide banned in the 1970s).
- PAH (polycyclic aromatic hydrocarbons, mainly in water waste from uses of coke in the making of steel).
- Mercury (a heavy-metal toxicant discharged from chlor-alkali and pulp paper industries).
- Dieldrin (a chlorinated insecticide, banned in the 1970s).
- Chlordane (a chlorinated insecticide, all uses currently canceled).

The size of the fish listed in the advisories is important. The larger and older fish are a predator species high on the food chain. Because they feed for longer periods of time, toxic buildup in older fish is higher. At the lowest link of the food chain are tiny organisms on which small fish feed. Larger fish consume the small fish, and then larger, older fish higher on the food chain consume the subordinate species. With each link, toxic chemicals multiply in surviving fish and the concentration of toxins in them can be millions of times greater than the chemicals in the water.

What are consequences of eating them?

While some scientists argue against consuming any Great Lakes fish, others direct fishing enthusiasts to the advisories. "The point is not to scare people or discourage fish consumption because we don't really know whether the contaminants at the levels we find in fish adversely affect humans," said Donald Westin, PhD, a biologist with the Habitat and Contaminant Division of the U.S. Fish and Wildlife Service. "The purpose of fish advisories is to assist consumers in selecting fish for eating that have the lowest contaminant levels or no contamination at all," Westin said.

Is there any agreement about the consequences?

Bureaucratic disagreement

Controversy surrounds the standards for judging the purity of fish habitats. The jurisdictions use separate criteria to estimate water quality. Some argue for uniform criteria and tighter water quality standards. Others believe standards set by the Environmental Protection Agency (EPA) and FDA are adequate and that uniformity overlooks location and differences in water depth and concentrations of waste.

What are the standards of judgment?

Who makes them?

What's the IJC?

In the midst of the conflict, the Great Lakes Water Quality Board of the International Joint Commission (IJC) stepped into the arena in 1990 to declare that current standards were inadequate in light of accelerating pollution. They recommended stricter guidelines. The IJC is a binational organization formed by the 1909 Boundary Waters Treaty under which the U.S. and Canada cooperatively resolve problems along their common border, including problems of water and air pollution.

The IJC recommendation followed on the heels of the 1985 study and several additional studies showing the extent of contamination in fish. One of these was a 1989 study by the Michigan Department of Natural Resources (DNR). They found that about one in four of the more than 700 Great Lakes fish tested during the past two years were polluted at levels deemed unsafe for human consumption.

Also that year, a group of researchers at the University of Michigan, under a grant from the National Wildlife Federation, concluded that consumers of sport fish may face substantial cancer risks when concentrations of DDT and dieldrin in the fish are at or near FDA level standards, which the researchers described as outmoded. Toxicologist Alex Bannister, PhD, with the Great Lakes office of the National Wildlife Federation, said he cautions child-bearing women, including female offspring who may bear children in the future, against eating any fish from either the Great Lakes or the rivers into which they flow. "It's chemical soup," he said. "Those toxics get into the bloodstream of child-bearing women and if a woman bears a female child and the child ingests sport fish regularly and she has a child, the ensuing buildup of toxins in people's bodies is measureable six generations thereafter."

There seems to be a lot of controversy about GL fish.

How am I supposed to know what to do?

Other scientists say informed use and moderation is the key. The way to reduce exposure to toxins is careful preparation, thorough cooking, and limited consumption, according to Martin Ogilevsky, PhD, an epidemiologist with the Office of Science for the Council for Environmental Quality, MDPH. "Organic contaminants like PCBs, DDT, chlordane, and dieldrin can be reduced by skinning the fish and trimming fatty deposits before cooking," he said. "Mercury accumulates in the muscles of the fish and cannot be significantly reduced by these methods. However, persons such as vacationers, who only eat sport fish one or two weeks during the year, can safely eat several fish meals during that time period because mercury is eliminated from the body relatively rapidly and does not build up to a toxic level in the short time period."

As a general rule, Dr. Ogilevsky recommends following the state fish advisories and to limit fish consumption to no more than once a week. Advisories may be obtained by writing to your state health department or your regional Department of Natural Resources.

Pre-regulation legacy

When scientists began detecting traces of inorganic and organic contaminants in edible portions of Great Lakes fish in the 1960s, they determined that uncontrolled industrial discharge was part of the problem. They called for regulatory measures.

In 1972, Congress passed the Clean Water Act giving the Environmental Protection Administration (EPA) responsibility for regulating industrial discharge loads. The EPA set limits on discharge loads according to the type, size, and location of an industry. Then by 1982, all the Great Lakes states and the province of Ontario had programs for sport fish sampling and analysis.

Most scientists agree those programs have served their purpose. "They've achieved remarkable success in detecting contaminants in fish to guide fishermen and contributed a great deal in the assessment of water quality." Dr. Ogilevsky said.

However, controls and programs may not have come soon enough. Chemical pollutants discharged before 1972 have since attached to sediment particles on the Great Lakes floor where organisms feed and flourish to provide food for fish which, in turn, provide food for waterfowl and nearshore wildlife and, finally, people who regularly fish for meals.

Although industrial discharge points are now monitored and measures taken to stop discharge of harmful substances, whatever was discharged before regulation remains in the water and penetrates lake beds and surrounding land areas. For example:

If they've had regulations since '72, how come pollution isn't under control?

Exactly what's in the lake beds now?

Where did it all come from?

- Researchers continue to find traces of DDT and PCB in the lakes despite the 1972 ban on DDT and the ban on PCB in 1978 under the Toxic Substance Control Act (TSCA).
- Before 1985, tetra-ethyl lead had been discharged into Lake Ontario. Tetra-ethyl lead is a toxic substance used as an additive in gasoline to reduce vehicle vibration (anti-knock gasoline).

Production of the additive is limited under 1986 amendments to TSCA passed by Congress in 1976. Tetra-ethyl lead is insoluble in water.

- Prior to 1972 controls, industrial plants discharged a wide range of pollutants into the Great Lakes. Organic and inorganic pollutants, including PCB and mercury, accumulated in lake bed sediments which now slowly release contaminants to the water and food chain.

Since 1929, 20 million gallons of PCBs had been manufactured worldwide and 60 percent of that total is still in use as electrical coolants or is buried in dumps; most of the rest is in the environment. Less than five percent has been destroyed.

Ghostly presences

Many points of pollution are felt but unseen. Runoff from pesticide-treated farms and lawns and leakage from buried toxic waste number among them. Nor are all unseen sources local. Air currents carrying toxic substances from southern states and the other side of the globe have found a home in the Great Lakes basin.

Just how much contamination is in GL now?

"Air deposition is another major source polluting the Great Lakes, adding more layers of chemicals to those already in the lake bed," said Telford Roberts, PhD, a chemist with the Great Lakes Environmental Research Lab, U.S. Oceanic-Atmospheric Administration. "We've only recently turned our attention to this problem and now have some idea of the level of airborne chemicals entering the Great Lakes each year.

"We estimate that of the PCBs in Lake Superior, 90% were airborne, as well as 97% of all lead-based chemicals. In Lake Michigan, 60% of the PCBs were deposited by the currents and over three quarters of the chemical pollutants in Lake Huron were also air deposited." Canadian researchers believe they know why the

Why in the GL basin?

Great Lakes act as a magnet for airborne toxic substances. They plotted North American wind patterns and concluded that the lakes are near the core of where large air masses from the Pacific coast, the Arctic, and the tropics meet. One study estimates that air from

Tennessee travels to the Great Lakes within a five-day period.

Those findings may explain why toxaphene, a pesticide rarely used in the Midwest but once sprayed extensively on cotton fields in the South and still used in South America, ends up in a lake as far north as Isle Royale in Lake Superior. Researchers have also learned that DDT is coming in on air currents from South America where it is also still in use.

Great Lakes limitations

Once thought capable of sustaining any kind of organic or man-made onslaught, researchers say the turnover capability of the Great Lakes is not swift enough to flush out the pollutants in the quantity now entering them. Because of their depth and size, centuries pass before the largest lakes renew their waters.

GL are powerful seas. How come Nature can't take care of the pollution?

- Lake Superior takes 200 years. (The lake is 1,333 feet deep, 160 miles wide and 350 miles long).
- Lake Michigan takes 100 years (923 feet deep, 118 miles wide, 307 miles long).
- Lake Huron, 20 years (750 feet deep, 183 miles wide, 206 miles long).
- Lake Ontario, 8 years (802 feet deep, 53 miles wide, 192 miles long).
- Lake Erie, 3 years (210 feet deep, 57 miles wide, 241 miles long).

Recovery prospects

Despite the grim outlook, Roger Ellis, PhD, an environmental biologist with the Michigan DNR, feels renewal of the Great Lakes is possible. "Once called the 'dying lake,' Lake Erie was revived and the Clinton River, once called '30 miles of sewer,' is in better shape now than it was in 1966," Ellis said. The Clinton empties into Lake St. Clair which, in turn, flows into the Detroit River, a connecting channel to Lake Erie.

Is there any hope for the GL?

What's Clinton River got to do with the GL?

"Today it's a veritable fish factory, and mainly because its marshes not only filter impurities in the lake water, they also act as nurseries for fish."

Marshes in the Great Lakes area are protected against violation for development purposes under the Goemaere-Anderson Wetlands Protection Act adopted in the 1970s. "It's a constant battle keeping remaining wetlands out of the hands of developers who seem sensitive only to profit," Ellis said.

Remedies ahead

Recent Congressional action and support from the Oval Office may mark the 1990s as the decade of renewal for the Great Lakes. With a new mandate from Congress, the EPA has selected the Great Lakes as a national laboratory for an assault on pollution. In 1990, President George Bush proposed a 1991 allocation of $82 million for Great Lakes programs administered by the EPA, the U.S. Fish and Wildlife Service, and the National Oceanic and Atmospheric Administration.

What's the government doing about the ruin of the GL?

The federal gift is a raindrop in the ocean according to some observers. In 1989, a Washington-based research group estimated that it would take $2.9 billion to $3.4 billion to clean up just 10 of the most contaminated sites out of the 42 polluted areas of concern. At the time, complete contamination data were available only on the 10 sites. The other 32 areas are still undergoing analysis by Remedial Action Plan committees supervised by IJC.

The 45-page study was prepared by the Northeast-Midwest Institute, a nonprofit research and public education center which works closely with bipartisan coalitions of House and Senate members from 18 Northeast and Midwest states.

A two-year study by the Institute for Research on Public Policy at Ottawa and the U.S. Conservation Foundation, Washington, DC, reported that $100 billion is needed to prevent further deterioration of the Great Lakes. Hugh Ashford, PhD, environmental scientist and researcher at the Ottawa institute, said immediate action must be taken to avoid continuation of wildlife damage and health risks to humans. "No one's going to fall over dead tomorrow. It's future generations I'm worried about." The federal allocation may fall far short of the need, Ellis said, "but at least it's a beginning."

Restoration action

In 1990, Congress also enacted the Great Lakes Critical Programs Act, which sets firm deadlines for the EPA to draft uniform water quality standards for the eight Great Lakes states and to complete cleanup plans for the 42 "hot spots" in the region. Scientists have been recommending uniform criteria in water quality programs since 1985, partly to avert relaxed discharge regulations in states' efforts to attract more industry.

When can we expect to see some results?

Remedial action goes a long way, but results will not show up tomorrow. "Even if all toxins were eliminated from the lakes, it would take 30 years before they were no longer found in the fish and wildlife, Ellis said. "In that sense, the federal commitment to restoration of the Great Lakes only represents a starting point of a prolonged and expensive process."

Ellis believes much of the government's current interest in Great Lakes renewal is due to public pressure for a cleaner environment. "Conservation activists, annual Earth Day observances, and citizen participation in conservation efforts have put politicians on the alert. But more changes and decades of effort lie ahead," he said.

Closure

The Wells family may not be able to return to Lake Michigan's shores next year or even in the years that follow. What matters to them is whether the once Great Lakes will be Great again for future generations of their family.

* * *

ENDANGERED NEARSHORE SPECIES

How bad is the threat to wildlife?

The level of chemicals found in Great Lakes wildlife is nearing the point where some face extinction, according to environmental biologist Ernest Lenz, PhD, of the U.S. Fish and Wildlife Service. "The fact is, just in Michigan, some 300 plant and animal species are currently on the endangered or threatened list. And we're seeing increases in the numbers of species on the list each year." Endangered means any species of fish, bird, or wildlife in danger of disappearing. Threatened means any species likely to become endangered.

What chemicals are doing the damage?

Mercury, PCBs, DDT, and PAHs are the principal sources of harm, he said, adding that research has shown decreased reproduction levels in wildlife and increasing cases of tumors in some fish.

"We're also seeing more and more cormorants with crossed bills and birth defects in caspian terns," Dr. Lenz said. "Especially worrisome is that these and other birds, fish, and animals are not reproducing at rates we're accustomed to seeing.

What are the effects of these chemicals on wildlife?

"The low reproduction rate of the bald eagle, for instance, which feeds on fish and animals, is just one of the ominous signs." The differences between nearshore and inland reproduction rates are striking, he said, noting that 1989 studies of eagle nests near the shoreline showed decreased yields of eaglets when compared to hatchings at inland areas. For example, the rate of eaglet hatchings in nests near the shorelines of Lakes Michigan and Huron is 36 and 19 percent, respectively, in comparison to the inland rate at the upper peninsula which is 63 percent.

Contaminants have also been found in otter and mink, Lenz said, particularly in habitats near Green Bay, Wisconsin, and around Lake Michigan on the Michigan side. The substantially low level of mink reproduction near Lake Erie at the northern tip of Ohio is another cause of concern.

* * *

HERITAGE OF INDUSTRIAL GROWTH

Formed by Arctic glaciers tens of thousands of years ago, the once pristine Great Lakes no longer resemble the glacial purity of just a half a century ago. Today the lakes, which contain ⅕ of the earth's supply of fresh surface water, have become trash baskets for industrial, agricultural, and municipal waste.

How did this problem get started?

This largest inland body of water in the world contains over 360 toxic contaminants. The Great Lakes Water Quality Board lists 24 of them as hazardous to the living.

Water quality of the Great Lakes began to suffer

when the area became the center of industrial and human growth in the 1800s. So important was Great Lakes maritime trade that in the 1890s Chicago was named the fourth largest port in the world, even though ice closed the port up to five months a year.

To make way for more commerce, construction of four canals began in 1799 and ended in 1955, opening the way between the upper lakes and lower lakes to the Atlantic. By 1959 ocean-going vessels entered inland and traveled the 2,342 mile distance from the mouth of the St. Lawrence River to Duluth, Minnesota, at the western end of Lake Superior.

Shortly before and after the seaway opened, more development came with growing public needs, including chemical products. Development of petrochemicals, particularly, grew by leaps and bounds in the years following the end of World War II until production limitations were set in 1986 under the Toxic Substance Control Act.

Other chemical plants flourished as well, including the coal, copper, steel, and paper industries. Waste treatment, hydroelectric, and nuclear power plants filled out the string of pollution source points that line the shores of the Great Lakes today. The area, which also houses over 35 million people, is said to harbor the highest concentration of industries on the continent.

* * *

Now that you have seen the possibilities for opening, closing, and developing a story, keep the recommendations made in this chapter in mind next time you have to "put it all together." Begin by asking Critical Self-Inquiry 12: *What information for elaboration is relevant, informative, interesting, provides a thorough and balanced account, and stands up to question?*

Here's how the professionals interviewed in this book pulled their data together for presentation.

* * *

HOW THE PROFESSIONALS DO IT

Presenting and Writing the Copy

The media writers quoted here could not explain how their presentation idea popped into their minds, but you will. And like these professionals you will perform as reliably and creatively as they do, but with less of the stress that comes with trial and error. Here the writers described the last phase of their assignment, putting their work on paper.

Print News: The Navy Story

This is how Mr. Ashenfelter opened his story:

> For five years, Roy and Helen Collum believed their son fell overboard and drowned during flight operations on the USS Ranger. That's what the United States Navy told them.
>
> The telegram notifying them of Terry's death said he "died while serving his country," and the Navy posthumously promoted him. His body was never recovered.

Several introductory graphs follow giving additional background and context, all of which ends on this sentence suggesting the development that follows in the next paragraphs:

> Last month, Roy and Helen Collum finally learned the truth about how their son died.

Development of introductory details ran across a quarter of the front page and continued on a full page and a half on the inside pages. The body of print is broken up at appropriate places with subheads and the italicized paragraphs to which Mr. Ashenfelter had referred. These brief italicized inserts presented witness statements and evidence from Navy reports, messages, and manuals to tell the Collum story. One of them is shown here and represents an eyewitness statement concerning the Collum incident:

> *I was about 10 feet from where the Marines were (exercising the prisoners). One of the prisoners wasn't keeping up with the rest of the group. The Marines told him to get up and he got up on his feet and they started yelling the s. . . . out of him like they always do. The guy just couldn't take it anymore so he grabbed the rail and just went over.*
> —Airman Neal Flax, from the Navy report on Terry Collum's death.

Mr. Ashenfelter chose to close with a quote.

> "I can understand why they would try to save us some anguish," says Helen Collum. "But we could have taken it. They should have told us."

Methodical habits and critical thinking produced a series of stories worthy of a Pulitizer award, but the series also brought the Ashenfelter-

Freedberg team the reward of fulfilling the needs of families who had made the ultimate sacrifice, loss of a son. As importantly, the team's investigations led to correction of abuses inflicted on servicemen placed under guard.

> **Ashenfelter**: We were right on. And then during the summer, I believe it was in August, the Navy finally brought charges against 28 Ranger crewmen including the officer in charge, the captain of the ship. The bottom line was that everybody was either acquitted of charges of misconduct or found guilty and given relatively light punishment. Navy Secretary Warner apparently was so outraged he put an official letter of censure in the file of the captain of the ship and the one second in command. What those letters of censure did was, well, their careers were dead in the water. In the Collum case, we concluded early on that he was not murdered, that he simply went over the side of the ship. The murder thing just didn't wash in the initial investigation. But the whole issue of how prisoners are treated in the brig, well, the Navy completely rewrote its correctional manuals. Then, for the first time since 1775, Marines were relieved of guarding sailors, which was pretty significant.

Notice that in his final comment Ashenfelter again alluded to the modification of first predictions. Notice, too, that the issue of Navy abuse became part of the final statement, but only after vigilant verification which went beyond the usual check and to the extent of conducting a survey.

Print News: The Ford Plant Fire

Again Mr. Cain reaffirmed his final statement is a modification of earlier beliefs concerning the fire. Here he also explained how he presented his story and prefaced it with this explantion:

> **Cain**: Because the paper appears the following afternoon after the fire started, I have to assume that most of the readers of the paper [*Ann Arbor News*] will be aware from radio, television and just word of mouth that there was a heck of a fire out in Saline. So I'm going to want something in the lead that will be new. So that's why I picked the state police arson investigators poking through the blackened slag heaps of incinerated plastic trying to pinpoint who or what touched off this big blaze [observations of the aftermath]. Then I tried to summarize in the next few, eight paragraphs what I considered to be the most significant things that happened or didn't happen. They didn't lose the plant. Nobody got badly hurt. Having done that, the easiest way to handle the story is chronologically, gives a sense of dramatic flow and it allows me to counterpoint the general with the particular.

Here's how Mr. Cain began his story:

> State police arson investigators today were poking through blackened slag mounds of incinerated plastic trying to pinpoint who — or what — touched off

a Thursday afternoon blaze in a storage area behind the Ford Motor Co. Saline plastics plant.

A billowing black cloud of hydrogen cyanide-dashed smoke routed some 4,000 school children, workers, and area residents but sent only three people to Saline Community Hospital for treatment of mild smoke inhalation.

The plant was back in operation today.

Introduction and context end on the above sentence suggesting the development of details inherent in the opener and introduction and which Mr. Cain fulfilled in the next paragraphs. The story ends on one of the final details rather than a formal closure, which is customary in a breaking news story.

Broadcast News: The TWA Hijack

Mr. Meisner described the rationale for handling both the evening newscasts and the final hour-long documentary. His suggestion for presentation focus on the documentary turned out to be much the same as the one he used for the nightly newscasts: the international incident and its relationship to the St. Louis victims.

> **Meisner:** In this story, we had to have the political element, but that was the backdrop for the human element. That [the human element] was the story. It [the whole coverage, the 6 p. m. newscasts for the hour program] was much greater than I expected. I was very concerned. I had very little time to work with. I was extremely concerned about the quality. At the outset of the story it was very difficult to know [the story focus]. What we were looking for was the human element as well as the political element and to follow the story through the process and when the story ended to be there to cover it, to bring it [the international incident and the local interest] all together. Most times you're not fortunate enough to get those elements.

The story that initiated the series of 6 o' clock evening broadcasts began with a straightforward opener:

> A tense hostage situation is unfolding in the Middle East.

Details of how the seige occurred came next and then the story broke away to a UPI reporter in Beirut who gave an update on the incident. This was followed by a return to the homefront and an interview with family members of one of the hostages. The newscast closed on another straightforward sentence informing the audience that Eyewitness News would follow the story and update the incident as reports became available.

The prime time documentary opened on the released hostages deplaning on American soil, followed by events that led to their release. These scenes were intercepted with scenes showing reactions of family members. The story closed on reunions of the hostages with their families. And the whole was drawn from the evening newscasts of the 14-day hostage situation.

Broadcast News: Illegal Use of Public Land

In the previous chapter, Ms. Timmons referred to three segments in the presentation of her story, in essence her synthesis statement. Ms. Timmons also differentiated this story from other stories she has worked on where the backgrounding, researching, and interviewing extended into months because the deadlines were longer.

> **Timmons**: The story didn't change much [after it was established there was a problem in Michigan, that only drug farmers and survivalists were involved]. We did not have a problem with squatters so that did not relate to the California people. There had been a few instances involving survivalists which they [TV staff in California] relayed to me. And there had been some instances of marijuana growers who had threatened some people and they related that information to me.
>
> There was a fine line here. I didn't want to scare people off from using public lands. You don't want to use scare tactics on something like this. You want to make the public aware, give the public some preparation and warning that if they are confronted, this is what they should do. This was the last piece in the three-part presentation of: *Yes, this is happening, these people are doing this and it is happening in Michigan* [part 1]. *This is why* [part 2]. *The public lands are there for you to use, but if you are confronted, this what you should do to protect yourself* [part 3].
>
> I did minimal research on this story. I had ready material [California tapes and government data] that really gave me a boost in starting on it. It also cut down the shooting schedule. Normally research [and shooting] would take at least a month, if not a year. There are some stories I'm working on now where I've been building files for two or three years.

Public Relations: The Converted Ambulance Crisis

Mr. Snearly's next comment illustrates again the importance of an audience directed presentation. The facts were there, the data was complete and substantiated, but reasons for the mishaps were not what the public, or the media, wanted to hear. They first wanted to hear the Ford Motor Company express concern for public safety and then to explain the reasons. The overriding PR principle at Ford's, that they are *customer driven*, got lost because the message was delivered upside down, that is, the reasons came first and then Ford's ethic about being customer oriented. Notice Mr. Snearly's synthesis statement remains the same; only the presentation plan undergoes revision. That plan is embodied in a guiding construct which he names as their *key phrase*.

Snearly: Unfortunately, the public wasn't totally convinced by our message, even though it was the truth, mainly because the papers, and especially television news, focused on the fires. The news was that Ford ambulances were blowing up, and they reduced the reasons for the explosions to a graph, or a couple of sound bytes, or ignored them. The public perception became the media's perception—that this was a Ford cop-out, that we were foot dragging, pointing the finger at someone else. We had to modify the message.

So I said: *Let's back up.* I knew we were concerned, that we were committed, that this was a complex problem. We had to let them [the media] know they're talking to other human beings [the Ford Motor Co.] who are very concerned about this. We're what we call customer driven around here. The reality, the reasons for the situation didn't change, all that was the truth to begin with, but the real message of our concern and dedication wasn't getting through.

The message had to be modified from a PR message to the Ford message. So the key phrase that guided us was what I called: *the three C's . . . Concern, Commitment, Complexity.* When asked we would say: *Yes, we are concerned with this problem and we're committed to resolving it.* Then we would drag out the statistics, the man hours we spent, the resources that we committed. All that got lost before.

Now we tried to explain our concern about this issue and commitment to resolving it and explained this first. Then, we would say: *There's third-party manufacturers, there's poor maintenance practice, there's severe vehicle misuse* [the development]. It seemed to come across better when you first reassured people that you were concerned and were working hard to resolve it, and then explained the causes [rather than explaining causes first and the Ford commitment last]. It was our concern and commitment that wasn't coming across at all before.

When PR products are solid and delivered with audience in mind, the PR purpose is fulfilled, including that of the news media. The return for writers in all mediums is gratifying.

Snearly: One newspaper, the *Wall Street Journal*, did an in-depth front-page article on this story.They asked all the right questions: *How many fires have there been? How many injuries? What are you doing about it? Why was this was happening?* Others just wanted to hear that Ford had goofed.

Of course, we spent about four months with the *Wall Street Journal* before the article was published. They took the time to understand the facts and when you understand the facts, that makes a difference for the public's understanding of the situation. It wasn't a great story for the Ford Motor

Company, but we didn't come across as corporate criminals, or as uncon-
cerned about the issue.

We felt somewhat vindicated recently [April 1989]. The NHTSA has a
monthly investigation report in which they announce new investigations, and
in it they announced they were investigating 83-87 ambulances based on
third-party manufacturer's additions to the chassis, which is what we had been
talking about all along. They're investigating the converter manufacturers, the
alterations they're making on the heater hoses, but they're not investigating
Ford. In addition, the Environmental Protection Agency has announced new
guidelines to reduce fuel volatility, air pollution which, in turn, will reduce the
likelihood of fires. So besides the new approach, I now have news sources
other than myself repeating my message.

Public Relations: The Motorsports Promotion

The press notebook was the hook that resolved the original problem—a
new device to anchor media attention to the Ford name. And information
obtained from research and interviews (regarding Ford racecars and drivers,
other racecars and their drivers, along with data on racetracks, past races,
anything the media would find informative, relevant, useful and interesting)
was organized and arranged in the press notebook for easy reference.
Writing was limited to introductions to facts and information that the news
media would find useful and could pick out quickly. From the start, Mr.
Preuss knew what he had to do on this one. Research confirmed it and from
there it was a matter of updating facts he knew would contribute to the
organization and presentation of the press notebook.

The device was a novel one, but had to be augmented with other projects
to promote the Ford product. Mr. Preuss explained that some of these side
products included placing Ford racecar winners in the *Win* ad program,
Racing Into the Future, arranging interviews on talk shows featuring
winning drivers and team members, and readying file photos and videotapes
of Ford racecars on the track for use by the media. All this activity, even
when there is no "win," exemplifies the basic purpose of a public relations
effort, which Mr. Preuss effectively expressed in the last sentence of this
comment.

Preuss: The whole thing is image. What we're trying to do is create the
impression that Ford Motor Company products, the production cars, are
reliable, durable, well built. Racing a car 215 miles an hour at Daytona is heck
of an achievement. The trick is to get the press, first of all, to tell people how
difficult it is to win races. Then they have to get the relationship across that
the Thunderbird [the model raced at Daytona] is as solid as the race model
and to say: *Okay, we have a great Thunderbird running down at Daytona, so
go into your local Ford dealer and take a look at the production version.* The

other trick is to say to the world in all your advertising and promotion that the Ford Motor Company builds one solid car, and proof of this is the fact that this car runs this well against the best competition in the world. Even when you lose the Daytona race, you try to make something of how well your product did perform.

If, as Mr. Preuss said earlier, the *homework* never ends, neither does evaluation, including questioning one's own creative work.

Preuss: After every decision on a strategy, you always have to know: *Is it working, or not?* We could test, for example, by observing the success our press notebooks were having on the field. We'd put them out on a tray and within a half-hour they were all gone. But even after that, you have to ask: *Is anybody promoting his product at the racetrack any better than we are?*

One of the things our PR agency does is to monitor what the other guys are doing. Occasionally, I go down to the track and sit around the press room and talk to a lot of friends, have casual conversations, just to check how we're doing with them. I'm more convinced than ever that press kits don't work any more with these people. But I have to ask [in reference to the press notebook and other Ford PR products]: *Should we be doing something different? Have our products become old hat?* It's a constant re-examination of how you're doing things. Nobody out there is doing anything better than we are, but I suspect in the next year or two we're going to have to devise something more novel than what we're doing now. Something else the others can imitate again.

Advertising: The Pizza Campaign

Once approved, the campaign idea is developed for final presentation in print and broadcast media for the public market. Here, Mr. Thornton described the development for TV. Notice his criteria for selecting the main and sub-themes for the visual campaign: *easy to say, memory value, alliteration, good sound, fit the idea.* And notice he used the narrative approach to present the campaign idea. Also, that he adjusted the visual to the demands of a radio audience.

Thornton: We made a story out of all the ideas. Each had a beginning, middle, and end. In the promotion with the guy in the white coat, he was the antagonist against the imagined concerns the consumer held about Domino's Pizza. In the Noid promotion, the Noid character was the antagonist and Domino's was the hero coming to the rescue to overcome the villain [the annoyances of delivered pizza]. We had a collection of commercials and other promotions to show the client how we could keep all this going. Incidentally, the Noid theme didn't work too well on radio. It just didn't go over. People had to see the character and the animation, so we used another campaign for radio just based on the *Domino's Pizza Difference* theme.

In our visual campaigns, we used *Avoid the Noid* as the main theme and *Domino's Pizza Difference* as the sub-theme. Both were easy to say, had memory value, alliteration, a good sound and both fit the idea that Domino's pizza was the answer to overcoming the usual shortcomings of delivered pizza.

The evolution of the Noid character was an integral part of the campaign project and Mr. Thornton's comments about it are included here because they illustrate certain aspects of the strategy and critical thinking when applied to a specific part of the final product. Notice the number of times they juggled with visualizations of the Noid character before they designed the one figure they knew was "the right one." As Mr. Thornton pointed out, it took "a lot of thinking."

Thornton: It wasn't as easy it sounds. Even with the research data, a lot of thinking went into all of this, the character's name, the themes, the campaigns. The Noid wasn't a human figure. It couldn't speak. But it moved about, showed emotion, and had the ability to think. It was a humanoid, not human, just a noid. That's how we came up with the name ["humanoid" is a term from science fiction which may have figured in the reading background of someone in the creative group]. The *Avoid the Noid* theme was a natural follow-up of the conclusion we drew from the data [see chapter 11], and it rhymed.

Then we asked our writers and artists to give us their ideas for a figure that characterized all the consumer concerns that came out of the research. I gave the artists and writers a list of characteristics that the Noid might have. The Noid is clever, industrious, energetic, etc. We started out with little men, sort of dwarfs and gnomes, things like that from the mystic world. The character was emotional and could think, but it didn't speak, so it had to have a lot of body language. That's how we came up with the Bugs Bunny ears. The ears served the purpose of language very well and added to the animated action.

After we had a figure that we liked fairly well, we decided it should be animated and in clay. We sent it off to Will Vinton in Oregon. He does animation visuals. We kept adding things to the drawings. We tried him with gloves, without gloves. We tried different kinds of shoes on him. We sent Vinton our sketches. He sent us his. We went back and forth like that for a hundred or more sketches until we hit on the final sketch of the Noid. We knew the right one when we saw it [characteristic of continuous visualizations of an idea that ends in confident choice]. Vinton did the animation, and the rest is history.

The Noid theme worked and was sustained for the next five years, but not without frequent checks with consumer and competitive markets. When competitors moved into delivery service to compete with Domino's, the pizza company took another advertising direction.

Thornton: No one could have predicted the success of the Noid campaign. It was more successful than we could have anticipated. As we continued with the research and updated our data, we kept enlarging on the original idea. The figure of the Noid, particularly, was a phenomenal success. Yet some people didn't like it, about 20 percent, we learned in the marketing test. But it was tremendously popular with the young age group, the early teens to late twenties and early 30s. As the age level increased, the popularity of the image lessened. A good index of its popularity with the younger group is that Domino's share of the market increased from 12 to 20 percent in the first years. When you compare that with Pizza Hut's share of the market, which had shown a level course for the past five years, that's a remarkable rise and the Noid image had a lot to do with it. In fact, we discovered that the Noid had exceeded the popularity of Mickey Mouse and Bugs Bunny.

Advertising: The TV Spot Ad

If you recall in chapter 11, Ms. Gahagan explained the process that led to preliminary presentations. Now these are reviewed by group supervisors, and this review is followed by additional checks by several levels of supervisors.

Gahagan: [Describing verification procedures for content, Gahagan said]: Our checks [at this point] deal mainly with the creative idea. I mean whether it will catch the viewer's interest, how people might respond to the script itself. We ask: *Is it clear? Is it what we set out to communicate?* And when the copy goes to the account people, they check to see if everything the client has requested is in the copy.

We have several layers of supervisors. You run something by one first, and once you get something through with that person, then you go to the next level, and they approve something or choose their favorite, and after that it goes up to another level. So there's quite a bit of checking that goes on as far as making sure that the message is clear, that it's communicating, that it's entertaining, that it's breaking through. It has to be interesting so that people will watch and remember it.

Here, Ms. Gahagan explained the development of two TV spots, one of which went into the final product. It is also here that she described the source of her idea as something that occurs spontaneously (reminiscent of Norman's findings) unaware, of course, that she was, as Bruner put it, perceptually ready to confront the task.

Gahagan: I opened with dialogue for one idea. [Asked how she came up with her ideas, Gahagan's response was:] Well, a lot of us would love to know where that comes from. I don't know. It just comes. I really can't explain it.

On this one, we [the team of two writers, two artists] just put together a number of ideas, first on paper and then storyboards. These go through the agency for approvals and then to the client and they select the ones they like. We [the creative team] worked up two of these.

They chose one I had done with my writing partner and one by another team. The one my partner and I did showed a country fair and judges were testing several products [of the same kind as the client's]. The judge goes down the line of entries. Right at the end of this line a little kid squirms her way through the crowd of adults and puts up a container of [the client's product] as her entry. Everyone kind of smiles tolerantly and says, "Isn't that cute." Then, of course, the judge half seriously takes a taste and decides the kid's entry is really the best. The one the other team did showed the outrage of the townspeople over the release of their prized country recipe to outsiders. The recipe had been guarded secretly by the townspeople for many years. No one knows who gave their secret recipe away until one of the town's ladies drives by in a big, brand new car.

Both spots were well received in the focus group test and proved consumer effective. Both were aired, but on the research group's recommendation the second commercial was aired first. The two ads demonstrated a solid job, passed all the checks and balances, measured up to editorial expectations, and hit home with the client.

That's the name of the media game. Do a solid job for an audience and you will achieve the purpose of your medium, whether it is print or broadcast news, magazine, PR, or advertising. The means for players in that game are there for anyone's use—*the right strategy, the right questions.*

Epilogue: Looking Back

You have just completed a study of the right strategy, the right questions. You now know the inner workings of the dynamics of mass media writing and the critical questions they require. Use the outline of the strategy and its questions in chapter 1 as a guide for your next assignment or personal project. Refer to critical questions listed in chapters detailing the stages in the strategy. It will be difficult at first, but put to practice, the routine and the habit of critical thinking will become part of your reflexive nature. The alternative is to fall back on old and chaotic habits, mainly trial and error.

Make no mistake, the strategy is not a magic code, nor is it a "formula" that guarantees gripping prose. What it will do is help you perform systematically instead of chaotically, critically instead of passively, and confidently instead of doubtfully. The reward is professional performance that can lead to the kind of creative originality editors are looking for.

When Bruce DeSilva, writing coach at the *Hartford Courant*, spoke before a group of students at the University of Michigan, he said, "Stories play an important cultural role, and no one else is doing it very well right now." Then referring to the TV series, which was based on Larry Mc-Murtry's novel, *Lonesome Dove*, he said, "When television does it [the story] well, it is so unusual that it gets billed as a national TV event." It's a need newspapers must fill, he added, "readers love it."[1]

---

[1]During the spring 1991 term, Bruce DeSilva taught a 2-week mini-course in journalism as literature at the University of Michigan, Department of Communication. Some of his comments, including those above, were published in the spring 1991 issue of *The Michigan Journalist*, a department publication produced by graduate students and faculty.

William Taubin, a member of the Art Directors Hall of Fame, expressed similar sentiments about advertising. When asked about advertising, he said, "Advertising today is the bland leading the bland. Advertising today is imitative." In the same interview, he added, "Good advertising . . . has to incorporate ideas based on creative principles. Each product has something unique. The advertiser must discover this uniqueness and deliver it to the audience."

In all fairness to Mr. Taubin, it must also be said that he believes "advertising is not a science. It is an art, an instinct for something. And in many ways it is intuitive." Perhaps Mr. Taubin is unaware of how the "uniqueness" he seeks is found. If he were aware of the characteristics of the scientific/creative thinker and writer, perhaps he would realize that creativity has its source in systematic habits and critical thinking. In fact in his closing comments he at least recommends the latter, "As creative people, we need to remember that, if everyone is moving in one direction, we ought to be thinking about the other direction. We need to stop accepting things as they are and learn to ask why."[2]

With that point of view, perhaps Mr. Taubin might agree with Rudolph Arnheim's quote at the beginning of chapter 1 and Oscar Wilde's comment at the beginning of chapter 12:

> *Without any idea of what sort of process is at work, how is one to comprehend why certain conditions enchance understanding whereas others hamper it? And how is one to discover the best methods of training the mind for its profession?*

> *The imagination imitates. It is the critical spirit that creates.*

You have just read about the process at work in your profession. You are aware it can be as systematic as science and that intuition is less an instinct about something and much more a "perceptual readiness" for the creative demands of the art *and* science you practice, writing to communicate.

---

[2]Alan Dennis, a faculty member in the Department of Advertising and Public Relations at the University of Alabama, interviewed Mr. Taubin during the period when Mr. Taubin served as visiting professor of advertising at the university. The interview was published in the department's publication, *Perceptions*, March 1991.

Appendix A: Some Do's About Writing and Editing

Although this book assumes the novice media writer has had some basic training in both writing and editing skills, some reminders about writing and, above all, close scrutiny of one's written work are always helpful. Even after the final editing, a critical evaluation should follow.

Test your copy against the following list of guidelines. The list by no means covers every writing weakness. It is merely a representation of frequently made errors you should try to avoid. To resolve other problems about grammar, punctuation, and capitalization, refer to any one of the useful texts recommended at the end of these guidelines. Then check your written work against the criteria given in the last section of this appendix. It is easy to forget about the "rules" of communication, especially in the heat of writing, and sometimes you are so close to your own copy, the things that need correction escape your eye. Nobody's perfect, including those who issue these precautions. But the point is to try to be as error free as one possibly can.

1. Be specific.
- This applies to names of people, places, things, action words, and feelings. If you mean a certain senator among several mentioned, give his name, *Senator John Jones,* rather than saying, *the senator.* Otherwise, you force the question, "Which senator?"
- Help the receiver visualize the place of action. If the argument took place on the courthouse steps, say so, rather than *in front of the courthouse.* If you are talking about a *situation,* identify it. Otherwise, you invite guesswork or raise questions in the receiver's mind.

- Help the receiver visualize the action or feeling. *He leaped across the aisle* gives the reader an actual photograph of the true action. *He walked across the aisle* does not.

- Help the receiver understand by using the word that conveys the precise meaning you intend. If you mean *eager*, then avoid using *anxious*, which means to be worried or distressed. If you mean worried or distressed, then use *anxious*. Use the verb specific to the action or feeling, but make sure you are using it correctly. Look up meanings of even simple words in the dictionary. Always work with a dictionary close by.

- To select the most precise word, adopt the habit of searching for the specific word you believe describes the person, place, thing, action, or feeling you have in mind. Even if you think you know its meaning, look it up.

2. Use simple, familiar words.

- Words with more than four or five syllables are either not understood or misunderstood, especially when delivered on the air. Remember, you are communicating with a general audience from the not-so-well educated to the very well educated. You have to reach every level in that range with words every person will understand. Besides, they are not interested in how smart you are, only in what you can tell them. So, instead of tongue twisters like *dis-sem-i-nate*, say *scatter*, or *spread*. The meaning is the same. Everyone will understand.

3. Write plainly.

- It is one thing to use simple and familiar words; it is another to put them together in a sentence that sounds like common speech and not like pompous double talk. This sentence, for example, is just pure puffery: *The forbearing review policy poses a danger to the public because of the tendency of persons on probation to commit more crimes*. Rewritten, the following sentence gets rid of some of "p" words, sounds more down-to-earth, is more specific, and takes less space and time: *The review policy encourages parolees to repeat crimes and threatens public safety*.

4. Use active, descriptive verbs.

- No need to be shy, even when writing about the tragic. For example, this sounds wimpy and flat: *Four people are dead as a result of the blaze*. Use of *are*, a "to be" verb, weakens the whole sentence. This sentence addresses the tragedy: *Four people died in the blaze*.

- Use the same principle here: *He said this year the company had a poor start. He said the company started out poorly this year*.

5. Place modifiers where they belong.

Clarity is lost when words are misplaced in a sentence. Keep words together that are related in thought. Keep apart those that are not related. For example: *Twenty passengers were injured in the train accident including the engineer and ticket master*. The phrase beginning with *including* modifies *passengers*, not *accident*. Also, get rid of the passive verb "were." Rewrite to read: *Twenty passengers, including the engineer and ticket master, suffered injuries in the train accident.*

• Here's an adverb that is frequently misplaced: *The pilot only had 30 hours of flight training.* Rewrite to read: *The pilot had only 30 hours of flight training.* The meaning of *only* is not in reference to the pilot, but to the pilot's limited experience.

• This is a dangling participial phrase: *Watching the ball sail into the bleachers again, relief of pitcher Rand was Coach Martin's decision.* The opening phrase modifies Coach Martin, not Rand. The participial phrase dangles away from its rightful owner. Proper placement also gets rid of the passive *was* so that the sentence now reads: *Watching the ball sail into the bleachers again, Coach Martin decided to relieve pitcher Rand.*

6. Use adjectives and adverbs wisely.

• Piling up adjectives on a noun and piling up adverbs on a verb means you have probably selected an imprecise noun or a weak verb. Too many of these modifiers slow a sentence down to a screeching stop, as they do here: *The uncertain, inconclusive, and unproductive meeting ended in a stalemate. The bright, brisk, refreshing May day was a welcome change from the usual bitter, bone chilling, below zero Moscow winter.* See how CBS broadcaster Dan Rather described these thoughts concisely and far more vividly in the next paragraph. Sometimes it takes more than two modifiers to characterize the noun or verb they modify, but whenever there is a single word modifier that is more precise, use it.

• Steer clear of modifiers like *well built* athletes, *stunning* actress, *happy young* faces. They are clichés, stereotypes. Use adjectives and adverbs that create a picture, communicate the feeling that you actually saw and felt. In a May 18, 1990, broadcast from Moscow, Dan Rather described the uncertain exchanges between Soviet and U.S. diplomats as a *diplomatic ballet*. He described the weather as *sunflash bright* and a pleasant change from the usual *Napoleon retreat cold* of the Soviet capitol. Dan Rather used his memory bank of sights, senses, and data knowledge to associate what he saw and felt to his observations in Moscow. His words create a scene. These do not: the *uncertain, inconclusive, and unproductive* meetings, the *bright, brisk, refreshing* May day was a welcome change from the *usual bitter, bone chilling, below zero* Moscow winter.

Watch out for adjectives and adverbs that reflect your bias. These are not modifiers. They are labels and give notice of your imprecision as well as your bias. *She's only five feet tall* is a value judgment. *The senator still hasn't finished his speech* suggests the senator has talked too long. *The student effectively challenged the teacher* indicates you have taken sides.

7. Write active sentences.

• Means placing subject, verb, and object in that order, an S-V-O structure: actor, action, object of the action. It also means using the active voice wherever possible instead of passive voice. Together, those two meanings stand for declarative style, one for which John McPhee, former writer for *The New Yorker,* is noted. Declarative style moves the copy forward and avoids twisted structures and ambiguity. The secret here is to identify the true actor, the true action of that actor, and the true object of that action. Active sentences become passive sentences when the "to be" verb replaces an active, descriptive verb (see Items 4 and 5 above). Sometimes the passive voice is unavoidable, even appropriate, especially if you intentionally want to slow down the copy for emphasis or to establish an observed mood: *The refugees at first objected, then wept. They were forced to relinquish any valuables they had with them.*

8. Write direct sentences.

• A direct sentence draws the receiver's attention to the subject of the sentence at the outset, rather than at the end. Interest wavers by the time the receiver gets to the subject of this sentence: *The strikers, who have been out of work for six weeks and face dwindling strike pay from the union, even though they continue to pay union dues, also requested intervention by a labor mediator.* Rewritten and reduced, the sentence puts the main point up front and breaks up an overweighty sentence into two sentences: *Union members also requested a labor mediator to intervene in this six-week-old dispute. Strikers face dwindling strike pay even though obliged to pay monthly union dues.*

9. Write coherent sentences.

• Fragment, fused, and run-on sentences represent three of the most frequent sentence faults. A *fragment* is not a sentence because it lacks a subject and predicate, a complete thought. The following sentence has a subject and verb and is punctuated with a period, but it is not a complete thought; it is a dependent clause: *Although she withdrew her name.* The next sentence is a complete thought and an independent clause: *She withdrew her name.* The following sentence, too, is a complete thought, but it includes both a dependent and independent clause: *Although she withdrew her name, she did so reluctantly.*

• Sometimes fragments serve to emphasize a thought or feeling: *What! Up, up, up, and then no more. Ah, sweet victory. Cooling, refreshing and nourishing, too!* Other times they serve as directives: *Try it.*

• *The fused* sentence combines two or more sentences when they should be separated with a punctuation mark: *He fled from the room the officer ran after him.* These are to two independent clauses and should be separated with a period: *He fled from the room. The officer ran after him.*

• The *run-on* sentence is like the fused sentence. It does not know when to stop: *The city's schools face troubling times, voters defeated the school millage proposal for the second time.* This is a run-on sentence with a *comma-splice* error. The comma links two independent clauses when a period should separate the two clauses: *The city's schools face troubling times. Voters defeated the school millage proposal for the second time.* If the intention is to indicate a close relationship between the two clauses, a semi-colon may be used: *The city's schools face troubling times; voters defeated the school millage proposal for the second time.*

• Another common run-on error is misuse of the conjunction "and." Used properly, it indicates two thoughts are related, or that the second thought follows in sequence to the first. Misused, the sentence jars the reader because it forces the reader to jump into another frame of mind without an appropriate transition. If the intention is to show a relationship between two independent clauses, "and" does the job: *The city's schools face budget deficits, and voters defeated the school millage proposal for the second time.* It is a little less jarring if one of the independent clauses is turned into a dependent clause: *Even though the city's schools face budget deficits, voters defeated the school millage proposal for the second time.*

10. Write readable sentences.

• In chapter 8 you learned questions should be framed within a 20-word limit, but not at the expense of the intended meaning. The same good sense holds true in general copy. However, no sentence should unnecessarily burden the reader or listener with a choker like this one: *A government spokesperson said release of the hostages was delayed but would not explain why, and others close to the White House said the State Department was awaiting assurance from Beirut that the hostages would be released to representatives of the U. S. government.* A series of items in a long sentence is permissible, but there are too many thoughts in this one. Broken up, the second and longer independent clause follows easily: *A government spokesperson said release of the hostages was delayed but would not say why. Others close to the White House said the State Department was awaiting assurance from Beirut that the hostages would be released to representatives of the U.S. government.*

11. Strike out excess prepositional phrases.

• Too many prepositional phrases complicate the sentence: *The City Council Friday proposed the consideration of two companies for supplying estimates for the repair of potholes on Main Street.* Get rid of some of them: *The City Council Friday proposed consideration of estimates made by two companies to repair potholes on Main Street.*

12. Beware of agreement traps.

• A singular subject takes a singular verb: *Our report in past years has been incomplete.* And not: *Our report in past years have been incomplete* because the verb modifies *report*, not *years.* Here's an example of a singular subject which takes a singular verb because the verb agrees with the subject: *The committee is James Brown, Margaret Smith, and Bill Jones.* Correct, but awkward. Rewrite: *The committee members include James Brown, Margaret Smith, and Bill Jones.*

• A plural subject takes a plural verb: *The representatives are James Brown, Margaret Smith, and Bill Jones.* The verb is still plural when: *James Brown, Margaret Smith, and Bill Jones are the committee.* Correct, but awkward. Rewrite: *James Brown, Margaret Smith, and Bill Jones make up the committee.* Or, *committee members include James Brown, Margaret Smith, and Bill Jones.*

• Watch out for tricky structures: *None of these recommendations requires approval.* *None* is the subject, not *recommendations.* The first word is not always a clue to the subject. The subject may be elsewhere in the sentence. If you are not sure where the subject is, turn the sentence around: *Here come the athletes now (The atheletes come).* But, in this sentence it is: *Here comes the winner now (The winner comes).* *There are the books I borrowed (The books are there).* Look for the word that performs the action. That is the word with which the verb must agree.

• Try not to let other words that are part of the main subject mislead you. This sentence has three items in it that look like they should take a plural verb. But they are really part of the principal subject which is singular: *Each document, statement, and photograph was destroyed. Every document, statement, and photograph was destroyed.*

• When one subject is singular and the other is plural in sentences with "or" or "nor" let the verb agree with subject nearest to the verb: *Neither the assailant nor the victims were wounded. A student pass or library card is required.*

• When "and" joins two subjects, use the plural form: *The lawyer and judge knew they had to make a quick decision. Her talent and charm have served her well. Several documents and a photo were destroyed.* This is correct, but if you switch the subjects around, the sentence falls more gently on the ear: *A photo and several documents were destroyed.*

• When several subjects connected with "and" are preceded by "each," "every," "everyone," "everybody," "either," "nobody," "someone," use a singular verb: *Each cabinet, chest, and drawer needs repair.*

13. Strike out redundancies.

• Some redundancies are obvious: *seldom ever, coming future, absolutely perfect.* Some redundancies are less obvious: *The raging flames burned out the center portion of the building where the terrorist had purposely placed the bomb.* A few of these words are unnecessary because the words that precede or follow them already convey the meaning intended. Flames rage. A center is a portion of the whole. Terrorists operate with purpose.

14. Identify ambiguous pronouns.

• Make sure your point of reference is clear. A reader or listener would have to guess about the antecedent reference in this sentence: *These delays increase the possibility of error because control over the department is not maintained.* Where is the root reference of departmental inefficiency? Is it *delays*? Or, is it *error*, or lack of *control*? All three? Take your pick. Any interpretation is justified, but why force the receiver to make choices? Tell the receiver precisely what you mean. Assuming the following is the author's meaning, the sentence might read: *Control over the department is necessary in order to reduce errors and delays.* But we cannot be sure.

• When you use pronouns such as *it, they, them, theirs, this, these, those, which*, make sure the subject to which those pronouns refer is close by. If not, identify the referent again: *Senator Arnold Miller said Proposal A passed and Proposal B was defeated because women activists campaigned for it the hardest.* Which one? A or B? Should the reader assume the referent is A? Not really, because it is your aim to make your meaning clear, not force assumptions: *Senator Arnold Miller said Proposal A passed and that Proposal B was defeated because women activists campaigned the hardest for Proposal A.*

15. Look for parallelism errors.

• Words joined by *and, or* should be equal in form to one another. This is not a parallel structure: *Planning, counseling, and prescriptions for medication are part of the program.* The first two words are activities. The third one is the name of a thing. All three should have parallel form: *Planning, counseling, and prescribing medications are part of the program.*

16. Check your paragraph breaks.

• Strunk and White define the paragraph as "a convenient unit" of composition and suggest that you should devote as much space in a paragraph as it takes to explain what you are writing about. The length of it may be a single, short sentence or a lengthy passage.

• Usually, it is best to divide subjects requiring lengthy explanations into topic paragraphs. It serves as an aid to the reader. The beginning sentence tells the reader that you have launched a new step in the development of your subject. Whenever possible begin each paragraph with a sentence that suggests the topic or serves as a transition from the previous topic to the next. Ordinarily, single sentences should not stand alone as a paragraph. However, for effect, a word, phrase, or sentence often appear as a single paragraph:

Freedom!
Never again.
The artist's voice thrilled the audience.

Try to avoid large blocks of copy. They look formidable on the page and discourage the reader. Too many short paragraphs give a staccato effect and can break the flow of thought. However, use of several short paragraphs in a series is accepted as effective style in advertising. The point about paragraphing is to understand what you are trying to communicate and then to use good judgment about setting up a user friendly order for the ideas you do communicate.

Although transitions were discussed in chapter 5, the subject is reviewed in the next item along with pace.

17. Check the flow.

• Help the reader move from one paragraph idea to another with transitions. Some paragraph transitions operate with one word or phrase, the shorter the better: *meanwhile, later, elsewhere, moreover, on the other hand, in addition, on the same note, in closing, unlike his predecessor, recalling the error, aware of murmurs in the audience.* Transitions, as you know, alert the reader for a change and avoid an abrupt break in the flow.

• A transition often connects sentences within a paragraph simply by repeating the referent: *A response from the supervisors must come first. To obtain the opinion of the supervisors, we distributed a questionnaire.* That's not redundancy. It links the second sentence to its proper referent in the first sentence.

• Flow also involves pace and rhythm. If you had nothing but long sentences in your copy, no short sentences in between them, the reader would soon tire or lose interest. For a model of good pace and rhythm read *The John McPhee Reader,* W. L. Howarth, editor (1977). Read McPhee's stories not only for copy flow, but for illustrations of all the writing clues discussed here. Be sure to read the introduction first.

18. Check the spelling.

• Careless spellers dismay editors. Comb your copy for typos and words that may look right but leave a doubt. Always look up words you are using for the first time. Even check words you think you are sure about. For plurals ending in "i" and "y" and other such confusing problems, check the spelling rules in the back of your dictionary. Most dictionaries have a section on the rules of spelling.

• It is very easy to overlook misspelled words. It helps to have someone review your copy for you, not only for misspelling, but for other infractions, as well.

• Avoid dependence on phonetics. Some people pronounce *prescriptions* as *perscriptions* and misspell words like this the way they say them. Or, they may pronounce *referent* so that it sounds like *refferant*, but the former is correct.

• Use the spelling aid in your computer program with caution. The speller cannot tell the difference when a word is used in another sense — *the trusties* could mean trustees of an endowment or an uncommon expression related to a group of trusted persons. The computer is unable to make the distinction, but you can. Use the dictionary. It is a more reliable reference than your spelling checker.

19. Look for punctuation errors.

Three troublesome punctuation marks are the comma, hyphen, and dash.

• *Commas* separate items in a series, but writers tend to create a series where one does not exist. If the items in a series are equal in rank, then commas separate them: *The wavering, weaving man tried to turn back as the policeman approached.* If the relationship is absent, leave out the comma: *Professor Jones is a kind old gentleman.* Here's a convenient test of whether commas should separate adjectives: If you could use "and" between the adjectives, then the comma is appropriate; if "and" seems awkward or suggests a relationship between the adjectives when there is none, then do not use the comma.

• Writers often forget the second comma to set off a phrase or clause: *Allen Martin, former director of the Becker Art Museum is no longer manager of the acquisition committee.* The missing comma should come after *Museum.*

• In sentences where the clause is essential to the meaning of the overall sentence, avoid setting it off with commas: *Two hostages who had escaped from the compound were crushed by the armored tank.*

• Use a comma between two independent clauses joined by "and" or "but." If the second clause is related to the first and is short, the comma may be eliminated: *The speaker spoke for over an hour in a room filled with sympathetic listeners and they applauded enthusiatically.* Include the comma in other instances, especially where emphasis is intended: *The bombing finally stopped, but the terror remained.*

• Use a *hyphen* in compound adjectives that come before the noun they modify: *That's an out-of-date story. He's a 15-year-old contestant.* No hyphen when: *He's 15 years old.*

• Hold the hyphen after adverbs: *It was hardly noticeable.* However, don't assume that includes adjectives that end in "ly": *The bakery is a family-owned business.*

• Keep the hyphen away from words that sound like compounds: *holdout, laundrywoman, lawn mower, vice versa.* When in doubt, check the dictionary.

• Use the *dash* to set off a parenthetical that appears in the middle of a sentence: *The whole team—the center, forwards, guards—left the floor.* Use the dash to set off a word, phrase, or sentence you want to emphasize: *She always gives you smile—well, almost always.* Some computers do not have a dash on the keyboard. Use two hyphens.

This brief list in no way covers all error possibilities regarding the comma, hyphen, and dash. Rely on a text devoted to these problems and other punctuation problems such as use of *parentheses, semicolon, colon, apostrophe, quotation* marks. Most good dictionaries include a section on punctuation. Other good references are listed below.

20. Tighten, tighten, tighten.

• Some tightening techniques were suggested in the above sections, but don't stop there. Without sacrificing clarity, comb your sentences for extra verbiage: *In order that I may improve my skills in the arena of business managment, I have determined that registering for this training program will be helpful.* Remove the excess and rewrite to read: *This training program will improve my management skills.*

• Cut out unnecessary words in a phrase: *get in contact with, grant approval, sufficient enough notice.* Reduce these to *contact, approve, sufficient notice,* or *enough notice.*

• On the issue of using *that* for *which* and vice versa, publishers and editors like to make a distinction between them. They recommend "that" for a limiting or defining clause and "which" to introduce a nondefining or parenthetical clause. Here's an example: *The machine, which is broken, is being repaired. Which* is used because the clause is set off parenthetically by commas. The parenthetical indicates which machine is being repaired. *The machine that is broken is being repaired. That* is essential here because there are no commas setting off a parenthetical and the reader must be referred to the particular machine requiring repair.

*   *   *

SUGGESTED REFERENCES ON ENGLISH USAGE

Bernstein, T. M. (1965). *The careful writer: A modern guide to English usage.* New York: Atheneum.

Cappon, R. J. (1982). *The word: An Associated Press guide to good news writing.* New York: Associated Press.

French, C. W. (Ed.). (1987). *The Associated Press stylebook and libel manual.* Reading, MA: Addison-Wesley.

Martin, P. R. (Ed.). (1987). *The Wall Street Journal stylebook.* New York: The Wall Street Journal.

Strunk, W., Jr. & White, E. B. (1979). *The elements of style* (3rd ed.). New York: MacMillan.

*   *   *

EVALUATION CRITERIA FOR YOUR COPY

General Review (re: audience, references, data, sources, interview questions) — Have you:

- Served audience interest and/or provided needed information, a service, some insight?
- Selected most appropriate references, persons from all sides of the problem, issue, or question?
- Selected most appropriate references, persons involved in the announcement of some recent event?
- Correlated your visuals with the copy?
- Missed any likely references, persons?
- Failed to ask any questions of references, persons?
- Verified, validated references used, persons interviewed?
- Verified, validated data collected?
- Included appropriate IDs of persons, places, things?
- Included all the relevant, informative, interesting data that stands up to question?
- Edited and revised your copy using critical self-inquiry?

The Opener and Introduction (re: the problem, issue, question or announcement, plus background/context) — Have you:

- Suggested or set up the problem?
- Answered the *who*, *what*, *when*, *where*, *why*, and *how* questions?
- Placed these in their most logical order?
- Provided the most recent incident if handling an ongoing story?
- Identified all persons, places, things, times accurately, fully?

The Middle (re: development and fulfillment of promise established in the opener and introduction) — Have you:

- Answered all receiver questions regarding any details related to the *W* questions introduced in the opener, in the introduction?
- Answered all possible receiver questions regarding any details related to *why* and *how* questions suggested in the opener, in the introduction? What is missing?
- Used relevant, informative, interesting, reliable data?
- Presented details accurately and interpreted them accurately, fully?
- Presented these details in their most logical order?
- Balanced your presentation of information?
- Fully identified sources used?
- Quoted these sources accurately, fairly?
- Avoided ambiguity, weighty sentences, weak structures, etc.?
- Contradicted yourself, left a gap, revealed bias? What is missing?

The Close (depending on narrative type you are dealing with) — Have you provided any of the following?:

- A wrap-up of everything that has gone before in a memorable way.
- What the receiver can expect next.
- Question or quote.
- A source where receiver can obtain additional information.

* * *

SUGGESTED READING LIST

The following list includes works of poetry, drama, and various forms of prose. The list reflects this author's personal choices and is a mere peekhole look into the world of nourishing reading from the time of the ancient Greeks to current times. Many great works of literature are missing. Read what appeals to you. Discard those that do not. If you find an author you really like, look up other works by him or her. By all means try Homer, Vergil, the Greek dramatists, Dante, Chaucer, Shakespeare, Milton, William Blake, John Donne. They are not easy reading, but they are an education in themselves and worth the struggle. Meet Defoe, the 18th-century novelist who set the style for journalistic writing. You will find Saint-Exupéry a delight, Pound mystifying but memorable, Jane Austen and the Bronte sisters engaging, Brown, Erikson, and Young enlightening, as are so many others.

If you cannot find some of the works in quotes, you will find them in collected works of those authors. Read for content, but also notice the way the content is composed. Study the poetry for literary techniques such as alliteration, assonance, imagery, phrasing, rhythmical beat, tone, and language. Read drama for its movement from problem, to complications, to climax to resolution; for the development of its characters, their triumph or demise. Read fiction for overall structure, characterizations, descriptions, order of words in sentences, content rhythm and pace. Read these works for their wisdom, as well.

Aeschylus (translation of)
  Agamemnon
  Prometheus Bound
  Eumenides
Anderson, Sherwood.
  Winesburg, Ohio
  A Story Teller's Story
Aristophanes (translation of)

The Wasps
Lysistrata
The Women in Politics
Aristotle (translation of)
  Nicomachean Ethics, Rhetoric and Poetics
Arnheim, Rudolf
  Visual Thinking
Auerbach, Eric
  Mimesis
Austen, Jane
  Pride and Prejudice
  Emma
Babbitt, Irving
  "The Critic and American Life"
  On Being Creative
Benét, Stephen Vincent
  John Brown's Body
Bible, The
Blake, William
  "Songs of Innocence"
  "Songs of Experience"
  "The Marriage of Heaven and Hell"
Boccaccio, Giovanni (translation of)
  The Decameron
Bronte, Charlotte
  Jane Eyre
Bronte, Emily
  Wuthering Heights
Brown, Norman A.
  Life Against Death
Browning, Robert
  "Pippa Passes"
  "Fra Lippo Lippi"
Butler, Samuel
  The Way of All Flesh
Byron, Lord
  "Childe Harold"
Capote, Truman
  In Cold Blood
Carlyle, Thomas
  Sartor Resartus
Carroll, Lewis
  Alice in Wonderland

Cather, Willa
  One of Ours
  Obscure Destinies
  A Lost Lady
Chaucer, Geoffrey
  Book of the Duchess
  The Romance of the Rose
  Troilus and Crisyede
  The Canterbury Tales
Chekov (translation of)
  Three Sisters
  The Cherry Orchard
  Uncle Vanya
  The Sea Gull
Clark, Kenneth
  Leonardo Da Vinci
Coleridge, Samuel Taylor
  "Kubla Khan"
  "Rime of the Ancient Mariner"
Conrad, Joseph
  Lord Jim
  Youth
Dante (translation of)
  La Vita Nuova (The New Life)
  La Commedia (The Divine Comedy)
  The Paradiso
  The Purgatorio
DeFoe, Daniel
  Robinson Crusoe
  Moll Flanders
  A Journal of the Plague Year
Dickens, Charles
  Great Expectations
  Oliver Twist
  Hard Times
  A Tale of Two Cities
Donne, John
  His sermons, usually in collected works of Donne
Dos Passos, John
  Three Soldiers
  42nd Parallel
Dreiser, Theodore
  An American Tragedy

Jenny Gerhardt
Sister Carrie
Du Maurier, Daphne
  Rebecca
  My Cousin Rachel
  Tales from the Macabre
Eliot, George
  The Mill on the Floss
  Silas Marner
Eliot, T. S.
  The Wasteland
  Four Quartets
  Murder in the Cathedral
Emerson, Ralph Waldo
  His essays, usually in a collection of same
Epic of Gilgamesh (translation of)
Erikson, Erik H.
  Identity: Youth and Crisis
  Childhood and Society
  Insight and Responsibility
Euripides (translation of)
  Medea
  Electra
  Iphigenia in Tauris
Faulkner, William
  Absalom, Absalom!
  The Sound and the Fury
  As I Lay Dying
Fielding, Henry
  The History of Tom Jones, A Foundling
  The History of the Adventures of Joseph Andrews
Flaubert, Gustave
  Madame Bovary
Franklin, Benjamin
  An Autobiography
Frost, Robert
  "Mending Wall"
  "The Gift Outright"
  "The Road Not Taken"
Ghiselin, Brewster
  The Creative Process
Gibran, Kahlil
  The Prophet

The Wanderer
Goethe (translation of)
  Faust
Hardy, Thomas
  Tess of the d'Urbervilles
  The Return of the Native
  The Mayor of Casterbridge
Hawthorne, Nathaniel
  The Scarlett Letter
  The Marble Faun
Hemingway, Ernest
  The Sun Also Rises
  A Farewell to Arms
  Death in the Afternoor
Homer (translation of)
  The Iliad
  The Odyssey
Houghton, W.E.
  The Victorian Frame of Mind
Howarth, William L.
  The John McPhee Reader
Hugo, Victor (translation of)
  Les Miserables
  Notre Dame de Paris
Huxley, Aldous
  Brave New World
  Point Counter Point
Ibsen, Henrik
  An Enemy of the People
  A Doll's House
Ionesco, Eugene
  The Bald Soprano
  The Chairs
  The Lesson
James, Henry
  Daisy Miller
  The Portrait of a Lady
  The Golden Bowl
Jefferson, Thomas
  (his autobiography, speeches, and letters)
  Democracy
Joyce, James
  Ulysses

In Defense of Women
Mill, John S.
  Essay On Liberty
Millay, Edna St. Vincent
  The Harp Weaver and Other Poems
Miller, Arthur
  The Crucible
  Death of a Salesman
Milton, John
  "Paradise Lost"
  "Paradise Regained"
Nietzsche (translation of)
  Thus Spake Zarathustra
O'Casey, Sean
  The Plough and the Stars
  The Silver Tassie
  Within the Gates
O'Neill, Eugene
  Mourning Becomes Electra
  Strange Interlude
  Beyond the Horizon
Ovid (translation of)
  Metamorphoses
Plato (translation of)
  Apology
  Crito
  Gorgias
  Symposium
Platt, John R.
  The Excitement of Science
Plutarch (translation of)
  Lives of the Noble Grecians and Romans
  "On the Right Way of Hearing Poetry"
Poe, Edgar Allen
  "The Bells"
  "To Lenore"
  "Anabel Lee"
  "The Raven"
  "The Murders in the Rue Morgue"
  "The Purloined Letters"
  (any of Poe's short stories)
Popper, Karl R.
  The Logic of Scientific Discovery

Porter, Katherine Anne
  Ship of Fools
  Flowering Judas and Other Stories
  Pale Horse, Pale Rider
  Noon Wine
Pound, Ezra
  Cantos
  Personae
  Pavannes
  Divisions
  ABC of Reading
  Make it New
Rousseau, Jean Jacques (translation of)
  The Social Contract
  Émile
Saint Augustine (translation of)
  On Christian Doctrine
Saint-Exupéry, Antoine de (translation of)
  The Little Prince
Salinger, J. D.
  Catcher in the Rye
Saroyan, William
  My Name is Aram
  The Human Comedy
Scott, Sir Walter
  The Lady of the Lake
  Waverley
Shakespeare, William
  (any work of, particularly *Macbeth*)
Shaw, George Bernard
  Man and Superman
  Candida
Shelley, Percy Bysshe
  Prometheus Unbound
  "A Defence of Poetry"
  Triumph of Life
Sophocles (translation of)
  Oedipus the King
  Oedipus at Colonus
  Antigone
Steinbeck, John
  The Grapes of Wrath
Sterne, Laurence

The Life and Opinions of Tristram Shandy
Stevenson, Robert Louis
   Treasure Island
   The Strange Case of Dr. Jekyll and Mr. Hyde
Strindberg, Johan August
   The Father
   A Dream Play
   Miss Julia
Swift, Jonathan
   A Tale of a Tub
   The Battle of the Books
   Gulliver's Travels
Tennyson, Lord Alfred
   "The Poet"
   "The Charge of the Light Brigade" (based on a news dispatch)
   "Crossing the Bar"
Thoreau, Henry
   Walden
Tocqueville, Alexis de (translation of)
   Democracy in America
Twain, Mark
   The Prince and the Pauper
   The Adventures of Huckleberry Finn
Upanishads, The (translation of)
Vergil (translation of)
   The Aeneid
Watson, Robert I.
   The Great Psychologists: Aristotle to Freud
Wells, Herbert George
   The Time Machine
   The Invisible Man
   The War of the Worlds
Welty, Eudora
   The Robber Bridegroom
   Delta Wedding
   The Ponder Heart
West, Rebecca
   The Return of the Soldier
   The Judge
Whitman, Walt
   Leaves of Grass
Wilde, Oscar
   Lady Windemere's Fan
   The Importance of Being Earnest

Williams, Tennessee
  A Streetcar Named Desire
Wolfe, Thomas
  You Can't Go Home Again
  The Story of a Novel
Wordsworth, William
  The Prelude
Yeats, William Butler
  The Wind Among the Reeds
  Kathleen ni Houlihan
Young, J. Z.
  Doubt and Certainty in Science
Zola, Emile (translation of)
  Nana

Appendix B: Writing the Technical/Instructional Video Script

Jack Imes, Jr.

Jack Imes, Jr., is a creative executive in the Marketing Communications Group at the Sandy Corporation, Troy, Michigan (a Detroit suburb). The Sandy Corporation produces many of the same communication products as other agencies such as direct mail, product promotion and public relations brochures, product service and specification manuals, and the like, but the company specializes in consulting and custom-designed training programs and educational films.

As one of Sandy Corporation's visual designers and scriptwriters, Mr. Imes directs concept and script development for various types of media including video, film, interactive videodisc (similar to music compact discs) and videowall multi-screen presentations (projections of videos on super-size screens).

Here he describes how he developed a proposal and a series of video treatments as a preliminary to creation of a 50-minute video. The client, a major tire company, was moving out of the tire supply business and wanted to direct more attention to their nationwide chain of auto service facilities. They were entering a field that was dominated by automobile dealers whose customers were accustomed to taking their cars to dealer garages for maintenance. The client needed a program that would serve as good public relations, yet would subtly advertise its national chain. They requested a videotape that dramatized their services, but taught owners how to recognize the sources of their automobile problems. The intent was to help car owners learn more about their automobiles by distributing the video to male and female audiences for home use and in high school classes for student drivers.

The client expected to see a formal *proposal*, some *treatments*, and a *storyboard*. A *proposal* can be a simple or complex report that sets up the aim of the project, profiles the audience, and reveals what the research uncovered. It also describes how the research translates in terms of theme and content for the designated audience, clarifies video time, suggests a production schedule, includes other production details and a cost estimate.

Writing a proposal before audience communication can begin is often expected of a media writer, not only in advertising, but in PR and news, as well. Here you will get a look at how one proposal is put together. The process is similar in kind to the one required for any media project — systematic strategy and critical thinking.

Treatment is simply another term for a preliminary script, usually the divided sheets of paper described by Ms. Timmons and Ms. Gahagan. In this case, it was a short description of the video items and a brief summary of the copy that would accompany the visuals.

Once the proposal and treatments go through in-house approvals, a *storyboard* (a visual scenario of the proposed video) is developed for the client. Upon client approval, work for any one of the treatments is available for easy transfer into a full-blown shooting script. Development of the proposal, treatments, and final video are described here.

Like other professional writers, Mr. Imes followed a systematic work process and applied a series of self-inquiries that were relevant and specific to each task in the operation. In addition, although this assignment is instructional and calls for far more technical content than the assignments you read about earlier, the final video product is as entertaining and as scientifically and creatively derived as the previous ones. Mr. Imes described his methods, almost apologetically, as *not quite mechanical*, but close to it. The client's name and product are left unnamed at the request of the agency. Much of this particular interview was necessarily shortened due to limited space.

Notice Mr. Imes identified the problem before translating it into a tentative working statement:

Imes: The client . . . needed an idea that had wide-range audience appeal offering an uncomplicated story about the way automobiles function. The client believed that if drivers understood how a car worked, then they would better understand the need for proper maintenance. Service is what the client wanted to promote [identification of problem] . . . the general requirements for the car that most people don't want to attend to themselves because it's messy or time consuming . . . maintenance they didn't want to do, nor could they handle things like major transmission repairs and major engine over-hauls.

With that focus, the client needed a program with broad appeal, but not get too technical in the sense that: *We're not going to teach the technical nitty-gritty of the car in a dry way* [working statement]. Entertainment value would be one of the No. 1 measures of the program. At that point the client said, "Okay, what we'd like to see is a proposal about how you would develop this videotape."

In the following comment, notice Mr. Imes' preliminary questions and sources for research and backgrounding for the proposal. He later explained that he pre-coded his collected data in several three-ring binders calling one a "resource book," another a "script book," and divided their contents under tabbed headings.

Imes: First I had to do some reviewing. I looked at the material the client had provided in terms of their general marketing campaign, that is, the general marketing materials they had on other videotapes. I wanted a clear sense of the client's required level of quality. Then I looked at their particular services and promotional materials of those services. From the client, I obtained the official service dealers' operational manual and a step-by-step book of maintenance procedures.

All this gave me a good understanding of what the boundaries were for this particular program in terms of the services being offered. Then I researched magazines and directories of similar or comparable programs that are already out in the market. I wanted to know: *How unique is this program? Has this been done before and in what way?*

As I reviewed, I kept some basic questions in mind: *What was the presentation style? What's the particular level of expertise required by the viewer? Could I figure out what kind of budget they* [other advertisers] *had to work with? How do they focus the information delivery? Was it through a narrator alone, or actors in a scene?*

Then as I began to get ideas for my program, I kept up the flow of questions: *Where could it be different than what I had seen? Where could I better use information? What could I build on more dramatically? What ideas would serve my client's special needs in terms of the quality they wanted?*

I looked at home video markets in general to see what kind of basic trend was going on. Again, more questions, but tougher: *How can I create a program that would intrigue but not be so different that it would be ignored?* I wanted something that would fit in line with something the consumer would like to see. I had a basic commercial message, but the program had to deliver that message without becoming a blatant commercial.

Following this initial research, Mr. Imes wrote the proposal. It contained many of the items already mentioned here, and it included four suggested video treatments with accompanying storyboards. Research for the proposal also served the purpose of initial preparation for the treatments and video.

The client liked two of the treatments, so these were merged and attention turned to developing the final video for this six-figure project. To do this, Mr. Imes had to interview key people to find out more about how an auto owner should carry out ordinary maintenance procedures. He found he had to return to research for a demographic profile of the auto owner, certain video cost charges, and basic information to develop a glossary. He also conducted a survey of auto owners, which ultimately provided the dialogue he needed for the script as well as the specific information he sought to obtain.

Imes: This [interviewing] generally entailed conversations with an actual service person to check information and to check on the practicality of certain maintenance procedures. If I needed a clarification or a broader explanation of some procedure in the client's service manual, I'd call a garage and talk to an expert on that particular procedure and say: *Can you elaborate on this? Can you tell me how this is followed in your operation? Can you think of divergences from this procedure and the reasons why you altered the procedure?* In that way, I would get what I call a "reality check" of the procedures.

It also required some reference checking, getting a demographic profile of the typical customer, obtaining cost charges of various video techniques, and developing a glossary of commonly used words for the writer's use. It's one thing to have the technical word, but it's also useful to have the common usage, too. It also required research into what ordinary people knew about their cars [the survey].

We questioned some car owners on what they would like to know about their cars. We wanted to determine how much of a mystery there was about their cars. Because Sandy Corp. deals a lot with the automotive industry, we have very car-smart people within the company. But I needed to know more about the consumer's perspective. I started talking to friends first. Expanding the research, I talked to people who would be least likely to know technical details: the new driver, somebody who had a new car, people who didn't do their own maintenance at all.

I usually make a list of questions that I myself would like answered. Then I would say: *If that's what it's like in my case, then what's it like in someone else's case? Is this something that's just common knowledge?* Such as, we all have to fill tires with air: *Using a tire gauge, is that something I learned to do because my Dad showed me, or did I see somebody do that?* Then when I talked to people, I'd ask: *When the oil needs changing, how do you get it done? Do you know what the carburetor is for? Do you know that your car has different kinds of brakes? Do you have any idea how to maintain any of those things?*

That gave me a sense of the common knowledge. People were generally willing to talk because, as you know, automotive repair is a rather frustrating thing in itself. So people had a lot of stories about the problems that they had. They didn't refer to things by their proper names. They just said: *The whatcha-ma-callit*, or *do-hickey*, and that was important to capture for the script dialogue because a viewer immediately relates to that and the situation.

Here, Mr. Imes explained how he organized and coded all his research and interview data. His explanation detailed quite clearly the orderly management required of a writer who must handle a mass of data.

Imes: All this research data was compiled into a three-ring binder that I call the "resource book." This book holds my ongoing notes of information, notes to myself, articles that I would pick out of competitive information. I put those under tabs and label them under their categories and label the book under the project name. This gives me a one-stop archive for answering any questions I had during the script writing. And because this particular videotape involved ordinary people talking, it gave me a good source of quotes for my video characters.

I also put together a second binder that I call the "script book." This holds all the documents sent to the client, including the actual proposal, the script drafts and treatments, anything to do with the script and ongoing development. The two binders are kept together at all times. Together they give me a continuous thread of information, all explainable, and a script development with no gaps. As often happens, later on somebody wants to know: *Where did this idea, or scene, come from? Was this dialogue in the previous script?* To answer, I can go back to the script book to show a reference and date. From a writer's standpoint, the two binders are solid gold to solve unexpected, last minute rewrites.

In his review and analysis of data, note his thinking process which he called the *fusion*, his use of the term *translates* for reference to the equation/conclusion, and that he *fleshes* out the copy, visualizing to *make it happen*. Notice, too, that he is quick to check his own imaginative tendencies with self-inquiries and frequent references to his "resource book," and that his selection criteria for copy is based on what he calls *must lines* and *certain facts* (relevant, informative, and reliable data).

Imes: So far I've been planning ahead with my resource and script books. Given the ongoing script, the resource material, knowing my material, the fusion begins in my head. I start to fuse and translate and try to develop the scenes and flesh them out and make it happen. It's not quite mechanical, but sometimes it almost approaches a mechanical translation, especially if there are certain facts that have to be quoted in certain ways.

I know what facts have to go in. I also have "must lines," links that appear in the script for one reason or another, such as the client's ad slogans or marketing lines. When I'm in a creative or writing mode, I don't try to be judgmental. I try to split idea "creation" from idea "criticism." I try to be as free as possible. So I give myself these little promptings: *Don't confine yourself. Try to be as free as you can.* Then when I move over to the writing phase, I try to become a translator at this point of those ideas, and ask: *How can I describe them? How can I work with that?* After I've finished with that, I get into this revision mode and say: *Okay, what's practical here? How can I fit these ideas within the goal that we've established in this program?*

Keep in mind that the presentation idea is the merged version of two treatment ideas the client has already approved. And, at this point, Mr. Imes is developing that idea into nearly an hour's video script. Here his comments refer to the structure he had given to the four proposed treatments and the result of the two combined treatments.

Imes: All four treatments had a beginning, middle, and end. We wanted to give the client the feeling that each program had a start, a content, and a finish, and wasn't just a fragment unable to carry the video length. My treatment sketches out my scenes. Let's say it contains two people and they're going to be discussing something. That gives me my basic spine and now I have to include some sample dialogue. So I look in my resource book under "Features." Then I take that material and bring it into my scene. The visual image is very important. What I try to do is write descriptions that create a strong picture. In scripts, the narration and visuals work together.

As often happens, one treatment totally satisfied them, but they liked the elements of two treatments together, [one entitled] "Fantastic Voyage," and the music video treatment [entitled] "Music of the Times." The first one used the idea of shrinking a car owner to a one-inch height to accompany a magical guide on a close-up tour of his car's mechanical maintenance. The other one was done in lively music video style. So we merged the two treatments . . . taking the best of each and that's how we derived our final treatment. That was enhanced with details fully researched. . . . [the merged treatments] became the basis of the 100-page script for a 50-minute video.

Critical review of the creative work continues with a check by the project supervisor. Notice Mr. Imes first checks to see if he fulfilled his responsibility and client expectations before the work is sent to supervisors or the client.

> **Imes**: The project manager looks for consistency and makes sure everything is within the approved budget. Because he works from the basic assumption that this is not on-the-job training, that the writer and producer know how to do their creative job, the rewriting, visuals, or production planning is up to us. The account executive keeps the client informed as to the progress of the overall project, but is not on a day-to-day basis with the material. Because the account executive is juggling several major projects for various clients, there's no time to get heavily involved in the details of any one project. The account executive may meet formally with us only about three times during the whole project.

> When the project's finished, it goes to the client for final approval. Often this final review brings in the client's top senior people. They may or may not know the details of the project, but they are the ones who will make the final approval. We plan for possible objections and that's part of our ongoing development. The initial conception is always seen in the much brighter light of one's imagination, but the reality is that you can never quite achieve what you set out to do. You have to stay close to what the client expects. And because we keep everyone and the client informed, we reduce surprises [for the client and the agency] during final reviews.

Mr. Imes explained that the review itself is just as much a promotion as the project itself, that the overall project, its details, and the special effects used must be sold even though the client has agreed on the nature of the presentation. As he said, everything is cleared before the review in order to reduce surprise, yet the "pitch," as he characterized it in a later comment, carries over into the final review. The proposed video was approved and production on it followed.

Appendix C: The Free-Lance Project

Jeffrey Larsen

Jeffrey Larsen, formerly a writer and senior producer with the Sandy Corp., is now president of his own media production company, Cinéma de Liberté, San Francisco, California. Here he describes preparatory work on a free-lance film project that later evolved into a series of 10 half-hour television programs. The initial work on the film was developed and written by Mr. Larsen and co-producer, John Kelin, a Detroit news producer for the ABC network. Larsen, Kelin, and another free-lance producer, Cliff Ewald, formed a partnership to produce the film.

Some time later, Larsen and Kelin began collaboration on the series for television with jazz artist and filmmaker Christopher Pitts. Entitled "Jazz Masters, Keepers of the Flame," the TV series centers on jazz in Detroit and features a number of the city's talented jazz artists. Larsen and Kelin were curious about the hidden forces that drove dedicated musicians to pursue a living composing and playing jazz music instead of chasing after fame and riches in a more popular market. Projects like this require funding, not always easy to raise, but the writers persevered.

Like the professionals who write media products for commercial organizations, this writer uses a similar approach for this entertainment project. First he explained how it all came about and then identified the problem and, at the same time, set up the boundaries of preliminary research and anticipated the tentative working statement. The problem was: *to get to the source of these people's inspiration to play the kind of music they were so passionate about.*

> **Larsen:** This project really began during a conversation with a colleague of mine, John Kelin, about applying for a Michigan Council for the Arts grant. We discussed possibilities and agreed that jazz in Detroit was an attractive subject for a documentary. We wanted to get at the source of these people's inspiration to play the kind of music they were so passionate about.
>
> We knew this would involve a great deal of research, past and ongoing, looking at Detroit jazz history through archival footage, photographs, and filmed interviews, becoming familiar with the artists and their music, their life experiences. The purpose was to create a film that would get at the inspiration which compels these highly talented individuals to create jazz music.
>
> [The writers applied for and received grants from the Michigan Council for the Arts and the Detroit Council for the Arts]. We dealt with several organizations [other than the two councils mentioned], their membership, their board of directors, trying to secure funding. They'd say we love it, think it's wonderful, but we've seen thousands of these and only one will ever make it, so forget it before you start. We just fortified our commitment and went back to somebody else and wrote the others off our list.

In these comments, Mr. Larsen mentioned the types of research he knew he would have to do. Here, he named the sources he relied on initially and later more fully described his sources of primary research—interviews with the jazz musicians. Mr. Larsen's reference to a *trailer* refers to a 10-minute film that was put together from the first filmed interview and "jam" session. A trailer is ordinarily a short preview film attached to a major studio release so that movie distributors and theater owners can preview a coming film release.

As you will notice here and must have realized by this time, a media writer's resources are many and varied. The key is: Whatever is relevant to the problem at hand.

> **Larsen:** A good source for us was a group called the National Association of Jazz Educators. They held their annual conference in Detroit last year and we had the opportunity to showcase the trailer we had put together in their media resource section. The conference also gave us the chance to meet many renowned jazz artists and to interest some of them in participating in the project. Another source was a 1984 publication, *Who's Who in Detroit Jazz,* by a Detroit writer living in New York, Herb Boyd. We also sought advice from Lazaro Vega, jazz historian and columnist with the *Grand Rapids Press.*

The staff at WEMU [a Michigan radio station affiliated with Eastern Michigan University], where I had been a broadcast journalist, was helpful, as was Jim Dulzo, jazz columnist of *The Detroit News*, Michael G. Nastos, a regular contributor to the *Ann Arbor News,* and James Jenkins. He, James Jenkins, created and now manages the Greystone International Jazz Museum. The Greystone [a popular Detroit ballroom that faded into history in the 60's] was a regular stop for the biggest jazz artists and bands during the swing and early bop eras. More than that, it was just a matter of getting closer to the artists themselves, meeting with them, establishing relationships, making connections through Christopher Pitts and his network of working musicians. The primary question these sources answered was: *Who's out there playing now?*

For this project, verifications and validations included checks on the data and checks by the sponsors.

Larsen: Information is easily cross-referenced. A couple of facts I didn't get straight so I checked them with someone else—historians, musicians, radio jazz directors—who would remember. There's also a formal procedure for reporting to the Michigan and Detroit Councils for the Arts. They don't look at each line particularly, and if we modified the budget, they would come back saying, "We can't give you this much, but here's something and resubmit a budget that shows how you will apply that to your budget."

Preliminary research brings the working statement into sharper focus and leads to a revision that sets the tone for the film documentary. Notice that even after revision of the working statement, Mr. Larsen moved against bias and said that he readily modified any initial direction if the data warrants it. Part of that defense is not only keeping a record of the data, but reviewing it periodically to steer clear of bias. Also, another part of the check on bias includes his pre-coded set of notes organized in looseleaf notebooks.

Larsen: During our original research, we discovered that there was a very interesting story to tell regarding the development of new jazz talent in the city. Our attention turned toward why certain young musicians, in the face of the nearly bankrupt nightclub scene, chose to devote themselves to jazz. So our original concept of Detroit jazz history [what inspired jazz artists in the past] turned towards: *What was inspiring musicians now?* We wanted to find out about the young musicians who were coming up, and what their hopes were for the future. So rather than looking back, we started looking toward the future.

You have to hold the vision of what you want the final piece to be like, so keeping that final film in mind is important. But I check myself by balancing the core concept with the entire team [the co-producer and other members of the film crew] and whatever else we discover that needs correction in the process of making the film. Part of that is keeping track of things with my production book, a way of keeping all this information in one place with three-ring binders. I have a whole stack of things I haven't put into it yet. Makes it a lot easier to find things later. I categorize them under certain headings. For this one, I have such headings as "contributors," "production," "post-production," "interview," "research."

Before production began, a formal proposal was assembled for review by the sponsors. When approval came through, the team moved into the next phase that included interviews. Here, Mr. Larsen described the questions that were designed for primary interviews and the artists who were chosen to answer them. Notice his definition of the creative artist in his references to *technical proficiency*. It is reminiscent of Bartlett's and Bruner's "perceptual readiness." Notice, as well, his references that are characteristic of Bartlett's scientific/creative thinker. They echo the meaning of "going beyond the information given": *to carry them beyond what's been done before . . . developing his own voice.* Finally, notice Mr. Larsen's effort to create a comfortable climate for his interview subjects in order to evoke easy, yet thoughtful response.

> **Larsen**: Once we had a handle on what we wanted to do, we went through the process of creating a budget and a production plan and submitted that with a proposal to the Michigan Council of Arts. And once we received the grant, we put our production plan into effect by hiring a crew and scheduling a shoot on the opening night of the 1987 Detroit Montreaux Jazz Festival.
>
> We had meetings with two of the artists chosen for the film and established what the focus of their discussion would be. Out of that came a brief outline for a dialog scheme, and I developed that into a shooting script. Christopher Pitts developed a question list that I have here in my production book: *When was the moment you felt the inspiration for a career in jazz? What influence toward music did your parents and family have on you? What was your first gig? Is there a Detroit style? What is it? Who inspired your style? Why? What roles did the following have in the development of jazz: Louis Armstrong, Duke Ellington, Charlie Parker, John Coltrane. What did jazz do for you?* [Larsen called out several additional questions].
>
> I knew that most jazz artists spent their lives looking for inspiration to carry them beyond what's been done before. Once you reach a level of technical proficiency, the artist has to begin developing his own voice. With artists, where you're trying to find out more about their personalities [during an interview], the whole point is to keep it open, conversational. What you're trying to do is create an atmosphere where stories are told and feelings are expressed. My interviews took place over dinner and involved conversation about music in general and about the project and where we were going with

it. Interview questions for the actual filming came out of these conversations. Part of my objective to hold these over dinner was to discover how effectively they would come across visually on camera and part of that includes dialog, how comfortable they feel, and how well they can express themselves, that kind of thing.

In the following comment, Mr. Larsen explained how he analyzed his data to arrive at some final insights. He described his analysis as looking for something that *tells the story*, that is, informs; that he looked for the *turning point* that triggered an artist's moment of inspiration. All came out of an examination of data in his "production book." Characteristically, he suggested his decisions are intuitive. The fact is, he knows *when you hear it you know it's true* because he manifests the productive choices that accrue to a writer who practices "perceptual readiness," and because he operates like a scientific/creative thinker.

Larsen: I really don't know how I decide what to use, what to eliminate. You just know. For the script I guess it's, *What really tells the story? What communicates and what doesn't?* You look for stories that have particular significance as turning points for the artist [Larsen explained he looked for the event, person, or experience that triggered the inspirational point in each artist's life and compelled that artist to devote singular attention to creating jazz music]. And when you hear it you know it's true. I came away with more than I expected. I had to eliminate. For example, Rodney [one of the featured artists] talks about who he's gigging with right now, spending time with the band members, the venues. All that is too removed, probably too obscure for most people.

The next comment reflects another characteristic of the scientific/creative thinker. Mr. Larsen described the source of his creative inspiration, something outside his data collection. He had heard a poetic tribute to an American war hero and made an association between the soldier's dedication to the cause of freedom and the selfless devotion of Detroit artists to keep jazz art alive. He then used that similarity, and part of the poem's title, to guide his work and the opening of his film presentation.

Larsen: I knew exactly how I wanted to open the trailer, scenes of fireworks over the Detroit River and Rodney Whittaker, the young double bass player, reading a poem written by Chris Pitts. From that point Ernie Rogers, the veteran saxophone player, and Rodney talk about this poem, that it could have been written about those who keep the spirit of jazz alive today. "Keepers of the Flame" is the title of Chris' poem, and I had that title in mind when Chris told me about the poem. He had written it some time before in memory of his grandfather who had given up his life fighting with the French resistance [against German occupation of France during World War II]. I wanted to find out about that poem and there seemed to be some connection there.

In another portion of the interview, Mr. Larsen, explained how he developed the script. Rather than interviews with each of the individual jazz artists, Larsen had the two artists he had chosen, Whittaker and Rogers, discuss jazz music and the Detroit artists who had made significant contributions to it. When they began discussing a particular artist, Larsen broke away from the two conversationalists and brought in scenes drama-tizing events in the life of the artist being featured. The documentary closed with Rodney playing the bass with Ernie Rogers and his ensemble and Rodney's voiceover saying he knows he will not make much money playing accoustic jazz, but that he is going to follow his heart's calling anyway.

To date, the video series, "Jazz Masters" (directed by Christopher Pitts and co-produced by Mr. Larsen) airs regularly on cable stations and arrangements for European distribution are currently under way. In 1989 when this interview was taped, Mr. Larsen did not anticipate working on a TV series. His goal then was to produce an hour-long jazz film.

Larsen: We hope to distribute all 10 videos primarily to schools through broadcast outlets, to public broadcasting stations, either independently or through PBS. Cable channels have expressed an interest, and there is also a network of videotape distributors for jazz films that some of the distributors have expressed an interest in seeing the finished product [a full-length jazz film].

For descriptions of career backgrounds on Mr. Larsen and Mr. Imes and the other eight media professionals, see Appendix D.

Appendix D: Career Backgrounds of Interviewed Media Professionals

David L. Ashenfelter, investigative news reporter at the *Detroit Free Press* since 1982, was formerly with *The Detroit News* where he began as a suburban reporter. During his 12 years at *The Detroit News,* he served as city-county reporter, as state capital bureau chief, and then as assistant national editor. He had joined the *News* staff in 1971 following graduation from the journalism program at Indiana University, Bloomington. While in Bloomington, he also worked alternately for two newspapers as a police reporter. In 1981, Mr. Ashenfelter and Ms. Sydney P. Freedberg teamed up on a series of stories that revealed a Navy practice of misleading families about peacetime deaths. *The Detroit News* series by the Ashenfelter-Freedberg team won the 1982 Pulitzer Prize for Meritorious Public Service. Later that year, Mr. Ashenfelter joined the *Detroit Free Press* where he has worked almost exclusively as an investigative reporter.

Since 1981, he has won more than two dozen local, state, and national newswriting awards, including three distinguished service awards from the Society of Professional Journalists/Sigma Delta Chi, the American Bar Association Silver Gavel Award, the Worth Bingham Prize for investigative reporting, and three public service medallions from the Detroit Press Club.

Stephen Cain, news reporter at the *Ann Arbor News* (Michigan), specializes in several areas of news coverage including federal and state criminal justice systems, medical research, public health, and municipal finance. He also served as general assignment and investigative newswriter at *The Detroit News* for nearly 14 years and was made head of its city-county bureau for 2 years before joining the *Ann Arbor News* in 1982. Prior to his association with *The Detroit News*, Mr. Cain was a reporter with several other Michigan newspapers, *The Ypsilanti Press*, *Saline Reporter*, and *Grand Haven Daily Tribune*.

A veteran news journalist, Mr. Cain has won 18 first place awards in statewide AP, UPI, and Detroit Press Club competitions. He was also nominated twice for the Pulitzer. Both nominations were for stories concerning an 18-month investigation he had conducted in 1974 and 1975 along with co-Pulitzer nominee, Douglas Glazier. The team had written a series of stories which resulted in freedom for four motorcyclists who had been imprisoned and were waiting execution in New Mexico for a murder committed by a former DEA informant. Another one of Mr. Cain's stories that drew wide attention concerned his extensive investigation of the activities of CIA agent David Henry Barnett. Agent Barnett proved to be the only CIA agent ever prosecuted as a KGB mole.

Along with his other responsibilities at the *Ann Arbor News*, Mr. Cain has also acted as co-director of the Law Writer's Project for third-year law students at the University of Michigan Law School and served as an instructor of journalism in the Department of Communication at the University of Michigan. Mr. Cain majored in journalism and geology at Amherst College and continued further studies in American history and social psychology at the University of Michigan.

Mort Meisner, news director at WJBK-TV2, CBS Detroit, began his career in 1977 with WXYZ-TV Detroit where he worked as an assignment editor for 4 years. He then went to WBBM-TV, Chicago, as assignment manager, moved on to WLS-TV, Chicago, as director of news operations for 2 years, then to KSDK-TV, St. Louis, Missouri, as assistant news director for 3 years and returned to his home state in June 1988 to serve as assistant news director for WJBK-TV2.

Mr. Meisner is the recipient of three Emmy awards. In 1980 and 1986, he won an Emmy for best newscast, and in 1982 he won an Emmy for best investigative series. Born and raised in Oak Park, a suburb of Detroit, Mr. Meisner studied communications and journalism at the University of Detroit.

Robbie Timmons is anchorwoman, reporter and writer at WXYZ-TV7, ABC Detroit. A Detroit television broadcaster since 1976, she was also anchorwoman, reporter, and producer for 4 years at WILX-TV at Lansing, Michigan, before joining Channel 7 in 1982.

Ms. Timmons has won numerous broadcasting awards including Emmy awards for two TV documentaries. One documentary, entitled "Some Call it Cattlegate," concerned the poisoning and loss of cattle contaminated by PBB, and the other was a news series on the volunteer Army entitled "This is the Army, Ms. Jones." She also won seven Emmy nominations for her special reports, some of which included a report on air safety, the fur industry, and laser surgery. In 1983, Ms. Timmons was named "Outstanding Woman in Broadcast News" by the American Women in Radio and Television. Ms. Timmons is a graduate of Ohio State University where she majored in communication and business.

Charles L. Snearly, manager of Public Affairs at the Lincoln-Mercury Division of the Ford Motor Company, Dearborn, Michigan, joined the corporation in 1977 as a reporter for *Ford World*, the company's employee newspaper. He then served as the paper's regional editor at St. Louis and Kansas City until 1980 when he joined the Consumer and Dealer Publications Department as publications editor.

Mr. Snearly's media career expanded into other areas of PR work in 1984 when he was named assistant public affairs manager of the Parts and Service Division. In 1985 he was made assistant public affairs manager for the Lincoln-Mercury Division, and in 1986 he joined the Corporate News Department as a media representative. Shortly thereafter, Mr. Snearly was named public affairs manager of the Parts and Service Division and in 1989 became public affairs manager for the Lincoln-Mercury division.

Before joining the Ford Motor Company, Mr. Snearly was a newswriter at *The Detroit News*, the *Oakland Press*, and *Observer* (the latter two are suburban Detroit newspapers). Mr. Snearly is a graduate of Wayne State University where he majored in journalism and minored in English.

Paul M. Preuss is manager of the Product and Technology Dept. in the North American Public Affairs operation of the Ford Motor Company. In this capacity, which he has held since 1985, Mr. Preuss supervises the product publicity launch of all of the company's North American-sold cars from his department offices at Dearborn, Michigan. He is responsible, as well, for administering Ford's motorsports publicity.

Mr. Preuss joined Ford Motor in 1965 after a 12-year career as a sportswriter with *The Detroit News*. Prior to his current Ford position, Mr. Preuss served as manager of Public Affairs, Ford Parts and Service Division. Earlier in his career at Ford, he worked for several years in the company's Los Angeles Public Affairs office serving the needs of West Coast auto enthusiast publications. Mr. Preuss has represented the Ford Motor Company at national and international racecar competitions and is known to sportswriters around the world, many of whom depend on him as an authoritative source concerning Ford race models and drivers. Born and raised in Detroit, he is a journalism graduate of the University of Detroit.

Mathew Thornton is one of the principal creative directors for Hummingbird Productions, which has its headquarters in Nashville, Tennessee, with satellite offices in New York, Chicago, and Detroit. At Hummingbird, Mr. Thornton specializes in composing music and lyrics and directing production of commercials for the company's national accounts, some of which include Pepsi-Cola, McDonald's, Wrigley's Gum, Shell Oil, Chrysler Corp., and Radio Shack.

Formerly vice-president of Creative Services at Group 243, Ann Arbor, Michigan, Mr. Thornton had joined Group 243 in 1983 as the firm's first advertising and design copywriter and rose quickly to become associate creative director of copy. During early merger negotiations (1988-1989) with the Ross Roy Group of Troy, Michigan, Mr. Thornton was named vice-president of Creative Services for Group 243, but in 1991 he chose to join Hummingbird Productions.

While at Group 243, Mr. Thornton directed work for clients in retail, health care, industrial, high-tech, and automotive supply industries. He also directed the initial campaign strategy that moved Domino's Pizza to the forefront of a highly competitive market and transformed a local consumer product into an international commodity. Mr. Thornton won several national awards for this campaign as well as other local and national awards for his creative work on a number of other accounts. Before entering the advertising world, Mr. Thornton had achieved a successful career in theater and music. He is a graduate of the School of Music at Oakland University, Oakland, Michigan.

Anne Gahagan, a senior writer at W. B. Doner & Company in Southfield, Michigan, had joined the Doner agency in 1985 as a junior writer, left 3 years later to become part of the creative staff at Ross Roy, then returned to W. B. Doner in 1989 as a senior writer.

She has produced copy for several client accounts including Chiquita Products, Blue Cross-Blue Shield, the Humane Society, and the Michigan Lottery. She is the recipient of the International Broadcasting award for a Perry Drugs TV spot, has won numerous awards given annually by the Creative Directors Club of Detroit, and was a finalist for a Cleo (TV spot) award. Ms. Gahagan is a graduate of Michigan State University where she majored in advertising in the College of Communication.

Jack Imes, Jr., creative executive in the Marketing Communications Group at the Sandy Corporation, Troy, Michigan, was a free-lance writer and graphic artist and served in the U. S. Army as a television production specialist before joining the Sandy Corp. in 1985. As creative executive at Sandy, Mr. Imes designs visuals and writes scripts. He has designed and scripted award-winning video programs for many clients, including General Motors, IBM, Firestone, Sheraton Hotels, and other Sandy clients. His articles on special effects have appeared in *Cinemagic* and *In Motion* magazines and he is the author of the 1984 text entitled, *Special Visual Effects*. Mr. Imes holds a bachelor's degree in fine arts and visual design from the University of Iowa.

Jeffrey Larsen, is president of his own media company, Cinéma de Liberté, Inc., San Francisco, California, where he produces training, product, and promotional film, and television and multi-media scripts for clients such as Apple Computer, Inc., Sun Microsystems, Amdahl, Hewlett-Packard Corp., and others.

Before establishing his own company, Mr. Larsen was a writer and senior producer at the Sandy Corp. He wrote and produced award-winning films, videos, and multi-media presentations for General Motors, Pontiac, IBM, Hyatt Hotels, and Pepsi-Cola. His awards include top honors from the International TV and Video Artists.

Prior to his association with Sandy, he served as business, public affairs, and general news broadcaster for radio stations in Michigan and Phoenix, Arizona. While in Phoenix, he wrote and produced promotional videos and television commercials for hotel and real estate clients and acted as creative consultant for the Hollywood entertainment division of Universal Studios. Mr. Larsen is a graduate of Michigan State University where he earned a bachelor's degree in telecommunications and philosophy. He also studied filmmaking at New York University and is a member of the Association of Independent Video and Filmmakers.

References

Abelson, R. P. (1976). Script processing in attitude formation and decision making. In J. S. Carroll & J. W. Payne (Eds.), *Cognition and social behavior* (pp. 33-45). Hillsdale, NJ: Lawrence Erlbaum Associates.

Allen, H. L. (1983). Methods of literary masters rub off on feature class. *Journalism Educator, 38*, 50-51.

Arnheim, R. (1969). *Visual thinking*. Berkeley, CA: University of California Press.

Aronson, E. (1980). *The social animal* (3rd ed.). San Francisco, CA: W. H. Freeman.

Babbie, E. (1983). *The practice of social research* (3rd ed.). Belmont, CA: Wadsworth.

Baker, B. (1981). *Newsthinking*. Cincinnati, OH: Writer's Digest Books.

Barol, B., & Brailsford, K. (1987, November 23). Men aren't her only problem. *Newsweek,* p. 76.

Barrett-Connor, E. (1989, August 3). Postmenopausal estrogen replacement and breast cancer. *New England Journal of Medicine, 321*(5), 319-320.

Bartlett, F. C. (1958). *Thinking, An experimental and social study*. London: George Allen & Unwin.

Bartlett, F. C. (1977). *Remembering: A study in experimental and social psychology*. New York: Cambridge University Press. (Original work published 1932)

Beed, T. W., & Stimson, R. (Eds.). (1985). *Survey interviewing: Theory and techniques*. Boston, MA: Allen & Unwin.

Belson, W. A. (1981). *The design and understanding of survey questions*. Aldershot, England: Gower.

Bergkvist, L., Adami, H., Persson, I., Hoover, R., & Schairer, C. (1989). The risk of breast cancer after estrogen and estrogen-progestin replacement. *New England Journal of Medicine 321*(5), 293-319.

Biagi, S. (1987). *News talk I: State-of-the-art conversations with today's print journalists*. Belmont, CA: Wadsworth.

Blundell, W. E. B. (1986). *Storytelling step by step: A guide to better feature writing*. New York: Dow Jones.

Bogart, L. (1968). Social sciences in the mass media. In F. T. C. Yu (Ed.), *Behavioral sciences and the mass media* (pp. 153-174). New York: Russell Sage.

Bostrom, R. N., Ray, E. B., & Coyle, K. (1989, May). *Differential aspects of listening skill and the retention of medical messages: A study in validity.* Paper presented at the annual meeting of the International Communication Association, San Francisco, CA.

Bradburn, N. M., & Sudman, S. (1981). *Improving interview methods and questionnaire design* (3rd ed.). San Francisco, CA: Jossey-Bass.

Brady, J. (1976). *The craft of interviewing.* Cincinnati, OH: Writer's Digest Books.

Bruner, J. S. (1957). Going beyond the information given. In J. S. Bruner (Ed.), *Contemporary approaches to cognition* (pp. 41-69). Cambridge, MA: Harvard University Press.

Bruner, J. S. (1964). On perceptual readiness. In J. C. Harper, C. C. Anderson, C. M. Christensen, & S. M. Hunka (Eds.), *The cognitive processes* (pp. 225-257). Englewood Cliffs, NJ: Prentice-Hall.

Buller, D. B., Comstock, J., & Aune, R. K. (1989, May). *The effect of probing on deceivers and truthtellers.* Paper presented at the annual meeting of the International Communication Association, San Francisco, CA.

Cannell, C. F. (1985a). Experiments in the improvement of response accuracy. In T. W. Beed & R. J. Stimson (Eds.), *Survey interviewing: Theory and techniques* (pp. 24-62). Winchester, MA: Allen & Unwin.

Cannell, C. F. (1985b). Interviewing in telephone surveys. In T. W. Beed & R. J. Stimson (Eds.), *Survey interviewing: Theory and techniques* (pp. 63-84). Winchester, MA: Allen & Unwin.

Cannell, C. F., Fowler, F. J., & Marquis, K. H. (1968, March). The influence of interviewer and respondent psychological and behaviorial variables on the reporting in household interviews. *Vital and Health Statistics, Series 2, No. 26* (pp. 1-65).

Cannell, C. F., & Kahn, R. L. (1968). Interviewing. In G. Lindzey & E. Aronson (Eds.), *Handbook of social psychology* (Vol. 2, 2nd ed., pp. 526-595). Reading, MA: Addison-Wesley.

Cannell, C. F., Kalton, G., Oksenberg, L., & Bischoping, K. (1989). *New techniques for pretesting survey questions.* Ann Arbor, MI: University of Michigan, Survey Research Center, Institute for Social Research (with F. J. Fowler, Center for Survey Research, University of Massachusetts) for the National Center for Health Services Research and Health Care Technology Assessment, Washington, DC.

Cannell, C. F., Miller, P. V., & Oksenberg, L. (1981). Research on interviewing techniques. In S. Leinhardt (Ed.), *Sociological methodology* (pp. 389-437). San Francisco, CA: Jossey-Bass.

Converse, J. M., & Presser, S. (1986). *Survey questions: Handcrafting the standardized questionnaire.* Beverly Hills, CA: Sage.

Davis, J. A. (1964). Great books and small groups: An informal history of a national survey. In P. E. Hammond (Ed.), *Sociologists at work: Essays on the craft of social research.* New York: Basic Books.

Dillman, D. A. (1978). *Mail and telephone surveys: The total design method.* New York: Wiley.

Dionne, E. J., Jr., & Morin, R. (1990, December 17-23). Good news for the GOP — if it's true. *The Washington Post, National Weekly Edition,* p. 37.

Donaldson, S. K. (1979). One kind of speech act: How do we know when we're conversing? *Semiotica, 28,* 257-297.

Dutta, S., & Kanungo, R. N. (1975). *Affect and memory.* Oxford: Pergamon.

Erdelyi, M. H. (1974). A new look at the new look: Perceptual defense and vigilance. *Psychological Review, 81,* 1-24.

Feasley, F. G. (1985). Copywriting and the prose of Hemingway. *Journalism Quarterly, 62*(1), 121-126.

Ghiselin, B. (Ed.). (1963). *The creative process: A symposium* (7th ed.). New York: Mentor.

Gibson, J. J., & Gibson, E. J. (1955). Perceptual learning: Differentiation or enrichment? *Psychological Review, 62,* 32-41.

Giles, R. H. (1987). *Newsroom management: A guide to theory and practice.* Indianapolis, IN: R. J. Berg.

Graham, M. (1991, January). The quiet drug revolution. *The Atlantic,* pp. 34-40.

Gray, P. (1989, July 10). *Time,* p. 62.

Greene, J. O., & Sparks, G. (1983). Explication and test of a cognitive model of communication apprehension. *Human Communication Research, 9*(4), 349-366.

Grey, D. L. (1972). *The writing process: A behaviorial approach to communicating information and ideas.* Belmont, CA: Wadsworth.

Hagenaars, J. A., & Heinen, T. G. (1982). Effects of role-independent interviewer characteristics on responses. In W. Dijkstra & J. van der Zouwen (Eds.), *Response behavior in the survey interview* (pp. 91-130). San Diego, CA: Academic Press.

Hayes-Roth, B., & Thorndyke, P. W. (1979). Integration of knowledge from text. *Journal of Verbal Learning and Verbal Behavior, 18,* 91-108.

Henson, R. M., Cannell, C. F., & Lawson, S. A. (1973). *Effects of interviewer style and question form on reporting of automobile accidents.* Ann Arbor, MI: University of Michigan, Survey Research Center, Institute for Social Research.

Higgins, E. T. (1981). The "communication game": Implications for social cognition and persuasion. In E. T. Higgins, C. P. Herman, & M. P. Zanna (Eds.), *Social cognition: The Ontario symposium* (Vol. 1, pp. 343-392). Hillsdale, NJ: Lawrence Erlbaum Associates.

Higgins, E. T., Kuiper, N. A., & Olson, J. M. (1981). Social cognition: A need to get personal. In E. T. Higgins, C. P. Herman, & M. P. Zanna (Eds.), *Social cognition: The Ontario symposium* (Vol. 1, pp. 395-420). Hillsdale, NJ: Lawrence Erlbaum Associates.

Higgins, E. T., McCann, C. D., & Fondacaro, R. (1982, March) The "communication game": Goal-directed encoding and cognitive sequences. *Social Cognition, 1*(1), 21-37.

Hite, S. (1987). *Hite report: Women and love: A cultural revolution in progress.* New York: Knopf.

Hochschild, A. R. (1987, November 15). *New York Times Book Review,* p. 3.

Howarth, W. L. (Ed.). (1977). *The John McPhee reader* (13th ed.). New York: Vintage.

Kahn, R. L., & Cannell, C. F. (1957). *The dynamics of interviewing: Theory, technique, and cases.* New York: Wiley.

Kaplan, A. (1964). *The conduct of inquiry: Methodology for behavioral science.* San Francisco, CA: Chandler.

Korbel, P. J., & Bell, I. R. (1985). Fieldwork methodology: A survey of buyers' concerns and doubts. In T. W. Beed & R. J. Stimson (Eds.), *Survey interviewing: Theory and techniques* (pp. 158-170). Winchester, MA: Allen & Unwin.

Labow, P. J. (1980). *Advanced questionnaire design.* Cambridge, MA: Abt Books.

Levine, M. (1980, July). Investigative reporting as a research method. *American Psychologist, 35*(7), 626-638.

Lindsay, P. H., & Norman, D. A. (1977). *Human information processing: An introduction to psychology* (2nd ed.). New York: Academic Press.

Loftus, E. F. (1974, December). Eyewitness testimony. *Psychology Today,* pp. 117-119.

Loftus, E. F. (1979). *Eyewitness testimony.* Cambridge, MA: Harvard University Press.

Mandler, J. M. (1978). A code in the node: The use of a story schema in retrieval. *Discourse Processes, 1,* 14-35.

Mandler, J. M., & DeForest, M. (1979). Is there more than one way to recall a story? *Child Development, 50,* 886-889.

Marquis, K. H., & Cannell, C. F. (1969). *A study of interviewer-respondent interaction in urban employment survey.* Ann Arbor, MI: University of Michigan, Survey Research Center, Institute for Social Research.

Marzano, R. J., Brandt, R. S., Hughes, C. S., Jones, B. F., Presseisen, B. Z, Rankin, S. C., & Subor, C. (1988). *Dimensions of thinking: A framework for curriculum and instruction.*

Alexandria, VA: Association for Supervision and Curriculum Development.

Maslow, A. H. (1962). Emotional blocks to creativity. In S. J. Parnes & H. F. Harding (Eds.), *A source book for creative thinking* (pp. 93-103). New York: Scribner's.

Matarazzo, J. D.,Wiens, A. N., Saslow, G., Dunham, R. M., & Voas. R. B. (1964). Speech durations of astronaut and ground communicator. *Science, 143,* 148-150.

McAdams, K., & Sweeney, J. (1985). Copywriting and newswriting need similar skills. *Journalism Educator, 4,* 38-40.

Mehrabian, A. (1972). *Nonverbal communication.* Chicago, IL: Aldine-Atherton.

Metzler, K. (1977). *Creative interviewing.* Englewood Cliffs, NJ: Prentice-Hall.

Meyer, P. (1979). *Precision journalism* (2nd ed.). Bloomington, IN: Indiana University Press.

Mitford, J. (1979). *Poison penmanship.* New York: Knopf.

Nisbett, R., & Ross, L. (1980). *Human inference: Strategies and shortcomings of social judgment.* Englewood Cliffs, NJ: Prentice-Hall.

Norman, D. A. (1979). Perception, memory and mental processes. In L.-G. Nilsson (Ed.), *Perspectives on memory research* (pp. 121-144). Hillsdale, NJ: Lawrence Erlbaum Associates.

Palmer, L. M. (1982). The scientific method, A writer's best friend. *Humanist, 42*(2), 29-34, 61.

Parsigian, E. K. (1987). News reporting: Method in the midst of chaos. *Journalism Quarterly, 64*(4), 721-730.

Payne, S. L. (1951). *The art of asking questions.* Princeton, NJ: Princeton University Press.

Platt, J. R. (1962). *The excitement of science.* Boston, MA: Houghton Miflin.

Reitman, J. S., & Rueter, H. H. (1980). Organization revealed by recall orders and confirmed by pauses. *Cognitive Psychology, 12,* 554-581.

Rivers, W. (1975). *Finding facts.* Englewood Cliffs, NJ: Prentice-Hall.

Rumelhart, D. E. (1980). On evaluating story grammars. *Cognitive Science, 4,* 313-316.

Runkel, P. J., & McGrath, J. E. (1972). *Research on human behavior.* New York: Holt, Rinehart & Winston.

Schneider, D. J., Hastorf, A. H., & Ellsworth, P. S. (1979). Person perception and nonverbal cues. In D. J. Schneider, A. H. Hastorf, & P. S. Ellsworth. *Person perception* (2nd ed., pp. 117-150). Reading, MA: Addison-Wesley.

Schuman, H., & Presser, S. (1981). *Questions and answers in attitude surveys: Experiments on question form, wording, and context.* New York: Academic Press.

Selltiz, C., Jahoda, M., Deutsch, M., & Cook, S. W. (1959). *Research methods in social relations.* New York: Henry Holt.

Selltiz, C., Wrightsman, L. S., & Cook, S. W. (1976). *Research methods in social relations* (3rd ed.). New York: Holt, Rinehart & Winston.

Sharples, M. (1985). *Cognition, computers and creative writing.* New York: Wiley.

Shell, A. (1990, December). VNR update: An easy guide to VNR suppliers. *Public Relations Journal*, p. 28.

Sizemore-Elliott, D. (1990, December). Developing public-private partnerships. *Public Relations Journal*, pp. 26-27.

Smith, T. (1989). Sex counts: A methodological critique of Hite's *Women and Love.* In C. F. Turner, H. G. Miller, & L. E. Moses (Eds.), AIDS: *Sexual behavior and intravenous drug use* (pp. 537-547). Washington, DC: National Academy of Sciences Press.

Snyder, M. (1981a). On the influence of individuals on situations. In N. Cantor & J. F. Kihlstrom (Eds.), *Personality, cognition and social interaction* (pp. 309-329). Hillsdale, NJ: Lawrence Erlbaum Associates.

Snyder, M. (1981b). Seek, and ye shall find: Testing hypotheses about other people. In E. T. Higgins, C. P. Herman, & M. P. Zanna (Eds.), *Social cognition: The Ontario symposium* (Vol. 1, pp. 277-303). Hillsdale, NJ: Lawrence Erlbaum Associates.

Stice, J. E. (1987). Further reflections: Useful resources. In J. E. Stice (Ed.), *Developing critical thinking and probleming-solving abilities* (pp. 101-110). San Francisco, CA: Jossey-Bass.

Sudman, S., & Bradburn, N. M. (1982). *Asking questions*. San Francisco, CA: Jossey-Bass.

Tankard, J., Jr. (1976). Reporting and the scientific method. In M. E. McCombs, D. L. Shaw, & D. Grey (Eds.), *Handbook of reporting methods* (pp. 42-80). Boston, MA: Houghton Miflin.

Taylor, S. E., & Crocker, J. (1981). Schematic bases of social information processing. In E. T. Higgins, C. P. Herman, & M. P. Zanna (Eds.), *Social cognition: The Ontario symposium* (Vol. 1, pp. 89-134). Hillsdale, NJ: Lawrence Erlbaum Associates.

Thorndyke, P. W. (1977). Cognitive structures in comprehension and memory. *Cognitive Psychology, 9*, 77-110.

Tversky, A., & Kahneman, D. (1974). Judgment under uncertainty: Heuristics and biases. *Science, 185* , pp. 1124-1131.

Wallis, C., & McDowell, J. (1987, October 12). Back off, buddy: A new Hite report stirs up a furor over sex and love in the '80s. *Time*, pp. 68-73.

Walters, B. (1970). *How to talk with practically anybody about practically anything*. New York: Dell.

Watson, J. D. (1968). *The double helix: A personal account of the discovery of the structure of DNA*. New York: Atheneum.

Weaver, D. H., & Wilhoit, G. C. (1986). *The American journalist*. Bloomington, IN: Indiana University Press.

Webb, E. J., & Salancik, J. R. (1966, November). The interview or the only wheel in town. *Journalism Monographs*, 2.

Wileman, R. E. (1980). *Exercises in visual thinking*. New York: Hastings House.

Williams, P. N. (1978). *Investigative reporting and writing*. Englewood Cliffs, NJ: Prentice-Hall.

Wimmer, R. D., & Dominick, J. R. (1983). *Mass media research*. Belmont, CA: Wadsworth.

Zajonc, R. B. (1980). Feeling and thinking: Preferences need no inferences. *American Psychologist, 35*(2), 151-175.

Author Index

Subject Index